THE TRANSFIGURATION OF HISTORY AT THE CENTER OF DANTE'S *Paradise*

THE TRANSFIGURATION OF HISTORY AT THE CENTER OF DANTE'S *Paradise*

JEFFREY T. SCHNAPP

PRINCETON, NEW JERSEY
PRINCETON UNIVERSITY PRESS

COPYRIGHT © 1986 BY PRINCETON UNIVERSITY PRESS
PUBLISHED BY PRINCETON UNIVERSITY PRESS, 41 WILLIAM STREET
PRINCETON, NEW JERSEY 08540
IN THE UNITED KINGDOM: PRINCETON UNIVERSITY
PRESS, GUILDFORD, SURREY

ALL RIGHTS RESERVED

LIBRARY OF CONGRESS CATALOGING IN PUBLICATION
DATA WILL BE FOUND ON THE LAST PRINTED PAGE OF THIS BOOK

ISBN 0-691-06679-5

PUBLICATION OF THIS BOOK HAS BEEN AIDED BY THE PAUL MELLON
FUND OF PRINCETON UNIVERSITY PRESS

THIS BOOK HAS BEEN COMPOSED IN LINOTRON JANSON

CLOTHBOUND EDITIONS
OF PRINCETON UNIVERSITY PRESS BOOKS ARE
PRINTED ON ACID-FREE PAPER, AND
BINDING MATERIALS ARE CHOSEN
FOR STRENGTH AND
DURABILITY

PRINTED IN THE UNITED STATES OF AMERICA
BY PRINCETON UNIVERSITY PRESS, PRINCETON, NEW JERSEY

for Venus   against Mars

CONTENTS

LIST OF ILLUSTRATIONS ix
ACKNOWLEDGMENTS xi
ABBREVIATIONS xiii

I. Introduction: History and Eternity
at the Center of Dante's *Paradise* 3

II. Bella, Horrida Bella: History in the
Grip of Mars 14

III. Marte/Morte/Martirio: The Dilemma
of Florentine History 36

IV. Unica Spes Hominum, Crux,
O Venerabile Signum 70

V. Sant' Apollinare in Classe and Dante's
Poetics of Martyrdom 170

BIBLIOGRAPHY
Primary Sources 239
Secondary Sources 246
INDEX TO PASSAGES CITED FROM
DANTE'S WORKS 259
SUBJECT INDEX 262

ILLUSTRATIONS

following page 176

1. The Cross against a background of stars with the four Evangelists. Mosaic, central vault of the mausoleum of the Galla Placidia, Ravenna. P: Alinari/Art Resource, N.Y.
2. The Cross against a background of stars over altar. Mosaic, chapel of the Archbishop's Palace, Ravenna. P: Deutsches Archäologisches Institut, Rome.
3. Four Angels supporting central Christogram surrounded by the four Evangelists. Mosaic, central vault of the Archbishop's Palace, Ravenna. P: Alinari/Art Resource, N.Y.
4. The Lamb of God against a background of stars supported by four angels. Mosaic, central vault of the Presbyterium, San Vitale, Ravenna. P: Alinari/Art Resource, N.Y.
5. Saint Apollinaris as orant. Detail from apse mosaic, Sant' Apollinare in Classe, Ravenna. P: Alinari/Art Resource, N.Y.
6. The Vision of the Cross against background of the heavens. Central area of apse mosaic, Sant' Apollinare in Classe, Ravenna. P: Alinari/Art Resource, N.Y.
7. Clipeus with portrait of Christ. Detail from cross, apse mosaic, Sant' Apollinare in Classe, Ravenna. P: Alinari/Art Resource, N.Y.
8. Christ as universal sovereign with attendant angels, presenting martyr's crown to Saint Vitalis. Apse mosaic, San Vitale, Ravenna. P: Alinari/Art Resource, N.Y.
9. The Transfiguration with figure of orant Saint Apollinaris below accompanied by sheep. Full horizontal view of apse mosaic, Sant' Apollinare in Classe, Ravenna. P: Alinari/Art Resource, N.Y.
10. The Evangelists John and Matthew (above); procession of sheep out of Jerusalem (below). Mosaic, left side of triumphal archway, Sant' Apollinare in Classe, Ravenna. P: Deutsches Archäologisches Institut, Rome.
11. The Evangelists Mark and Luke (above); procession of sheep out of Bethlehem (below). Mosaic, right side of triumphal archway, Sant' Apollinare in Classe, Ravenna. P: Deutsches Archäologisches Institut, Rome.

12. The Transfiguration. Full vertical view of apse mosaic including triumphal arch, portraits of Ravenna's Bishops and altar, Sant' Apollinare in Classe, Ravenna. P: Alinari/Art Resource, N.Y.
13. The Granting of Ravenna's *Privilegia*. Left panel, apse mosaic, Sant' Apollinare in Classe, Ravenna. P: Alinari/Art Resource, N.Y.
14. The Symbolic Sacrifices. Right panel, apse mosaic, Sant' Apollinare in Classe, Ravenna. P: Alinari/Art Resource, N.Y.
15. The Vision of the Cross with orant Saint Apollinaris. Central axis of apse mosaic, Sant' Apollinare in Classe, Ravenna. P: Art Resource, N.Y.
16. The Good Shepherd and the story of Jonah, with accompanying orant figures. Ceiling painting, chamber of the Good Shepherd, catacomb of Saints Peter and Marcellinus, Rome. P: Benedettine di Priscilla, Pont. Comm. di Arch. Sacra, Rome.
17. Pagan Orants. Roman sarcophagus, Vatican Museum, Rome. P: Archivio Fotografico Vaticano, Vatican City.
18. Pagan Orant. Roman Statue, Vatican Museum, Rome. P: Archivio Fotografico Vaticano, Vatican City.
19. Christian orant (the "Donna Velata"). Wall painting, chamber of the *Velatio*, catacomb of Priscilla, Rome. P: Benedettine di Priscilla, Pont. Comm. di Arch. Sacra, Rome.
20. Noah as orant. Ceiling painting, catacomb of Pamphillus, Rome. P: Benedettine di Priscilla, Pont. Comm. di Arch. Sacra, Rome.
21. Veiled Christian orant. Ceiling painting, catacomb of Saint Callixtus, Rome. P: Snark/Art Resource, N.Y.
22. Saint Agnes as Orant. Altar façade, Sant' Agnese fuori le Mura, Rome. P: Alinari/Art Resource, N.Y.

ACKNOWLEDGMENTS

First and foremost I would like to thank my teacher, friend, and colleague John Freccero, without whose encouragement and learning this book would not have been possible. I would also like to express my deep gratitude to my friend Rachel Jacoff, for her valuable readings of the manuscript at various stages. Among the many other friends and colleagues who have contributed directly or indirectly to this book I would like to single out Kevin Brownlee, whose support was invaluable to me during my years at Dartmouth. Finally, I would like to thank the Mabelle McLeod Lewis Fund for its generous research grant for the academic year 1982–1983, without which this work could not have been completed.

ABBREVIATIONS

AH	*Analecta Hymnica Medii Aevi*, eds. Clemens Blume and Guido Dreves (Leipzig, 1886–1922)
CCSL	*Corpus Christianorum, Series Latina*
CSEL	*Corpus Scriptorum Ecclesiasticorum Latinorum*
DS	*Dante Studies*
JACh	*Jahrbuch für Antike und Christentum*
Migne PG	*Patrologiae Cursus Completus: Series Graeca*, ed. J. P. Migne (Paris, 1857–1894)
Migne PL	*Patrologiae Cursus Completus: Series Latina*, ed. J. P. Migne (Paris, 1844–1864)
MLN	*Modern Language Notes*
PMLA	*Publication of the Modern Language Association of America*
SIR	*Stanford Italian Review*

All citations from Dante's *Commedia* are from Singleton's version of the Petrocchi text as published in *The Divine Comedy*, translation and commentary by Charles S. Singleton (Princeton, N.J.: Princeton University Press, 1970–1975). English translations of all indented quotations from Dante's poem, except where noted, are by Singleton; in-text translations are my own. Quotations from the *Convivio* are from Maria Simonelli's critical edition (*Il Convivio*, Testi e Saggi di Letterature Moderne, Testi 2 [Bologna: Casa Editrice Prof. Riccardo Pàtron, 1966]). Translations of the Latin Vulgate are adapted with minor modifications from the Douay/Rheims edition. Translations of Virgil's *Aeneid*, when so indicated, are from Robert Fitzgerald's *The Aeneid* (New York: Random House, 1983). (Since Fitzgerald's line numbers diverge from those of the original, they are listed after each quoted passage for the convenience of the reader.)

THE TRANSFIGURATION OF HISTORY AT THE CENTER OF DANTE'S *Paradise*

I

INTRODUCTION: HISTORY AND ETERNITY AT THE CENTER OF DANTE'S *Paradise*

> Medium enim, cum amissum est in circulo, inveniri non potest nisi per duas lineas se orthogonaliter intersectantes.
>
> BONAVENTURE, *Collationes in Hexaemeron* 1.24.

Introduction

Approaching the periphery of Dante's limbo, Virgil has occasion to recall to memory an event which dramatically altered the landscape of Hell:

> ... Io era nuovo in questo stato,
> quando ci vidi venire un possente,
> con segno di vittoria coronato. *Inf.* 4.52–54
>
> (I was new in this condition when I saw a Mighty One come here, crowned with sign of victory.)

To the Christian reader of the *Divine Comedy*, for whom the identity and significance of the *possente* in question are hardly insignificant matters, Virgil's words can only seem those of a tragic outsider. Virgil recognizes the *power* of Christ, just as he recognizes in the cruciform nimbus a sign of *victory*. Yet it is clear that he is speaking from within the discourse of Classicism, for the specificity of Christ's power and victory go unmentioned. The harrower of Hell is consequently depicted as the last in an apparently endless series of conquerors, a bolder Theseus, a more powerful Hercules, a more courageous *Mars Ultor*: a rescuer of souls but not a universal saviour. Nowhere are we reminded that in the Christian conception Christ's power must by necessity transcend the boundaries of Classical epic, nor that the term "victory" must here suggest no less than the irreversible swallowing up of death into eternal life.

What Dante has Virgil dramatize in his description is that, in the end, the gap between Christian truth and Classical vision is unbridgeable. The hopelessness of limbo is the consequent fate of Classicism: without access to the proper name of Christ, without a mastery of the Word, it is forever condemned to a tragic state of hermeneutic suspense, forever alienated from its own words and meanings. Like the Virgil that Statius describes in *Purgatory* 22, Classicism advances like a somnambulant along the path of history, facing the starless immensity of the night, and yet bearing behind its back—and for the exclusive benefit of future men—the very principle that renders it intelligible: the light of Christ.

All the more poignant is that, despite the essential role performed by the *Aeneid* in the disclosure of Christ's historical mission, Virgil remains in death as in life a tragically flawed reader. The concrete signs of the Christ-event (the immediate carnal presence of the actual harrower of Hell), and the fact of Classical Elysium's topographical marginality to Christian paradise, have no real impact: the ultimate meanings of all events and signs, so long as Christ remains hidden in anonymity, will be a mystery to Classical man. Virgil's predicament in canto 4 clarifies the central place of Christ in Dante's literary system. It is not that all linguistic and literary alterity simply vanishes for those who, like the poet-pilgrim, take up their cross and follow Christ. Nor is poetic vision in any way guaranteed in the wake of the Christ-event. On the contrary, the gap dividing sign and signified, letter and spirit, appearance and essence, virtue and reward, persists: indeed it continues to define what Dante saw as the essential dynamism of human history.

Christians born into the hiatus between Christ's first and second advents thus live in suspense, occupying their own sort of historical limbo. But since they are inhabited by hope, their predicament is not a tragic one. Unlike Virgil, they are even able to

HISTORY AND ETERNITY 5

read behind their backs because they gaze directly into the light of the *sol Christi*: a principle of intelligibility which animates not only individual and collective life, but also the general movement of human history toward those ultimate events in which all creation will be bound up into eternity.

In the course of the present study I show the full extent to which the central cantos of *Paradise* may be regarded as Dante's Christian response to the dilemma of *Inferno* 4. In the heaven of Mars—against an explicitly Virgilian backdrop—Dante reaches the center of his own celestial Elysium: a truly Christian Elysian homeland and Hall of Fame in which the name of Christ is fully known and over which his sign of victory shines like a resplendent sun. Dante scholarship (and such names as Cosmo, del Lungo, Momigliano, Pascoli, Rajna, Rheinfelder, Vallone, Vianello, and Vossler come to mind) has tended to divide into two camps over these cantos, one emphasizing their "true Flemish miniatures and everyday household scenes," to paraphrase de Sanctis; that is, the concrete poetic particulars of Cacciaguida and of his narrative and prophecies; the other emphasizing their links to the overarching structures and themes of the poem as a whole.[1] If the persistence of Croce's distinction between the "poetry" and "structure" of Dante's text can still be felt in this division, I have tried to bypass any such dichotomy. What is proposed in its place is a comprehensive reading, attentive to broader intertextual and structural matters, but whose principal aim is to reconstruct the link—a properly "figural" link, as Auerbach would have had it—between the historical *minutiae* of cantos 15–17 and the abstract cross of cantos 14 and 18; the link, to

---

[1] "Sono vere pitture fiamminghe, scene di vita domestica" (Francesco de Sanctis, *Lezioni sulla Divina Commedia*, 300). For a general bibliography of Italian and German scholarship on the Cacciaguida cantos, see the entry on "Cacciaguida" by Fiorenzo Forti in the *Enciclopedia Dantesca* 1.739. A list of the principal Italian *lecturae Dantis* is given on pp. 585–586 of the Appendix volume of the *Enciclopedia*. For additional bibliographical sources, see the bibliography of secondary sources at the conclusion of this study.

evoke another dyad familiar to students of Dante's poem, between the "poetry" and the "theology" of Dante's heaven of Mars.

While this reconstruction begins with an in-depth inquiry into Dante's rewriting of Book 6 of Virgil's *Aeneid*, the central relay from the Classical to the Christian is provided, not by a literary work, but rather by a visual one. Dante's vision, I suggest, is modeled not only after Virgil (and, to a lesser extent, Cicero's *Dream of Scipio*), but also after the apsidal mosaics of Sant' Apollinare in Classe, Ravenna: mosaics in which the iconographies of Christ's Transfiguration or *Metamorphosis* and of the Exaltation of the Cross are uniquely blended in a celebration of the victorious Christ. These sixth-century mosaics Dante modifies and adapts for his reworking of the Elysian encounter of Aeneas and Anchises in a Christian key. Their celebration of martyrdom as a *repraesentatio Christi*, of the martyr's heroic triumph over death, and of his resulting powers of prophetic vision, are thus pointedly juxtaposed with the epic heroism, the limbic hopelessness, and the terrifying prophetic riddles of the Classical world.

Such contrasts serve to underscore the centrality of the cross in the scheme of things: only it, Dante believed, could truly bind history to eternity and man to God, and bring to poetry the firmer hermeneutic and epistemological foundations which make available to human utterance and interpretation those ultimate meanings that eluded Virgil and Classical civilization. Yet the central message of the cross in cantos 14–18 remains a more immediate and personal one as well: it exhorts the poet-pilgrim to persevere, to rise up and conquer the adversities of history, and, most of all, to complete without hesitation or fear the exemplary act of faith which is the writing of his *Commedia*.

History and Eternity

In the opening chapter I set out in general terms a dialectic which will reappear under a multiplicity of guises in the course of the present study: the dialectic of "history" and "eternity." It is this dialectic, sometimes conceptualized as a play of perspectives, sometimes as an equation of sacrifice and reward, or death and transfiguration, which serves as the underlying structural mechanism in the otherworldly encounters of father and son found in cantos 14–18 of Dante's *Paradise*, Book 6 of Virgil's *Aeneid* and Book 6 of Cicero's *Republic*. Each involves an exchange of contrasting paternal and filial views whose ultimate objective is the conversion of the son—the "protagonist of history"—to an epic task: a sacrificial endeavor occupying a special place in the providential ordering of history.

In the chapter that immediately follows, I explore this complex of themes with respect to *Aeneid* 6 and Anchises' representation of Roman history, concentrating on a number of unresolved tensions in Virgil's text which make it available to a "tragic" Christian reading. Dante's "tragic" reading of Book 6 does not, as does that of Saint Augustine, lead to a refutation of the entire Virgilian construct, but it does insist on the anarchic presence within Roman history of Mars: the most politically corrosive and destabilizing of the planets and Gods but—paradox of paradoxes—the mythical founder of the city and the presiding force behind its rise. Yet Mars's role in Book 6, as in cantos 14–18, extends far beyond this propagation of political flux, for Mars becomes the symbolic bearer of an even deeper more elemental negativity. His grip on human history is ultimately revealed as the tyrannical reign of *death* and of its blinding perspectives over the human city.

This presence of Mars at the heart of the human city condemns Rome and Florence alike—the latter is the subject of my third chapter—to the incessant cycles of natural history: the city rises, it falls, it is regenerated, it is corrupted, but most of all it undergoes the constant cycle of transmutations known to the Middle Ages as Fortune. And this is true whether the Mars in question is he who presides over Rome's internecine struggles, or rather he who animates the ontological violence Dante associates with

Florentine mercantilism. If in Classical political theory and historiography such naturalist metaphors arise as a matter of course, there is in Virgil, as in Dante, a powerful will to uncover a higher logic, a providential pattern, an overarching moral in the text of history. It is this desire that lends the particular pathos to both texts which is so distinctively Virgilian and Dantean: the history of the city must be *more* than just eternal cyclicality, and it is this symbolic *more* that both texts set out to uncover and represent.

But the supplement required to remedy this situation could not come from "within" an urban order in which Mars himself was the city-father. The central portions of chapters 2 and 3 are concerned with the remedy to this founding negativity that Virgil and Dante propose: the father's prophetic intervention from the beyond, whether Classical Elysium or Christian Paradise. With the father's fictional intrusion into the text of history comes the supplement that is required if history is to transcend its own hermeneutic and epistemological limitations.

For Providence's plan to be fulfilled, the son must see beyond the tragic immediacy of the present. Yet the effect of Mars is precisely to render this impossible. Only the "eternalized" father can supply the necessary perspective: a prophetic vision of the otherworld, of the ultimate rewards that await the son, and of the meaning of the task assigned him. The father's role is to bridge the gap between history and eternity, present and future, present and past; making plain the *logos* that underlies the apparent anarchy of historical events, and revealing history's obstacles to the achievement of the epic endeavor as what they "truly" are: mere shadows, temporary detours on a road to eternal glory.

The paradigm then that emerges in the course of chapters 2 and 3 is one structured around a number of polarities: father and son, eternity and history, reward and sacrifice. Bridging the gap between each opposing pair is the father's prophetic intervention, the success or failure of which hinges on his conversion of the son to his own otherworldly perspective. It is here that Dante locates the underlying "tragedy" of *Aeneid* 6, for without an understanding of the role of Christ such otherworldly perspectives could only partially overcome the blinding effects of Mars's rule. In chapter 4 I explore Dante's own solution to the apparent negativity of human history and to the incompleteness of Virgil: the sign of the cross, a sign which in the course of cantos 14–18 will indeed provide a definitive bridge between history and eternity right at the center of Dante's celestial paradise.

The cross of light which appears over Dante's heaven of Mars plays a number of highly charged symbolic roles in cantos 14–18, and it is these that I explore in my fourth chapter. The chapter is divided into three distinct sections: Exaltation, Transfiguration, and Revelation—each concerned with a specific dimension of Dante's cross of light. In "Exaltation" I consider the cross's iconographic origins, its numerological peculiarities and symbolic implications, and its relation to Dante's Classical prototypes as well as to the various liturgies of the cross. In "Transfiguration" I turn instead to a specific gospel incident in Christ's biography which was long viewed as a clarification of the Christian theology of the cross: Jesus' metamorphosis before his disciples on the road to Jerusalem. The Transfiguration of Christ, I argue, plays a decisive supplementary role in cantos 14–18, and unveils not only an eschatological "higher logic" which apparently solves the dilemma of history under the destabilizing rule of Mars, but also the Christian analogue to Classicism's epic reward: not deification but transfiguration—a metamorphosis of the self into Jesus Christ. This is to say that it entirely redefines the genealogical themes that are so important to the encounter of Aeneas and Anchises and provides a key model for the general process of poetic "trans-humanization" (*trasumanar* [1.70]) characteristic of *Paradise* as a whole.

In "Revelation" I return to a theme with which I opened chapter 2: the theme of Mars as the god of discord, ontological violence, and disorder. I suggest, via an examination of Dante's identification of Mars as the heaven of music in *Convivio* 2.13, that what is figured in the sign of the cross is a grand resolution of all of history's apparent differences: a harmonization so complete that it points beyond the Classical formula *harmonia est concordia discors* (harmony is discordant concord), with its implicit theory of irreconcilable opposites, to the differentiated *discordia concors* (concordant discord) of the citizens of the apocalyptic city. All negativity, all tragic and/or discordant perspectives, will be revealed as illusory in the end: such is the radical promise of the eschatological cross of light which Dante places at the center of his celestial paradise. Negative signs will become positive signs, history's tragedies, eternity's comedy. This hermeneutic harmonization makes of the cross of light a particularly apt symbol of the oracle of Christ: an oracle which at the center of *Paradise* will displace the inadequate oracles of Apollo. The Christ/Apollo confrontation, I suggest, produces one especially audacious substitution in the course of cantos 14–18: the cross of light is disclosed as the *true* Helios of Dante's Christian cosmos, taking the place of the actual sun in the universal symphony.

In my closing chapter I turn to the apsidal mosiacs of Sant' Apollinare in Classe which, like cantos 14–18—at least in my interpretation—represent a unique fusion of the iconography of the Exaltation of the Cross and of Christ's Transfiguration. Although my reading of the Cacciaguida cantos does not rest upon this association, I suggest that a number of important structural, iconographic, symbolic, and visual features in these mosaics are relevant not only to Dante's Martial vision, but also to his appropriation of Virgil's Book 6. I focus in particular on the substitution of the transfigured (i.e., solar) Christ with the cross of light, the structural role given the bishop-martyr Saint Apollinaris and its analogies to that of Cacciaguida, and on the orant pose adopted by both in their respective paradisiac settings.

Out of this analysis emerges a more distinct vision of Dante's fate as delineated in Cacciaguida's prophecy: of just *how* the poet-pilgrim is to be a literary martyr and imitator of Jesus Christ. His task is to make the full vision manifest—"tutta tua visïon fa manifesta" (17.128) Cacciaguida commands—transforming his words into literary crosses, into heroic acts of public testimony and confession. In my conclusion I emphasize the transformation of Classical conceptions of epic heroism that results from the Christian understanding of heroism as martyrdom in imitation of Christ's sacrifice on the cross. The central paradox of Christian martyrdom, I propose, is that it inextricably identifies *epic action* with *verbal action*, thus making possible Dante's reenactment of Book 6 as the story of the writing of his own *Commedia*. How can the tale of Aeneas' foundation of Rome be retold as that of the writing of a poem? Or, for that matter, how can the poet-pilgrim be both Aeneas and Paul? The answer I think lies in the Christian theology of martyrdom and its characteristic conflation of *heroic word* and *heroic act*.

Transfiguration and History

Last of all, a word of explanation regarding my choice of title. Dante's conception of "history" is so complex as to require a separate study well beyond the scope of the present investigation.[2] But it should be said that in the Cacciaguida cantos the term "history" encompasses everything from the poet-pilgrim's personal history to the particular history of a city (Florence) to the universal drama of human history in its progress towards apocalypse. All three are joined together in a dense typological nexus, but remain, nevertheless, clearly distinguishable.

The first level, which is that of biography, fuses the epic prototypes of figures such as Aeneas, Ulysses, and Jason with the individualized and interiorized "epic" of conversion and confession that we associate with Saint Augustine. It is further enriched by the additional presence of Boethius as a model, for as

---

[2] A number of major studies of Dante's historiography have appeared in recent years, most notably Giuseppe Mazzotta's *Dante, Poet of the Desert: History and Allegory in the Divine Comedy*; Charles T. Davis' essays collected in *Dante's Italy and Other Essays* (pp. 1–70 in particular); and Joan M. Ferrante's *The Political Vision of the Divine Comedy*.

in the *Consolation of Philosophy*—at least according to *Convivio* 1.2.13—the poet's self-representation at the center of *Paradise* is justified by its virtuous goal: to denounce an unjust sentence of exile and to fight off infamy in the name of truth.[3]

The second level, which is that of the "discourse of the city," places individual biography in a broader typological-ethical setting. As in Dante's Classical models, we thus encounter a number of exemplary urban types and figures such as Cacciaguida: the symbolic bearer of ancient Florentine virtues and model citizen who serves to identify Florence with Rome and also with a number of biblical cities. This more "public" conception of history, however, is tied in cantos 14–18 to the tradition of the Medieval civic chronicles (which finds itself, as will be seen in chapter 3, both embellished upon and subverted). Cacciaguida's capsule history of Florence thus views the history of the city not only as a reenactment of that of Rome and/or Babylon, but also as a *narratio rei gestae*: a succession of events, battles, heroic actions, and dynastic struggles.

The third level, whose focus is primarily eschatological, insists on the vaster drama within which the history of the individual city is inscribed. Since the "story" of Dante's Martial cantos is essentially that of the poet-pilgrim's exile from the "historical" (i.e., his native) city, it is this level that will ultimately prevail. Cacciaguida's emphatic view that ours is a "fallacious world" (15.146) will sharply reinforce in cantos 14–18 the call for participation in the construction of the eschatological city, over and against any hope of a return to the "historical" *patria*. These three

---

[3] There are two preeminent reasons for speaking of oneself in Dante's view: "l'una è quando sanza ragionare di sé grande infamia o pericolo non si può cessare. . . . E questa necessitate mosse Boezio di se medesimo a parlare, acciò che sotto pretesto di consolazione escusasse la perpetuale infamia del suo essilio, mostrando quello essere ingiusto, poi che altro escusatore non si levava. L'altra è quando, per ragionare di sé, grandissima utilitade ne segue altrui per via di dottrina; e questa ragione mosse Agustino ne le sue Confessioni a parlare di sé" (*Convivio* 1.2.13–14).

"texts" of history are symbolically joined through the sign of the cross which rises over the heaven of Mars: a personal model for the poet-pilgrim's own literary askesis, an emblem of utopian cohesion and urban order, and a sign of Judgment marking the end of the historical city and the advent of the city at the end of time.

The choice of the term "Transfiguration" I would hope suggests a distinctively Christian theology of history, which, rather than insisting on the escape or transcendence of historical lack that is promised in Virgil and Cicero, emphasizes instead the "resurrection" of this very lack. As I indicate in chapter 4, Christ's Transfiguration reveals the individual reward that awaits those who take up their personal cross and follow him. It also unveils Christ, the eschatological Messiah: the apocalyptic sun which was to rise at the end of history, marking Jesus' triumphal return and the advent of the Holy Jerusalem. And in between these two, "transfiguration" refers to the action by means of which the text of history is, in anticipation of the end, prophetically re-viewed. What appears from the son's perspective a tragic narrative of exile and loss can be seen as a tale of individual and/or collective redemption. The role of Cacciaguida is thus to insist upon the *meaningfulness* of the sacrifice the poet-pilgrim shall be called upon to make, and not, as is the case with Anchises and Africanus, to promise a simple escape from the prison of history. To take on the historical (literary) task and follow Christ is to accept not only its transfiguring reward, but also the preeminent need for martyrdom and self-sacrifice in human history.

II

BELLA, HORRIDA BELLA: HISTORY
IN THE GRIP OF MARS

O tandem magnis pelagi defuncte periclis   *Aeneid* 6.83–86
(sed terrae graviora manent), in regna Lavini
Dardanidae venient; mitte hanc de pectore curam;
sed non et venisse volent. . . .

Bella, horrida bella: wars, savage wars. With these ominous words the Sibyl welcomes the wandering Aeneas into the confusing world of Book 6 and discloses the tragic circularity of human history under the schizoid rule of Mars. Both as planet and divinity, Mars had long been considered a privileged harbinger of death and devastation, the force presiding in the company of Saturn over all corruptive and degenerative processes: "oppressor of the human species and source of disharmony in nature as a whole," Bouché-Leclercq writes, "Mars, the astrological Satan, is of those who bring about the 'works of darkness.' "[1] Included among such works were the promotion of acts of violence, violent deaths, bodily suffering and exile, as well as the disordering of father/son relations and successions (the latter accounted for less by Mars's link in myth to the story of Thebes and hence to Oedipus, than by the astrological ascendancy he was commonly

---

[1] "Le tyran de l'espèce humaine et perturbateur de la nature entière," "Mars le diable astrologique, est de ceux qui font des 'oeuvres de ténèbres' " (*L'Astrologie grecque*, 99, 104). On the planet Mars, see also 98–99, 422–425, 509–510. For a complete catalogue of Mars's attributes see Alan of Lille's *Anticlaudianus* 5.414–443. A more general survey of both the positive and negative attributes of the god Mars can be found in Uguccione of Pisa's *Magnae Derivationes*, one of Dante's major sources on etymology. Uguccione places Mars under the rubric of *mas, maris* and then proceeds to derive his name from matrimony (*marito/marita*) and from *amas*. He identifies Mars as the god of war and warriors, refers to his role as the founding father of Rome, and insists on his masculinity (*mas*) and role in the transmission of the male seed (*Magnae Derivationes*, Ms. misc. 626 Laud [a] Bodleian, Oxford, fasc. 107).

granted over the central fifteen years of the son's life: the turbulent period of the son's metamorphosis into a father). Pointing out Mars to his grandson Scipio, Africanus thus refers to the planet as "the ruddy one . . . dreaded on earth."[2] Firmicius Maternus writes of the "great evils and great ill-fortune" brought about by Mars, and of his impious sons as "hot headed, impudent, filled with rage, always wandering . . . unstable in all matters."[3] Albumasar (Abu Ma'shar), Dante's source via Albert the Great for the important discussion of Mars in *Convivio* 2.13, summons up images no less catastrophic: "wars in Babylon," "plagues," "deaths of rulers," "ravenous wolves," "battles between the Romans and the Turks," "the destruction of the king of the Romans."[4]

[2] "Tum rutilus horribilisque terris quem Martium dicitis" (*De Re Publica* 6.17). Macrobius comments on this passage: "quod vero fulgorem Iovis humano generi prosperum et salutarem, contra Martis rutilum et terribilem terris vocavit, alterum tractum est ex stellarum colore—nam fulget Iovis, rutilat Martis—alterum ex tractatu eorum qui de his stellis ad hominum vitam manare volunt adversa vel prospera, nam plerumque de Martis terribilia, de Iovis salutaria evenire definiunt" (*Commentarii in Somnium Scipionis* 1.19.19). Macrobius goes on in paragraph 26 to cite the traditional argument that Mars's role as a discordant planet is founded on its negative harmonic ratios to the other planets. Mars, unlike the sun and moon but like Saturn, is not one of the *vitae auctoribus*. It is, rather, an instrument of cosmic disorder and a force of death. On Mars in the *musica mundana*, see Bouché-Leclercq, 109–110, 319–326.

[3] The full passage reads: "Per diem vero si in horoscopo partiliter fuerit inventus, calidos audaces furiosos peregrinos facit et in omnibus semper instabiles et [qui], quicquid ausi fuerint, nulla poterunt ratione complere, sed semper de manibus eorum quicquid nacti fuerint defluit; patrimonia autem eorum, qui sic Martem habuerint, dissipantur" (*Matheseos* 3.4.3). Cf. Ptolemy, *Tetrabiblios* 3.165–169, on the astrological character of Mars.

[4] *De Magnis Coniunctionibus*, fol. 146 (recto). Albert writes: "ita demum Martis bella et mortem continentium et regentium turbas signat sicut inclinans primum ad hoc per iram et calorem et siccatem, ex quibus provenit animositas: sed concitatio populorum ad invicem, et ideo significatum cometae prius est super Martem qui est causa belli et destructionis populorum" (*De Meteoribus* 1.3.11 [Borgnet, vol. 4, 508]). For a more contemporary discussion of Mars's astrological attributes, see Restoro d'Arezzo, *La composizione del mondo colle sue cascioni* 2.2.3.1ff.

Now it is true that, in the proper astronomical configuration, Mars's vast negative energy might be turned to the benefit of the forces of life and good. His call to war might then induce not internecine strife, but instead the fighting of a just and holy war like the crusade of *Paradise* 15 "against the iniquity of that law whose people usurps . . . what is your right" (142–144). But still Mars's effects were conceived as so overwhelmingly negative that it was on the orbital dialectics of a tempering Jupiter and a wrathful Mars that the entire system of political prognostication of Perso-Arab (and to a lesser degree, Classical) astrology would be based.[5]

In Classical and post-Classical mythography Mars appears as an equally resolute *eversor vitae*. In Statius' *Thebaid*, for example, he is less the war-god of Homeric epic whose personal loyalties are at stake than an abstract personification of War: "His business is not to influence wars but to inspire them; he is in fact 'an accident occurring in a substance,' the martial or pugnacious spirit as it exists in the mind now of one nation, and now of another, at the bidding of Fate."[6] His temple, the subject of an extended ecphrasis in Book 7 of the *Thebaid*, is the site of a most hideous court. Guarded by Wild Passion (47), Blind Sinfulness (48), Burning Wrath (48), Pallid Fear (49), Armed Discord (50), and by Treachery bearing a concealed sword (49–50), it rises from the wastelands of northern Thrace, battered at all times by violent storms. Within its iron walls, are such courtiers as Ill-humored Valor (51), Rage Exultant (52), and Armed Death (53); and in their midst the god of war, covered with fresh Hyrcanian gore.[7] Like the city of Dis in *Inferno* 8–10, it is ringed by ferocious

---

[5] Saturn was of course the third key element, especially in its relation to Mars. Mars was often referred to as the "Lesser Infortune" and Saturn as the "Greater Infortune" in Classical astrology. See once again Bouché-Leclercq, 104ff.

[6] C. S. Lewis, *The Allegory of Love: A Study in Medieval Tradition*, 50–51. On Mars in the *Thebaid*, see also David Vessey, *Statius and the Thebaid*, esp. 85–88.

[7] Cf. the description of Dis in *Inferno* 8.78ff., which, like the portion of the *Thebaid* under discussion, is filled with echoes of *Aeneid* 6.270–280 and 6.566–576.

Furies, no less than a thousand in fact: "mille furoribus illi / cingitur averso domus immansueta" (7.41–42). And everywhere about are blood and the stench of death, the ruins of cities, the detritus of war.[8]

With no less ingenuity than the astrologers, however, mythographers too confronted the problem of rendering productive the negativity of Mars. As mythic embodiment of musical, and by extension, political and ontological discord, the god of war was dialectically counterbalanced by Venus, goddess of love, in a formula which serves as the foundation of Classical and Medieval musical theory, and whose influence has been studied by Edgar Wind and Leo Spitzer: *Harmonia est concordia discors* ("Harmony is discordant concord" or "Harmony is the concord of discordant elements").[9] Others, less sanguine perhaps about the prospects for so ideal a harmonization of war and love, would instead dream with Lucretius of a less conciliatory (but more temporary) solution to the destructive powers of Mars:[10]

> Effice ut interea fera moenera militiai
> per maria ac terras omnis sopita quiescant;
> nam tu sola potes tranquilla pace iuvare
> mortalis, quoniam belli fera moenera Mavors
> armipotens regit, in gremium qui saepe tuum se
> reiicit aeterno devictus vulnere amoris,
> atque ita suspiciens tereti cervice reposta
> pascit amore avidos inhians in te, dea, visus,
> eque tuo pendet resupini spiritus ore.
> hunc tu, diva, tuo recubantem corpore sancto
> circumfusa super, suavis ex ore loquellas
> funde petens placidam Romanis, incluta, pacem.

---

[8] For a contemporary version of Mercury's ecphrasis in the *Thebaid*, see Giovanni Boccaccio, *Teseida delle nozze d'Emilia*, 7.29–38 in particular. An even more comprehensive catalogue of Martial *terribilia* is found in the *Genealogie Deorum Gentilium* 9.3.

[9] *Pagan Mysteries of the Renaissance*, 86–96; and Leo Spitzer, *Classical and Christian Ideas of World Harmony: Prolegomena to an Interpretation of the Word "Stimmung."*

[10] *De Rerum Natura* 1.29–40. Eng. trans. by W.H.D. Rouse.

(Cause meanwhile the savage works of war to sleep and be still over every sea and land. For you alone can delight mortals with quiet peace, since Mars mighty in battle rules the savage works of war, who often casts himself upon your lap wholly vanquished by the ever-living wound of love, and thus looking upward, with shapely neck thrown back, feeds his eager eyes with love, gaping upon you, goddess, and, as he lies back, his breath hangs upon your lips. There as he reclines, goddess, upon your sacred body, do you, bending around him from above, pour from your lips sweet coaxings, and for your Romans, illustrious one, crave quiet peace.)

In the famous proem of *De Rerum Natura*, Venus, the mother of Rome and of the Trojans, is thus entreated to extend her dominion over the recumbent body of the city's wounded father, the war god Mars. Then at last peace would be at hand, war would be vanquished, and discord subdued.

Yet for poets as concerned as were Dante and Virgil with the harmonization of human history with the providential perspective of eternity, the problem of Mars could not simply be abstracted away into a neat astrological, musicological, metaphysical, or aesthetic paradox, or resolved by the momentary victory of the forces of love. Mars, the martial arts and martial violence were all too intimately bound up in the mythical origins of the city (the fratricide of Romulus, the Catilinian war), its historical ascent (Rome's imperial expansion, Florence's imperial service), and tragic fall (Rome's civil wars, Florence's factional wars) for any of the latter to be possible. Mars was, most troubling but inescapable of all, the founding father of Florence, Rome, and even Thebes—the principal dystopian model for the city of Dis in Dante's Hell.

This is in a sense the central paradox of the city narratives of Virgil, Statius and Dante: the city originates in Martial violence and yet its transcendent function is to maintain the social peace, (a peace it must—all the more paradoxically—sometimes *impose*).[11] But whether it is a fratricide like that of Romulus or a war

---

[11] The only systematic study of the role of Mars in Dante's understanding of

of Fiesolan/Catilinians against Roman Florentines that marks the origins of the city, once the spiral of fratricidal violence is unleashed its effects are uncontrollable: the city born of fratricide ends in fratricide.

While this tragic understanding of Rome's Martial origins surfaces with great frequency in Virgil's poem, it is a "generative" Mars that Virgil must first and foremost emphasize in Book 6: a Mars who is the father of Rome, the builder of the city, the driving force behind its growth into an empire, and the guarantor of its national cohesion, heroic vigor, moral rectitude, and restraint. This is the Mars of the astrological *thema Romae* which had reputedly marked both the city's foundation and the advent of Augustus: his powers held in fragile equilibrium by the harmonizing embrace of the sign Libra, special protectress of Rome and Italy, symbol of Roman justice and jurisprudence.[12]

In the prophetic scenario advanced by Anchises to propel Aeneas' conversion to the historical task, Mars is likewise present as the promoter of a different sort of energy: of bodily heat and progenation, of the coronary production of the seed, its im-

---

the epic cities of Thebes, Rome, and Florence is Ronald L. Martinez's "Dante, Statius, and the Earthly City," diss. University of California, Santa Cruz, 1977. Martinez exhaustively documents the place of Statius' *Thebaid* in Dante's urban representations, particularly in the first canticle. On Mars, see esp. 27–52.

[12] See Bouché-Leclercq, 368–371, on the astrology of the foundation of Rome. Speculations on the *thema Romae* can be found in Varro and Cicero, among others, and were imitated in the Florentine chronicles, as in Giovanni Villani's *Cronica* 3.1, which places Florence under the astrological rule of a rising Mars: "E dissesi ancora per li antichi, ch' e' Romani per consiglio de' savi astrologi, al cominciamento che rifondaron Firenze, presono l'ascendente di tre gradi del segno dell' ariete, essendo il sole nel grado della sua esaltazione, e la pianeta di Mercurio congiunta a grado col sole, e la pianeta di Marti in buono aspetto dell'ascendente, acciocchè la città multiplicasse per potenzia d'arme, e di cavalleria, e di popolo sollecito e procacciante in arti, e ricchezze, e mercatanzie, e germinasse d'assai figliuoli e grande popolo" (Dragomanni, vol. 1, 125). The notion of Libra as the sign of justice which stands in opposition to Mars and Martial signs such as Scorpio is a commonplace in astrological treatises. See, for example, Restoro d'Arezzo, *La composizione del mondo* 2.2.5.10–14.

plantation and historical fruit—the orderly succession of human generations. Here as in *De Rerum Natura* it is Venus (and not Libra) who provides the true symbolic/genealogical counterforce. Aeneas must found Rome so that the line of Trojan Venus may intermarry with the native line of Mars, bringing (as Augustine was perhaps the first to point out) the laws of *Amor* and *Roma* into euphonious accord. The result, to judge from Anchises' description of Rome's ascent, shall be the absence of genealogical corruption: Aeneas, Ascanius, Albanus, Silvius, Romulus . . . in an uninterrupted parade the seed of Troy shall have been passed from father to son without any falling away from origins. Their ultimate historical progeny will be the universal harmonization of mankind decreed by Providence from the very start: the Augustan reconstitution of Rome's originary Saturnian age, when the arts of Mars faithfully served under the rule of Reason and Love.

But for every triumphal vision of empire without end, there is in Book 6 an equally haunting one of the tragic price: visions of rupture, meaningless suffering, but most of all war, interminable war. Virgil contrasts each triumphalist prophecy with a representation of the persistence within history of a seemingly uncontainable sacrificial logic. The downward turn begins already at the gates of Phoebus' temple, onto which are etched the tragedy of Icarus, the yearly Athenian tribute of seven sons, and the tale of Ariadne's bestial offspring. It is completed on an even more somber note: the terrible cries of mourning that sweep across the city of Mars at the loss of the young Marcellus, who could have been the most glorious of Rome's commanders, the envy of the gods, but was not. The father's parade of Mars's triumphant sons is recast as a procession of victims of Mars: lost sons, sons cremated before their fathers' own eyes, monstrous progeny, disfigured carcasses.

Or worse still, his generative model of succession is interrupted by Oedipal strife and internecine conflict:[13]

[13] All quotations in this study from Virgil's *Aeneid*, including the one that fol-

> heu quantum inter se bellum, si lumina vitae
> attigerint, quantas acies stragemque ciebunt,
> aggeribus socer Alpinis atque arce Monoeci
> descendens, gener adversis instructus Eois!   6.828–831
>
> (What war, what grief, will they provoke between them—
> Battle-lines and bloodshed—as the father
> Marches from the Alpine ramparts, down
> From Monaco's walled height, and the son-in-law
> Drawn up with armies of the East, awaits him.)   vv. 1115–1119,
> Fitzgerald

This is the mark of a second Mars in Roman history counterbalancing the upward-driving progenerative Mars: a Mars now free from tempering Venus and Jupiter, outside the reach of Libra's scales of justice, a Theban Mars. Known to the reader of the *Aeneid* as the source of man's blind lust for the madness of combat (the *insani Martis amore* of 7.550) and as the "blood-stained Mars" or *sanguineus Mavors* (12.332) in whose company are always to be found the dark visages of Terror, Wrath, and Treachery ("atrae Formidinis ora / Iraeque Insidiaeque" [12.335–336]), he is the god of self-devouring war and ritual blood-letting, the spirit of faction in the city and of rebellion in the family.[14] It is he who in a number of different guises will, in the course of Book 6, in the *Inferno* and in cantos 14–18 of *Paradise*, severely test the son's determination to implement the father's plan (and were it not for the father's prophetic intervention from the beyond he might well succeed). Behind all natural and political corruption stands this wrathful Mars, perverting all erotic and semiotic order, and

---

lows, are from the 1892 Oxford edition of Virgil's complete *Opera* edited by Papillon and Haigh.

[14] On the attributes of the "infernal" Mars, see also the description of the "House of Orcus" in *Aeneid* 6.279–280 ("mortiferumque adverso in limine Bellum, / ferreique Eumenidum thalami et Discordia demens"); and the shield of Vulcan in 8.700–703 ("Saevit medio in certamine Mavors / caelatus ferro, tristesque ex aethere Dirae, / et scissa gaudens vadit Discordia palla, / quam cum sanguineo sequitur Bellona flagello").

bringing into being uncontrollable passions, blind egoism, and the madness of sons.

Is history then a zero sum? Does the rule of Mars condemn the history of the city to eternal cycles of peace and carnage? On these questions hinge all interpretations of Virgil's relation to the Augustan project as a whole. Answering in the affirmative, we follow the skeptical Virgil most recently emphasized in W. R. Johnson's *Darkness Visible*; in the negative, instead, the view that makes of Virgil an Augustan apologist.[15] The truth probably lies less in between than in a simultaneous yes *and* no: the tension is irreducible, no happy synthesis fuses the "political" with the "skeptical" Virgil. Ultimately, however, such a state of suspense must be understood as an affirmative answer: history under the sign of Mars is essentially natural history—a seemingly endless succession of generative and degenerative cycles ungoverned by any higher principle than alteration itself.

It is thus that before the *ruina* of *Inferno* 12 Dante has Virgil invoke the Empedoclean theory of history in the midst of another of his important misprisions of the Harrowing of Hell:

> Ma certo poco pria, se ben discerno,
> che venisse colui che la gran preda
> levò a Dite del cerchio superno,
>   da tutte parti l'alta valle feda
> tremò sì, ch'i' pensai che l'universo

[15] W. R. Johnson, *Darkness Visible: A Study of Virgil's Aeneid*, 152: "in the *Aeneid* there grows a constant impulse towards awful dualism that mocks the splendid unities of classical humanism, with its belief in an intelligible universe and in purposeful human activity inside the universe. The metaphors for evil have become, here below, the truths." Cf. Charles Norris Cochrane, *Christianity and Classical Culture*, 27: "Vergil constitutes a supreme embodiment of the optimism of his age. In him we may perceive the scope and character of those aspirations to fulfilment which were stirring in the contemporary world and which had come into focus in the programme of the Caesars. But this, in itself, by no means exhausts the significance of his work. For, while revealing the substance of the Augustan hope, Vergil at the same time disclosed its essential basis, relating it to a vast background of human history and giving it, indeed, a cosmic setting."

sentisse amor, per lo qual è chi creda
  più volte il mondo in caòsso converso. . . .   *Inf.* 12.37–43

(But certainly, if I reckon rightly, it was a little before He came who took from Dis the great spoil of the uppermost circle, that the deep foul valley trembled so on all sides that I thought the universe felt love, whereby, as some believe, the world has many times been turned to chaos. . . .)

While Virgil's statement is somewhat equivocal due to the noncommittal "è chi creda," it freely acknowledges its inability to find an alternative to Empedocles' endless cycles of eros and chaos, love and war. Such a view brings us back to Lucretius' proem, implying that history is little more than flux and that its determining events, whether linked to the ascendancy of eros over chaos or vice versa, are fundamentally military. The forces of either Venus or those of Mars, whichever are strongest, rule the universe; a dualism which clearly encompasses the figures of Christ the Crucified ("tremò sì") and Christ the Harrower—the intrepid commander who seized the glorious prey ("la gran preda") from *Dite*—as present in Virgil's description. In either event *Harmonia*, the most cherished progeny of Venus and Mars, remains elusive.

Virgil's Mars may accordingly be viewed as an epic avatar of the Boethian goddess Fortuna. Turning her wheel this way and that, Fortune too is forever upending the very foundations of human history, though in so doing she always serves a providential end.[16] The end which for Boethian man lies beyond the experience of this infernal circularity is to be found in Philosophy's invitation to seek a private form of consolation above and beyond the vicissitudes of historical becoming: a site uncontaminated by

---

[16] On Boethius and Fortune in general, see Howard E. Patch, *The Tradition of Boethius* and *The Goddess Fortuna in Medieval Literature*. On Dante's attitude toward the Boethian view of history, see especially Giuseppe Mazzotta, *Dante, Poet of the Desert*, 319–328, which approaches Dante's relation to Boethian *fortuna* in terms of St. Augustine's historiography. See also Vincenzo Cioffari, *The Conception of Fortune and Fate in the Works of Dante*.

unstable temporal perspectives, a site from which all of history's discordant events may be transcended and even harmonized. This is the end sought and achieved by Virgil's Anchises, Cicero's Africanus, and Dante's Cacciaguida. All are in a sense Boethian men: men of action transformed into men of contemplation, gazing back into history from the perspective of eternity. Each is the paternal counterpart of Boethius' *Philosophia*, bearing a message of comfort and consolation to the son immersed in the violence of the earthly city.

Yet there is a powerful countercurrent in Virgil's and Dante's texts that refuses this contemplative posture. The Boethian paradigm necessarily implies a partial abandonment of the Christian insistence on the meaningfulness and high drama of human history, as well as of Virgil's seeming belief in the providential design of Roman history.[17] Both of these views amount to a call—a characteristically epic call—to bring the perspectives of eternity and history into a more dynamic interplay, to supplement one's contemplative *theoria* with a militant historical *praxis*. This is what for Dante made the pagan Virgil a figure precisely comparable to the greatest Hebrew prophets: the conviction that behind the apparent circularity of Martial history lay a dialectical machine driving humanity as a whole toward a universal and climactic event.

---

[17] In *Christ and Time: The Primitive Christian Conception of Time and History*, Oscar Cullmann has argued that the most radical anti-Classical idea found in early Christian thought is that of a temporality in no way dialectically opposed to an atemporal "eternity." Cullmann suggests that even the term "eternity" is understood in an entirely temporal sense in early Christian thought, and that the story of the first four centuries of Christian intellectual history is that of the re-Hellenization of the Christian understanding of time. Dante clearly stands at the end of this process, so when I speak of a "Christian" theology of history here, I am referring more to the synthesis of Hellenic and properly Christian (in Cullmann's sense) modes characteristic of Dante's period. On Dante's own theology of history, see Charles Till Davis, "Dante's Vision of History," *DS* 93 (1975): 143–160 (reprinted in *Dante's Italy and Other Essays*, 23–41) and, once again, Mazzotta's *Dante, Poet of the Desert*.

It is not that history could for Dante or Virgil generate a progressive internal logic of its own. Nor could history appear as anything but a tragic circle, an empty exodus, when viewed in the son's strictly human terms. An external logic was required to give form and meaning to the text of history, an ordering from the perspective of eternity which could render the negativity of Mars *productive*. The locus of such a perspective would have to be above and beyond historical flux, while remaining accessible to history-bound man, so as to permit its active intervention in human affairs. This privileged site was for Virgil Elysium, for Dante Paradise, for Cicero the celestial Elysium of Plato's *Republic*, and it was from here that the eternalized genealogical father—empowered with the dual authority of origins and ends—could articulate the perspective of eternity, open up the Book of the Future for his sons, and reveal to them both the precise character of their task and the rewards that would result from its accomplishment.

Only here can an interpretive conversion be completed which is structurally essential to the *Aeneid* and the *Commedia*: the son's symbolic rupture with the Book of Memory and its retrospective images of peace and home, and his adoption of the father's future perspective as his own. Once this is accomplished, the father is no longer needed as an external support: the son is now fully empowered as the bearer of the holy paternal seed. Erasing the legendary Troy of Aeneas' forebearer and the epic Florence of Dante's exemplary *radice*, Mars had rendered such a metamorphosis inevitable, indeed, largely *conservative* in character. But certain resistances and symbolic obstacles remained, and with them the terrible burden of sadness and nostalgia. These only the father's prophetic intervention could truly conquer, and it is his intervention that serves as the symbolic turning point in each of these texts.

In the Classical context such a dynamic exchange between the perspectives of history and eternity could be achieved only through Helios Apollo: god of light and prophetic illumination, god of music, of poetry and of oracles. It is he who presides, through the *pii vates et Phoebo digna locuti* (6.662)—the prophets worthy of Phoebus' prophetic song—over the visions of Book 6. And it is his authority that is at stake in the conversion of Aeneas to the father's *comic* perspectives.

But can Apollonian vision truly rise up above the confusion of history under the rule of Mars? Can Apollo transform all of history's *tragic* signs into *comic* ones, make eternal gains of the son's tragic sacrifices and losses? Can man genuinely affiliate himself with eternity through Apollo? Despite the success of Aeneas' conversion—here Dante would have seen Christian hope secretly at work—for the Christian reader of the *Aeneid* the answer could only be "no."

This "no" in the case of Augustine was so resounding in its implications as to effectively deconstruct the very foundations of Virgil's representation in Book 6 of Roman history, from its providential claims to its highest moral and juridical ideals. In the preamble to the *City of God*, Augustine refers to Anchises' climactic formulation of Rome's most exalted aspirations:

> tu regere imperio populos, Romane, memento;
> hae tibi erunt artes; pacisque imponere morem,
> parcere subiectis et debellare superbos.   6.851–853
>
> (Roman, remember by your strength to rule
> Earth's peoples—for your arts are to be these:
> To pacify, to impose the rule of law,
> To spare the conquered, battle down the proud.)   vv. 1151–1154,
>   Fitzgerald

With brilliant acuity Augustine finds in Virgil's recourse to militarist verbs (*imponere, parcere,* de*bellare*) the key disclosure that the law of *Roma* is the antithesis of the law of *Amor* which resides exclusively in Jesus Christ.[18] (That R-O-M-A backward should spell A-M-O-R makes the antithesis all the more elegant of course.)

---

[18] *De Civitate Dei* 1.1.praefatio.

Rome's is in reality nothing but a law of uncontainable violence, an insatiable *libido dominandi*. Behind the humanist rhetoric exalting to the stars Rome's authority founded on reason, its model institutions of justice and law, lies an ever more tragic enslavement to the wrathful Mars.

The scenario is much the same in another Christian account which was equally authoritative for Dante and the Middle Ages: Paulus Orosius' apologetic continuation of the Augustinian anti-*Aeneid*, the *Historia Adversos Paganos*. Pagan history again unfolds under the exclusive hegemony of Mars. Its motto is *bella, horrida bella*. The ideals of Ciceronian humanism and the accomplishments of Roman jurisprudence are mere bubbles in a sea of blood.

For Dante there could be no radical antithesis between the laws of *Roma* and of *Amor*. The Augustinian formulation was at once too idealistic and too skeptical. Placing the law of Christ resolutely above any conceivable political implementation, it was naturally led to express profound doubts concerning all human political institutions. In his treatise on *Monarchy*, Dante sets out to construct in the hiatus between the two liminal Augustinian cities an actual historical—and not merely metaphorical—point of secular mediation: the universal Roman emperor "half-way between things corruptible and incorruptible" (*medium corruptibilium et incorruptibilium*) engaging Mars in the service of Christ, directly translating God's providential plan into historical action.[19]

That Virgil should remain to some degree entrapped within a Martial formulation of the meaning of the *pax Romanorum* was not for Dante the result of some fundamental misunderstanding of Roman history, but rather of a relative hermeneutic and epistemological incompleteness. Once the revelation of Christ's law of love is added to the Anchisean representation of history, the con-

---

[19] *Monarchia* 3.15.3. On Dante's defense of the Martial arts and his critique of Augustine's Christology, see in particular his treatment of duels in *Monarchia* 2.9. See also Davis' *Dante and the Idea of Rome*, 139–194, which is primarily concerned with Dante's attitude toward Augustine and Orosius.

taminated elements fall away, and Virgil's text at last becomes complete.

The missing master-signifier of the *Aeneid* and yet its secret protagonist, the cross of Christ, could alone provide the basis, in Dante's view, for any fully adequate act of reading or interpretation. In its absence, Virgil could envision no instrument powerful enough to expose all historical and hermeneutic *insomnia* as illusory, or to exorcise the paralyzing sign of Mars/*mors* from the text of history, leading us to the higher meaning beyond the madness of the letter.[20] Nor could the higher productivity at work beneath the negative surfaces of Martial history be fully known: whether the cataclysmic violence of Golgotha or Apocalypse, or the simple devastation of the epic cities of Florence, Thebes, and Troy. Through the cross, Dante believed, a genuine perspective of eternity becomes available within human history that permits the full absorption of the catastrophe of Troy into the splendor of Rome, the fall of Roman Florence into the composition of a divine *comedy*, the negativity of Mars into the fullness of time which preceded Christ's birth.

Such a hermeneutic conversion is after all the explicit point of the advent of Beatrice in canto 30 of *Purgatory*: the metamorphosis of a funerary cry ("manibus date lilia plenis" [6.883]) into a hymn celebrating the return of an ancient love from the grave. Like a victorious prefiguration of the *sol Christi* which triumphs at the center, then at the two-thirds point (canto 23) and then at the end of *Paradise*, Beatrice rises over the eastern horizon in a veil of light, resurrecting through love all the lost promise, the ancient honor ("prisca fides" [6.878]), the immense hopes raised by Mars's most tragic sacrificial victim: the youth enshrouded in

---

[20] Dante underscores the incompleteness of Virgil's comprehension of the sign of the cross on a number of occasions in the first canticle. The most important of these comes in *Inferno* 23.124–126, when we see Virgil in a state of wonderment before the crucified hypocrites Annas and Caiaphas. Although it is conceivable that his *meravigliar* is due to their absence on his earlier descent, it seems more likely that the punishment itself provokes his amazement.

HISTORY IN THE GRIP OF MARS

darkness at the conclusion of Book 6, whose absence is now revealed as that of Virgil himself.[21]

Virgil disappears because it was not he, but his successor Dante, who would explore the realm of paradise that the cross opens up in its wake. Without an understanding of the genuine perspective of eternity implanted into history through the cross, Virgil and his characters—Dante always meshes their respective plights—were entrapped in the fatal circularity of Mars. Listening to the voice of Apollo, they listened in reality to that of Mars; calling again and again for blood sacrifice (6.38–41, 6.249–267), demanding the cremation of Misenus (6.149–155), seizing its intermediaries with *furia*, drunken stupors and the confused images of sleep rather than with the full wakefulness of revelation.

The language it speaks is that of madness: a Babelic dialect of circumlocutions, conundrums, palindromes, recursive phrases ("bella, horrida bella"), and utterances with mutually self-cancelling meanings.[22] Such circular "riddles of terror . . . enshrouding in darkness its truths" ("horrendas canit ambages . . . obscuris vera involvens" [6.99–100]), issuing forth from one hundred gaping mouths/tunnels/doors or textualizing themselves in a pile of unbound leaves forever on the verge of becoming literary nonsense, could only be those of a profoundly decentered speaking subject. In promising at the beginning of Book 6 to bind these leaves to a stable institution—a shrine to Phoebus at the center of Rome—Aeneas looked forward to Christ's final restoration of semiotic order to the world, yet unaware of the true identity of Helios.

[21] In "Theological Semantics: Virgil's *Pietas* and Dante's *Pietà*," *SIR* 2 (Spring 1981): 76–77, Robert Ball has proposed a highly suggestive psychoanalytic reading of this crucial succession scene, further developing a number of important ideas from John Freccero's lectures on *Purgatory* 30.

[22] An *ambages*, defined literally, is a "circuitous path" or labyrinthine "winding" (see *Metamorphoses* 8.161); defined figuratively it is "circumlocution, evasion, digression" or obscure and enigmatic speech (*A Latin Dictionary*, eds. Lewis and Short, 101). On the textualization of madness, see Paolo Valesio, "The Language of Madness in the Renaissance," *Yearbook of Italian Studies* (1971): 199–234.

The pagan confusion of the language of revelation with that of madness could only be the sign of an imbalanced civilization: a *gente folle*, a "mad people," as Dante will put it in canto 17 of *Paradise*. Seeking in madness a guide to the otherworld, and through methods marginal to consciousness its insights into the future, Classicism was led, in Dante's view, to a fatal *inviscamento* (17.32): a sense of paralysis, of oppressive fate, a sense that man was forever condemned to repeat the errors of the past.[23] It was consequently blind faith that must bring Aeneas to sacrifice everything for the building of a future city he shall never know. Faced, furthermore, with the prospect of wars present, past, and future, haunted by the shades of their tragic victims and by the seeming arbitrariness of the laws of the Classical otherworld—the souls' hard (and even, perhaps, unjust) lot, their "sortemque animo . . . iniquam" (6.332)—it is hardly surprising that the son should be brought to question the historical condition itself:

> O pater, anne aliquas ad caelum hinc ire putandum est
> sublimes animas iterumque ad tarda reverti
> corpora? quae lucis miseris tam dira cupido?   6.719–721

> (Must we imagine,
> Father, there are souls that go from here
> Aloft to upper heaven, and once more
> Return to bodies' dead weight? The poor souls,
> How can they crave our daylight so?)   vv. 965–969, Fitzgerald

Or in the case of Scipio, at the conclusion of Cicero's *Republic*, the son is led to doubt the very necessity of the historical task:[24]

---

[23] The equation between divinity and madness would have seemed particularly striking in the light of Isidore of Seville's well-known etymology of the term Sibyl: "Sibyllae generaliter dicuntur omnes feminae vates lingua Graeca. Nam σιὸς Aelico sermone deos, βουλὴν Graeci mentem nuncupant, quasi dei mentem" (*Etym.* 8.8.1).

[24] *De Re Publica* 6.15; Eng. trans. by George H. Sabine and Stanley B. Smith from *On the Commonwealth*, 259.

HISTORY IN THE GRIP OF MARS

> Quaeso, inquam, pater sanctissime atque optime, quoniam haec est vita, ut Africanum audio dicere, quid moror in terris? Quin huc ad vos venire propero?

> (O father most excellent and holy, since true life is here, as Africanus tells me, why, I ask you, do I linger upon earth? Why may I not hasten to come to you?)

The answer to such questions is an ambivalent one, at least in the central book of the *Aeneid*.

Against the prison of the body and the nightmare of history under the rule of Mars, Virgil imagines an Elysium in that most urban of literary genres: the pastoral mode. Arcadia in Book 6 is all too uncanny a double of human history: a representation not of a radical otherness but of a fully recognizable sameness. It is history's Hall of Fame, a humanist analogy to the immortality that Christian salvation claims to provide, a place of sopor and/or release from temporal cares, where the machinery of war provokes nostalgia in the blessed:

> Quae gratia currum
> armorumque fuit vivis, quae cura nitentes
> pascere equos, eadem sequitur tellure repostos.   6.653–655

> (All the joy they took, alive, in cars and weapons,
> As in the care and pasturing of horses,
> Remained with them when they were laid in earth.)   vv. 874–876,
> Fitzgerald

And if this "contamination" by history were not enough, the eternal peace of Elysium is even more threatened by a tragic human forgetfulness: a strange compulsion to return from Arcadia to the scene of sacrifice and suffering, to submit the soul anew to the prison of the body and the inequities of death. Virgil's escape from history was thus for Dante fully immersed in historical flux.

The logic of Cacciaguida's conflation in canto 17.31–36 of the Sibyl's "riddles of terror" with Anchises' Elysian prophecies is now clear: both speak from the same incomplete perspective of eternity. The extraordinary disparity of the two figures, Anchises the pious Roman father speaking in the voice of Classical wisdom, the Sibyl the incarnation of the forces of madness and unreason, renders the conflation all the more powerful and astute a dramatization of the hermeneutic chaos wreaked by Apollo.[25] If the only transcendance of the sibylline *bella, horrida bella* that

[25] This disparity must be juxtaposed with the ideal complementarity of Cacciaguida and the poet-pilgrim's own Sibyl, Beatrice, who appear both as mirrors of divinity and as mirror-images of one another. Dante's conflation confirms a structural feature of Virgil's poem that has not usually been noted: the prophecies of the Sibyl and Anchises are not only closely related, but also begin and end on the same note. In the speech with which she opens Book 6, the Sibyl first expresses dire forebodings concerning the Trojans' new home (83–90), then refers to the many *bella, horrida bella* that are to come, alludes to the new Achilles (Turnus) whose blows Aeneas shall have to parry, and concludes with a promise: the Trojans' persistence shall eventually pay off and a mysterious "Graia . . . urbe" (97)—Evander's Pallanteum—will provide the "via prima salutis" (96). Anchises returns quite precisely to the Sibyl's themes in the closing speech of Book 6: "exin bella viro memorat quae deinde gerenda, / Laurentesque docet populos urbemque Latini, / et quo quemque modo fugiatque feratque laborem" (890–892). Alluding here to the Sibylline *bella*, to their locus—an oblique reference, at the very least, to Turnus—and to an eventual but still mysterious overcoming of fate's blows, Anchises completes the prophetic circle opened up by the Sibyl, binding their two discourses together and setting the stage for Dante's conflation of the two in *Paradise* 17. The link is further reinforced by an additional detail: near the end of Book 5 Anchises clearly foreshadows the Sibyl's words of gloom, announcing the presence of a "gens dura atque aspera cultu / debellanda tibi Latio est" (5.730–731). One final point: it is self-evident that the phrase "quo quemque modo fugiatque feratque laborem" (6.892) recalls the promise made by Helenus in 3.458–460 that a *woman* shall tell Aeneas of "Illa tibi Italiae populos venturaque bella, / et quo quemque modo fugiasque ferasque laborem, / expediet, cursusque dabit venerata secundos." Virgil would seem to contradict himself on this point since the self-quotation in 6.892 implies that it is Anchises (and not a woman) who has made this disclosure. But the difficulty is more apparent than real, for the Sibyl too refers with great precision to the "venturaque bella" faced by the Trojans and, like Anchises, offers a hint as to the *cursus* to victory: the mysterious "via salutis" of 6.96. Cf. Marguerite Mills Chiarenza's "Boethian Themes in Dante's Reading of Virgil," *SIR* 3 (Spring 1983): 25–35, which underscores Virgil's self-contradiction as well as parallels in the Cacciaguida episode.

the Classical father can propose is Fame—an eternity resulting from service to mankind and oddly dependent upon historical remembrance—then there is indeed something nightmarishly circular about the central book of the *Aeneid*.[26]

As Dante saw it, Virgil's vision was in the end a true *insomnium*: a nightmare which for Aeneas does not simply "flee when he awakes and quickly vanish into the thin air" ("cum somno avolant et pariter evanescunt"), as Macrobius would pretend in his commentary on the *Dream of Scipio*.[27] But this is not due to any inherent flaw in the Virgilian vision of history. Rather, it is due to the insufficiency of the hermeneutic of Apollo and its Elysian locus: their inability to differentiate the truths of revelation from the mad enigmas of the Sibyl, their inability to penetrate the ultimate meaning of Roman history—Christ's cross.

[26] In *Purgatory* 11 the pursuit of fame is identified by the illustrator Oderisi da Gubbio with the sin of pride and with *artistic* pride in particular. (Both are sins that Dante openly confesses on a number of occasions, the opening of *Paradise* 16 being a case in point.) Eternal *fama*, Oderisi insists, is but an illusion: "non è il mondan romore altro ch'un fiato / di vento, ch'or vien quinci e or vien quindi, / e muta nome perché muta lato" (*Purg.* 11.100–102). These words follow his description of the shifting fortunes of Cimabue and Giotto and of the two Guidos, Guido Guinizelli and Guido Cavalcanti. A third contender for the literary throne goes unnamed ("forse è nato / chi l'uno e l'altro caccerà del nido" [11.98–99]), but is of course none other than Dante himself. The question of fame and its subordination to the Christian writer's prophetic vocation is raised anew (and resolved) in canto 17 of *Paradise*.

[27] In his discussion of dream typologies Macrobius classes the *insomnium* among those with no prophetic significance. As a result, Virgil's Book 6 represents less an *insomnium* in the technical sense than a hybrid vision, encompassing modes as diverse as the *insomnium*, the oracular dream, and the enigmatic dream. But by identifying the *caelo* of 6.896 ("Falsa ad caelum mittunt insomnia Manes") with the earth and Virgil's *falsa* with the realm of temporal becoming, Macrobius effectively undermines the entire Virgilian—or at least Anchisean—vision of Roman history. For Macrobius human history is indeed a meaningless dream that vanishes when death awakens us to the transcendent realm of ideas. See *Commentarii* 1.3.1–14 on the general matter of dream visions. Cf. John of Salisbury, *Policraticus* 2.15.

So the passage of Aeneas and the Sibyl out the ivory gate at the end of Book 6 through which "false dreams are sent by the shades of the dead to the upper world" ("falsa ad caelum mittunt insomnia Manes" [6.896]), could not have meant to Dante what it did to Macrobius: namely, that the realm of becoming was forever to be a place of madness and meaninglessness.[28] Nonetheless, it must have seemed a startling confession on Virgil's part that the sun shining over his Elysium—the "solemque suum" of 6.641—could neither overcome the blinding negativity of Mars, nor provide human reason with an adequate foundation for knowledge of matters historical and suprahistorical alike.

Like the imperfect nimbus that appears suspended over Dante's limbo in *Inferno* 4.68–69 ("io vidi un foco / ch'emisperio di tenebre vincia"), always on the verge of victoriously dispersing (*vincere*) a horizon of darkness but itself tragically bound (*vincire*), this Elysian sun had never truly emerged from behind a veil of sleep—a Sleep which is no less than Death's blood-brother ("consanguineus Leti Sopor" [6.278]).[29] But whether the master-sig-

---

[28] This was a favorite passage of Virgil's commentators. The most complete study of their interpretations is that of Pierre Courcelle, "Les Pères de l'église devant les enfers virgiliens," *Archives d'Histoire Doctrinale et Littéraire du Moyen Âge* 22 (1953): 5–69. See also his "Interprétations néo-platonizantes du livre VI de l'*Enéide*," *Entretiens sur l'Antiquité Classique de la Fondation Hardt* 3-"Recherches sur la tradition platonicienne," (1955), 117–118, esp. For a recent view which supports Macrobius' insistence on Virgil's absolute skepticism toward human history, see R. J. Tarrant, "Aeneas and the Gates of Sleep," *Classical Philology* 77 (January 1982): 51–55.

[29] The consanguinity of Sleep and Death is a notion derived from Homer's *Iliad* 14.231. The passage is cited in Augustine's treatise on the soul: "Now, although even those objects which we suppose to be like bodies are of the same class, yet so far as the dead are concerned, we can form an after guess about them from persons who are asleep. For it is not in vain that the Holy Scripture describes as 'asleep' those who are dead, were it only because in a certain sense 'sleep is akin to death' " (*On the Soul and its Origins in Saint Augustine: Anti-Pelagian Writings*, trans. Phillip Schaff, 4.28). Augustine is associating the passage from Virgil with 1 Thessalonians 4:13—an important Christian text for the metaphorics of resurrection as awakening.

nifier of Classicism was to be *death* or simply *sleep*, the tragic grip of Mars/*mors* on human history would remain inescapable so long as Classicism could conceive of no force powerful enough to convert history's tragic signs into comic ones, history's temporary losses into eternal gains. This, Dante believed, Christ alone could bring about: the true *solemque suum*, as shall be seen in a subsequent chapter, at the center of his Christian *Paradise*. And restoring Elysium to its proper celestial site, this Christian sun sadly left Apollo's Hall of Fame just where Virgil had situated it: in limbo between the eternal tortures of Hell and the eternal sopor of its entryway and vestibule.

III

MARTE/MORTE/MARTIRIO: THE DILEMMA OF FLORENTINE HISTORY

> Et sachés que la place de tiere ou Florence est fu jadis apelee chiés Mars, c'est a dire maisons de batailles; car Mars, ki est une des .vii. planetes, est apelés deus de batailles, ensi fu il aourés ancienement. Por ce n'est il mie merveille se li florentin sont tozjors en guerre et en descort, car celui planete regne sor aus.
>
> BRUNETTO LATINI,
> *Li Livres dou Tresor*
> 1.37.2–3

Adapting the Virgilian precedent to the concrete circumstances of his biography, Dante proposes at the center of the third canticle a reenactment of Book 6, but *with a difference*: the cross of Christ which rises victoriously over the heaven of Mars. It is this difference that cantos 14–18 explore in a constant counterpoint of comic and tragic perspectives. If through the cross the providential principle which governs historical becoming was disclosed and a new foundation provided for the city of man, the disruptive Mars of Virgil's *Aeneid* and Statius' *Thebaid* nevertheless survives, but only as the blood-red field against which Christ's triumphant sign is profiled.

The particular density and hue of this Martial background, however, is not only Virgilian and Statian but also quite specifically *infernal*. Omnipresent in the *Commedia*'s first canticle, Mars appears as the virtual lord of Dis, the city of Martial dis-cord by antonomasia.[1] At the gate of the *città roggia*, his art of war is practiced against Virgil and the pilgrim by an army of gruesome guardians: a thousand wrathful souls, the Medusa and three of

---

[1] On Mars in the *Inferno*, see Georg Rabuse, *Der kosmische Aufbau der Jenseitsreiche Dantes: ein Schlüssel zur Göttlichen Komödie*, 11–77. In "Dante 'Apollinian' " (*Annali dell'Istituto Universitario Orientale, Sezione Romanza* 12 [Naples, 1970]: 181), Erich von Richtofen terms Mars "a simile representing the evil spirit in Florence as opposed to Christian ideals."

the war god's favorite Furies, all bent on revenge for the assault of Theseus (9.54). Within its walls and showered by fire—the element of the planet Mars—are the violent: murderers, suicides, blasphemers, sodomites, and usurers, destroyers of their own substance and of God's. Right before them come the heresiarchs, and among them Farinata degli Uberti, a great practitioner of the terrible art of Mars. "You shall know how much that art weighs" ("tu saprai quanto quell' arte pesa" [10.81]), he promises the pilgrim-poet, alluding to the definitive character of the latter's explusion from Florence in 1302 (while also avenging an earlier reference to a military setback suffered by his own political party).

As it turns out, Farinata's promise, implicating Mars in the future of the pilgrim and of his native Florence, is not the exception but the rule. In *Inferno* 6, Mars appears as the spirit of faction and discord (6.63), inflaming Florentine hearts with "pride, envy and avarice" ("superbia, invidia e avarizia" [6.74]).[2] In canto 13 he is explicitly named and appears, as in *Paradise* 16, as Florence's vengeful *primo padrone* or "first guardian," who, once displaced by John the Baptist, "will with his art forever make her sorrowful" ("sempre con l'arte sua la farà trista" [13.145]). In Vanni Fucci's prophecy of 24.143–151, Mars's presence is at once meteorological and military: he shall gather an "impetuous and bitter storm" ("tempesta impetüosa e agra" [24.147]) over Campo Pi-

---

[2] Mars's presiding role over all sins of *political incontinence*—later thematized in terms of the prostitution both of Florence as well as Papal and Imperial Rome—may already be foreshadowed by the place of the she-wolf in the poem's opening prophecy. Symbolic bearer of sins of incontinence and principal antagonist of the salvific *veltro*, the she-wolf was commonly associated with the Roman prostitutes and their trans-Tiburtine bordellos and identified as the tutelary beast of Mars. In Servius' words: "Nam et meretrices lupas vocamus, unde et lupanaria, et constat hoc animal in tutela esse Martis" (*Commentarii in Vergilii Carmina* 1.273 [Thilo/Hagen, vol. 1, 102]). Cf. *Aeneid* 9.565–566 ("quaesitum aut matri multis balatibus agnum / Martius a stabulis rapuit lupus") and Horace, *Carminum* 1.17.9 ("Nec Martiales haedulae lupos"). For further references to this commonplace of Roman mythography, see W. H. Roscher's *Ausführliches Lexikon der griechischen und römischen Mythologie* 2.2430.

ceno, only to strike down the Whites, Dante's own party, with a crushing bolt of lightning.

What this brief survey of Martial *terribilia* reveals—and many further examples could be cited—is firstly the extent to which cantos 14–18 of *Paradise* are central to the *Commedia*'s prophecies as a whole. They provide the poem's climactic clarification of what by now has emerged as a crucial question: how does Mars intersect the future trajectories of pilgrim and *patria*? Secondly, our survey reveals that even under the cross history will continue to be a place of loss and wandering: a "fallacious world," as Cacciaguida, echoing Boethius, will put it at the end of canto 15.[3] Confronting his fate in canto 17, Dante must confront no less than Aeneas a frightening *insomnium*. His nightmare, indeed, is all the more clearly cast in the Macrobian mold. Exhorting Dante to complete his text, Cacciaguida must first address "the worries that afflict his spirit or body and vision of the future"; and exposing the "insidious snares that are concealed behind a few circlings" ("le 'nsidie / che dietro a pochi giri son nascose" [17.95–96]) Cacciaguida recalls the fears of "insidious plots and the physical might of an enemy" that haunt the Macrobian insomniac.[4]

---

[3] In the heaven of the sun Dante describes Boethius as "l'anima santa che 'l *mondo fallace* / fa manifesto a chi di lei ben ode" (*Par.* 10.125–126; my italics). The self-quotation is probably a re-quotation since the adjective "fallax" is a privileged one in Boethius' *Consolation of Philosophy*. In the text's opening poem we find the following description of unstable Fortune: "Nunc quia fallacem mutavit nubila vultum" (1, metrum 1.19). In *prosa* 6, Lady Philosophy promises to unveil the true light that is concealed behind man's deceitful affections: "ut dimotis fallacium affectionum tenebris splendorem verae lucis possis agnoscere" (1, prosa 6.61–62). Again in the opening verses of Book 2, the adjective recurs in a discussion of Fortune: "Humilemque victi sublevat fallax vultum" (2, metrum 1.4). In meter 10 of Book 3, the chain that binds the human mind to earthly cares is described as "fallax": "Huc omnes pariter venite capti / quos fallax ligat improbis catenis / terrenas habitans libido mentes" (3, metrum 10.1–3). The self-quotation in canto 15 thus appears to be a direct echo of Boethius' own discourse on the fallaciousness of the realm of appearances.

[4] *Commentarii* 1.3.4. The complete text of Macrobius' definition runs as follows: "est enim ἐνύπνιον quotiens cura oppressi animi corporisve sive fortunae, qualis vigilantem fatigaverat, talem se ingerit dormienti: animi, si amator deliciis

But the poet-pilgrim's conversion to the epic (literary) endeavor is considerably eased, or such is Dante's claim, by the victorious precedent of Christ on the cross: a concrete model for imitation and a guarantee that history's losses are only temporary and its sufferings the divine *paideia* which alone can transform man into a true Son of God.

As it is mapped out in the narration of cantos 14–18, the text of Florentine history, which is to say the text of Dante's own biography, extends between the two liminal poles of post-incarnational history. At one extreme appears the Saturnian Rome of Augustus and Christ (figured in the epic Florence of Dante's great-great-grandfather Cacciaguida) and, at the other extreme, Apocalypse as associated by veiled allusion with the rise of Cangrande della Scala. In a rapid alternation which calls to mind that of Anchises in Book 6, the crusader Cacciaguida narrates the history of the city as a dialectic of generative and degenerative forces whose point of departure is an idyllic originary state.

He lingers in his description on the virtuous *Fiorenza* of the "cerchia antica" or "ancient circle" (15.97), not out of nostalgia, but rather putting into practice the didactic poetics he will formulate at the end of canto 17 (and which we may take as Dante's own):

> Però ti son mostrate in queste rote,
> nel monte e ne la valle dolorosa
> pur l'anime che son di fama note,
>   che l'animo di quel ch'ode, non posa
> né ferma fede per essempro ch'aia
> la sua radice incognita e ascosa,
>   né per altro argomento che non paia.   17.136–142

(Therefore only the souls known of fame have been shown to you within these wheels, upon the mountain, and in the woeful valley; for the mind of him who hears rests not nor confirms its faith by an

---

suis aut fruentem se videat aut carentem, si metuens quis imminentem sibi vel insidiis vel potestate personam aut incurrisse hanc ex imagine cogitationum suarum aut effugisse videatur" (*ibid.*).

example that has its roots unknown or hidden, nor for other proof that is not manifest.)

It should first of all be noted that the poetics of exemplarity here described—and this is a subject I will return to in my final chapter—constitutes an exact negative double of the Pauline definition of faith: "Est autem fides sperandarum substantia rerum, *argumentum non apparentium*" (Heb. 11:1; emphasis mine), or as rendered by Dante in *Paradise* 24.64–66, "fede è sustanza di cose sperate / e argomento de le non parventi" ("Faith is the substance of things hoped for and the conviction of things unseen"). Translating the mysteries of faith into exemplary figurations, poetry acts to confirm and strengthen the reader's faith while providing models for imitation. It thus imitates the "condescensional" movement of Scripture which attributes appendages such as hands and feet to the divine Father because, as Dante states in *Paradise* 4.40–42: "Così parlar conviensi al vostro ingegno, / . . . che solo da sensato apprende / ciò che fa poscia d'intelletto degno" ("It is necessary to speak thus to your faculty . . . which only through the senses apprehends that which it then makes fit for the intellect").[5] Such a principle of didactic "translation" can be shown to govern the structural relation of Cacciaguida to the cross of light, the poet-pilgrim to Cacciaguida and the reader to the poet-pilgrim, in descending order. For the moment, however, it is the particular exemplarity of Cacciaguida himself and of his Florence that is of interest, especially inasmuch as they illuminate the figure of the pilgrim—the poem's central *exemplum*.

In cantos 14–18 Cacciaguida appears literally as Dante's "treasure" (the actual appellation "mio tesoro" occurring in 17.121): an ideal paternal paradigm, a personal treasure-house of wisdom, a Book of Memory filled with political, moral and lin-

[5] In "*Paradiso* X: Dance of the Stars," *DS* 86 (1968): 85–111, John Freccero offers a brilliant exposition on the principle of accommodation and "condescension" in relation to the poetics of *Paradise*.

guistic models for imitation.⁶ And as Dante's "padre" (16.16), "primizia" (16.22), and "piota" (17.13), his role is to unfold the origin and meaning of the sacred family name, the "cognazione" (15.92) or "sopranome" (15.138) which, like Scipio, Dante now possesses only by inheritance.⁷ So this treasure is also the mirror in which the poet-pilgrim comes to recognize himself and the precise character of his endeavor—the literary act by which he shall take full possession of his cognomen. In and through Cacciaguida are represented Dante's symbolic inheritance, the "unknown and hidden root" ("radice incognita e ascosa" [17.141]) to which he is the frond, the powerful native voice which he is called upon to adopt and preserve even in exile, the promise of origins that is his responsibility to fulfill.

This promise, as we discover it in cantos 15–17, is a hybrid

---

⁶ Fulgentius' interpretation of Virgil could have influenced Dante's reading of Book 6 as the incomplete climax of Aeneas' *Bildung*, especially in its emphasis on the importance of memory. Fulgentius writes: "Next he [Aeneas] fastens the golden bough on the dedicated gateposts and so enters Elysium, where, the labor of learning now over, he celebrates the perfecting of memory, which is to be fastened in the brain as enduringly as the golden bough on the gateposts. He enters the Elysian fields—*elisis* in Greek means release—that is, the liberated way of life after finishing with the fear of teachers. As Proserpine is the queen of the lower world, so the queen of knowledge is memory, which as it advances reigns forever supreme in liberated minds. In this way is the golden bough dedicated to learning. Cicero used to say that memory was the 'treasure house of wisdom' " (*Exposition on the Content of Virgil*, in *Fulgentius the Mythographer*, trans. Leslie G. Whitbread, 132). Bernard Silvestris ends on a similar note: "But since committing to memory follows discovery by wit, Aeneas places the branch (*ramum*)—philosophy—across the threshold (*adverso limine*), the rear chamber" (*Commentary on the First Six Books of Virgil's Aeneid*, trans. E. G. Schreiber and T. E. Maresca, 107). As Dante's personal "treasure house of wisdom," Cacciaguida clearly exemplifies the three Augustinian divisions of the faculty of memory as stated in *Confessions* 11.20: memory concerned with the present of things past (retrospection), the present of things present (vision), and the present of things future (expectation).

⁷ See, for instance, *De Re Publica* 6.11: "Videsne illam urbem, quae parere populo Romano coacta per me renovat pristina bella nec potest quiescere . . . ad quam tu oppugnandam nunc venis paene miles? hanc hoc biennio consul evertes, eritque cognomen id tibi per te partum, quod habes adhuc hereditarium a nobis."

Christian-Roman one. Early Florence in Cacciaguida's narrative appears exactly as it was depicted in the city's first chronicles: as a *piccola Roma*, a perfect scale model of Augustan Rome.[8] The relation could not have seemed an accidental one to Dante: for defeating the Catilinian-Fiesolan conspirators, Cicero and Julius had in a single move constructed the city walls and cleared the way for the advent of the *pax Romanorum* (causally related events in the chronicle tradition).[9] As such, Florence emerges as the last

[8] *Chronica de Origine Civitatis*, in *Quellen und Forschungen zur ältesten Geschichte der Stadt Florenz*, ed. Otto Hartwig, 54ff. The following extract is characteristic: "E Giulio Cesare disfece la cittade di Fiesole, e fece la città nuova e popololla di gente fiesolana e di gente romana: e volle che per lui fosse chiamata Cesaria. La qual cosa non piacque a' sanatori, nè al consiglio di Roma: ma consigliarono e ordinarono che uno de' nobili cittadini di Roma dovesse far fare le mura della detta cittade: e le torri spesse per lo giro delle mura, e che tutta fosse edificata al modo di Roma: e anche un altro nobile cittadino dovesse far fare lo smalto della città a similitudine di quel di Roma: e un altro nobile cittadino dovesse far fare le piazze e il Campitoglio come quello di Roma: e un altro nobile cittadino . . . sicché non ebbe altro nome questa città a quella volta: poi fue chiamata *la piccola Roma*" (*Il libro fiesolano* [Hartwig, 54–56]; my italics). The comparable passage in Villani can be found in *Cronica* 1.38 (Dragomanni, vol. 1, 59ff.). On Dante's relation to Villani and Ricordano Malispini, see Charles T. Davis, *Dante and the Idea of Rome*, 244–262, and "Recent Work on the Malispini Question" in *Dante's Italy and Other Essays*, 290–299. On Dante and the chronicle tradition, see Giovanni Aquilecchia's "Dante and the Florentine Chroniclers," *Bulletin of the John Rylands Library* no. 48 (1965): 30–55, reprinted in *Schede di italianistica*, 45–72. As might be surmised from my emphasis on Dante's ties to the early chronicles, I am thoroughly persuaded of Villani's debt to Dante (and not of the inverse). Villani's standard practice is to compile and paraphrase secondary sources whenever possible, whether literary texts, like Dante's *Commedia*, or actual chronicles, making the case for Dante's dependence on Villani highly unlikely. The early chronicles, in any event, constitute a popular tradition which would have been familiar to literate and illiterate medieval Florentines alike, and it is they that appear to have been Dante's primary source. This is not to imply that the chronicles were in any sense authoritative for Dante: they are in fact freely modified, adapted, and even undermined, to better suit the *Commedia*'s literary and political ends.

[9] See especially the *Chronica de Origine Civitatis* (Hartwig, 45–61) and Giovanni Villani's *Cronica* 1.38 (Dragomanni, vol. 1, 59–62). The phrase *flore hominum Romanorum* is always present in the chronicle tradition in explanations of the city's

DILEMMA OF FLORENTINE HISTORY   43

of the genealogical descendants of epic Troy and epic Rome: a city of epic, the "church of Mars" of Brunetto's *Tresor*, always under the sign of the god of battle and war.[10]

The city's civic order is presided over by Florence's analogue of the pure senatorial race of Rome: the martial *flore hominum Romanorum*, the bearers of arms or *armipotens*, "color ch'a quel tempo eran ivi / da poter arme tra Marte e 'l Batista" ("All those who were there at that time able to bear arms between Mars and the Baptist" [16.46–47]). Its interiors are the domain not only of the feminine arts of weaving, spinning wool, and child-rearing, but also of an epic *paideia*. To properly shape the character of future citizens of the republic, mothers orally recite—"favoleggiare" is Cacciaguida's verb—the epics of Troy, Fiesole, and Rome (15.126), remember the exemplary virtues of a Cincinnatus and a Cornelia (15.129), and practice the ideal sobriety and decorum of the Roman in matters of public conduct and dress (15.100–102). Like the inhabitants of Cicero's perfect republic, the individual citizens of Cacciaguida's Florence appear at the same time as distinct personalities and as generalized social types. This is because here, as in all utopian sites, no gap is conceivable between private and public self, no troubling disjunction between objective surface and subjective depth. Implicit is always the individual's observance of an indelible set of sociopolitical and familial markings and a complete internalization of the law such that no external instance of enforcement is required, no formalized code, no written text.[11]

---

name: a name selected not only to honor Florinus, one of the city's reputed founders and its first martyr, but also the other noble citizens who participated in its construction. Villani's version follows: "Poi la maggiore parte degli abitanti furono consenzienti di chiamarla Floria, siccome fosse di fiori edificata, cioè con molte delizie. E dicerto così fu, perocch'ella fu popolata della migliore gente di Roma, e de' più sofficienti, mandati per li sanatori di ciascuno rione di Roma per rata" (Dragomanni, vol. 1, 62).

[10] See *Li Livres dou Tresor*, ed. Francis J. Carmody 1.37.2.

[11] The key term in the Ciceronian model is that of *decorum*: in this regard, see

But if originary Florence is Roman in its architecture, language, civic virtues, and morality, it is equally a place where Rome is recast in a Christian mold: where Classical *pietas* is transformed into Christian *pietà*, where to follow the Emperor is to take on the cross and follow Christ, and where the Christian *tropaeum crucis* has displaced all regal trophies and imperial ensigns.[12] Identifying himself first as "cristiano" and then as "Cacciaguida" (15.135), Dante's ancestor calls attention to the political metamorphosis this implies: over and above all martial virtues, juridical distinctions, and social hierarchies, the Christian city is founded in the egalitarian institution of Baptism. And through baptism all proper names are firmly anchored in the name of Christ, all individuality located in His collective body—the *Ecclesia*.[13]

Here Cacciaguida tilts his description away from the ideal republics of Aristotle and Cicero and toward the world of pastoral, stressing the chastening interplay of Classical and Christian elements. In its pagan form, epic Florence appears as a *locus amoenus* enclosed in the verdant valley of the Arno: the city of the pagan goddess of fertility, the voluptuous Flora, and a perfect site for the implantation and fructification of the holy seed of Rome. In its Christian form, it appears, rather, as the type of Eden, with Cacciaguida adopting the role of the Adamic founding father: pious citizen and good shepherd, speaker of a pre-lapsarian *antica*

---

in particular Cicero's *De Officiis* 1.27–33, which is of special importance to the fourth tractate of Dante's *Convivio*.

[12] On *pietas* and *pietà*, see Robert Ball, "Theological Semantics," 64ff. A general reading of the *Commedia* based on the symmetry of the signs of the Emperor and of Christ is advanced in Luigi Valli's, *Il segreto della croce e dell'aquila nella Divina Commedia*.

[13] For a more complete discussion of the Christianization of the Classical "discourse of the city," see Etienne Gilson's "Eglise et société," *La Philosophie au Moyen Âge*, 155–178; and Charles N. Cochrane, *Christianity and Classical Culture*, 488ff. Other instances of double self-identifications in the *Commedia* are *Purgatory* 5.88 ("Io fui di Montefeltro, io son Bonconte"), *Paradise* 6.10 ("Cesare fui e son Iustinïano"); cf. *Inferno* 2.32 ("Io non Enëa, io non Paulo sono"), and *Purgatory* 22.73 ("Per te poeta fui, per te cristiano").

favella closer to Virgil's noble Latin than to the rhetorical perversions and affectations of contemporary speech.[14] Hence the curious reference in 16.33–34 to the need for translation ("ma non con questa moderna favella, / dissemi"), and Cacciaguida's continual melding of Classical and Christian citations.

But, as in Eden, there is something dangerously overripe about Flora's pleasure: an excess obliquely underscored in Cacciaguida's reiterative "a *così* riposato, a *così* bello / viver di cittadini, a *così* fida / cittadinanza, a *così* dolce ostello" ("to *so* peaceful, to *so* fair a life of citizens, to *so* trustworthy a community, to *so* sweet an abode" [15.130–132; my italics]). This, Dante—still smarting from the sting of recent exile—had already signalled during a digression on his beloved native city in the first tractate of *De Vulgari Eloquentia*: "ad voluptatem nostram sive nostre sensualitatis quietem in terris amenior locus quam Florentia non existat" ("in terms of our pleasure and our sensual contentment there exists no more agreeable place in the world than Florence" [1.6.3]).

We are, nevertheless, repeatedly assured that in Cacciaguida's time such a danger was always tempered by the chaste pastoral of the Christian shepherd and his flock: "[la] cerchia antica / . . . si stava in pace, sobria e pudica" ("[the] ancient circle / . . . abode in peace, sober and chaste" [15.97–99]); the reflexive "si stava," best translated as "to stand alone" or "unto oneself," reinforcing the impression of autonomy, enclosure, and self-presence.[15] And

[14] As regards the relation of pastoral and urban typologies in cantos 14–18 see Mazzotta's discussion in "*Communitas* and Its Typological Structure," in *Dante: Poet of the Desert*, 124–131. Cf. D'Arco Silvio Avalle, "L'età di oro in Dante," in *Modelli semiologici nella Commedia*, 77–95; Rafaello Ramat, *Il canto XV del Paradiso*, esp. 12–13; and concerning the historical details of Cacciaguida's discourse, Charles T. Davis' "Il buon tempo antico (The Good Old Time)," in *Dante's Italy*, 71–93. On the rhetorical topic of the *locus amoenus*, see E. R. Curtius, "The Ideal Landscape," in *European Literature and the Latin Middle Ages*, esp. 195–200.

[15] Cacciaguida's "dentro da la cerchia antica" (15.97) recalls a phrase employed in the opening description of the terrestrial paradise: "dentro a la selva antica" (*Purg.* 28.23). The Middle Ages usually imagined Eden as a circular enclosure with the tree of knowledge at its center.

at the center of this circle, as if its ontological spindle, rose the focus of the city's daily life: the Florentine Baptistry, the "bel San Giovanni" (*Inf.* 19.17), undistracted by all worldly ambitions and cares, calling the sheep into the sheepfold (and not merchants to their stalls) at terce and none.[16] So it should come as no surprise that from this ideal pre-mercantile state of peace and harmony to the eternal peace of the City of God the path should seem to our pilgrim an exceedingly short one.

But as is the wont of pastoral, such a delicate balance cannot resist even the most modest of intrusions. The same martial virtues that maintained the civic equilibrium by holding off the forces of corruption, exteriority, and difference, once unbalanced, will turn inward to devour the sacred enclosure they had engendered in the first place. Or, to shift to another set of terms, Florence's Edenic surfaces were in reality but the outermost layer of a troubling and complex architectural palimpsest at whose center remained Mars. The site of the "bel San Giovanni" was according to the Florentine chronicles none other than that of the Temple of Mars, and the edifice itself but the reconverted Temple of War.[17] Worse yet, Florence's *primo padrone* had survived his deposition by the *secondo padrone*, John the Baptist. The scowling marble idol that once rose above the sacrificial altar, first removed from the city's center to a tower on the fringes of the Arno, now stood as the guardian of the Ponte Vecchio, one of the

---

[16] Cf. Jacques Le Goff, *Time, Work, and Culture in the Middle Ages*, 43ff., which makes use of this image in an analysis of temporality and Medieval modes of production.

[17] Villani writes: "Il detto duomo si crebbe, poichè fue consecrato a Cristo, ov' è oggi il coro e l'altare del beato Giovanni; ma al tempo che 'l detto duomo fu tempio di Marti, non v'era la detta aggiunta, nè 'l capannuccio, nè la mela di sopra; anzi era aperto di sopra al modo di Santa Maria Ritonda di Roma, acciocchè il loro idolo Iddio Marti ch'era in mezzo al tempio fosse scoperto al cielo. Ma poi dopo la seconda redificazione di Firenze nel 1150 anni di Cristo, si fece fare il capannucio di sopra levato in colonne, e la mela, e la croce dell'oro ch'è di sopra. . . . E per più genti che hanno cerco del mondo, dicono ch'egli è il più bello tempio, ovvero duomo, del tanto che si truovi" (*Cronica* 1.60 [Dragomanni, vol. 1, 83]). The passage is noted by most of Dante's commentators from Boccaccio onward.

city's major thoroughfares.[18] So, though displaced, mutilated, and worn, the pagan father remained within the ancient circle, ever hungry for revenge, ever anxious to regain his former throne.

Seduced, however, by the utopian prospects of canto 15 and puffed up with blood-pride, the pilgrim is at first impervious to such images of urban instability, contamination, and decay. He represses them—a move I have earlier troped by stressing the positivity of Cacciaguida's representation of originary Florence—holding out instead for a continuation of the narrative in a strictly nostalgic and pastoral mode.[19] It is in this spirit that

---

[18] The story as told by Villani is somewhat more complicated. The Florentine's lingering fear of Mars was held responsible for the idol's survival: "E nella nostra città di Firenze si cominciò a coltivare la verace fede, e abbattere il paganesimo al tempo di . . . che ne fu vescovo in Firenze fatto per Papa Silvestro; e del bello e nobile tempio de' Fiorentini, onde è fatta menzione addietro, i Fiorentini levaro il loro idolo il quale appellavano lo Iddio Marti, e puosonlo in su un'alta torre presso al fiume d'Arno, e nol vollono rompere nè spezzare, perocchè per loro antiche memorie trovavano, che il detto idolo di Marti era consegrato sotto ascendente di tale pianeta, che come fosse rotto e commosso in vile luogo, la città avrebbe pericolo e danno, e grande mutazione" (*Cronica* 1.60 [Dragomanni, vol. 1, 82]). According to Villani (*Cronica* 2.1 and 3.1 [Dragomanni, vol. 1, 89 and 124–125]) the actual disfigurement of the statue occurred in the year 450, when Florence was destroyed by Attila.

[19] It so happens that this pastoral tension can be translated into genealogical terms, since Cacciaguida—as Dante must certainly have known—was quite literally a "son of Adam." That his father's name was indeed "Adamo" we know from a 12th-century document discussed in the first volume of Robert Davidsohn's monumental *Geschichte von Florenz*, vol. 1, 440. This literal dimension further enhances the already rich ambiguities of Cacciaguida's role in cantos 15–18. He speaks, on the one hand, from a strictly post-Edenic perspective: insisting on the inexorability of the city's fall, calling for a repudiation of all nostalgia, and a conversion to his own eschatological perspective, and stating that in his own time Florence was "già nel calare" (16.90). On the other hand, he is set up as the central embodiment in the *Commedia* of the poet-pilgrim's origins: Dante's "radice" (15.89), "padre" (16.16), "primizia" (16.22), "piota" (17.13), and "tesoro" (17.121). And as the Edenic father he displaces the fallen historical father (Dante's own is pointedly absent): the only missing genealogical link in the narrative of cantos 15–16.

Dante adopts the honorific "voi" first spoken in Rome ("che prima a Roma s'offerie" [16.10]) at the opening of canto 16: a radical misprision of Cacciaguida's account of his knighting and subsequent martyrdom.[20]

But returning with great insistence to the theme of historical cyclicality and flux, and confronting his descendant with the inexorable negativity of Florence's fall, Cacciaguida will drive home a point that is the cornerstone of the rhetorical structure of cantos 14–18: the gulf between the present and past is unbridgeable *except via the future*. The fall of the city was necessary and good. Only by abandoning the fallen city for exile, only by taking on without fear or hesitation the literary task, can the promise of origins be fulfilled and the paternal *cognazione* be fully earned. Between the peace of the ancient circle and that of paradise stands an ineluctable intermediate point: that of martyrdom—the exemplary "martiro" which brought the crusader Cacciaguida from the fallen city to the heaven of Mars ("venni dal martiro a questa pace" [15.148]), and the personal and literary act of martyrdom which alone can permit the poet-pilgrim to duplicate his ancestor's glorious course.[21] Such a detour represents but a

---

[20] The "voi" was said to have been originally reserved for the Emperor Julius. Despite the fact that its use here is severely undercut, it serves nevertheless to mark Cacciaguida's ideal *Romanitas*: a result of his dual service under the Emperor and the Pope.

[21] Cacciaguida's itinerary, as I later note, is modeled after that of Boethius as described in *Paradise* 10.124–129:

> Per vedere ogne ben dentro vi gode
> l'anima santa che 'l mondo fallace
> fa manifesto a chi di lei ben ode.
>
> Lo corpo ond' ella fu cacciata giace
> giuso in Cieldauro; ed essa da martiro
> e da essilio venne a questa pace.

Aside from the obvious self-quotations here—"mondo fallace" and its rhyme with "da martiro . . . a questa pace" clearly anticipating 15.146–148 ("disviluppato dal mondo fallace, . . . venni dal martiro a questa pace")—a number of additional links to cantos 15–17 make this an absolutely crucial passage for under-

temporary loss; indeed, it is the only means of avoiding a truly tragic tear in the fabric of history: a sense of unconquerable sadness, and the paralysis and self-loss that must ensue.

The principal aim, then, of the father's prophetic intervention at the center of *Paradise*, like that of Aeneas' descent into the underworld in Book 6, is to free the son from the hypnotic spell of tragic events, present, past and future. If the task of prophecy in cantos 15–18 is first of all to make the history of the city simply *appear*, disclosing to the inheritor of the paternal seed the precise character of his responsibilities and origins, prophecy's second task, and one perhaps of even more decisive importance, is to make it *disappear*: absorbing it into a higher anagogical perspective, effectively sundering past from present in the son's imagination.

From the opening of Cacciaguida's description of ancient Flor-

---

standing the role of Cacciaguida as Dante's model. Line 124 recalls 18.1 ("Già si godeva solo del suo verbo"); "l'anima santa" calls to mind "l'anima santa" of 17.101; and "fa manifesto" in turn Cacciaguida's "tutta tua visïon fa manifesta" (17.128), which is itself embedded in a passage filled with paraphrases of Boethius' *Consolatio*. In addition, the past participle "cacciata" followed by "giace" and "giuso" comes exceedingly close to actually pronouncing the name of Dante's ancestor. Finally, the emphasis in verse 126 on the need to listen carefully to the Boethian unmasking of worldly goods ("a chi di lei *ben* ode")—an allusion perhaps to the ideal state of attentiveness described in *Consolatio* 3, prosa 1.3—is of some importance to the opening of canto 16. Here the poet-pilgrim's switch to the " 'voi' che prima a Roma s'offerie" (16.10) misreads the closing words of canto 15, since the poet-pilgrim hears, not a message drawing attention to the fallaciousness of earthly loves ("mondo fallace, / lo cui amor molt' anime deturpa"), but rather the opposite: a message glorifying his own ancestry and hence himself. What all of this suggests is naturally that Cacciaguida is a double of Boethius-Martyr: a martyr as well as a theological *auctor*, a spokesman for Boethian *Philosophia*, and, like Boethius, a literary *artista* (18.51). This is important inasmuch as it all the more clearly establishes Cacciaguida's exemplarity vis-à-vis the poet-pilgrim's own future martyrdom. In order to play the central role assigned to him in cantos 14–18, Cacciaguida must be more than just an ancestral Alighieri, an Anchises and/or Africanus: he must in some sense be Dante's literary ancestor, a Boethius as well as a Paul, who makes it clear that martyrdom involves not only the *literal* crusade of canto 15.142–148 but also the *literary* crusade delineated at the close of canto 17.

ence with its nine emphatic negatives, the dominant theme had thus been the irrevocability of the city's fall:

> Non avea catenella, non corona,
> non gonne contigiate, non cintura
> che fosse a veder più che la persona.
>   Non faceva, nascendo, ancor paura
> la figlia al padre, ché 'l tempo e la dote
> non fuggien quinci e quindi la misura.
>   Non avea case di famiglia vòte;
> non v'era giunto ancor Sardanapalo
> a mostrar ciò che 'n camera si puote.
>   Non era vinto ancora Montemalo
> dal vostro Uccellatoio, che, com' è vinto
> nel montar sù, così sarà nel calo.   15.100–111

(There was no necklace, no coronal, no embroidered gowns, no girdle that was more to be looked at than the person. Not yet did the daughter at her birth cause fear to the father, for the time and the dowry did not outrun due measure on this side and that. Houses empty of family there were none, nor had Sardanapalus arrived yet to show what could be done in the chamber. Not yet was Montemalo surpassed by your Uccellatoio, which as it has been passed in the uprising, so shall it be in the fall.)

The spiral of decay is one we recognize from the Classical discourse of the city.[22] First an incursion of supplementary elements

---

[22] See, for instance, Cicero's adaptation of Plato's *Republic* (563a–566b): "eos, qui pareant principibus, agitari ab eo populo et servos voluntarios appellari; eos autem, qui in magistratu privatorum similes esse velint, eosque privatos, qui efficiant, ne quid inter privatum et magistratum differat, ferunt laudibus et mactant honoribus, ut necesse sit in eius modi re publica plena libertatis esse omnia, ut et privata domus omnis vacet dominatione et hoc malum usque ad bestias perveniat, denique ut pater filium metuat, filius patrem neglegat, absit omnis pudor, ut plane liberi sint, nihil intersit, civis sit an peregrinus . . . inque tanta libertate canes etiam et equi, aselli denique liberi sic incurrant, ut iis de via decedendum sit" (*De Re Publica* 1.43). The descent of the well-ordered city into the the pure horizontality of carnival is commonly associated in Classical texts with the anarchic influence of the marketplace on the social order. Dante's attack on Florentine

disturbs the city's pastoral equipoise. Internally this may take the form of a sudden excess of bodily ornamentation: subverting the equation between beauty and self-identity, a woman attempts to tyrannize the desires of the collectivity. Externally, it is thematized as the breakdown of barriers between country and city: the Fiesolan evil seed (whose symbolic constituents are both mercantile and Catilinian) infiltrates the sacred enclosure, gradually contaminating the unsullied seed of Rome.[23] Or, as in verse 107, natural geography is itself subverted: orient becomes occident (like Julius Caesar feminized by Cleopatra at the conclusion of Lucan's *Pharsalia*), the transvestite king of Assyria, Sardanapalus, makes of the chaste *Fiorenza* an Epicurean.[24] Soon the local im-

---

mercantilism thus participates in the most ancient of conservative polemics; to the question of whether the marketplace—a place of symbolic exchange, of shifting property, of uncontrolled social circulation and flotation of values—can be fully reconciled with the maintainance of a hierarchically structured social system, Dante answers "no," but with Plato, Aristotle, and Cicero standing behind him.

[23] The language of miscegenation is everywhere in the chronicles, and in the *Gesta Florentinorum Sanzanomis* is employed to suggest that Fiesole was founded by Mars's own monstrous progeny: the giants of *Inferno* 31.51. On this and on the Fiesolan "malum semen inutilem producentem," see Hartwig (2–3). Mars is also associated with the foundation of Fiesole by Villani, who reports in *Cronica* 1.9 (Dragomanni, vol. 1, 27) that the sons of Attalante, Italus, and Dardanus, in order to determine who was to rule the city of Fiesole, went to sacrifice to "il loro Iddio alto Marte, il quale adoravano." (The tale is of course a retelling of the story of Romulus' fratricide and the foundation of Rome.)

[24] The usual gloss on Sardanapalus referring the reader to Juvenal's tenth Satire (v. 362) originates with Pietro Alighieri, and is only partially complete. In "Dante's Obligations to the *Ormista*" (*Dante Studies and Researches*, 131), Paget Toynbee added the suggestion that Orosius and Aegidius Romanus' *De Regimine Principum* might both have colored Dante's views of the Assyrian monarch. But neither is exact. Sardanapalus was a relatively important figure in exemplarist and moralizing literature at least as far back as Aristotle. He is present in one of Aristotle's now lost early political dialogues, in the *Nicomachean Ethics*, *Eudemian Ethics* and *Politics*, always cited as an *exemplum in malo*. In the *Nicomachean Ethics* he appears as the embodiment of hedonism: "Now the mass of mankind are evidently quite slavish in their tastes, preferring a life suitable to beasts, but they get

balance extends to the whole, perverting and falsifying the person, both as an individual entity and in its social interrelations. Speech becomes rhetoric, procreation a form of commerce, politics a theatre of self-interest, the surface of the body a disguise. As the principle of identity is fragmented, the entire system of social differentiation breaks down; the body politic is dismem-

---

some reason for their view from the fact that many of those in high places share the tastes of Sardanapalus" (1095b.19–22). In the *Eudemiam Ethics*, likewise, he is seen as a voluptuary: "those who felicitate Sardanapalus or Smindyrides the Sybarite or any other of those who live the voluptuary's life, these seem all to place happiness in the feeling of pleasure" (1216a.16–20). In Book 5 of the *Politics* his case is cited as an example of how unbecoming behaviour on the part of a monarch can breed contempt among his subjects and lead to murder: "Another motive [for assassination] is contempt, as in the case of Sardanapalus, whom someone saw carding wool with his women, if the story-tellers say truly" (1312a.1–2). By the time of Cicero, Sardanapalus had become explicitly identified with that which the Middle Ages would understand by the term "Epicurianism." In *Tusculans* 5.35.101, for instance, Cicero describes the reputed epitaph inscribed over Sardanapalus' tomb as reading: "That which I possess is that which I have eaten and consumed to satisfy my lusts. Behold instead the thousand magnificent goods I have left to waste." This, Aristotle was said to have remarked, was an epitaph befitting of a cow. The Assyrian monarch is again mentioned in Cicero's *De Re Publica* (in Book 3 among the *fragmenta*) and in *De Finibus Bonorum et Malorum* 2.32.106. Dante's more immediate sources, however, are likely to have been Augustine's *De Civitate Dei* and Albertus Magnus' *Commentarium in Octo Libros Politicorum Aristoteles*. In 2.20 of his work, Augustine cites the reputed epitaph and suggests that, despite Cicero's assertions to the contrary, the early Romans worshipped, not at the temple of Romulus, but rather at that of Sardanapalus: a further instance of the ultimate moral bankruptcy of the City of Man. Albertus, on the other hand, writes: "Deinde cum dicit, *Hae autem propter contemptum*, etc. enumerat insurrectiones, quae contingunt propter contemptum. Et primo ponit exemplum, ibi, *Sicut Sardanapalum*, de quo dicitur quod semper voluit esse clausus cum mulieribus in cameris, quem *videns quidam cum mulieribus* se *percutientem*, id est alapizantem: in hoc enim delectabatur, ut dicitur in Primo Ethicorum, eo quod totus resolutus voluptatem summum bonum reputabat" (*Commentarium* [Borgnet, vol. 8, 516–517]). The apparent recall in 15.108 ("ciò che 'n camera si puote"), as well as the presence of such themes as the confusion of public and private roles, of false leadership, and sexual inversion, all make the connection with Albertus tenable.

bered, the body of Christ prostituted: the moment of carnival has arrived (the moment of democracy and then ochlocracy in the Classical discourse).[25] Mars first reemerges upon the scene in this strictly metaphorical form: instituting a reign of generalized ontological violence, a state of radical liquidity, a perpetual reshuffling of all values, signifiers, proper names, fashions, mores, and beliefs. The end result is, however, not renewal, but rather faction and civil war: the *locus amoenus* is left a desert, the *dolce ostello* is made a city of the dead.[26]

As Cacciaguida represents it in canto 16, the descent of Florence into carnival and civil war is the result of Mars's cruel revenge: "conveniesi, a quella pietra scema / che guarda 'l ponte, / che Fiorenza fesse / vittima ne la sua pace postrema" ("it was fitting that to that broken stone which guards the bridge, Florence should offer a victim in her final days of peace" [145–147]). One of his titles, after all, was *Mars Ultor* (Mars the Avenger): a title

---

[25] On "carnival," see Mikhael Bakhtin, *Rabelais and His World*, and Julia Kristeva, "Le Carnaval ou l'homologie corps-rêve-structure linguistique-structure du désir," in *Sèméiôtiké: Recherches pour une sémanalyse*, 160–163. The extreme use of parataxis in Cacciaguida's speech is characteristic of the mechanism by which satirical texts, from the time of Juvenal to that of Wordsworth (cf. the "Residence in London" portion of the *Prelude*), stage the "carnivalesque" only to contain and supress it. The suspension of social codes is represented by means of a complex two-fold syntax. On the one hand, it "de-hierarchizes" the sentence, displacing the laws of syntactical subordination with a more elementary, and hence potentially anarchic, principle: that of purely quantitative accumulation. On the other hand, this procession of a potentially limitless series of terms is itself rigidly law-bound, chanelled in and out of the strictest sort of syntactical grid. In satire, "carnival" is the "parade" which immediately precedes the reinstatement of order.

[26] Dante is exceedingly consistent in his political metaphors and imagery, associating political strife with: (a) the presence of Mars; (b) the breakdown of the pastoral order (usually manifest in the metamorphosis of shepherds into wolves); and (c) with images of prostitution, disfigurement, and masquerade. Major examples are the "Ahi serva Italia" speech of *Purgatory* 6.76–151, Folquet of Marseille's denunciation of Florence in *Paradise* 9.127–142, the narrative of *Paradise* 15–17, and Saint Peter's denunciation of the papal "rapacious wolves dressed in shepherd's clothing" in *Paradise* 27.40–66.

granted so that he might punish a murder emblematic of Rome's own fissured body politic—Brutus' murder of Julius. The mutilated and/or cleft stone of canto 16 is also linked to a founding murder, the murder of Buondelmonte: the act which triggers the whole economy of factional revenge and blood exchange, whose end result is that the city is made a sacrificial victim ("vittima fesse"). In a deliberate parody of the Christian act of *devotio* or self-offering to Christ, Florence thus becomes an offering on the altar of Mars. Instead of making herself holy in a quite literal *sacri-ficium*—the sacrificial logic figured through Cacciaguida and the cross of light—Florence victimizes herself not in the name of Christ, but only to assuage the eternally bloodthirsty God of War.[27]

Yet the violence of her disfigured/disfiguring guardian stone is no less sacrificial than it is genetic and mercantile. Mars presides over the miscegenation of Florentine and Fiesolan seed, whose historical fruit is the substitution of Florence's epic Christianity by the religion of the marketplace and its god of exchange: the Juvenalian *sanctissima divitiarum maiestas*, her divine majesty Wealth, to whom God and Good are merely goods and Truth but a rhetorical trick.[28] And with this new deity arrives a new mercenary Mars: the individualized wars of commerce with their law of minimum risk and maximum return, taking the place of Conrad III's idealistic crusade "against the iniquity of that law whose people usurps . . . what is your right" ("incontro a la nequizia / di quella legge il cui popolo usurpa, / . . . vostra giustizia" [15.142–144])—an ideal harmonization, in Dante's view, of Roman and Christian ideals.

[27] "Fare vittima" was for Dante the definition of the verb "sacrificare," as we know from Beatrice's discourse on broken vows in *Paradise* 5.19–45: "nel fermar tra Dio e l'omo il patto, / vittima fassi di questo tesoro" [i.e., man's free will] (28–29). In verse 44 she refers back to the act of vowing as "questo sacrificio." Cf. Isidore, *Etym.* 6.19.30–39.

[28] The quotation is from Juvenal's *Saturae* 1.112–113, one of the many background texts for Cacciaguida's discourse. On satire as the epic of the fallen city, see *Saturae* 1.1–30.

In this satirical Florence, the market's wheel of fortune spins with dizzying rapidity, making and unmaking new dynasties (16.76), bringing about a constant confusion of persons (16.67), an endless shuffling of proper names, places, and events. Cacciaguida's long listing of Florentine families, in fact, serves to dramatize the absolute instability of all social and political Fortune in a post-lapsarian world: there are, as Charles Till Davis has written, "those already past their prime (16.88–90), those still in the midst of their prosperity (16.91–93), and those which had lately become prominent (16.100–108)."[29] Likewise, the consoling epic mother of canto 15 disappears, only to be replaced by a string of jealous stepmothers: the cruel and perfidious Phaedra (Florence) driving the chaste Hippolytus (Dante) into exile and to his death (17.46–48), the gluttonous clergy not beneficient like a mother to her son, but instead a maleficent stepmother unto Caesar (16.59–60). Such transgressions of both Roman and Christian piety extend to the family as a whole: the son becomes like Phaeton and Hippolytus a tragic victim, the father his executioner, and the pastoral urban flock of the sheepfold of Saint John—even in exile—a "wicked and senseless company" ("compagnia malvagia e scempia" [17.62]), its locus a valley of ingratitude, madness and cruelty ("questa valle . . . tutta ingrata, tutta matta ed empia" [17.63–64]).[30]

[29] *Dante and the Idea of Rome*, 259.

[30] Hippolytus was commonly paired with Phaeton in Latin exemplarist literature to illustrate how it was sometimes necessary for fathers to break certain promises made to their sons. See, for example, Cicero, *De Officiis* 3.94, and Ovid's *Fasti* 6.733–762 (in which Hippolytus is resurrected by the same herbs with which Aesculapius transformed Glaucus into an immortal). The question of family tragedy aside, the identification of Phaeton and Hippolytus rests on the similarity of their deaths. On the figure of Virbius as the resurrected Hippolytus and the important themes of exile, death, and resurrection in cantos 15–17, see Marguerite Mills Chiarenza, "Hippolytus' Exile: *Paradiso* xvii, vv. 46–48," *DS* 84 (1966): 65–68, and "Time and Eternity in the Myths of *Paradiso* xvii," in *Dante, Petrarch, Boccaccio: Studies in the Italian Trecento in Honor of Charles S. Singleton*, 133–150. Although I generally agree with Chiarenza's interpretation, I think it should be noted that the central attribute of Hippolytus in both Classical and Medieval

But from the very start this rapidly shifting tableau of carnivalesque inversions and falsifications, imposing as it seems to the poet-pilgrim, is unmasked by Cacciaguida as amounting to nothing in the gaze of eternity: nothing at all, a mere dance of the dead, a mere preface to life in the City of God. So if in the course of Florence's descent into the anarchy of the marketplace "all fast-frozen relations with their train of ancient and venerable prejudices and opinions" are "swept away," and "all new formed

---

traditions is his *chastity*. It cannot, hence, be accidental that Dante presents himself in canto 17 as someone who like Hippolytus must overcome the seductive advances of a corrupt stepmother and suffer calumny as a result. Dante's figurative chastity is at stake. Nonetheless, Chiarenza's view is reinforced by the longstanding Christian confusion of the mythological Hippolytus with the third-century martyr Saint Hippolytus. The Hippolytus of myth was thus identified as a martyr crucified on his chariot but brought to life again by the medicine of the cross. This confusion appears to have contaminated the *Ovide Moralisé*, from which I quote the concluding verses:

> Par Ypolite ou par Virbie
> Si com dist l'autre alegorie,
> Peut l'en les convertis entendre
> Qui pour sainte Yglise déffendre
> Souffrirent mort et passion,
> Et par la prédication
> De sainte Yglise s'esbahirent
> Tant qu'a la foi se convertirent.

Ovide Moralisé: Poème du commencement du 14ème siècle, ed. Christian de Boer, vv. 6377–6384. The specific link to Christ's martyrs and crusaders seems incongruous if one does not take into account the intertwining of the respective tales of mythical figure and martyr which goes back at least as far as the earliest liturgies celebrating Saint Hippolytus. On this subject, see Baudoin de Gaiffier, "Les Oraisons de l'office de Saint Hippolyte," in *Etudes critiques d'hagiographie et d'iconologie*, 97–102. One last point needs to be made regarding the Christianization of the figure of Hippolytus. A number of details in Ovid's narrative in *Metamorphoses* 15 render his identification with Christ and with His martyrs especially tenable. First, the story of Hippolytus is told as an "exempla dolentem" (15.495) to console Egeria for the loss of her husband and to show that behind every tragic blow there lurks a comic outcome. Second, it is noted in 15.531 that the deceased Hippolytus visited Hell before his resurrection: "vidi quoque luce carentia regna / et lacerum fovi Phlegethontide corpus in unda." Both are unmistakably applicable to the story of Christ as well as to Dante's own *imitatio Christi*.

DILEMMA OF FLORENTINE HISTORY

ones" become "antiquated before they can ossify," it is not in anticipation of revolution, or of a great commercial efflorescence like that out of which the nascent culture of civic humanism had just emerged.[31] Rather, it is to stage the triumphal return of the sign of the cross: a sign of the human city's anchorage in an immutable transcendent order; but most of all (and this will be a major theme in the chapter that follows) a powerful eschatological sign capable of overturning all merely historical perspectives from the perspective of the end and hence a remedy to Florence's fall.[32]

In the course of his discourse Cacciaguida thus returns with special insistence to the theme of history's *end*:

> Se tu riguardi Luni e Orbisaglia
> come sono ite, e come se ne vanno
> di retro ad esse Chiusi e Sinigaglia,
>   udir come le schiatte si disfanno
> non ti parrà nova cosa né forte,
> poscia che le cittadi termine hanno.
>   Le vostre cose tutte hanno lor morte,
> sì come voi; ma celasi in alcuna
> che dura molto, e le vite son corte.   16.73–81

(If you regard Luni and Urbisaglia, how they have perished, and how are following after them Chiusi and Senigallia, it will not appear to you a strange thing or a hard, to hear how families are undone, since cities have their term. Your affairs all have their death, even as have you; but it is concealed in some things that last long, whereas lives are short.)

His lesson is a simple one: history under Mars is history under the sign of mutability and, finally, death. Mutability teaches us that ours is a fallacious world, a *mondo fallace* whose greatest fal-

[31] The quotation is from the "Manifesto of the Communist Party," by Karl Marx and Friedrich Engels, cited from *The Marx-Engels Reader*, 476.

[32] The crucifixion of Lady Fortune by ungrateful mortals, as described by Virgil in *Inferno* 7.91–93, serves as an ironic double here of Christ's crucifixion: "Quest' è colei ch'è tanto posta in croce / pur da color che le dovrien dar lode, / dandole biasmo a torto e mala voce."

lacy would be to hope that it could provide any definitive sense of justice, peace, or home. Far from representing an exceptional punishment for which Dante is singled out, exile is the fundamental condition of all historical becoming: we are as "strangers [*peregrini*] and nomads [*hospites*] on earth," reads Hebrews 11:13—a crucial text for the interpretation of cantos 14–18.[33] But this realization need not be a source of sadness, once it is accepted that death, more than the tragic end-term of all historical experience, is truly the gateway to man's celestial homeland.

Identifying death as the master-signifier of human history, Cacciaguida no doubt alludes to an etymology well known in the Middle Ages, which appeared to confirm Mars's association with violence, death, and sin: "His name is Mars since he produces death, for the word *mors* comes from *Mars*," and later in Isidore's text, "Death is called *mors* because it derives from *amara* (bitter), or from *Mars* the producer of death, or from the *morsu* (bite) of the first man, who, eating of the fruit of the prohibited tree, incurred death."[34] While Cacciaguida's allusion unifies the complex of ref-

---

[33] In Cacciaguida's itinerary from martyrdom to peace ("venni dal martiro a questa pace" [15.148]), no direct mention of exile is made. But that exile or its symbolic analogue, pilgrimage, is the key link between martyrdom and eternal peace we know from Boethius' trajectory in canto 10.128–129: "da martiro / e da essilio venne a questa pace." (The term "pilgrim" or "peregrinus" was of course understood throughout the Middle Ages as referring to the "stranger" or "foreigner," and crusades were themselves conceived as pilgrimages.) On exile in the *Commedia*, see C. S. Singleton, "In Exitu Israel de Aegypto," in *Dante: 20th Century Views*, ed. J. Freccero, 102–121; and *Dante's Commedia: Elements of Structure*, 18–44.

[34] "Martem quasi *effectorem mortium*. Nam a Marte *mors* nuncupatur" (*Etym.* 8.11.51). "Mors dicta, quod sit amara, vel a Marte, qui est effector mortium [sive mors a morsu hominis primi, quod vetitae arboris pomum mordens mortem incurrit]" (*Etym.* 11.2.31). Isidore's etymology is very likely derived from a more ancient Stoic etymology found in Cornutus' *Theologia Graeca*, also employed to justify Mars "anaeretic" astrological character. Uguccione of Pisa fuses the two passages from Isidore in his etymology of *mors* in *Magnae Derivationes* (Bodleian fol. 115). Isidore's etymology is also cited in John the Scot's *Annotationes in Marcianum* 211.6 ("Mars dicitur quasi *mors* . . . *mors* a Marte derivatur"), Hrabanus

DILEMMA OF FLORENTINE HISTORY

erences in cantos 15–17 to the loss of Eden and to the bitter blows of Fortune that have already been discussed, it also brings about an accommodation that is of decisive importance to the polemical strategy of cantos 14–18: an accommodation between the planetary scheme of the third canticle and the Father's message at the center of Book 6 both of Virgil's *Aeneid* and of Cicero's *De Re Publica*, Dante's primary and secondary Classical models for the encounter of father and son in the heaven of Mars.

After all, Anchises too had spoken to Aeneas of life as a protracted death and of the body as a death-bound prison that plagues man with warring emotions and inevitably blinds him to the light:

Igneus est ollis vigor et caelestis origo
seminibus, quantum non corpora noxia tardant
terrenique hebetant artus moribundaque membra.
Hinc metuunt cupiuntque, dolent gaudentque, neque auras
dispiciunt clausae tenebris et carcere caeco.   6.730–734

(And fiery energy from a heavenly source
Belongs to the generative seeds of these,
So far as they are not poisoned or clogged
By mortal bodies, their free essence dimmed
By earthiness and deathliness of flesh.
This makes them fear and crave, rejoice and grieve.

Maurus' *De Universo* 7.6 ("Mors dicta, quod sit amara, vel a Marte, qui est effector mortium" [Migne PL 111, col. 194]), and in Giovanni Boccaccio's *Genealogie Deorum Gentilium* 1.32.21a ("Mors dicta est . . . quia mordeat vel a morsu parentis primi, per quem morimur, vel a Marte qui interfector est hominum, vel mors quasi amaror, quia amara sit") and 9.3.94c. It is paraphrased in Pietro Alighieri's gloss on *Paradise* 14.96: "Unde fingitur *Deus bellorum et effector mortis*" (*Commentarium*, 648). Benvenuto speaks only of the Macrobian Mars: an "autor destructionis et corruptionis" (*Comentum super Dantis Aldigherij Comoediam*, vol. 5, 120). Besides the widespread play in the vernacular love poetry of the Middle Ages (including Dante's own) on *amor-amaro-morte* (and upon occasion *Marte*), there is one particular instance of the identification of Mars with death that Dante could have taken only very seriously: Guido Cavalcanti's masterpiece "Donna mi prega," in which Mars appears as a tragic god of love, always undermining the rule of reason.

Imprisoned in the darkness of the body
They cannot clearly see heaven's air.) vv. 981-988, Fitzgerald

Before him, Africanus had said no less to his grandson Scipio, adopting an even more paradoxical formulation: "In truth . . . only those who have escaped from the bondage of the body as from a prison are alive, for *what you call life is truly death* ("Immo vero . . . vivunt, qui e corporum vinculis tamquam e carcere evolaverunt, vestra vero, quae dicitur *vita mors est*" [*De Re Publica* 6.14; emphasis mine]).³⁵ In these two cases, as in Cacciaguida's discourse, the purpose is the same: to embolden the son's epic resolve by reducing human actions, emotions, and events to their "true" diminutive scale, revealing the son's greatest fears to be groundless, his greatest historical obstacles to be merely symbolic or illusory in character, and his greatest possible sacrifices to be minor and entirely dwarfed by the future reward that awaits him.³⁶

---

³⁵ The ultimate source of both formulations is an etymology in Plato's *Cratylus*: "For some say that the body is the grave (σῆμα) of the soul which may be thought to be buried in our present life. . . . Probably the Orphic poets were the inventors of the name, and they were under the impression that the soul is suffering the punishment of sin, and that the body is an enclosure or prison in which the soul is incarcerated, kept safe (σῶμα, σώζηται), as the name σῶμα implies, until the penalty is paid" (400c; B. Jowett trans.).

³⁶ To a lesser extent the same logic is at work in Boethius' *Philosophiae Consolatio*. The intervention of Lady Philosophy hinges on a demonstration that all of Fortune's goods are illusory ("Crede fortunis hominum caducis, / Bonis crede fugacibus. / Constat aeterna positumque lege est / Ut constet genitum nihil" [2, metrum 3.15-19]), and that the origin of this negativity is to be found in death: "Ullamne humanis rebus inesse constantiam reris, cum ipsum saepe hominem velox hora dissolvat? Nam etsi rara est fortuitis manendi fides, ultimus tamen vitae dies mors quaedam fortunae est etiam manentis" (2, prosa 3.46-50). The result of this intervention is, as in the other texts, an assertion on the part of the protagonist of his readiness to parry even the cruelest blows of Fortune: "adeo ut iam me post haec inparem fortunae ictibus esse non arbitrer! Itaque remedia quae paulo acriora esse dicebas, non modo non perhorresco, sed audiendi avidus vehementer efflagito" (3, prosa 1.6-9). Such is the effect of his careful and attentive listening to Lady Philosophy's "sententiarum pondere vel canendi etiam iucunditate" (3,

"Alte spectare si voles . . . neque te sermonibus vulgi dedideris nec in praemiis humanis spem posueris rerum tuarum," the father says, "If you wish to look on high . . . you will not give in to the flattery of the vulgar herd, nor place your hopes in human rewards" (*De Re Publica* 6.23). But to accomplish this transformation of the will, the son must be shown how the supplement of the otherworld acts to undermine all strictly terrestrial economies. He must be shown the secret workings of divine justice, the *anima mundi* and *to pan*: the great cosmological machine—whether cosmic cross or tree, heavenly whorl or golden chain—that binds earthly flux to a transcendental point of origin.[37] And, last but not least, he must be shown the special place of his endeavor in history's providential order and the location of his true eternal homeland.[38]

Death stands at the center of this inflation of eternal perspectives and deflation of strictly historical ones, because, as the most immovable of all of history's obstacles, it remains the key to the success or failure of the father's prophetic intercession. It is, as we have seen, the all-pervasive presence of death in human his-

---

prosa 1.5–6). The analogy with the sweet hymn of the warriors of the cross and with the various *sententiae* of Cacciaguida is reinforced by the declaration in 17.23–24 of Dante's readiness for the "blows of fortune" which immediately precedes his request for the prophetic "grave words."

[37] Macrobius, following perhaps upon Servius' remarks on *Aeneid* 6.724, links the cosmological discourses of Africanus and Anchises to the Plotinian formula *en to pan*: "totius mundi a summo in imum diligens in hunc locum [*De Re Publica* 6.17] collecta descriptio est et integrum quoddam universitatis corpus effingitur, quod quidem Τὸ πᾶν id est omne dixerunt, unde et hic dicit *conexa sunt omnia*. Vergilius vero magnum corpus vocavit" [a quotation of *Aeneid* 6.727 follows] (*Commentarii* 1.17.5). Cf. Servius on *Aeneid* 6.724 (Thilo/Hagen, vol. 2, 99–102); and also among Bede's *Spuria et Dubia*, the *De Mundi Coelestis Terrestrisque Constitutione* (Migne PL 90, col. 899): an analysis of Anchises' *to pan* speech filled with borrowings from Servius and Macrobius.

[38] This same structural program encompasses not only Cicero, Virgil, Boethius, and Dante, but also *grosso modo* the gathering of shades in Homer's *Odyssey* (Bk. 10) and the "Vision of Er" at the close of Plato's *Republic*; in a less restrictive sense it applies to the *Commedia* as a whole.

tory that first draws the son into the orbit of Mars: bringing him to doubt the rationality of his epic task; to wonder whether virtue, justice, and self-sacrifice go unrewarded; to ask whether his passage into fatherhood is really warranted—to doubt, in short, the existence of a transcendent plan or *logos*. It is death, likewise, that opens him up to the temptation of accepting history on its own corrupt and calculating terms: to seek out compromise and advantage in the place of excellence and virtue ("suis te oportet inlecebris ipsa virtus trahat ad verum decus" [*De Re Publica* 6.23]), Dido's Carthage instead of Augustus' Rome, the safe embrace of lascivious Flora instead of the dangerous friendship of uncensored prophecy and truth ("s'io al vero son timido amico" [17.118]).

Prophecy arrives upon the scene hoping to break the blinding grip of Mars/*mors* and to convert all of history's present signs of death into eventual signs of eternal life, all present bitterness into a transcendent future sweetness. But in the case of Book 6 of the *Aeneid* and of Cicero's *De Re Publica* its success, Dante believed, had been far from complete; and it was here that he staked out Cacciaguida's claim to primacy over his Classical predecessors. For while Anchises and Africanus rehearse the paradoxical logic of life as death and historical gain as eternal loss, they do so without the authority of the cross: the only instrument, in Dante's view, powerful enough to transform the tragedy of life as death into the comedy of death as eternal life.

Such was the victory of Christ on the cross that death itself was—paradox of paradoxes—finally laid to rest:[39]

---

[39] The quotation is from the hymn "O Crux, splendidior cunctis astris," based on the Antiphon sung at the mass of the Exaltation of the Cross. *Vita/mors* paradoxes abound in hymns to the Holy Cross, which, as I later show, exerted a significant influence on Dante's vision in canto 14. Venantius Fortunatus' "Vexilla regis prodeunt" (parodied in *Inferno* 34.1 by the hymn "Vexilla regis prodeunt inferni"), for example, begins and ends with the following strophes:

Vexilla Regis prodeunt:
Fulget Crucis mysterium,

> O, magnum Pietatis opus, mors
>   mortua tunc est:
> In ligno quando mortua vita fuit.
>
> (Oh, great work of Piety, for
>   death died
> on the cross when Life died.)

Without access to the power of Christ's cross, Dante believed, the Classical father's otherworldly disclosures are incomplete and hermeneutically flawed. The only real solution that he can propose to the son's present dilemma is an abstract one: the Stoic freedom from passionate disturbances, or *ataraxia*—a simple denial of the reality of human suffering. The alternative offered in the heaven of Mars is a more impassioned and carnal one: the complete program for transcending historical suffering through self-sacrifice and love dramatized by the transfigured warriors of the cross, those truly beloved Sons of God, who by taking on their own personal crosses participated directly in the power and victory of Christ's universal cross.

As such, prophetic vision in cantos 14–18 does not pretend to provide the miraculous panacea that would once and for all abolish pain and suffering. It insists, rather, on the inexorable reality of (even carnal) suffering and on the necessity for bearing public witness to the love that binds the individual to the cross of Christ—the necessity, that is, for martyrdom in history.

So, no matter how fully armed he is with foresight, no matter how determined and fearless, the son's conversion to the father's

---

> Qua vita mortem pertulit,
> Et morte vitam protulit.
> ....
> Salve ara, salve victima,
> De passionis gloria.
> Qua vita mortem pertulit,
> Et morte vitam reddidit.

For the full text, see Jacob Gretser, *De Sancta Cruce*, in his *Opera Omnia*, vol. 3, 353–357.

comic perspectives *must* be a difficult one. The overriding pessimism of Cacciaguida's prophecy seems to underscore the point: emphasizing the themes of exodus and self-sacrifice almost to the exclusion of any equivalent to the Anchisean glorification of Rome. Like Aeneas on his exilic "iter durum" (6.688), the poet-pilgrim shall have to abandon all that is most dear (17.55), leaving the city of his origins for the "duro calle" (17.59) of exile. Like Aeneas he will endure diverse trials and temptations, parrying the blows of fate through both flight and confrontation.[40] Of the many cities that lie along his path, few will offer anything but temporary haven. The soil of human history will be found strangely resistant, even hostile, to his attempted redissemination of the originary seed, and the grip of Mars will seem tragic and unrelenting. Grief and nostalgia will continue to haunt him, and with them lingering doubts regarding the meaning of his mission, and fears of Ulyssean hubris and Oedipal madness. And as for Aeneas, there is really no choice: Mars has disfigured the Book of Memory beyond recognition. It is only in the Book of the Future that the son can hope to find a place that he recognizes as his own.[41]

[40] Cacciaguida's prophecy is divided between exhortations to flight ("di Fiorenza partir ti convene" [17.48]) and exhortations to literary confrontation: "rimossa ogne menzogna, / tutta tua visïon fa manifesta; / e lascia pur grattar dov' è la rogna" (17.127–129). This, according to what we are told in 6.892, was precisely the structure of Anchises' closing advice to Aeneas: "quo quemque modo *fugiatque feratque* laborem" (my italics).

[41] In an important article on Dante, Virgil, and Boethius, Marguerite Chiarenza has recently proposed that there may be a deeper structural parallelism beyond this network of thematic links between the respective fates of Aeneas and the poet-pilgrim. In *Inferno* 10.130–132 and 15.88–90 the promise is made that a woman shall present the pilgrim with an important prophecy concerning his future. In reality, Beatrice merely *leads* the poet-pilgrim to Cacciaguida, the true speaker of these prophecies. Chiarenza calls attention to the presence of a similar disjunction in Virgil's text, where in 3.456–460 Aeneas is told by Helenus that his future shall be elucidated by a lady, when in point of fact it is Anchises who speaks the central prophecies in Book 6. Although in my own view there is a greater degree of complementarity between the prophecies of the Sybil and An-

Yet, painfully enough, the scenario that Cacciaguida unfolds lacks rather strikingly the scope and historical precision of Anchises' description of Rome's ascent. In canto 17 Cacciaguida can offer only the vaguest of historical rewards: promises of a *first* refuge, advice as to the period of exile, and veiled suggestions concerning the universal import of Cangrande della Scala's rise. If Cangrande cannot for certain bring about a new "translation" and restoration of Augustan Rome, he can at least provide a corrective *trasmutamento*: "per lui fia trasmutata molta gente, / cambiando condizion ricchi e mendici" ("by him the fortune of many shall be transmuted, / the rich and beggarly exchanging their condition" [17.89–90])—an action apparently combining the evangelical "He has put down the mighty from their seat and exalted the humble" (Luke 1:52) with the Virgilian "spare the conquered and battle down the proud" (6.853), but in a pecuniary sense appropriate to Dante's critique of Florentine mercantilism. Cangrande's astrological impress as a formidable son of Mars (17.76f.) and the presence of the symbols of the heavens of Jupiter and Saturn on his escutcheon (the Imperial eagle and the ladder) do identify him with the three planets governing political affairs and, for that matter, major upheavals.[42]

---

chises (and one which Dante powerfully exploits in his critique of Classical prophecy in canto 17), there can be no question that this structural parallel confirms both the acuity of Dante's reading of Virgil and the importance of cantos 14–18 to Dante's Christian rewriting of Book 6. See M. M. Chiarenza, "Boethian Themes in Dante's Reading of Virgil," esp. 26–29.

[42] On Cacciaguida's prophecy, see Colin Hardie, "Cacciaguida's Prophecy in *Paradiso* 17," *Traditio* 19 (1963): 267–294. The importance of astrology to the central cantos of *Paradise* is not exhausted by the references to Cangrande. The retrospective dating in 16.34–39 of Cacciaguida's birth by Martian (and not solar years), for example, calls to mind the common practice in astrological theories of history of associating major events—the birth of rulers, wars, natural cataclysms—with the planetary cycles of Mars, Jupiter, and/or Saturn. Examples of such systems are Albumasar's (Abu Ma'shar) *De Magnis Coniunctionibus*, Masha Allah's *Astrological History*, and Roger Bacon's *Opus Majus* (Bridges ed., vol. 1, 263–269). In the specific case of Dante's ancestor, the conjunction of the *stella forte*

The suspense is further heightened by the central position occupied by this particular prophecy; coming right at the midpoint (verse 77) of canto 17, itself the central canto of the thirty-three that make up the final canticle.[43] Our attention is also drawn to the mysterious nines ("per la *nove*lla età, ché pur *nove* anni" [17.80]) cited in the description of Cangrande's present age: a number whose symbolic import in Dante's works is of course considerable. And the extraordinary things ("cose incredibili" [17.92–93]) prophesied by Cacciaguida but left outside the margins of the text would seem to justify even the most extravagant of hopes. The only *certainty*, however, promised by Cangrande's rise falls entirely within the cyclical flux of Martial history: a *trasmutamento* like the "death of kings and transmutation of kingdoms" which are the effects of Mars's astrological rule according to *Convivio* 2.13.22. The poet-pilgrim must look elsewhere for his reward, just as he must look elsewhere for definitive images of peace and home.

This "elsewhere" suddenly appears to Dante upon his ascent in canto 14 into the fiery sphere of Mars. It arrives in an atmosphere already charged with apocalyptic expectation: everything seems to point to the advent of an extraordinary new "dawn" or

---

with the constellation Leo underscores the *masculinity* (Mars and Leo are masculine), *nobility* (Leo is a solar sign and "lo più nobele segno" [Restoro d'Arezzo 2.2.4.5]), and *martial strength* (Mars is the planet of warriors, Leo the "più forte e potente de tutti li altri segni" [*ibid*]) of Cacciaguida's natal horoscope. Following upon the work of Rudolph Palgen (in particular *Dantes Sternglaube: Beiträge zur Erklärung des Paradiso*), Georg Rabuse has developed a comprehensive astrological reading of the *Commedia*, and one in which the central cantos of *Paradise* play a major role. But the problem with his *Der kosmische Aufbau* is that, like Valli's theory of the eagle and cross and so many other supposed "keys" to Dante's poem, Rabuse's is frequently a reductive one and requires considerable twisting of Dante's text. On Dante's use of astrological concepts, see also Robert Durling's excellent notes in "*Io son venuto*: Seneca, Plato and the Microcosm," *DS* 93 (1975): 126–128.

[43] On the numerological structure of *Paradise* and the Cangrande prophecy, see the diagrams at the beginning of Chapter 4.

"illumination" (the *albor* of 14.108). First comes the striking series of syntactical criss-crossings with which canto 14 opens: "Dal centro al cerchio, e sì dal cerchio al centro" ("From the center to the rim and so from the rim to the center" [14.1]), "Quel uno e due e tre che sempre vive / e regna sempre in tre e 'n due e 'n uno" ("That one and two and three that forever lives and rules forever in three and two and one" [14.28–29]), to cite but the most obvious instances. Prefigured by two important criss-crossings in the heaven of the sun—the cosmological chiasmus of *Paradise* 10.7–9 (the "chi" in the sky formed by the intersecting ecliptic and equator) and the chiastic narrative of cantos 10–13 with its alternation between Thomas and Bonaventure, Francis and Dominic—these further point us towards the awaited sign and hint at its identity.

Next comes Solomon's discussion of the bodies of the blessed (14.37–60): what are they presently made of and how shall they be different after the Last Judgment? How shall the resurrected body function? Do the blessed look forward to their resurrection? Then, at the sounding of an affirmative "Amen," a third ring of light appears unexpectedly over the heaven of the sun as if a sunrise ("per guisa d'orizzonte che rischiari" [14.69]). Is a new era about to dawn, an era, for example, of the Holy Spirit? The unveiling remains tantalizingly incomplete: "la vista pare e non par vera" ("the sight seems real and yet not real" [14.72]). Finally, in enigmatic contrast to the Mars whose horrors are so exhaustively documented throughout the *Inferno* and at the center of *Paradise*, the pilgrim is "translated"—a verb usually reserved for martyrs—into the sphere of Mars only to be greeted by a glowing and ruddy smile:

> Ben m'accors' io ch'io era più levato,
> per l'affocato riso de la stella,
> che mi parea più roggio che l'usato.   14.85–87

(That I was more uplifted I perceived clearly by the fiery smile of the star which seemed to me ruddier than its wont.)

Out of this paradoxical smile, and as a reward for an internalized—which is to say figurative—"holocaust" (14.89), (also described as a "sacrificio" and a "litare" in vv. 92–93), will soon appear a vision of the mysterious key to the overturning of all of history's *insomnia*: an apocalyptic cross of light, the *signum Filii hominis in caelo*, a sign of the Son's coming into his eschatological kingdom. This sign, as will be seen in the following chapter, promises to bring into harmony the seeming discord of history and eternity, driving the paralyzing sign of Mars/*mors* out of the text of revelation, and shattering all tragic perspectives with the promise of eternal peace and victory.

The absence of concrete historical promises and predictions in canto 17 now reveals itself as an indication of the presence of the cross at the center of Dante's celestial Elysium. Personalized through the figure of Cacciaguida, the cross provides not only present hope and a paradigm for imitation, but also a representation of the reward which awaits the son's completion of his epic endeavor: that is, salvation. The disclosure and confirmation of this reward must, in *Paradise* 15.36–42 and 17.92–93, be partially relegated to the silent margins of the text, because, in the Christian view, it necessarily lies beyond the grasp of human reason. Through his cross Christ had transformed the sacrificial logic of Classical epic: remaking the epic hero in the image of the martyr-*imitator Christi*, identifying his endeavor with redemption and his reward with the mystery of salvation by grace, and insisting on the diverse and personal character of sacrificial imitation (to each a *crucem suam*). As a result, Christianity demands that those who take up their cross and follow Christ do so out of *faith* and not the desire for fame or honor, or for particular historical rewards like those adumbrated by Anchises.

The earlier cited Pauline definition of faith, accordingly, stresses belief in the invisible: "sperandarum substantia rerum, *argumentum non apparentium*" (Heb. 11:1; my italics). The power of faith is such, the Pauline author goes on to assure us, that it alone can transform the invisible into the visible, make genuine motivating substances out of *unknowable future rewards*, violate all rational methodologies and all reasonable expectations. This was the case of Moses (and of the other Old Testament examples remembered in Hebrews 11), who long before the advent of Christ's cross, led the Jews out of the Egyptian desert toward Jerusalem like a man who could see the invisible ("invisibilem enim tanquam videns sustinuit" [11:27]). So must the pilgrim persist along the road to Jerusalem and discern beyond all immediate historical obstacles and rewards, beyond the tragedy of his beloved native city, the invisible certainties of faith. In history's bitter *martiri* he must uncover the pattern of Christ's own transfiguring *martyrium*.

The call to perseverance issued at the center of *Paradise* thus joins the Virgilian thematics of epic sacrifice to the new epic of Christ and of His cross. Like Aeneas, urged in Book 6 to resist evil ("Tu ne cede malis" [6.95]), to complete his task and to persist against all odds ("Sed iam age, carpe viam . . . Acceleremus" [6.629–630]), Dante is spurred onward and upward, but in the language of the cross. Such is the mystery of Christ's universal cross that through Cacciaguida this generalized and abstract message can be translated into a distinctively personal one: a *literary* appeal to complete the text, to take up the poetic lyre against the most powerful of foes, and to make the full vision manifest without compromise or hesitation. It is precisely this literary perseverance that emerges in cantos 14–18 as the key to the certain victory and special honor that lie immediately beyond the tragic reality of the poet-pilgrim's individual cross, his personal exodus.

IV

UNICA SPES HOMINUM, CRUX, O VENERABILE SIGNUM

Vere crux Christi scala est a terra in coelum attingens, quia per fidem crucis, per imitationem passionis, redit homo de exsilio ad patriam, de morte ad vitam, de terra ad coelum, de deserto hujus mundi ad paradisum.

ALAN OF LILLE,
Sermo 2, De Sancta Cruce

1. EXALTATION

Dante's Sign of Difference

Since the earliest days of Christianity, the cross had been the central symbol of that which in the Christian faith was most incomprehensible and scandalous to Classical reason: "to the Jews an obstacle that they cannot get over, to the pagans madness, but to those who have been called, whether they are Jews or Greeks, a Christ who is the power and the wisdom of God" (1 Cor. 1:23–24). Likewise, the "language of the cross" or *verbum crucis* was necessarily "illogical to those who are not on the way to salvation, but those who are on the way see it as God's power to save [*Dei virtus est*]" (1 Cor. 1:18).[1] And as if to dramatize this gap in understanding, Medieval Christendom everywhere celebrated the polysemous promiscuity of the cross: imagining it at once as a ladder, an anchor, a lamp, a throne, a medicine, a military ensign, a secret gnosis, a science of salvation, a cosmological pattern, the signature of Christ, the book of life, the martyr's crown, the door to paradise, and the gateway to otherworldly visions.[2]

---

[1] This passage from I Corinthians, like the one that precedes it, is from *The Jerusalem Bible* translation.

[2] Aside from the secondary materials cited in the course of this chapter and, first and foremost, Gretser's *De Sancta Cruce*, the following are the principal primary sources I have relied upon in my treatment of the cross: pseudo-Athanasius, "Sermo in Passionem Domini in Parasceve" (Migne PG 28, cols. 1053–1062); John Chrysostom, "De Cruce et Latrone" 1 and 2 (Migne PG 49, cols. 399–418), "Homilia de Adoratione Crucis" and "Homilia de Confessione Crucis" (Migne PG 52, cols. 835–844); and "In Adorationem Venerandae Crucis" (Migne PG 62, cols.

These are but a few of the many meanings out of which, in the course of cantos 14–18, will emerge a higher, more generalized symbol: a cross which is the sign of the inexorable Christian *difference*, of that which elevates Dante's encounter with Cacciaguida, and on a larger scale the third canticle as a whole, above its Classical origins. For as sign of the well-foundedness of Christian hopes, as crux of the hermeneutic drama of revelation, as divine paradox and supernal *essempro* (14.105), the "venerable sign" at the center of Dante's *Paradise* comes to represent the new hermeneutic and epistemological conditions of the era of Christ. As such it will preside in cantos 14–18 over a revision of the sacrificial logic of Classical epic and a rectification of the balance between visible and invisible, revelation and mystery, human accomplishment and divine assistance. But most of all it will serve as the mark both of Christ's solution to the dilemma of epic history and of the gap that separates Christian paradise from Classical Elysium, the oracle of Christ from the oracle of Apollo, the eternal Jerusalem from historical Rome, Dante's *Paradise* from Book 6 of Virgil's *Aeneid*.

747–754); Andrew of Crete, "In Exaltationem Sanctae Crucis" (Migne PG 97, cols. 1017–1046); Augustine of Hippo, Sermo 155 ["De Passione Domini, VI, seu de Cruce et Latrone"] (Migne PL 39, cols. 2047–2053, a Latin abridgement of a sermon by John Chrysostom); Maximus of Turin, Homilies 49 ["De Passione et Cruce Domini 1"] and 50 ["De Cruce Domini 2"] (Migne PL 57, cols. 339–344); Peter Damian, Sermo 18 ["De Inventione Sanctae Crucis"] and Sermo 47 ["In Exaltatione Sanctae Crucis"] (Migne PL 144, cols. 601–610, 761–777); and Honorius of Autun, "De Inventione Sanctae Crucis" and "De Exaltatione Sanctae Crucis" (Migne PL 172, cols. 941–948, 1001–1006). On the general subject of cross lore, I have consulted Otto Zöckler, *Das Kreuz Christi*; on the early Christian theology and iconography of the cross, Peter Stockmeier, *Theologie und Kult des Kreuzes bei Johannes Chrysostomus: ein Beitrag zum Verständnis des Kreuzes im 4. Jahrhundert*; and on the "living cross," Robert L. Füglister, *Das Lebende Kreuz: Ikonographisch-ikonologische Untersuchung der Herkunft und Entwicklung einer spätmittelalterlichen Bildidee und ihrer Verwurzelung im Wort*, 167–220. For further bibliography, see Stockmeier, ix–xvi; Füglister, 189–190 and 221–225; R. E. Kaske, "A Poem on the Cross in the Exeter Book: *Riddle 60* and *The Husband's Message*," *Traditio* 23 (1967): 41–71; and William Wood Seymour, *The Cross in Tradition, History and Art*, xxi–xxx.

CHAPTER FOUR

The Cross at the Center

In this most meticulously constructed of poems, the cross in the heaven of Mars is both symmetrical and asymmetrical with respect to the main body of *Paradise*. Occupying the fifth or central rung in Dante's modified Ptolemaic system, its own mid-point precedes the text's arithmetic center (17.83) by approximately the length of a single canto; (out of deference, possibly, to the position of the encounter of Anchises and Aeneas in the *Aeneid*). Its location remains, however, no less of a mystery than the reflective pattern that Charles S. Singleton discovered radiating out from the center of *Purgatory*.[3]

---

[3] "The Poet's Number at the Center," *MLN* 80 (1965): 1–10. On this question, see also J. L. Logan, "The Poet's Central Numbers," *MLN* 86 (1971): 96–98. Cf. R. J. Pegis, "Numerology and Probability in Dante," *Medieval Studies* 29 (1967): 370–373. An attempt at a general numerological interpretation of the *Commedia* can be found in Roberto Sarolli's *Analitica della Divina Commedia: Struttura numerologica e poesia*. Sarolli and others have proposed that Singleton's pattern at the center is also present in *Paradise* and *Hell*, invoking the standard Medieval practice of adding up the integers of numbers ten and above. A pattern thus emerges at the center of the third canticle which, centered in canto 17, extends out symmetrically seven cantos in either direction. Canto 17, with its 142 verses, represents a 7 (1 + 4 + 2); cantos 16 (154 vv.) and 18 (136 vv.) represent 10's (1 + 5 + 4 and 1 + 3 + 6); cantos 15 and 19 (148 vv. each) represent 13's (1 + 4 + 8); cantos 14 (139 vv.) and 20 (148 vv.) represent 13's (1 + 3 + 9 and 1 + 4 + 8); cantos 13 and 21 (142 vv. each) represent 7's (1 + 4 + 2); cantos 12 (145 vv.) and 22 (154 vv.) represent 10's; and cantos 11 and 23 (139 vv. each) represent 10's (1 + 3 + 9); after which the paradigm breaks down even with a re-addition of two-integer numbers. The following scheme results:

10–10–7–13–13–10–[7]–10–13–13–7–10–10

While such a pattern reinforces my general reading of cantos 14–18, I think there are some reasons for caution about such a procedure. First of all, its recondite character makes it ultimately less convincing than the fully visible pattern at the center of *Purgatory*. There is, secondly, the problem of its statistical probability. In a system of progressions of three—*terza rima* makes this automatic—whose upper limit is 154 (canto 17) and lower limit 130 (canto 3), there are nine possible verse count figures: a number sufficiently large to render the random occurrence of Singleton's pattern highly unlikely. But the procedure of adding up integers reduces the possible outcomes from nine to only four—the numbers 4, 7, 10, and

UNICA SPES HOMINUM

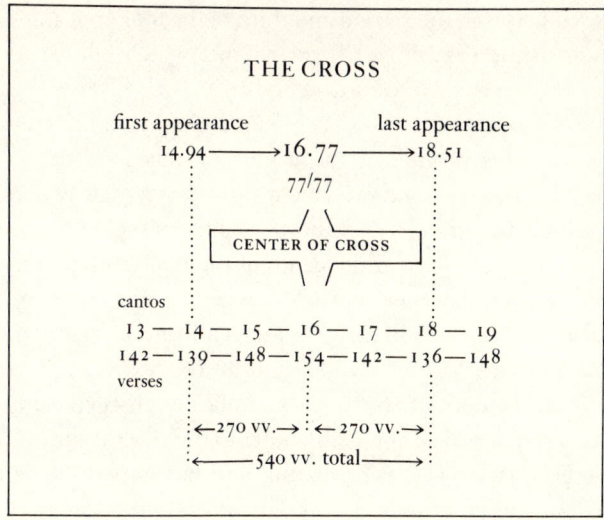

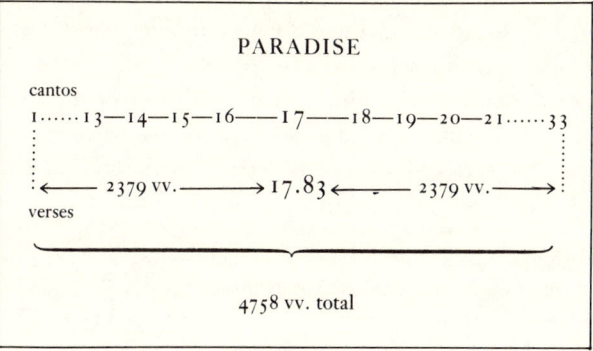

For, as the diagram indicates, the Martial cross extends exactly 270 verses to either side of the center of canto 16 (verse 77): first appearing in 14.94–95 ("con tanto lucore e tanto robbi / m'apparvero splendor dentro a due raggi") and disappearing by 18.52 ("Io mi rivolsi dal mio destro lato"), and cleaving canto 16 into two 77-verse halves. It should also be noted that the cross is itself

---

13—greatly increasing the probability of random patterns. Double addition leaves only three possible outcomes: 1, 4, and 7.

enclosed between the second and third of the four appearances in *Paradise* of the *Cristo/Cristo/Cristo* rhyme, which fall exactly on verses 104–106–108 of cantos 14 and 19.[4]

Dante's attentiveness to such numerological and structural matters in this portion of the poem is evinced, as earlier observed, by the strategic placement of Cacciaguida's prophecies concerning Cangrande and the poet-pilgrim's fate: found not only in canto 17 (the middle canto of the final canticle's thirty-three) and in the heaven of Mars (the central planetary sphere), but also near verse 83 of canto 17, which from the standpoint of versification marks the precise center of the text's 4,758 verses. The presence here of so many symbolically charged numbers, whether incidental or not, contributes to the general aura of mystery: the quadruple sevens of canto 16 (an important digit in Christian apocalyptics and in the hexameral tradition, and "the number that binds the universe together" according to *De Re Publica* 6.18—an allusion to the Pythagorean vision of the cosmos as a heptacord lyre), the double 270's or $3^3[3 + 3 + 3 + 1]$ associated with 27 (the highest number in the Pythagorean "lambda" diagram and hence the highest note in the harmony of the spheres), the secret nines of 17.80 ("per la *nove*lla età, ché pur *nove* anni"), and so on and so forth.[5]

---

[4] The other two instances are 12.71–73–75 and 32.83–85–87. For a suggestive exploration of the implications of Christ's self-rhyming, see John Freccero, "The Significance of Terza Rima" in *Dante, Petrarch, Boccaccio: Studies in the Italian Trecento*, 3–17. Giovanni Pascoli's *La mirabile visione: Abozzo d'una storia della Divina Commedia* (esp. 555–573) attempts a systematic interpretation of the various appearances of the *Cristo/Cristo/Cristo* rhyme in the final canticle. Frequently overlooked is the existence of one additional self-rhyme in *Paradise*: the triple "io vidi" of 30.95–97–99, which occurs precisely as the pilgrim enters the celestial rose. Here the self-rhyme would seem to proclaim the pilgrim's metamorphosis into a true *vates* (a title etymologically linked to the verb *video*), since abandoning "nature" for the entirely supernatural realm of the Empyrean, he gazes into the city at the end of time.

[5] All of these magic numbers are associated with Classical theories of harmony which adopt a macrocosmic/microcosmic paradigm for explaining the relation of

One last point (and one to which I will return in a subsequent section) must be made regarding the placement of the cross: it occupies the central rung of *Paradise* because it is in fact the celestial double of those two trees which, as stated as Genesis 2:9, stood at the center of the garden of Eden—the Tree of Knowledge and the Tree of Life.[6] According to a vast and authoritative exegetical tradition, the tragic tree of man's fall and/or its comic counterpart, the Tree of Life, were of the same wood as that tree through which man was redeemed and the way to paradise reopened: the tree of the cross. "This most dignified of trees," reads one of the hymns linked to the mass of the Exaltation of the Cross, "is situated at the center of Paradise."[7] Hence the historical procession of *Purgatory* 32 converges upon a certain "robust tree" (32.46) at the center of Eden, magically rejuvenating it as the "twin-natured animal" (47) or Christ, binds it to the chariot of the Church by its cross or rudder ("temo" [32.49]); a renewal which, as in cantos 14–18, bears ecclesiastical and imperial implications.

Whether cross of light or rudder, the cross remains a symbol of the providential force which binds history's tragic beginning to its comic end. But whereas the *temo* of canto 32 emphasizes Christ's "conservative" role, his role as Adam *redivivus* (or in the

---

human music to its cosmological model, while insisting on the ethical, moral, and political dimension of music. The immediate source for most Medieval speculations on celestial and earthly harmonics was Boethius' treatise *De Institutione Musica* (see esp. 1.1–12). On the number 27, see *Timaeus* 35b–36b, which arbitrarily makes 27 the largest numerical component of the world soul. As the third power of three it occupies the right foot of the Pythagorean "Lambda" diagram, opposite the number eight, the third power of two. On the *Timaeus* and Pythagorean arithmetic, see Cornford's notes in *Plato's Cosmology: The Timaeus of Plato*, 66–72.

[6] On this tradition, see Edward Moore, *Studies in Dante: Third Series—Miscellaneous Essays*, 219–220; and Eleanor S. Greenhill, "The Child in the Tree: A Study of the Cosmological Tree in Christian Tradition," *Traditio* 10 (1954): 323–371, a study of particular relevance also to the description of the cosmos in 18.29–30, as "l'albero che vive de la cima /·e frutta sempre e mai non perde foglia."

[7] "Haec est arbor dignissimum / in Paradisi medio situata." From "O Crux, splendidior cunctis astris," reprinted in Gretser, *De Sancta Cruce*, vol. 3, 357.

terms of our literary analogy, Dante's role as the restorer of Virgil); the cross of light emphasizes instead a radical rupture: it is the "sign of the Son of man in heaven" (Matt. 24:30), the sign of Christ the eschatological Messiah (Dante *poeta*) and one of the signs of the ἐσχάτη ὥρα (1 John 2:18), the "approaching last hour." As such, the cross of light of cantos 14–18 signals not so much a return to Eden, as the definitive supplement which Christ appended to the restoration of Eden and/or Elysium, the Christian *felicity* which transfigures Hebraic *culpa* and Classical *tristitia*: Christian paradise itself (Dante's final canticle), the eternal peace of the eschatological city.

Galassia

More than a simple numerological enigma, then, the cross which rises in canto 14 is a cosmic mystery which calls into question all merely human science and philosophy:

> Come distinta da minori e maggi
> lumi biancheggia tra' poli del mondo
> Galassia sì, che fa dubbiar ben saggi;
>   sì costellati facean nel profondo
> Marte quei raggi il venerabil segno
> che fan giunture di quadranti in tondo.
>   Qui vince la memoria mia lo 'ngegno;
> ché quella croce lampeggiava Cristo,
> sì ch'io non so trovare essempro degno;
>   ma chi prende sua croce e segue Cristo,
> ancor mi scuserà di quel ch'io lasso,
> vedendo in quell' albor balenar Cristo.   14.97–108

(As, pricked out with greater and lesser lights, between the poles of the Universe, the Milky Way so gleams as to cause even the wise to question, so did those beams, thus constellated, make in the depth of Mars the venerable sign which joinings of quadrants make in a circle. Here my memory outstrips my wit, for that Cross so flashed forth Christ that I can find for it no fit comparison; but he that takes

up his cross and follows Christ shall yet forgive me for what I leave
untold when he sees Christ flash in that dawn.)

Here scarcely a trace can be found of the Franciscan iconography
of the cross which, with its insistence on the carnal immediacy of
Christ's paschal drama, had transformed the visual arts in
Dante's time.[8]

This allusively dense passage recalls instead both the transfigurational Christology of the Eastern Church, and an early speculative tradition (predominantly Eastern as well) that had attempted the reconciliation of Plato's Timaean cosmology, the *logos* of the Stoics, the Orphic/Gnostic Aeon and the Christian mystery of the cross. As admirably documented by Dölger, Bousset, Rahner and others, the cross came to be viewed as "the fundamental schema imprinted on the cosmos by God (who from the very beginning looked secretly forward to the coming Cross of His Son)," and the "two great celestial circles, the equator and ecliptic, which intersect one another in the form of a horizontal X, and around which the whole vault of the starry firmament moves in miraculous rhythm" were thought to form a heavenly cross.[9]

While this tradition was one of the many which contaminated all later speculations on the cosmic cross, Dante's cross of light in cantos 14–18 belongs, properly speaking, to the iconographic

---

[8] Of the voluminous bibliography on this subject I have found Paul Thoby, *Le Crucifix des origines au Concile de Trente: Etude iconographique*, to be particularly useful. But see also Jacob Stockbauer, *Kunstgeschichte des Kreuzes: die bildliche Darstellung des Erlösungstodes Christi im Monogramm, Kreuz und Crucifix*.

[9] Hugo Rahner, "The Christian Mystery and the Pagan Mysteries," in *The Mysteries: Papers from the Eranos Yearbooks*, 372. On this tradition, see also Gretser, *De Sancta Cruce*, vol. 1, 84f.; Wilhelm Bousset, "Platons Weltseele und das Kreuz Christi," *Zeitschrift für die Neuetestamentliche Wissenschaft* 14 (1913): 273–285; Franz Dölger's posthumous "Beiträge zur Geschichte des Kreuzzeichens," *JACh* 10 (1967): esp. 23–30; and Peter Stockmeier, *Theologie und Kult des Kreuzes bei Johannes Chrysostomus*, esp. 92–123. Cf. Georg Rabuse, *Der kosmische Aufbau* (esp. 208–247) and *Gesammelte Aufsätze zu Dante* (205–208), which link Dante's cross to the Plato's *chi*.

conventions of the Exaltation of the Cross, as represented in the apsidal mosaics at Sant' Apollinare in Classe, Ravenna, and only indirectly to any Christianization of Plato's speculative cosmology. The cosmic mystery to which the cross in the heaven of Mars is assimilated is not the purely imaginary intersection of ecliptic and equator (an intersection already alluded to in *Paradise* 10.7–21), but an actual circle of light: the *Galassia* or Milky Way, the outermost and most steadfast of the visible heavenly spheres of Medieval astronomy, and the only celestial circle reputed to traverse the cosmic poles.[10]

If Dante's simile is astronomically precise, though, its principal thrust is symbolic: to emphasize the cross's all-comprehending embrace of the universe, its centrality and stabilizing role, the figurative act of binding it performs on the great scroll of creation, that *magno volume* (15.50) whose immutable celestial writing stretches out over the heavens.[11] The symbolic implications

---

[10] Concerning the Milky Way and the various theories as to its origin, see Dante's discussion in *Convivio* 2.14.1–13. Dante's source is Albert the Great's commentary *De Meteoribus* 1.1.2 (Borgnet, vol. 4, 493–498), which in turn rehearses much of Aristotle's *Meteorologica* 1.8 (345a–346b). The passage from Aristotle was the standard consideration of the matter and is repeated in one form or another in Manilius, Hyginus, Macrobius, and Averroes. On Dante's debt to Albertus, see Paget Toynbee, *Dante Studies and Researches*, 42–47, 88–89. Dante's major innovation in the *Convivio* is his elaborate allegoresis of the Milky Way's polar intersections. As I later demonstrate, the passage from *Convivio* 2.14, like the discussion of Mars in *Convivio* 2.13 which precedes it, provides an essential background for the understanding of cantos 14 and 15, and in particular the galactic simile.

[11] An elaborate Christian allegorization of the Milky Way which is suggestive in terms of the galactic simile of cantos 14–18 is found in the work of Giovanni of San Gimignano, a contemporary of Dante's:

Tertia gratia gratis data dicitur fides. Et haec assimilatur circulo galaxiae propter quator. Primo propter *puritatem*, quia Galaxia dicitur Via Lactea, in quo significant nitor puritatis quam fides facit . . . secundo propter *firmitatem* quia galaxia semper stat in eodem loco caeli (ut dicit Philosophus). Quod intelligitur quantum ad apparentiam propter tardissimum motum, quia in rei veritate expertum est, quod galaxia movetur in centum annis gradu uno.

of Dante's "subtle and noble comparison" (the words are Benvenuto's) are further illuminated by a passage from the apocryphal Acts of Andrew, which, in a mode characteristic of this entire tradition, describes the cross as a cosmic *lignum vitae* (Tree of Life) stretching from the nadir to the apex of the universe:[12]

> For you [the cross] are set up in the cosmos to establish the unstable. And one part of you stretches up to heaven so that you may point out the heavenly Logos, the head of all things. Another part of you is stretched out to right and left that you may put to flight the fearful and inimical power and draw the cosmos into unity. And another part of you is set on the earth, rooted in the depths, that you may bring what is on earth and under the earth into contact with what is in heaven. O Cross, tool of salvation of the Most High! O Cross, trophy of the victory of Christ over his enemies! O Cross, planted on earth and bearing your fruit in heaven! O name

---

Fides autem prout gratia gratis data, accipitur pro aliqua fidei excellentia, sicut pro constantia fidei, ut dicit glosa "Unde fides dicitur substantia propter firmitatem (Heb. 11.1)." Tertio propter *claritatem*. Nam galaxiae circulus tunc est clarior quando aura nocturna fuerit frigidior et serenior: quia scilicet constantia fidei tanto amplius clarescit, quando aura persecutionis vel frigus mundi tenebrosi magis contra eam excrescit.

Summa de Exemplis et Similitudinibus Rerum 1.34. The final justification for the allegory is that of the galaxy's *utility* in all earthly pilgrimages: by its pure light pilgrims proceed and sailors navigate through the sea of the world (the case of Moses leading the Hebrews through the Red Sea and across the desert being cited as evidence).

[12] From Edgar Hennecke, *New Testament Apocrypha*, vol. 2, 418–419. The text as cited was assembled by J. Flamion, and consists of a collage of fragments from the *Martyrium Andreae Prius*, the *Martyrium Andreae Alterum*, the "Narratio" or *Martyrium Sancti Apostoli Andreae*, the *Passio Sancti Andreae* ("conversante"), and the so-called "Epître grecque." The only elaborate consideration of the cosmic implications of the cross of cantos 14–18 is that of Rabuse (*Der kosmische Aufbau*, 195–247), but in his eagerness to prove the importance of the Third Vatican Mythographer to the microcosmic/macrocosmic structure of the *Commedia*, Rabuse considerably overstates his case with regard to the cross and the realm of Mars. Although his central thesis is sometimes suggestive, it is frequently undermined by such extravagant claims as that the *Weltentstehungshoroskop* or *thema mundi* is of central importance in Dante's poem.

of the Cross, filled with all things! Well done, O Cross, that you have bound the circumference of the world!

This is a cross as cosmic Aeon, a cross as Alpha and Omega; a cross linked not only to Nebuchadnezzar's vision of a towering heavenly tree in Daniel 4:7–10, and to the Tree of Life in Revelations 22:2 "bearing twelve fruits and yielding its fruit every month," but also to one of the closing images in the heaven of Mars: Cacciaguida's vision of the cosmos as a "tree that lives from its summit and is always in fruit and never sheds its leaves" ("l'albero che vive de la cima / e frutta sempre e mai non perde foglia" [18.29–30]).[13] This cross is cast in the image of the cosmic Christ of Colossians 1:17–20, in and through whom all fallen things are reconciled with their transcendental origin: "And he is before all, and by him all things consist . . . because in him it was pleasing that all fullness should dwell; and through him to reconcile all things unto himself, making peace through the blood of his cross, both as to the things that are on earth, and the things that are in heaven." Binding earth to Empyrean, history to eternity, and man to the divine Logos, drawing all that is dispersed throughout the universe together toward a single point, the cosmic cross makes of the Christian universe an exact antitype of the Sibyl's disordered songs (and thus can promise in cantos 14–18 a remedy to the disorder at the heart of Virgil's book).

The metaphorics of the book are particularly suggestive here because in the course of cantos 14–18, the cross inscribed in the depth of Mars (14.100–101) will indeed anticipate the mysterious volume of *Paradise* 33 and its triune circles:[14]

---

[13] Compare Giordano da Rivalto's sermon 84 (15 ottobre, 1305): "Vide Daniello uno albero, che la cima sua era infino al cielo, e' suoi rami si distendeano all'estremità della terra, sopra i quali rami eran diversi animali: e questo albero si è la benedetta croce di Gesù Cristo benedetto. Ogne uomo, il quale sostiene pena in questo mondo, come detto è, sì abita ne' rami di questo albero. I santi, perocchè si umiliarono e sostennero passione, sì sono onorati eternalmente in vita eterna" (*Prediche inedite*, 389).

[14] An important series of structural parallels join the cantos of the Sun and

Nel suo profondo vidi che s'interna,
legato con amore in un volume,
ciò che per l'universo si squaderna.   33.85–87

(In its depths I saw ingathered, bound by love in one single volume,
that which is dispersed in leaves throughout the universe.)

Like this transcendental Book in which eternal substance and temporal accident are radically fused, the cross will provide a literary and personal example ("essempro" [14.105]) for imitation. At the center of the only canticle in which Virgil is entirely absent, it will lead to the celebration of the poet-pilgrim's literary coming of age: his accession to a prophetic voice entirely his own and his ascendancy over all Classical literary models.[15]

Mars to the final vision of the poem: the latter offering in certain respects an instantaneous telescoping of what is temporalized in cantos 10–16 (and 16–22). This of course fits the fictive "double-temporality" of Dante's final canticle: on the one hand unfolding within realm of natural temporality and flux (within the planetary hierarchies whose movements govern natural events); and on the other (once we pass beyond the sphere of the fixed stars into the celestial rose), in a supernatural instant: a moment of mystical vision which, anticipating the end of time, collapses all spatio-temporal multiplicity into God's ineffable unity. It is conceivable thus that Dante wished that the seemingly disparate events of 10–16 and 16–22—the dance of the two rings in the heaven of the sun, the appearance of a third mysterious ring, the flashing forth of a cross of light in the heaven of Mars and its dual unfolding in Jupiter's imperial eagle and Saturn's contemplative ladder—reappear in canto 33 as spatially and temporally one: the three circles of 10–15 becoming the interwoven "three circles of three colors" (33.116–117) with the transfiguring Christ/cross defining their "magnitude" (33.117). Similarly, the mysterious effigy which proposes in 33.131–138 a solution to the squaring or "measuring" of the circle may be intended as a double of that sign in canto 14 which flashes forth the glorified Christ over a "joining of quadrants in a circle." For two equally speculative views on the relation of the central cantos of *Paradise* to the final vision, see Leone Tondelli's *Il libro delle figure*, vol. 1, 225ff., which explores the possible connection to Joachim of Fiore's *figurae*, and Georg Rabuse's *Der kosmische Aufbau* and *Gesammelte Aufsätze* (68–69 esp.), which postulate a number of Platonic, astrological, and hermetic links between the two parts of the poem. Cf. Marjorie Reeves and Beatrice Hirsch-Reich, *The Figurae of Joachim of Fiore* (317–329), which calls into question many of Tondelli's assertions.

[15] The literal force of the book metaphor ought not be underestimated, not

It is natural enough, then, that Virgil and Cicero should both lurk in the background of this astronomical simile. Given Dante's vital interest in all Virgilian "predictions" of the Incarnation, he might well have imagined that the galactic cross, as the symbol of Christ's universal empire, fulfilled Anchises' claim that under a certain *divi genus* or son of god, Rome would extend her domain out beyond even the zodiac's star-tricked wheel:

> Hic vir, hic est, tibi quem promitti saepius audis,
> Augustus Caesar, Divi genus, aurea condet
> saecula qui rursus Latio regnata per arva
> Saturno quondam, super et Garamantas et Indos
> proferet imperium; iacet extra sidera tellus,
> extra anni solisque vias, ubi caelifer Atlas
> axem umero torquet stellis ardentibus aptum.   6.791–797

> (this is the man, this one,
> Of whom so often you have heard the promise,
> Caesar Augustus, son of the deified,
> Who shall bring once again an Age of Gold
> To Latium, to the land where Saturn reigned
> In early times. He will extend his power
> Beyond the Garamants and Indians,
> Over far territories north and south
> Of the zodiacal stars, the solar way,
> Where Atlas, heaven-bearing, on his shoulder
> Turns the night sphere, studded with burning stars.)
>   vv. 1062–1072, Fitzgerald

The adaptability of this prophecy (especially through the mediation of the Fourth Eclogue and its reputedly Christological Sa-

---

only because of the symbolic tension that runs throughout *Paradise* between binding and unbinding (or between God's Book and the endangered sibylline leaves), but also due to the great frequency of bejeweled crosses on the bindings of Medieval books, especially on Bibles. The practice receives particular impetus from the bibliolatry of the Christian religion as from its Christocentric theology of history. On Dante's bookbinding metaphors in relation to Medieval book production, see John Ahern, "Binding the Book: Hermeneutics and Manuscript Production in *Paradiso* 33," *PMLA* 97 (October 1982): 800–809.

turnian age) to a Christian reading did not escape Dante, as we know from the fourth tractate of the *Convivio* among other places.[16] That it provides the model for Dante's own dedicatory prophecy in canto 17 addressed to the new Augustus, Cangrande della Scala, is self-evident and makes the case for a galactic cross-reference in canto 14 all the more telling.

Similarly, and perhaps even more apparent to the Medieval reader of the *Commedia*, would have been the reminiscence of Scipio and Africanus' galactic encounter (a scene whose structural relation to the center of *Paradise* has already been examined). Placing his own celestial Elysium in the Milky Way, Cicero provides a point of transition between Virgil's subterranean "place of joy" ("locos laetos" [6.638]), and Dante's planetary paradise. Cicero's Milky Way is the eternal homeland and privileged meeting place to which the beatified few—those who have imitated the harmony of the spheres, studied the movements of the heavens, cultivated justice and piety, or served their parents and/or fatherland—return for their final reward.[17] But stressing the

---

[16] In a famous passage from *Convivio* 4.5.6–8 Dante writes: "E tutto questo fu in uno temporale, che David nacque e nacque Roma, cioè che Enea venne di Troia in Italia, che fu origine de la cittad romana, sì come testimoniano le scritture. Per che assai è manifesto la divina elezione del romano imperio per lo nascimento de la santa cittade, che fu contemporaneo a la radice de la progenie di Maria. E incidentemente e da toccare che, poi che esso cielo cominciò a girare, in migliore disposizione non fu che allora quando di là su discese Colui che l'ha fatto e che 'l governa, sì come ancora per virtù di loro arti li matematici possono ritrovare. Né 'l mondo mai non fu né sarà sì perfettamente disposto come allora che, a la voce d'un solo principe di Roma, popolo e comandatore fu ordinato, sì come testimonia Luca evangelista."

[17] Restoro d'Arezzo may have had Cicero's text in mind when, adopting the theory of Anaxagoras and Democritus (rejected by Dante in *Convivio* 2.14.6), he assimilates the stars of the Milky Way to a circle of knights whose brilliant armor reflects the sun's rays: "vedemo che questa parte del cielo è piena e sofolta de grandissima moltitudine de stelle, unde aguardandoli lo sole, alluminando colli suoi ragi quelle stelle, che so' strette e sofolte asieme, repercote e recopre de lume l'una l'altra, e fano parere questa via luminosa e piena de lume quasi continua da l'uno polo a l'altro d'uno pezzo, en modo che fosse una schiera de gente stretta, armata

patriotic and even military dimension of this otherworld, Cicero draws us back toward the cruciform Hall of Fame of cantos 14–18, whose Christian epic heros (Roland, William of Orange, Renoart), martyrs (Judas Maccabeus, Cacciaguida), and rulers (Charlemagne), like the beatified souls described by Africanus, have saved, aided, or enlarged their fatherland: "omnibus, qui patriam conservaverint, adiuverint, auxerint, certum esse in caelo definitum locum, ubi beati aevo sempiterno fruantur" (*De Re Publica* 6.13).[18]

From Blood to Light or "per Crucem ad Lucem"

Whatever the relative significance of these and other Classical allusions, the association of Dante's vision in the heaven of Mars with the iconography and thematics of the Exaltation of the Cross remains the predominant one. This is confirmed by the presence in canto 14 of a network of references to the corpus of liturgical texts and hymns that accompany the celebration of this feast on September 14 of the liturgical year (the putative date of Dante's death in 1321 according to Giovanni Boccaccio).[19] To

d'elmi di 'ciaro embruniti, e avéssaro armi lucenti, unde aguardandoli lo sole, per la luce se nascondaréno li elmi, e parrea la schiera standoli delogne quasi tutto uno lume e quasi uno pezzo" (*La composizione del mondo* 2.2.5.16).

[18] Cicero also provides a point of transition inasmuch as Africanus is Scipio's grandfather and not his father. Dante will displace the blood-relation of "father" and "son" even further, Cacciaguida being neither the pilgrim's father nor his grandfather nor even his great-grandfather. The result, as I later show, is a subtle undercutting of the genealogical themes of Dante's Classical models: as all literal blood-ties are distanced, an alternative genealogy passing through Christ is interposed.

[19] The Feast of the Exaltation, or the "Encaenia" as it was first referred to, was originally linked to the celebration of the founding of the churches of the *Anastasis* (the Holy Sepulcher) and *Martyrion* (Calvary) in Jerusalem. Incorporated into the Roman liturgical calendar in the seventh century, it bears important thematic ties to the eighth century "Feast of the Invention of the Cross" celebrated on May 3, which inaugurates the legendary finding of the "true" cross by Heraclius and Helen, the mother of Constantine. For present purposes, the only distinction to

cite only a few: the galactic simile ("tra poli del mondo") is a conventional one for the cosmic Christ *scandens polorum sidera* (spanning the heavenly poles) found in a wide variety of hymns to Christ and to the Holy Cross; the "venerable sign" of verse 101 apparently quotes from the chorus of a relatively well-known processional hymn by the Ravennate Bishop Peter Damian "Unica spes hominum, crux, o *venerabile signum*"; and the later description of the cross as a "precious jewel" ("questa gioia preziosa" [15.86]) itself bejewelled with living gemstones, belongs to precisely the same iconographic framework as that cross "shining forth with supernal ornaments" celebrated in the Antiphon from the mass of the Exaltation.[20] But perhaps most of all, it is the vis-

---

be made between the two feasts is that while the Invention, because of its ties to the figure of Constantine and its incorporation of numerous *Constantiniana* (the legend of his conversion, of the apparition of the cross before the battle of Milvia Bridge), invokes a more earthly and political set of symbols, the Exaltation is more strictly eschatological in its focus. For a collection of liturgical texts associated with these two feasts see Jacob Gretser, *De Sancta Cruce*, vol. 3, 281–359.

[20] The phrase "scandens polorum sidera" in reference to the cosmic Christ is a rhetorical commonplace in cross and passion hymns. It is present, for instance, in John Donne's "Good Friday, 1613. Riding Westward" (vv. 21–25):

> Could I behold those hands
> which span the poles?
> And turn all spheres at once,
> pierced with those holes?
> Could I behold that endless height which is
> Zenith to us, and to'our antipodes,
> Humbled below us?

(I would like to thank my friend Albert Ascoli for first calling this poem to my attention.) For other examples of the same, see hymn no. 443 ("In Resurrectione Domini"), AH 42.229; hymn no. 21 ("De Sacra Cruce") strophe 7, in Pitra's *Analecta Sacra Spicilegia Solesmensi*, vol. 1, 507; Bede's hymn no. 13 ("In Natale Sancti Andreae") strophe 4, *Opera Rythmica* CCSL 122; and the anonymous hymn no. 7 ("Haec est praefatio . . .") strophe 1 reprinted in Migne PL Supplementa 4***, col. 1478. The full text of Peter Damian's Hymn no. 37 ("Paractericum Carmen de Sancta Cruce") is reproduced in Migne PL 145, col. 931. The expression "venerabile signum" is not one of the most common appellations for the cross, and I

ual construction of Dante's emblem—a cross of light superimposed not over the cosmos, but over the malefic heaven of Mars—that dramatizes the central theme of the Exaltation: the triumph of life over death, of the sign of Christ over the sign of Mars/*mors*.

Superimposed over the cosmos, the cross of light would have appeared a merely abstract figuration of the Christian antidote to the hopelessness of Classical limbo. Rising up instead against the red sky of Mars, it is a brilliantly polemical emblem of hope: a scandalous hope upending all tragic perspectives, infecting with activism all philosophies of skepticism and retreat, promising a true prophetic link between history and eternity, a true genealogical bond between man and his creator.[21] Ascending over Mars, the "venerable sign" rises over a Martian background of

---

have encountered it only in Dante, Peter Damian, and Godefridus of Viterbo (*Pantheon* 19.1, Migne PL 198, cols. 1007–1008). "O Crux venerabilis" is less rare and is present in the Antiphon to the mass of the Exaltation. In any event, both Peter Damian's and Dante's "venerabile signum" may be adapted from the standard appelation "O *admirabile* signum," also found in the above cited Antiphon ("O Crucis victoria, et *admirabile signum*, in caelesti curia fac nos captare triumphum"). On the general subject of the Holy Cross hymns, see Gretser, vol. 3, 281–359, and Joseph Szövérffy, "Crux Fidelis: Prolegomena to a History of the Holy Cross Hymns," *Traditio* 22 (1966): 1–41, and *Hymns of the Holy Cross: An Annotated Edition with Introduction*.

[21] The red/white color shift, crucial to the *Dream of the Rood* as well as to cantos 14–18, may have a precise scriptural analogue in Matthew 16:1–4, where, right before the Transfiguration, Jesus refuses the Pharisees a "sign from heaven" while referring to various interpretations of the red sky: "Facto vespere dicitis: Serenum erit, rubicundum est enim caelum. Et mane: Hodie tempestas, rutilat enim triste caelum" (Matt. 16:2–3). One standard interpretation of Christ's words held that these evocations of the reddened heavens were to be understood as anticipating his passion (prophesied in Matt. 16:21) and second coming (anticipated in Matt 16:27–17:6): "Signa temporum dixit de adventu suo vel passione cui simile est roseum coelum vespere. Ed item de tribulatione ante adventum futurum, cui simile est roseum coelum cum tristitia" (*Biblia Sacra cum Glossa Ordinaria*, vol. 5, 275). Cf. *Paradise* 27.28–36 on the cosmic blush at the time of the Crucifixion. The verb *rutilo* is of course associated with Mars, as in Book 6 of Cicero's *Republic*, where Africanus describes Mars as "tum rutilus horribilisque terris" (6.17). On red and white in the heaven of Mars, cf. G. Rabuse, *Gesammelte Aufsätze*, 63–65.

extraordinary symbolic density; a background into which are interwoven the infernal violence of the city under the rule of Mars, the person of Virgil and the text of his epic poem, the future and present sacrifices imposed upon Dante and Aeneas, the fruitful passions of Christ and of his martyrs, as well as the fruitless *martiri* of the damned.[22] Surfacing above this field of sacrificial blood, the cross bears both an imminent and an ultimate solution to the dilemma of history in the grip of Mars. To the epic hero it promises the eternal peace and salvific fame of Christian paradise; to the earthly city, the eventual and definitive victory of Christ's imperial Rome—the eschatological Jerusalem. Hence the apparent paradox that in cantos 14–18 it is as much a sign of peace as the military ensign of the warriors of the cross: a universal lyre intoning the ultimate reconciliation of all things opposed and an end to Martial sacrifice; and yet the crusader's personal cross, the battle *signum* that drives him along the arduous path ("la guerra / sì del cammino e sì della pietate" [*Inf.* 2.4–5]) that leads to his eternal homeland and reward.

Viewing the cross as a celestial cross of light and not as the blood-soaked rood of Golgotha, we step out of the frame of time and adopt (by anticipation) an eschatological perspective: a perspective above and beyond all Martial mutability, and hence only incompletely available to mortals. But no matter how great the difficulty, Christianity claims that it is only by adopting this higher gaze that we are able to penetrate the enigmatic *verbum crucis*, coming to see how an instrument of torture and abasement is really one of joy and exaltation, how a sign of death and darkness also signifies eternal life and eternal light. Or, as readers of cantos 14–18, how the heaven of Mars could be described as "this peace" ("questa pace" [15.148]), how the wrathful Mars could

---

[22] Again, see the celestial blush provoked by Peter's denunciation of the corrupt papacy in *Paradise* 27.22–36: a blush compared with a sunrise and/or sunset, which not only transforms Beatrice's semblance, but also recalls Christ's Crucifixion, the "eclissi . . . che 'n ciel fue / quando patì la supprema possanza" (27.35–36).

bear a glowing smile, how apparent bitterness could be converted into sweetness, and Martial discord converted into the rapturous music of the cross.

Before the spectacle of so dizzying a harmonization of things we thought so irreconcilably opposed, we stand with Dante in canto 14 at the vertical and horizontal limit of earthly wit ("qui vince la memoria mia lo 'ngegno" [14.103]), rapt in the cross's apocalyptic melody but "unable to follow the hymn" ("sanza intender l'inno" [14.123]), or, once again, "like he who understands not but hears" ("come a colui che non intende e ode" [14.126]). Such is the liminal state between blindness and prophetic vision described in Richard of Saint Victor's *Benjamin Maior*, a text whose presence is frequently felt in the third canticle:[23]

> And although we may retain in memory something from that experience and see it through a veil, as it were, and as though in the middle of a cloud, we lack the ability to comprehend or call to mind either the manner of seeing or the quality of the vision. And marvelously, in a way remembering, we do not remember; and not remembering, we remember; while seeing, we do not discern; looking at, we do not examine; and as we direct our attention to something, we do not penetrate it.

Indeed it is this same enshrouding and yet blindingly luminous veil, the fiery/vaporous atmosphere of the planet Mars, that hangs over much of cantos 14–18, setting up a characteristic mystical counterpoint between visions of crystalline clarity and of nebulosity, resistance, and visual impairment. The former in-

---

[23] "Et quamvis inde aliquid in memoria teneamus, et quasi per medium velum et velut in medio nebulae videamus, nec modum quidem videndi, nec qualitatem visionis comprehendere, vel recordari sufficimus. Et mirum in modum reminiscentes non reminiscimur, et non reminiscentes reminiscimur, dum videntes non pervidemus, et ascipientes non perspicimus, et intendentes non penetramus" (*Benjamin Maior* 4.23, Migne PL 196, col. 167). English translation by Grover A. Zinn from *The Twelve Patriarchs, The Mystical Ark, Book Three of the Trinity*, 306. The passage has been linked to the discussion of rapture in the Epistle to Can Grande (par. 28) by Edmund Gardner in *Dante and the Mystics*, 165.

sist, from the "still and cloudless evening sky" of 15.13 ("li seren tranquilli e puri"), through Cacciaguida's "clear words and precise Latin" ("chiare parole e . . . preciso latin" [17.34–35]) at the end of canto 17, on the power of the prophetic eye/word to penetrate all historical and cognitive barriers. The latter images begin with the profile of the Milky Way and an allusion to its vast sprinkling of sundry phosphorescent dots (14.97f.), immediately followed by the beautiful simile of a solar ray ("lo raggio" [14.115]) piercing a windowshade ("l'ombra" [14.116]) only to reveal the secret ferment of particles of dust. They continue in canto 15, as we see Cacciaguida gliding like a shooting star within a fulgurant constellation of light (15.13–21), and then his descent like a flame behind an alabaster screen ("parve foco dietro ad alabastro" [15.24]), two typical instances of *Paradise*'s poetics of white on white or light on light. And they reappear again in canto 18 with Cacciaguida's description of the lightning thrusts of Mars's spinning stars: "lì farà l'atto / che fa in nube il suo foco veloce" (18.35–36). Reinforced by the constant stupors and stoppages of cantos 14–18, they return us regularly to the theme of human fear and human error, providing evidence of the inadequacy of earthly language and perceptions, of the eternal tension between blindness and revelation.[24]

But where reason and perception falter, human faith seconded by grace—the "grace of God infused from above" first described in 15.28–29—marches onward, transforming discord into concord, adversity into advantage, sacrificial blood into transcendent light; empowering mortal eyes to penetrate, however partially, the enigmatic *verbum crucis*. What these and the earlier cited logical paradoxes describe is an inversion of perspectives or hermeneutic conversion which, as I have tried to suggest in chapters 2 and 3, serves as the key to Dante's epic metamorphosis at the center of *Paradise*, and hence to his Christianization of the transformations of Aeneas and Scipio. Figured abstractly

[24] See, for instance, 14.99, 14.103, 15.39–42, 15.79–84, 17.13–18.

through the celestial cross, its supernatural *exemplum* (14.105), this perspectival inversion must in turn be brought to bear upon the *personalized literary-biographical cross* that, via His Cross and the crusader Cacciaguida, Christ calls upon the poet-pilgrim to take up fearlessly.

The central objective of cantos 14–18 is, then, to bridge the gap between Dante's personal cross and the mysterious "joining of quadrants in a circle" of canto 14. To bring about this end the action of the text must be structurally two-fold. On the one hand, it must bring into gradual focus the precise character of this second cross: a task accomplished by the concrete prophecies of canto 17 and, in a more general sense, by the historical narrative that precedes them. On the other hand, it must link by a chain of didactic acts of condescension the universal cross of Christ to the particular cross of the poet-pilgrim, revealing in terms accessible to historical man how Dante's cross participates in the cross of Christ and, conversely, the cross of Christ in Dante's personal cross.

2. TRANSFIGURATION

Transfiguration and the Stumbling-Block of the Cross

From the opening " 'Rise up' and 'Conquer' " (" 'Resurgi' e 'vinci' " [14.125]) emanating from the cross of light, to Cacciaguida's spinning descent like a shooting-star off the cross (15.13–24), to his descent out of a gnosis above "the mark of mortals" ("il segno d'i mortal" [15.42]), to his embodiment and description of Dante's origins (15.97–16.154), and, finally, to the translation at the end of canto 17 of the celestial cross into a concrete literary program and praxis, the central cantos of *Paradise* set out to personalize the cross of Christ in terms of the pilgrim's epic *imitatio Christi*. As shall be shown in the following chapter, this programmatic rooting of the martyr's personal-historical cross in a celestial one defines not only the central action of cantos 14–18, but also that of the apsidal mosaics of Sant' Apollinare in

Classe, Dante's probable model. They share, I would suggest, a common theological background: the scriptural passage which in the view of centuries of Christian exegetes most fully dramatized the personal and individual implications of Christ's universal cross: the gospel account of the Transfiguration.

"The Transfiguration," as Otto Georg von Simson has written, "is the reality of the cross"; and in particular, one might add, its *eschatological reality*.[25] Suspended in all three synoptic gospels between the first and second predictions of Christ's crucifixion, the story of the Transfiguration or "metamorphosis" derives its name from an incident said to have occurred along the road to Jerusalem. On the summit of a lofty mountain, before Peter, James, and John—his most intimate disciples according to Mark 5:37 and 14:33—Jesus appeared suddenly metamorphosed into

---

[25] *Sacred Fortress: Byzantine Art and Statecraft in Ravenna*, 44. The most important Eastern treatises on the Transfiguration are those of Origen (*Commentarius in Evangelium Secundum Mattheum*, Migne PG 13, cols. 1065–1085 esp.), John Chrysostom (Homilies 55/56 and 56/57 in *Homiliae in Matthaeum*, Migne PG 58, cols. 539–558), the pseudo-Dionysius (*De Divinis Nominibus*, Migne PG 3, cols. 592–597 esp.) and John of Damascus ("Homilia de Transfiguratione Domini," Migne PG 96, cols. 545–576; and "Carmen in Transfigurationem Domini," Migne PG 96, cols. 848–852). Because the liturgical feast of the Transfiguration was not officially recognized in the West until 1475, the exegetical tradition is on the whole less rich, although discussions of the Transfiguration play a significant role in Medieval debates concerned with the metaphysics of light, and in mystical-contemplative texts. Major Western discussions are those of Jerome (*Commentarius in Evangelium Matthaei*, Migne PL 26, cols. 123–127); Augustine (Sermons 78 and 79 in *Sermones*, Migne PL 38, cols. 490–493); Pope Leo the Great (Homily 51, CCSL 138-A, 296–303); Gregory the Great (*Moralia in Job* 32.6, Migne PL 76, cols. 639–640); the pseudo-Bede (*In Evangelium Matthaei Expositio*, Migne PL 92, cols. 80–81); John the Scot (*De Divisione Naturae*, Bk. 5, Migne PL 122, cols. 998–1001); Albertus Magnus (*Super Dionysium De Divinis Nominibus*, vol. 37/1, 24–43 of *Opera Omnia*, ed. B. Geyer); Bonaventure (*Sermones de Tempore* 1 [Domenica Secunda in Quadragesima], vol. 9, 215–221 of *Opera Omnia*); and Thomas Aquinas (*Summa Theologiae* pars 3, que. 45 ["De Transfiguratione Christi"], arts. 1–4. For a general overview, see Peter A. Chamberaś, "The Transfiguration of Christ: A Study in Patristic Exegesis of Scripture," *Saint Vladimir's Theological Quarterly* 14, no. 1–2 (1970): 48–65.

glory, prefiguring his own ascension and the state of resurrected souls at the end of time: "Et transfiguratus est ante eos. Et resplenduit facies eius sicut sol [ὡς ὁ ἥλιος]: vestimenta autem eius facta sunt alba sicut nix" ("And he was transfigured before them. And his face did shine as the sun: and his garments became white as snow" [Matt. 17:2]). The specific solar attribute found in Matthew, so reminiscent of certain pre-Christian theophanies that scholars have sometimes doubted the provenance of the entire transfiguration story, is not preserved in Mark and Luke, though it remains nonetheless implicit.[26] Alongside the transfigured Christ in all three accounts, the equally fulgurant figures of Moses and Elijah reveal themselves: appearing briefly only to disappear abruptly as if to dramatize the absorption into Christ of Old Testament prophecy and law. Such at least was the standard interpretation among the Church Fathers. So, however fleeting, their appearance is of considerable importance, for just as Jesus' solar metamorphosis suggests that he is indeed the apocalyptic "Sol Iustitiae" or "Sun of Justice" prophesied in Ma-

---

[26] Among the doubters, see Wilhelm Bousset, *Kyrios Christos: A History of Belief from the Beginnings of Christianity to Irenaeus*, 342f. For a complete exposition on Christ as sun see John of Damascus, "Homilia de Transfiguratione Domini," Migne PG 96, cols. 564–569, which particularly emphasizes the exemplary character of Christ's metamorphosis. Mark elides the reference to the sun by emphasizing instead the glorified body: "et transfiguratus est coram ipsis. Et vestimenta eius facta sunt splendentia et candida nimis velut nix, qualia fullo non potest super terram candida facere" (Mark 9:1–2). Luke in turn even avoids the verb *transfiguro*, stating instead that Jesus, Moses, and Elijah were "visi in maiestate" (Luke 9:31). His description of the actual event identifies the Transfiguration with Christ's prayers at Gethsemane (Matt. 26:36–47, Mark 14:32–43) and on the Mount of Olives (Luke 22:39–47): "Et facta est, dum oraret, species vultus eius altera, et vestitus eius albus et refulgens" (9:29). There are a number of other divergences of greater or lesser importance, including the question of the number of days—six according to Matthew and Mark, eight according to Luke—between Christ's eschatological discourse and the Transfiguration. (This matter was resolved by most patristic interpreters both by calendrical slight of hand and by numerological allegory, as in John of Damascus' "Homilia de Transfiguratione," cols. 557–560.)

lachi 4:2, the presence of Moses and Elijah serves to confirm his identity as the eschatological Messiah. This, Peter, in a moment of prophetic insight, had just announced in Matthew 16:16: "You are Christ, the Son of the living God" ("Tu es Christus, filius Dei vivi") he states, to which Christ responds "your blood has not revealed it to you, but my Father, who is in heaven" ("sanguis non revelavit tibi, sed Pater meus, qui in caelis est" [Matt. 16:17]).

Jesus, Moses, and Elijah are engaged in a colloquium whose subject is only hinted at in Luke: "et dicebant excessum eius, quem completurus erat in Ierusalem" ("and they spoke of his decease, which he was to accomplish in Jerusalem" [9:31])—Jerome's choice of *excessus* here to translate the Greek ἔξοδον, evoking at once Christ's exodus and exile, the excessive love that was the origin of his sacrifice, and his crucifixion as a victorious *excessus* (exit) out of history.[27] Once Moses and Elijah have departed, the episode reaches a second climax as a bright cloud descends over Peter, James, and John—described in Luke 9:32 first as "heavy with sleep" ("gravati erant somno") and then as awakened ("vigilantes"). Out of this paracletic cloud emerges a voice repeating the Father's baptismal greeting of Christ (Matt. 3:17), "This is my beloved Son, in whom I am well pleased" ("Hic est Filius meus dilectus, in quo mihi bene complacui") but with the added command "hear ye him" ("ipsum audite" [Matt. 17:5]).[28] Overcome with fear, the apostles fall on their faces. They are, however, immediately comforted by Christ, who asks that they rise up and conquer their fears ("Surgite, et nolite timere" [Matt. 17:7]) and remain silent about the incident after their descent from the mountaintop—at least, that is, until after the crucifixion ("Nemini dixeritis visionem, donec Filius hominis a mortuis resurgat" [Matt. 17:9]). The narrative closes with their descent and

[27] In Matthew, Moses and Elijah are merely described as "cum eo loquentes" (17:3); in Mark "et erant loquentes cum Iesu" (9:3).

[28] Here again there are slight variants: in Mark "Hic est Filius meus charissimus: audite illum" (9:6), in Luke "Hic est Filius meus dilectus, ipsum audite" (9:35).

with Christ's veiled insistence that Elijah (in the form of John the Baptist) had already come: a further confirmation that all the messianic prophecies of the Old Testament had indeed been fulfilled by the time of His advent and that the time was now ripe for the final *parousia*.

The unusually dense conjunction of the characteristic gospel tensions between secrecy and proclamation, promise and fulfillment, present sacrifice and a rapidly approaching apocalyptic future—not to mention the imposing presence of the glorified Moses, Elijah, and Christ—all identify the story of Christ's Transfiguration as the "central knot" of the gospel narrative.[29] Or, as one contemporary theologian has put it:[30]

> The Transfiguration occurs in the Synoptic accounts as a kind of dramatic mid-point between the imminent exposure—one might almost say, explosion—of the messianic secret and the imminence of a messianic exodus. It is as though the whole history of Israel had gone into a sudden inversion. The protracted journey from Exodus to Advent had suddenly come full circle in a prodromal crisis of Advent and Exodus.

But if the structural significance of this biblical episode has sometimes been recognized by modern readers, its importance to the rest of the New Testament and to early Christian literature may not always seem as obvious. The Transfiguration remains, nevertheless, everywhere present: from the Christology of the gospel of John, to the discussions of metamorphosis and light in the Pauline epistles, to certain gnostically flavored apocryphal apocalypses, to the theology of Clement and Origen and the Al-

---

[29] These words are Frank Kermode's in *The Genesis of Secrecy: On the Interpretation of Narrative*, 142–143.

[30] Paul Lehmann continues: "Only the most casual and exterior reading of the gospel accounts of the Transfiguration and its setting could fail of being drawn into the mounting tension of time running out as the narrative moves from Jesus' scarcely veiled self-identification, elicited from his disciples in a confession of messiahship, through conflict, challenge, confrontation, to crucifixion. The time is indeed at hand!" From *The Transfiguration of Politics*, 82–83.

exandrian school as a whole. Because the gospel narrative emphasizes the confirmation of Christ's dual nature, his messianic identity, and the uniqueness of his sonship in God, it was employed polemically by the early Greek and Latin Church Fathers in combatting various heterodox Christologies, first and foremost Arius' subordination of Son to Father. As a result, it would play a significant role in the formulation of the trinitarian creed which was to be the principal fruit of the historic Council of Nicaea (A.D. 325).

Of equal importance to subsequent exegesis was its polemical usage, this time in opposing the "learned sophistries" of the Gnostics, in the Second Epistle of Peter (1:16–21), where it is adduced as proof of the truthfulness of all scriptural predictions and associated generally with prophetic vision:

> Non enim doctas fabulas secuti notam fecimus vobis Domini nostri Iesu Christi virtutem et praesentiam: sed speculatores facti illius magnitudinis. Accipiens enim a Deo Patre honorem et gloriam, voce delapsa ad eum huiuscemodi a magnifica gloria: Hic est Filius meus dilectus, in quo mihi complacui, ipsum audite. Et hanc vocem nos audivimus de caelo allatam, cum essemus cum ipso in monte sancto. Et habemus firmiorem propheticum sermonem: cui benefacitis attendentes quasi lucernae lucenti in caliginoso loco donec dies elucescat, et lucifer oriatur in cordibus vestris: hoc primum intelligentes quod omnis prophetia Scripturae propria interpretatione non fit. Non enim voluntate humana allata est aliquando prophetia: sed Spiritu sancto inspirati, locuti sunt sancti Dei homines.

> (For we have not by following artificial fables made known to you the power and presence of our Lord Jesus Christ; but we were eyewitnesses of his greatness. For he received from God the Father honour and glory; this voice coming down to him from the excellent glory: "This is my beloved Son, in whom I am well pleased; hear ye him." And this voice we heard brought from heaven, when we were with him in the holy mount. And we have the word of prophecy more firm: to which you do well to attend, as to a light shining in a dark place until the day dawn, and the morning star rise in your

hearts: understanding this first, that no prophecy of the Scripture is made by private interpretation. For prophecy came not by the will of man at any time; but the holy men of God spoke, inspired by the Holy Ghost.)

This passage, so filled with Dantesque reverberations, extends the Father's direct empowerment ("ipsum audite") of the Son's prophetic word into a universal empowerment of the word of Christ's privileged witnesses, his literal martyrs. With its emphasis on the individual Christian's participation in Jesus' paradigmatic transformation, it opens up the way for what, via Jerome, Ambrose, Augustine, John of Damascus, the pseudo-Dionysius, Leo the Great, Bede, and others would become by the twelfth century the systematic mystical interpretation of, for instance, Richard of Saint Victor's *Benjamin*. Here Christ's seamless and supernatural robe ("qualia fullo non potest super terram candida facere" [Mark 9:2]) would be contrasted with the torn garment of earthly *Philosophia*, his celestial (or mountain) *gnosis* with his terrestrial (or valley) teachings, the eschatological reality of transfiguration with the immediate reality of the cross, the ascent of the Christian *mystes* into the mystery of the trinity, with human reason falling on its face.[31]

---

[31] In his discussion of the Transfiguration, Richard writes: "Mox ut te dux tuus Christus collocaverit in summo, apparet tibi in habitu alio, et te coram induitur lumine sicut vestimento, et sicut evangelista testatur, fiunt mox vestimento ejus alba sicut nix, et qualia non potest fullo facere super terram, quia ille divinae sapientae splendor, qui ab alto speculationis vertice prospicitur, omnino definiri non potest per humani sensus prudentiam. Animadverte ergo quia aliam in valle, et aliam vestem Christus habet in monte. In valle sane habet vestem integram, sed in monte tantum, habet vestem gloriosam" (*Benjamin Minor* 80, Migne PL 196, cols. 56–57). For the contrast of pagan and Christian contemplation, see Chapter 75 (*ibid.*, cols. 53–54). Richard's mystical exegesis was founded on an authoritative tradition reaching back to the first exhaustive interpretation of the Transfiguration: that found in Origen's *Commentary on Matthew* (Migne PG 13, cols. 1065–1085). Origen too systematically foregrounds the mystical-visionary aspects of the event while emphasizing as well its eschatological dimension. The ascent takes place in the seventh day ("post dies sex" [Matt. 17:1]), thus, because it rep-

But from the privilege of ascent derived a concomitant moral responsibility, a responsibility to take on the historical task, whether cross or epic *labor*. Thus Augustine in his sermon on the Transfiguration calls upon those who have witnessed Christ's ultimate (which is to say, transfigured) glory on the mountain to:[32]

> Come down to labor in the earth, to serve in the earth, to endure humiliation and bear the cross in the earth. The Life came down in order to suffer death, the Bread came down to suffer hunger, the Way came down to suffer exhaustion along the path, the Fountain came down to suffer thirst: and you refuse to labor? "Seek not thy own." Have charity, preach the truth: only thus shall you come to that eternity where peace is found.

Here we touch upon the central polarity which identifies the Transfiguration with the great themes of the Dantean, Ciceronian, and Virgilian otherworldly encounters of father and son. For the entire vertical, ascensional, or, to coin a word to Dante's taste, "eternalizing," drive of the narrative serves not so much to describe an all-absorbing metaphysical alternative, as to promote an unequivocally didactic and "historicizing" end: to aid Jesus' followers in *overcoming the stumbling-block of the cross*. This, as Pope Leo the Great and subsequent commentators would insist, was the fundamental purpose of Christ's Transfiguration: "In this transfiguration the principal object was to remove the scan-

---

resents the vision of a new Sabbath beyond the six days of creation (cols. 1065–1068): a foreshadowing of the supernatural order that lies beyond the world of nature. See also cols. 992–1065 on the general setting of Christ's metamorphosis and its relation to martyrdom.

[32] "Descende laborare in terra, servire in terra, contemni, crucifigi in terra. Descendit vita, ut occideretur; descendit panis, ut esuriret; descendit via, ut in itinere lassaretur; descendit fons, ut sitiret: et tu recusas laborare? Noli tua quaerere. Habe charitatem, praedica veritatem: tunc pervenies ad aeternitatem, ubi invenies securitatem" (Sermo 78 ["De Diversis 69" in the old enumeration], Migne PL 38, col. 493). This "activist" reading is especially characteristic of the use of the Transfiguration in treatises on martyrdom. Its legacy can be felt in such contemporary exegetical works as Paul Lehmann's *The Transfiguration of Politics*.

dal of the cross from the hearts of the Apostles, such that their faith be not undermined by the humiliation undergone in His voluntary passion, revealing instead the magnificence of its concealed dignity."[33]

The symbolic stumbling-block in question is that which, in the immediate terms of the gospel narrative, is dramatized by Peter in Matthew 16:22-23 and Mark 8:32-33, where, confronted with Christ's prediction that he would be martyred in Jerusalem, Peter expresses understandable disbelief: "Lord, be it far from thee; this shall not be unto thee" ("Absit a te, Domine: non erit tibi hoc"). How, after all, could the living Son of God, the highest of beings, be subject to the most humiliating of fates? How could the one perfectly just man, the "Sun of Justice," be the victim of such an unspeakable act of injustice in a universe ruled by a benevolent and all-powerful God? Indeed, it does violence not only to the Platonist's sense of hierarchy and ontological order but also to simple common sense.

But Christ is quick to assert that this is precisely the point: transcendent mysteries like that of the cross must always prove a stumbling-block to human reason. Such objections are merely symptoms of the blindness characteristic of all temporal perspectives: "you do not relish the things that are of God" ("non sapis ea quae Dei sunt") Jesus tells Peter, reprimanding his disbelief, "but the things that are of men" ("sed ea quae hominum" [Matt. 16:23]). What Peter has failed to discern is something I have already thematized in terms of the iconography of the cross (and in a different setting, in Virgilian and Ciceronian terms): the eternal light which lies beyond the tragic immediacy of the coming blood-soaked rood, the "magnificence" of the cross's "concealed dignity," the honor and necessity of self-sacrifice.

Yet perhaps he is not to blame: Peter has not yet seen the

[33] "In qua transfiguratione illud quidem principaliter agebatur, ut de cordibus apostolorum crucis scandalum tolleretur, nec conturbaret eorum fidem voluntariae humilitas passionis, quibus revelata esset absconditae excellentia dignitatis" (Leo the Great, Sermon 51, CCSL 138-A, 298).

Transfiguration—the metamorphosis of the Son into that same supernatural sun which would shine over the Holy Jerusalem at the end of time. Hence, despite having just prophesied Christ's identity (Matt. 16:16), he stands like Virgil in *Purgatory* 22 on the brink of revelation but with the sun of Christ behind his back. And, like souls in Plato's cave, he still mistakes the shadows of historical becoming for the eternal Logos that is their animating principle.[34]

Peter's σκάνδαλον/cross is then none other than that which serves as the pivot of Dante's interpretive conversion in cantos 14–18. Dante too must overcome a symbolic stumbling-block; he must discern in a prophecy of sacrifice, injustice, humiliation, and death a necessary and overriding divine logic; and he must find the hidden dignity in his own personal *excessus* and the determination to take on his personal-literary cross. The structure of this conversion, whether in the synoptics, at the center of *Paradise* or, for that matter, in Virgil's or Cicero's Book 6, is essentially the same: on the one hand the son/hero/follower of Christ encounters the promise of eternity—fame, deification, metamorphosis, transfiguration; on the other, he must confront the primacy of sacrifice in history. To take on one's personal cross, an epic labor, or an unprecedented literary endeavor, is to accept not only the transfiguring reward but also the necessity and inevitability of sacrifice: this is above all what he must be brought to understand. If the motto of this conversion is *per crucem ad lucem* (through the cross to the light), its central theme is that the cross is not a detour but rather the only gateway to the beyond.[35]

---

[34] On Platonic "conversion" and Socrates' cave, see Werner Jaeger, *Paideia: The Ideals of Greek Culture*, vol. 2, 291–306. On conversion in the *Commedia*, see C. S. Singleton, *Journey to Beatrice* [Dante Studies II], 39–56; "In Exitu Israel de Aegypto," in *Dante: A Collection of Critical Essays*, ed. J. Freccero, 102–114; and Freccero's own "Dante's Prologue Scene," *DS* 84 (1966): 1–12.

[35] For a contemporary statement of this doctrine, see Giordano da Rivalto, sermon 27 (26 luglio, 1304): "Quegli dunque fanno vera penitenzia, che pigliano la croce di Cristo in loro medesimo; perchè il perdono di nostri peccati è sola la croce

How then does Christ help bring about this interpretive conversion through his Transfiguration? First, the exegetical tradition would respond, by assuming his own universal redemptive cross in an exemplary fashion: the Transfiguration is after all (like cantos 14–18) a kind of epic "recognition" scene in which the identity and the mission of the hero are revealed. The episode was thus thought to provide a model of filial piety and paternal pride, of a perfect adequacy of paternal promise to filial fulfillment, a harmonious paradigm of identity in difference and difference in identity: all for the benefit of future imitators of Christ and of his cross.[36] Secondly, by insisting on the presence in human history of a radical eschatological perspective from which history's "wrongs" are revealed as eternity's "rights": "For the Son of man shall come in the glory of his Father, with his angels" ("Filius enim hominis venturus est in gloria Patris sui cum angelis suis"), Jesus proclaims immediately before his transformation, "and then will he render to every man according to his works" ("et tunc reddet unicuique secundum opera eius" [Matt. 16:27]). Such is his promise of final justice beyond history's affronts and such the apocalyptic setting which identifies the Transfiguration with the Judgment prophesied in Matthew 24:29–31.[37]

But last yet most important of all, Christ facilitates the taking

---

di Cristo: chiunque la si reca più in se, e tienla in memoria, questi va, e sta ben sicuro. Chi per amor di Cristo diventa povero, afflige il suo corpo in digiunare, ed in affaticare, e crucifigerlo, come dice Santo Paolo, co' vizii, e con le concupiscenzie, questi con sicura faccia verrà al giudicio: chi più incorpora la passione di Cristo in se, questi è più sicuro, come i martiri, perocchè moriron per Cristo. Incorporaro sì la passione di Cristo in loro, che quando moriro, in uno punto, sanza nulla pena di Purgatorio, andavano in cielo, incontanente sanza nullo giudicio, nullo passavano a Dio" (*Prediche*, vol. 1, 211–212).

[36] See, for instance, Richard's treatment of "Hic est Filius meus dilectus in quo mihi bene complacui" (Matt. 17:5) in *Benjamin Minor* 82, Migne PL 196, cols. 58–59.

[37] The eschatological implications of the Transfiguration are prominent in patristic exegesis from Origen's *Commentary on Matthew* onwards (see Migne PG 13, cols. 1083–1086).

on of the hero's personal cross by revealing through his own metamorphosis into light the glorification that awaits those who follow his exemplary act of self-sacrifice and filial piety on the cross. (And this whether the act of imitation involves a literal [Cacciaguida] or figurative [Dante] martyrdom.) The solar Christ of the Transfiguration, therefore, discloses to those who suffer from the same history-bound blindness as Peter, how, paradoxically, sacrifice provides the necessary means to which transfiguration is the glorious end. The cross brings not punishment but the ultimate eternal reward, not Classical *fama* but the laurel crown of salvation, not deification but transfiguration, not so much the completion of morphosis as the self's complete metamorphosis into Christ.

As a result, the Transfiguration presents itself as conclusive proof of the veracity of Christ's description of the paradoxical economy of salvation:

> Si quis vult post me venire, abneget semetipsum, et tollat crucem suam, et sequatur me. Qui enim voluerit animam suam salvam facere, perdet eam: qui autem perdiderit animam suam propter me, inveniet eam. Quid enim prodest homini, si mundum universum lucretur, animae vero suae detrimentum patiatur? Aut quam dabit homo commutationem pro anima sua?

> (If any man will come after me, let him deny himself, and take up his cross, and follow me. For whosoever will save his life shall lose it: and he that shall lose his life for my sake shall find it. For what does it profit a man if he gain the whole world and lose his own soul? Or what shall a man give in exchange for his soul?) [Matt. 16:24–27]

These words, cited verbatim in canto 14, verse 106 ("ma chi prende sua croce e segue Cristo"), and paraphrased at the beginning of canto 15, immediately precede Jesus' transformation and provide a definitive gloss on the central cantos of *Paradise*. Apparent gain is eternal loss and eternal gain, apparent loss: such are the topsy-turvy perspectives opened up to humankind through

Christ's cross. And just as the pursuit of goods leads to the loss of the supreme Good, misplaced love will bring about the loss of love: "Bene è che sanza termine si doglia / chi, per amor di cosa che non duri / etternalmente, quello amor si spoglia" ("Right is it that he should grieve without end who for love of things that endure not eternally, strips himself of that love" [15.10–12]).[38] Dante's reflexive "si spoglia" simply reinforces a point implicit in Jesus' repeated use of the verb *velle*: the individual will must bear the full responsibility. Just as it alone can strip itself of the love of Christ, it alone can assume this sacred patrimony.

By way of this insistence on the will we are brought back to the grammatical subject of the opening verses of canto 15, the "benign will" of the crusaders in the heaven of Mars:

> Benigna volontade in che si liqua
> sempre l'amor che drittamente spira,
> come cupidità fa ne la iniqua,
>   silenzio puose a quella dolce lira,
> e fece qüietar le sante corde
> che la destra del cielo allenta e tira.
>   Come saranno a' giusti preghi sorde
> quelle sustanze che, per darmi voglia
> ch'io le pregassi, a tacer fur concorde?   15.1–9

---

[38] It is perhaps not coincidental that canto 15 of *Purgatory* is concerned with precisely the same paradoxical economy. The pilgrim has explained to him the extraordinary manner in which the Good of heaven is not quantitatively diminished by subdivision:

> Quello infinito e ineffabil bene
> che là sù è, così corre ad amore
> com' a lucido corpo raggio vene.
>   Tanto si dà quanto trova d'ardore;
> sì che, quantunque carità si stende,
> cresce sovr' essa l'etterno valore.   15.67–72

This logic which seems so incomprehensible from the perspective of earthly economies, founded as they are on scarcity and lack, serves to undermine (as does the cross of light) the ideology of the mercantile Florence described at the center of *Paradise*.

(Gracious will, wherein right-breathing love always resolves itself, as cupidity does into grudging will, imposed silence on that sweet lyre and quieted the holy strings which the right hand of Heaven slackens and draws tight. How shall those beings be deaf to righteous prayers, who, in order to prompt me to beg of them, became silent with one consent?)

What is immediately striking in this vision is the astonishing conformity of Christ's warriors to a single sign and will, especially so given the emphasis in canto 14 on the great diversity of their sacrificial acts, the varying magnitudes of their light (97), and their extreme kinetic agitation (109–117). Here, after all, is assembled the Christian Hall of Fame: the Christian heroes and martyrs who have made so great a name for themselves ("fuor di gran voce" [18.32]), as we later learn, that any poet or *musa*—even Dante's greatest muse ("maggior musa" [15.26])—would find abundant matter ("ne sarebbe opima" [18.33]) for epic treatment. And yet they seem to tolerate inequity even less than iniquity, for in an extraordinary act of humility they put off their individual names to form but a single proper name: the heavenly "X" which signifies Jesus Christ.[39]

As literal or figurative *cruciferi* (or bearers of the cross), Cacciaguida, Judas Maccabeus, Roland, William of Orange, Renoart, Robert Guiscard, Geoffrey of Bouillon, Charlemagne, and Joshua do of course belong to the same fraternity of the Holy Cross which the poet-pilgrim is now called upon to join. But the emergence of Christ's "venerable sign" out of history's anarchic plurality of personal crosses, of the name of Christ out of the he-

---

[39] The notion of the X of the cross as Jesus' signature, monogram, and proper name was so pervasive that it was a common scribal practice to substitute an X for the full transcription of his name. The same is true of Medieval legal documents, where the sign of Christ is often employed as a guarantee of the binding character of a contract upon two parties. On this subject see Dölger's "Beiträge zur Geschichte des Kreuzzeichens," *JACh* 3 (1960): 5–17. On the general matter of Christ's X in relation to his other monograms, see Jacob Stockbauer, *Kunstgeschichte des Kreuzes*, 81–120.

roes' illustrious names, provides a vivid demonstration of how the call of Matthew 16:24 is not a call for *individual* acts of heroism, for the pursuit of fame or glory, or for the *aristeiai* of Classical epic. Rather, it is a collective call to abandon such a deluded sense of self and to transform oneself fully in(to) Christ.

To take on one's personal cross is, thus, to participate directly in this universal eschatological cross. And it is simultaneously to begin one's personal metamorphosis into Christ: "But we all, beholding the glory of the Lord with face uncovered, are transformed into the same image from glory to glory, as by the Spirit of the Lord" ("Nos vero omnes, revelata facie gloriam Domini speculantes, in eandem imaginem transformamur a claritate in claritatem, tanquam a Domini Spiritu" [II Cor. 3:18]).[40] Only such a notion of mystical participation in Christ's victory on the cross can explain the ecstatic effect, at the close of canto 14, of the mysterious music of the cross:

> Ïo m'innamorava tanto quinci,
> che 'nfino a lì non fu alcuna cosa
> che mi legasse con sì dolci vinci.   14.127–129

(I was so moved to love [by it] that till then nothing had bound me with such sweet bonds.)

Listening to this music, with its militant call to rise up and conquer (" 'Resurgi' e 'Vinci' " [14.125]) and to join the august company of the *cruciferi*, the poet-pilgrim imagines himself as a Christ figure, bound ("legato") by sweet shackles ("dolci vinci") to the cross. The transformation can be only a preliminary one, but we know that the event is real because, as in canto 10 (59–60), the love of Beatrice is temporarily eclipsed (14.130–139). For a moment Christ's cruciform *Eliòs* has eclipsed the pilgrim's personal sun (herself frequently identified as a figure of the moon). What is anticipated is the total eclipse in the Empyrean of all mediate

---

[40] The passage from Corinthians is used in precisely this manner by John of Damascus in his "Homilia de Transfiguratione," Migne PG 96, col. 572b.

relations to divinity: Dante's metamorphosis, however momentary, into one of the glorified children of light of John 12:36, one of the transfigured holy strings of Christ's cruciform lyre.[41]

One last implication for cantos 14–18 is especially plain: once this logic of self-sacrifice and transfiguration has been fully clarified and it becomes evident how great is the cost of not taking up Christ's call ("quanto caro costa / non seguir Cristo" [*Par.* 20.46–47]), the cosmos of the marketplace with its always calculable risks and finite speculations falls away. And, with this falling away, the demons which haunt the story of Florence's fall are exorcised: the specter of an autonomous human subject freely pursuing his or her own private "interest," the capitalist's dream of self-engenderment, the humanist's cult of self-creation.

In the economy of salvation by grace there can be no place for the temptations of Carthage or Fiorenza, the mercantile harlot; no place for compromise, calculations, or the hedging of bets. There is only one eschatological city and a single gateway: the cross of Christ. Citizenship in this city is predicated upon an absolute and unconditional act of will; or, as the quotation from Matthew 16:25 unequivocally states, the total abandonment of the deluded "autonomous" self and the finding of oneself in the

[41] Like images of white on white and light on light, both "natural" and "supernatural" eclipses are of central importance to the poetics of the third canticle, linking *Paradise*'s cosmology to its rhetoric of the ineffable. Aside from their role in the iconography of the crucifixion (alluded to in *Par.* 27.35 and 29.102), they serve as mechanisms of interruption and anticipation, providing vivid demonstrations of the breakdown of human vision and language that in turn look forward to the definitive breakdown with which the poem comes to a close. In *Paradise* 10 (vv. 52–60) the "Sun of the angels" thus eclipses Beatrice "in oblivion," and in 25.119–120 the pilgrim attempts to see into the nature of the transfigured John and is as one who, looking into the eclipsed sun "in order to see, becomes sightless." If in the former example, the vision of the angelic hierarchies orbiting their divine center is explicitly anticipated, the latter also looks forward to the final vision, inasmuch as Beatrice reproaches the pilgrim for trying to look into a matter that *here* (that is, in the heaven of the Fixed Stars), "has no place" ("che qui non ha loco" [25.123]).

person of Jesus Christ: "Whosoever will save his life shall lose it, and he that shall lose his life for my sake shall find it."

Such is the movement of Dante's poem as a whole, from self-loss in the opening *naufragium* of *Hell* to the ultimate finding of "our effigy" inscribed into a triune circle to our final inscription at the close of *Paradise* within the circle of divinity. And such the general structure of Christian *comedy*: what I once lost now I have found. But cantos 14–18 of Dante's *Paradise* mark the privileged moment in this overarching structure when the theme of the paschal imitation (and finding) of Christ is directly identified with the literary-personal genesis of the entire poem. It is under the fulgurant sign of Christ in the heaven of Mars, thus, that the Classical father's exhortation to complete the epic endeavor is translated into a call to imitate Christ; or, more literally, that Cacciaguida's history of the city's fall and prophecy concerning his descendant's tragic fate is transformed into a call to complete the text and make the full vision manifest.

Trasumanar / Trasfigurar

The implications of the Transfiguration narrative to the interpretation of cantos 14–18 have not in any way been exhausted here. I have overlooked, for the sake of brevity, certain of the more obvious links: the lengthy discussion in 14.10–60 of the glorified body and of the radiant appearance of the blessed; the "O Eliòs" address to the cross in 14.96; the presence of Hippolytus as type of Christ and Phaeton as antitype in canto 17; the numerous stoppages and stupors recalling the apostles' reactions; the possible nexus between the bright cloud of Matthew 17:5 and the vapors of Mars; and Cacciaguida's reference to Dante as "my frond in whom I am well pleased" ("fronda mia in che io compiacemmi" [15.88]), a clear citation of God's Baptismal/Transfigurational greeting of Christ. (Some of these will be dealt with in coming sections.) Even less have I exhausted the significance of the Transfiguration to a canticle whose mode of vision is defined from the outset as an exemplary *trasumanamento*; a "trans-humanization" which, like Paul's rapture in II Corinthians 12:2 and the fulgurant beauty of the cross in canto 14, must ultimately thwart all human attempts to figure it linguistically: "Trasumanar significar *per verba* / non si poria" ("passing beyond the human *in words* cannot be set forth" [1.70–71]) Dante states in the opening canto, and later, in a characteristic moment of mystical aphasia before the solar Christ of canto 23, "così, *figurando* il paradiso, / convien saltar lo sacrato poema, / come chi trova suo cammin riciso" ("so, imaging paradise, the sacred poem must make a leap, like he who finds his path cut off" [61–63; my italics]).[42]

That Dante understood the Transfiguration in precisely such a mystical sense we know from the dedicatory epistle to Can Grande (whose authenticity I take for granted), in which Matthew is cited in defense of the epistemological marginality of Pauline rapture:[43]

> Ecce, postquam humanam rationem intellectus ascensione transierat, quae extra se agerentur non recordabatur. Hoc etiam est insinuatum nobis in Matthaeo, ubi tres discipuli ceciderunt in faciem suam, nihil postea recitantes, quasi obliti.
>
> (Behold, after the intellect had passed beyond the bounds of human faculty in its exaltation, it could not recall what took place outside of its range. This again is conveyed to us in Matthew, where we

---

[42] In canto 1, that which bridges the inevitable gap that separates transcendent realities from their linguistic representation is an *esperïenza* of divinity which can only be the result of grace ("l'essemplo basti / a cui esperïenza grazia serba" [1.71–72]). Similarly, in canto 14 Dante insists that it is only by taking on his or her own personal cross that the reader can accede to an adequate vision of the cross of light: "io non so trovare essempro degno; / ma chi prende sua croce e segue Cristo, / ancor mi scuserà di quel ch'io lasso, / vedendo in quell'albor balenar Cristo" (14.105–108). The implication is that the two are in some sense interchangeable: the imitation of Christ's passion leads to the supplement of grace which in turn leads to the "experience" of divinity's transcendent hieroglyphs. The term *essempro* is clearly highlighted in both passages, denoting that which Dante held to be the absolute expressive limit of human language: something marginal to the *logos*, but bearing nonetheless its vivid trace.

[43] *Epistolae*, ed. and trans. Paget Toynbee, 190–191 (lines 414–418).

read that the three disciples fell on their faces, and record nothing thereafter, as though memory had failed them.)

This interpretation—and an interpretation it is because the detail of the apostles' silence and oblivion can *only* be extrapolated from the gospel narrative—bears the stamp, once again, of Richard of Saint Victor, for whom the apostles' fall signified the breakdown of all human faculties: "For then bodily sense, then memory of external things, and then human reason are interrupted, when the mind is raised above itself, being snatched up into supernal things."[44]

But it is not only in *Paradise*'s "rhetoric of the ineffable" that the Transfiguration's presence can be felt, for, as cantos 23 through 26 powerfully suggest, the Transfiguration is of some importance to the overall design of the final canticle. These are cantos closely tied to cantos 14–18 insofar as their locus is a celestial sphere at the absolute limit of Dante's visible universe: the heaven of the fixed stars, site of the Milky Way and hence also the true site of the galactic cross imagined in the heaven of Mars (14.95–108). It is in the opening canto of this sequence (seven cantos from the center of the cross of light) that the pilgrim first attains a fleeting vision of Jesus Christ:

> vid' i' sopra migliaia di lucerne
> un sol che tutte quante l'accendea,
> come fa 'l nostro le viste superne;
> e per la viva luce trasparea
> la lucente sustanza tanto chiara
> nel viso mio, che non la sostenea.   23.28–33

---

[44] "Ibi enim sensus corporeus, ibi exteriorum memoria, ibi ratio humana intercipitur, ubi mens supra semetipsum rapta in superna elevatur" (*Benjamin Minor* 82, Migne PL 196, col. 58). English translation by G. A. Zinn, *The Twelve Patriarchs*, 140. Dante's mention of Matthew 17:6 immediately precedes a direct allusion to Richard's "De Contemplatione" (*Benjamin Maior*), coming in a portion of the letter to Can Grande filled with Victorine language. The notion, however, that the apostle's reaction represents the breakdown of human faculties goes back at least as far as Origen.

(I saw, above thousands of lamps, a Sun which kindled each one of them as does our own the things we see above; and through its living light the lucent Substance outglowed so bright upon my vision that it endured it not.)

That Christ should triumph here as a sun igniting an entire galaxy of souls may not seem surprising since the triumph of Beatrice in *Purgatory* 30 is also imagined as the dawning of an apocalyptic Sun of Justice. Yet, leaving aside the apparent echo of the "Elïòs" and constellated "Galassia" of the Martial cross, the emphasis on Christ's corporeal luminous substance, later termed "the wisdom and the power that opened the roads between heaven and earth" ("la sapïenza e la possanza / ch'aprì le strade tra 'l cielo e la terra" [*Par.* 23.37–38]) can only call to mind the Transfiguration when its effect upon the pilgrim is precisely the same rapturous oblivion experienced by Peter, James and John according to Dante's dedicatory epistle:[45]

> Come foco di nube si diserra
> per dilatarsi sì che non vi cape,
> e fuor di sua natura in giù s'atterra,
>   la mente mia così, tra quelle dape
> fatta più grande, di sé stessa uscìo,
> e che si fesse rimembrar non sape.
>   . . . Io era come quei che si risente
> di visïone oblita e che s'ingegna
> indarno di ridurlasi a la mente. . . .   23.40–51

(Even as fire breaks from a cloud, because it dilates so that it has not room there, and, contrary to its own nature, falls down to earth, so my mind, becoming greater amid those feasts, issued from itself, and of what it became has no remembrance. . . . I was as one that wakes from a forgotten dream, and who strives in vain to bring it back to mind. . . .)

---

[45] Giovanni Busnelli seems to have been the first to note the relevance of the Transfiguration to *Paradise* 23 and the ensuing examination. See *Il concetto e l'ordine del 'Paradiso' dantesco. Parte I: Il concetto*, esp. 114–116.

The pilgrim's *ekstasis* is not "upward" but instead "downward" ("in giù"): an *atterrare* like that of the Apostles who "fell upon their face" (Matt. 17:6).[46] It is richer still in its implications, however, implying a movement that runs counter to the laws of nature: just as fire in the form of lightning is thrust downward out of the clouds—its nature is to rise—so the body is raised into a vision of Christ's transfigured nature and itself transformed "out of its own nature" ("fuor di sua natura"). And like the ecstatic forgetfulness ("quasi obliti") of the Apostles, the pilgrim's condition too is "come . . . oblita": *oblito* being a self-evident Latinism as well as a *hapax legomenon* in Dante's *Commedia*.

That the sudden appearance and then disappearance of the transfigured Christ in canto 23 should give way in cantos 24–26 to an examination on the theological virtues administered by none other than Peter (faith), James (hope), and John (charity) places the Transfiguration once again at the center of our attention. For, as Beatrice notes in 25.33, the selection of these three examiners is based on the fact that Jesus showed most favor to these three: "Iesù ai tre fé più carezza." Of the three occasions, however, on which Jesus singles out Peter, James, and John for a special *carezza* or *chiarezza*, as many manuscripts read—the Garden of Gethsemane (Matt. 26:36–46), the resurrection of Jairus' daughter (Luke 8:50–56), and the Transfiguration—only the latter is of major significance to the gospel narrative and only the latter can be interpreted as involving the transmission of a secret *gnosis* of supernatural character. Moreover, the choice of James as Dante's examiner on hope—an examination whose climax comes in a discussion of the glorified white robes ("bianche stole" [25.95]) of the beatified souls—would seem particularly difficult

---

[46] The directional inversion appears all the more extraordinary in light of Beatrice's use of the simile in *Paradise* 1.130–135 to exemplify man's freedom to fall: "così da questo corso si diparte / talor la creatura, c'ha podere / di piegar, così pinta, in altra parte; / e sì come veder si può *cadere* / *foco di nube*, sì l'impeto primo / *l'atterra* torto da falso piacere" (my italics).

to explain, unless his presence at Christ's Transfiguration is taken into account.

There is considerable evidence, therefore, that the Transfiguration serves as a key link in Dante's theory of mystical illumination and Pauline rapture. I would in fact go so far as to suggest that, broadly speaking, the Transfiguration is Dante's primary model in the first thirty cantos of *Paradise*—the cantos of the natural heavens—and that it is nót until cantos 30–33—the cantos of the Empyrean—that the truly Pauline phase of the pilgrim's journey can be said to commence. Only in the final and climactic phase of Dante's poem does the pilgrim's sole objective become that vision of the ultimate mysteries of the Christian faith which Paul himself was reputed to have received: namely, a glimpse into the Incarnation and the Holy Trinity.[47]

But, leaving such larger questions aside, it is important to underscore the extent to which these references to Christ's Transfiguration are not isolated ones. Dante makes frequent use of the Transfiguration in both his late and early works. In the *Convivio*, for instance, the Transfiguration is interpreted in the moral sense as signifying that "in the most secret matters we should have but few companions" ("a le secretissime cose noi dovemo avere poca compagnia" [2.1.5]). The passage is framed by Dante's famous discussion of the "allegory of the poets" versus that of the theologians (2.1.2–4) and by his anagogical exegesis of Exodus

---

[47] Since the conventional view held that Paul's rapture consisted of a vision of God and the Trinity, the Transfiguration was thought to involve an intermediate form of vision somewhere between mystical illumination in the ordinary sense, and Pauline rapture. Giordano da Rivalto thus writes of Paul: "Ancor li fece Iddio la maggior grazia quasi che potesse essere, cioè, che stando in questa vita presente, il menò in cielo, e vide Iddio, la beata Trinitade; non si trova dono così singolare. Grande dono ebbero gli Apostoli, che videro Cristo in questo mondo; ma maggior l'ebber quelli, che 'l vider transfigurato in Monte Tabor, ch'assaggiaro allotta della dolcezza di Paradiso. Ma questo fu somma grazia; troppo fu grande dono questo" (Sermon 21 [30 giugno, 1303] in *Prediche*, vol. 1, 166–167).

(2.1.6–8).⁴⁸ In the treatise on *Monarchy* (3.9.11), it is cited, instead, to exemplify the frivolity of Peter, and in so doing to buttress Dante's argument that to the Empire belong all temporal responsibilities and to the Church all supratemporal ones—again, a theme important in cantos 14–18.⁴⁹

But perhaps most interesting of all is the Transfiguration's presence in the *Vita Nuova*, where it is already conceived as an allegory of spiritual metamorphosis and amorous martyrdom. Transformed in Chapter 14 by the vision of Beatrice into a "strange figure" ("figura nova"), the figure of an other ("in figura d'altrui"), he declares to an unnamed friend that in his "transfiguration": "Io tenni li piedi in quella parte de la vita di là da la quale non si puote ire più per intendimento di ritornare" ("I had my feet in that realm of life beyond which one cannot pass with the expectation of returning").⁵⁰ While here "transfiguration" is

---

⁴⁸ In *Convivio* 2.1.5, illustrating the four-fold theory of interpretation, Dante writes:

> Lo terzo senso si chiama morale, e questo è quello che li lettori deono intentamente andare appostando per le scritture, ad utilitade di loro e di loro disce[n]ti; sì come appostare si può ne lo Evangelio, quando Cristo salìo lo monte per transfigurarsi, che de li dodici Apostoli menò seco li tre; in che moralmente si può intendere che a le secretissime cose noi dovemo avere poca compagnia.

In their notes Busnelli/Vandelli (vol. 1, 99) associate this interpretation with Hugh of St. Cher's *Commentary on Matthew*, but, because of Christ's imprecation to silence in the three synoptic gospels, the interpretation is a relatively self-evident one found, among other places, in Thomas Aquinas's commentary on the Transfiguration in the *Summa Theologiae* 3, que. 45, art. 3. (Ad Quartum). The numerous allusions in the Gospel of Mark (5:37 and 14:33 in particular) to the privileged status of the Apostles Peter, James, and John further reinforce Dante's emphasis here on privilege and secrecy.

⁴⁹ Dante is obsessed with the political allegory of Peter's investiture in Matthew 16:18–19, a passage inadvertently parodied by Pier della Vigna in *Inferno* 13.58–63 and alluded to in *Inferno* 19.93, among many other places. Almost every major discussion of the relation of Emperor to Pope in Dante's works hinges on the interpretation of this passage.

⁵⁰ *Vita Nuova* 14.8. The Transfiguration narrative provides a constant point of reference from 14.7 through 15.2, and suggests, because of the importance of the

adapted to the ends of a stilnovist psychology of love and associated with the mostly secular metamorphoses of the lover tyrannized by desire, the clear allusion to mystical vision, Pauline ascent and ineffability, as well as the verbal staccato of "de la . . . di là da la," all bring us back to the opening of *Paradise* and the verse which elicited the mention of Matthew in the Letter to Can Grande: "vidi cose che ridire / né sa né può chi di là sù discende" ("I saw things which he that descends from up there neither has the knowledge nor the power to retell" [1.5–6]).

The situation in canto 1 of *Paradise* may be viewed, consequently, as palinodic with respect to the *Vita Nuova*. Amor, the capricious deity that haunted the lover of the *Vita Nuova*, has been displaced in Eden by a Beatrice who has come in the guise of Christ. So the contact with her once "homicidal" eyes now initiates not a recrudescence of the inner war of the passions with its perpetual cycle of transmutations, but rather, the spiritual *trasumanare* or transfiguration of the soul's accession to paradise.[51] The poet-pilgrim is thus in canto 1 "like Glaucus when he tasted of the herb" ("qual si fè Glauco nel gustar de l'erba" [1.68]):

Ovidian theme of metamorphosis through love, that Dante was already entirely aware of the sense in which Christ's "metamorphosis" might be viewed as unveiling the secret meaning of pagan metamorphosis. This metamorphic imagery is linked to the theme of martyrdom in 15.4–8, the next verse section, in which Dante imagines, playing perhaps on the double meaning of "passion," that even the stones seem to cry out for the lover's death: "le pietre par che gridin: Moia, moia." The death of Stephen Protomartyr is described in similar terms in canto 15 of *Purgatory*:

> Poi vidi genti accese in foco d'ira
> con pietre un giovinetto ancider, forte
> gridando a sé pur: "Martira, martira!" 15.106–108

The model for these double calls for death, like the "Mora, mora!" reportedly shouted at the armies of Charles Martel in *Paradise* 8.75, is the Jews's double call for Christ's crucifixion in John 19:6: "Cum ergo vidissent eum pontifices et ministri, clamabant, dicentes: Crucifige, crucifige eum."

[51] One need only recall Guido's "Donna mi prega," with its Martial god of love, to see how the Stilnovist transmutation/transfiguration theme might fit in with my earlier analysis of Mars's relation to *mors*.

a consort of the gods; or, to penetrate the truth beneath the Ovidian *bella menzogna*, one of the adoptive Sons of God through Jesus Christ, "who shall not taste death, till they see the kingdom of God" ("qui non gustabunt mortem donec videant regnum Dei" [Luke 9:27]).

Once the Transfiguration has been properly situated in Dante's works and the unifying principle behind its various occurrences shown, it will perhaps come as no surprise that its most explicit appearance in the *Commedia* is found in canto 32 of *Purgatory* under that tree "situated at the center of paradise" already referred to in a prior discussion. With his usual vertiginous powers of self- and cross-reference, Dante brings together in a single passage many earlier references to the Transfiguration, while setting the stage for its return at the center of *Paradise*, both as a mystical allegory and an epic/martyriological paradigm. In canto 32 the Transfiguration is linked not only to the transfiguring Beatrice—now guide to *Paradise*—of the *Vita Nuova* and to mystical and eschatological visions, but also to the restoration of paradise itself, to Christ's harmonization through the cross of Empire and Church, *Roma* and *Amor*. And this expansion of its meaning, as we discover from the perspective of the final canticle, takes place in a constant play of earthly and celestial doubles: a juxtaposition of the tree, the cross, the hymn, the paradise of Eden, with the cosmic tree, the cross of light, the eschatological song, the celestial rose of Christ's heavenly paradise.

Given the complexity of the scene in question, it is worth recapitulating at least briefly. The symbolic procession which begins its march across Eden in *Purgatory* 29, and represents the general movement of human history with a griffin (or Christ) at its head, pulling the chariot of the Church behind the yoke of the cross, accompanied in turn by representatives of the seven virtues and the Holy Scriptures, comes to a sudden halt in canto 32 at the base of the Tree of Knowledge.[52] Since this was the same

---

[52] The three most complete explorations of the allegory of the final cantos of

tree, according to the legend of Seth, from which by seed or severed branch—the tradition differs on this point—would grow the wood of the cross, their joining marks in reality a *re*-joining: a restoration at history's mid-point (the Incarnation) of its originary state (Eden).[53]

But because this was also the tree of the first divine interdiction ("de ligno autem scientiae boni et mali ne comedas". [Gen. 2:17]) and hence of the first human act of lawlessness, canto 32 invests it with an additional and specifically political meaning: it is the Tree of Law, a symbol of the ideals of Roman jurisprudence and Mosaic law, and of the Empire and the Church through which they were translated into a concrete historical praxis. It first appears in its postlapsarian condition, as sterile and disfigured: "dispogliata / di foglie e d'altra fronda in ciascun ramo" ("stripped of its flowers and other foliage on every bough". [32.38–39]). Once the chariot of the Church, however, is bound ("legato") to it by the cross, the Tree of Law is restored to its luxuriant original state: from a tree of death it is made a tree of life (just as the cross of Christ's death is made a sign of eternal life). At the precise moment of renewal an intoxicating hymn is heard, a hymn which, like the militant resurrectional hymn of *Paradise* 14 (" 'Resurgi' e 'Vinci' " [14.125]), mostly escapes the poet-pilgrim's understanding. But, unlike *Paradise*, where the song goes unheard and yet is heard, is disclosed and yet undisclosed, the incompre-

---

Purgatory are those of Moore, *Studies in Dante: Third Series*, 178–220; Singleton, *Journey to Beatrice* [Dante Studies II], 141–287; and R. E. Kaske, "The Seven *Status Ecclesiae* in *Purgatorio* XXXII–XXXIII," in *Dante, Petrarch, Boccaccio: Studies in the Italian Trecento*, 89–113.

[53] On this subject, see Edward Moore, *Studies in Dante: Third Series*, 219–220. One of the many possible direct sources for Dante's knowledge of these traditions is Jacobi a Voragine's popular *Legenda Aurea Vulgo Historia Lombardica Dicta*, which is the principal source as well of Piero della Francesca's splendid mural cycle devoted to the finding of the Holy Cross painted at the Church of Saint Francis in Arezzo. See especially chapter 68 ("De Inventione Sanctae Crucis"), pp. 303–311, in the standard Graesse edition.

hension here is absolute: "Io non lo 'ntesi, né qui non si canta" ("I did not understand it, nor is it sung here" [32.61]).

The omission, as the double negative makes plain, is no accident: this is a hymn to be sung in paradise proper and not in Eden—a point which the ascent of Christ and his retinue singing a "song more sweet and profound" ("più dolce canzone e più profonda" [32.90]) is about to dramatize. Its theme is none other than the Pauline *plenitudo temporis* or "fullness of time" (Gal. 4:4) which, fulfilled by Christ under the lawful rule of Augustus, brought the eternal spring of Eden back to earth. But because this peace only entered human history to mark the beginning of the end, its ultimate meaning is eschatological and can only be figured at the end of another canticle. Its true locus is the Holy Jerusalem described in Revelations 21–22, but seen by anticipation in the celestial rose of canto 32 of *Paradise*: the beatific city to come at the end of time, the "Rome where Christ is a Roman" (32.102) foreshadowed by the historical Rome of Augustus and Christ.[54] This is why the apostles' sleep is about to be associated with the sudden vision of the "blossoms of the apple tree whose fruit makes the angels hunger and makes for perpetual wedding feasts in heaven" ("fioretti del melo / che del suo pome li angeli fa ghiotti / e perpetüe nozze fa nel cielo" [32.73–75])—a description that unmistakably recalls that of the celestial rose in *Paradise* 32.

The poet-pilgrim is entranced at the sound of the hymn of peace and eternal spring, first comparing himself to Argos in Book 1 of Ovid's *Metamorphoses* fighting off the sweet but mortal sleep brought upon him by Mercury's song ("pugnat mollis evincere somnos" [1.685]). In an elaborate simile he then likens his state to that of the wakeful but slumbering apostles:

> . . . un splendor mi squarciò 'l velo
> del sonno, e un chiamar: "Surgi: che fai?"

[54] In his commentary Singleton has pointed out the shift here to the Augustinian two cities: "the Garden of Eden becomes in some sense the earthly city of the saints or the justified" (*Purgatorio: 2. Commentary*, 794).

> Quali a veder de' fioretti del melo
> che del suo pome li angeli fa ghiotti
> e perpetüe nozze fa nel cielo,
>   Pietro e Giovanni e Iacopo condotti
> e vinti, ritornaro a la parola
> da la qual furon maggior sonni rotti,
>   e videro scemata loro scuola
> così di Moïsè come d'Elia,
> e al maestro suo cangiata stola;
>   tal torna' io. . . .   32.71–82

(. . . a splendor rent the veil of my sleep, and a call, "Arise, what are you doing?" As when brought to see some of the blossoms of the apple tree that makes the angels greedy of its fruit and holds perpetual wedding feasts in Heaven, Peter and John and James were overpowered, and came to themselves again at the word by which deeper slumbers were broken, and saw their company diminished alike by Moses and Elias, and their Master's raiment changed, so I came to myself. . . .)

He awakes from this sleep only to find that Eden has in the meantime been transformed. The scene has shifted from a pre- to a post-incarnational setting: from a Tree of Law that has just been renewed through the cross, to a Tree of Law at whose root sits Beatrice alone. Just as Elijah and Moses (or prophecy and law) appeared in the gospel narrative only to be absorbed into the transfigured Christ, here Christ and his retinue have reascended into the heavens, leaving Beatrice as their sole representative.

Before we address the question of the doubling of cross and tree, an apparent divergence requires some attention: the particular emphasis here on sleep, which recalls the previously cited passage from the Epistle to Can Grande, but not the central cantos of *Paradise*. The difference is, however, more one of relative stages of spiritual advancement than of substance, for the "veil of sleep" is in all three cases not to be taken literally. It is a hybrid cognitive, hermeneutic, and epistemological obstacle akin to the "deeper slumber" brought on in cantos 14–18 by Mars/*mors*. The sleep of canto 32 of *Purgatory* is in fact a figurative sleep of death: the sopor that "was so costly" ("costò sì caro" [32.66]) to the about-to-be-assassinated Argos, but also that apostolic sleep (or collapse) long interpreted by Christian exegetes as a symbolic death followed by resurrection. "When they fell to the earth, thus, they signified that we die," Augustine writes, "when they were raised up by the Lord, the resurrection was signified."[55] In Dante's allegory, moreover, the resurrection that follows "sleep" or "death" takes on a distinctively visionary-mystical character: it opens the individual's eyes to the "perpetual wedding feasts" of a paradise *in heaven* (*Purg.* 32.75), or, going back to an earlier formulation, plants his or her feet in "that realm of life beyond which one cannot pass with the expectation of returning" ("quella parte de la vita di là da la quale non si puote ire più per intendimento di ritornare" [*Vita Nuova* 14.8]).

The major difference at the center of *Paradise* is that the "veil of sleep" has partially lifted. The shift from pre- to post-incarnational perspectives (whose hub is the sleep of *Purgatory* 32) has been accomplished, Moses and Elijah have disappeared into the triumphant Christ, and earthly perspectives have long been abandoned. We have suddenly leaped ahead from the Exodus of *Purgatory* to the Apocalypse of *Paradise*. And the evidence of Jesus' victory over "deeper slumbers" spreads over the heaven of Mars before the dazzled eyes of the pilgrim in the form of a resplendent cross of light: a guarantee of the transfigurational reality that lies beyond the tragic immediacy of the cross.

Sleep and its analogues (paralysis, sin, and death) remain nonetheless in the background of the central cantos of *Paradise*. Like the epic *insomnia* of Mars and the dream-visions of Cicero's Scipio and Virgil's Aeneas, they provide the necessary backdrop for a proper understanding of the implications of Christ's victory

---

[55] "Quod illi ergo ad terram ceciderunt, hoc significaverunt, quod morimur. . . . Quando vero eos Dominus erexit, resurrectionem significavit" (Sermo 78, Migne PL 38, col. 492).

on the cross. Yet halfway between Eden (which, after all, is still an earthly site) and the celestial rose, the poet-pilgrim need no longer fall on his face out of fear before the prospect of Christ's martyrdom or his own, nor need his understanding of eschatological mysteries be clouded by somnolescence. For now the dark prophetic riddles of his Classical forebearers and of his own *Inferno* can finally be completed in the "clear words and precise Latin" ("chiare parole e . . . preciso latin" [17.34–35]) of Christian prophecy.

The analogy between the sleep of *Purgatory* 32 and that of *Paradise* may seem somewhat forced, but it should be noted that Dante goes to some trouble to underscore their visual-iconographic interdependency. In doing so he touches upon one of the most ancient of Christian traditions—the belief that the Edenic *lignum vitae* was either the actual or the figurative structuring mechanism of the entire cosmos. As Hugo Rahner describes it:[56]

> Between the tree of life in paradise and the tree of life in the heaven to come, the early Christian beheld a tree of life on which the fate of the race of Adam was decided: the Cross. And with his feeling for mystery, he saw these trees as a single image. The tree of paradise is only a prefiguration of the Cross, and the Cross is the center of the world and of the human drama of salvation. It rises from Golgotha to heaven, embracing the cosmos.

In the earlier analysis of Dante's galactic simile I have examined one aspect of this tradition, but it now becomes clear how the *temo* of 32.49, the Edenic tree, the cross of light, the cosmic cross, and the cosmic tree can all participate in the same symbolic genealogy. Cacciaguida directly calls our attention to this progression in *Paradise* 18.28–30, where he describes the planetary system as an immutable and eternally fructifying tree: "l'albero che vive de la cima / e frutta sempre e mai non perde foglia" ("the tree that lives from its summit and is always in fruit and never sheds

[56] Hugo Rahner, "The Christian Mystery and the Pagan Mysteries," 382.

its leaves" [18.29–30]).[57] The image, with its evocation of an eternal (cosmic) spring, inevitably calls to mind not only Nebuchadnezzar's dream in Daniel 4:7–10 and Revelations 22:2, but also the downward-tapering Tree of Law rejuvenated—as was, in Dante's view, the whole universe—by Christ's sacrifice on the cross.[58] (The retrospective glances at the cosmic mechanism in Cicero's *Republic* and Plato's "Dream of Er" also come to mind.) The mirroring is not an incidental one since in Cacciaguida's tree we discern the heavenly prototype of the mutable earthly Tree of Law: the Father's model government of the universe with its regular motions and invariable laws. That in the heaven of flux and discord, however, Christ's celestial sign should be grafted onto the middle rung ("questa quinta soglia" [18.28]) of this cosmic Tree of Life recalls once again the paradoxical formula with which this study opened: "harmonia est concordia discors," or, as shall be seen at the close of the present chapter, its transformation into the eschatological theme of concordant discord. The tree that at the very navel of the earth once stood alongside the tree of mankind's fall is thus poetically reevoked as a cosmic tree, no less than the central pivot of the entire universe. And within this tree is another tree, a virtual double of the cosmic tree. It rises at the center of the final canticle, the center also of Dante's celestial paradise.

[57] The most comprehensive study of the figure of the cosmic cross is Giorgio de Santillana and Hertha von Dechend's *Hamlet's Mill: An Essay on Myth and the Frame of Time*. On pp. 196–197 Santillana and von Dechend refer to Dante's heaven of Mars, citing Georg Rabuse's contention in *Der kosmische Aufbau* (57–95 *passim*) that Dante's final canticle is structured around the system of planetary rivers which had in antiquity long been connected with the rivers of the underworld, forming a unified hydrographic system.

[58] On the Incarnation as a cosmic and political renewal, see *Convivio* 4.5.3–4: "Volendo la inmisurabile bontà divina l'umana creatura a sé riconformare, che per lo peccato de la prevaricazione del primo uomo da Dio era partita e disformata, eletto fu, in quello altissimo e congiuntissimo consistorio de la Trinitate, che 'l Figliolo di Dio in terra discendesse a fare questa concordia. E però che, ne la sua venuta, lo mondo (non solamente lo cielo, ma la terra) convenia essere in ottima disposizione."

3. REVELATION

The Sign of the Son of Man

If this long digression on Christ's Transfiguration has served a single purpose besides that of pinpointing the place of a key gospel episode in Dante's works, it has been to address what I take to be the central question of cantos 14–18: how does the hieratic cross of light intersect Cacciaguida's prophecy and the text of Florentine history? Or, to put the issue in terms which apply equally to the mosaics at Sant' Apollinare in Classe, how does history intersect the abstraction of the cross? Although the ultimate answer to this question (and the one proposed in the next chapter) must be "through prophecy" or "through the public witness borne by the warriors of the cross," the Transfiguration provides the essential scriptural link. It suggests just how this binding of individual to Christ, cross to Cross, and history to abstraction might take place through the imitation of Christ, and it clarifies the mystical-visionary implications of taking on one's personal cross. But as concerns the more general hermeneutic and epistemological framework within which the individual's act of imitation is enclosed we must once again turn to the preeminent mystery of cantos 14–18: the Martial cross of light, which now reveals itself as the eschatological "sign of the Son of man in the heavens" and as the oracle of the true Apollo—Jesus Christ.

The cross of light is from an iconographic standpoint a most distinctive cross. Unlike the blood-soaked rood celebrated at Easter, it has usually been conceived as strictly apocalyptic in character: "the epitome of the structural law of the universe, it will shine in the heavens at the end of the earth's visible history to foreshadow the coming of the transfigured Christ."[59] This

[59] Rahner, 375. On the identification of the "sign of the Son of man" with the cross of light, see Gretser, vol. 1, 154–156; Cornelius a Lapide's gloss on Matthew 24:30 in vol. 1, 233–236, of his *Commentaria in Quatuor Evangelia*; as well as Wilhelm Bousset, *The Antichrist Legend: A Chapter in Christian-Jewish Folklore*, 232–237. Also useful on the patristic background of the iconography of the cross of

view, held continuously from the *Didaché* through Ephraim the Syrian, Hippolytus, Methodius, and John Chrysostom, through Jerome, Augustine, Leo, and Bede to the Jansenists and Jesuits of the seventeenth century, rests on the identification of the cross of light with the mysterious "sign of the Son of man" prophesied by Jesus in his "apocalyptic discourse":

> Statim autem post tribulationem dierum illorum sol obscurabitur, et luna non dabit lumen suum, et stellae cadent de caelo, et virtutes caelorum commovebuntur: *et tunc parebit signum Filii hominis in caelo*: et tunc plangent omnes tribus terrae: et videbunt Filium hominis venientem in nubibus caeli cum virtute multa et maiestate.
>
> (And immediately after the tribulation of those days, the sun shall be darkened, and the moon shall not give her light, and the stars shall fall from heaven, and the powers of the heavens shall be moved: *and then shall appear the sign of the Son of man in heaven*: and then shall all the tribes of the earth mourn: and they shall see the Son of man coming in the clouds of heaven with great power and majesty.) [Matt. 24:29–30; my italics]

The link between this prophecy and the Transfiguration was self-evident to the Church Fathers (at least after John Chrysostom), for it clearly seemed to recall the prophecy which precedes Christ's glorification before Peter, James, and John: "Filius enim hominis venturus est in gloria Patris sui cum angelis suis: et tunc reddet unicuique secundum opera eius" ("For the Son of man shall come in the glory of his Father, with his angels, and then will he render to every man according to his works" [Matt. 16:27]). (A careful reading of the gospel narrative does suggest that the mirroring is far from accidental: the passages share a similar apocalyptic setting and a common concern with glorified bodies, brilliant clouds, and Christ as sun.) This nexus between the Transfiguration and the Last Judgment is of considerable import, providing a scriptural basis for what is without a doubt the

---

light are Erich Dinkler, *Das Apsismosaik von S. Apollinare in Classe*, 77–87; and Peter Stockmeier, *Theologie und Kult des Kreuzes bei Johannes Chrysostomus*, 84–90.

most distinctive iconographic feature of both cantos 14–18 of *Paradise* and the apsidal mosaics of Sant' Apollinare in Classe: the substitution of the transfigured Christ with an eschatological cross of light.[60]

Like the multiple seals of the Johannine Apocalypse, then, the cross of light was imagined as one of the signs of that last hour when Christ would return as judge. This is the sign celebrated in the vespertine Antiphon to the masses of the Invention and the Exaltation of the Cross, and in the related hymn "O Crux, splendidior cunctis astris":[61]

> Hoc signum crucis erit in caelo,
>   cum Dominus ad judicandum venerit.
> Tunc manifesta erunt abscondita cordis nostri:
> Cum sederit Filius hominis in sede maiestatis suae
> et coeperit judicare saeculum per ignem.
>
> (This sign of the cross shall be in heaven
>   when the Lord comes in judgment.
> Then shall be manifest that which is hidden in our heart:
> For the Son of man shall sit on his throne of majesty
> and shall begin to judge this generation by fire.)

Around this apocalyptic sign an important literature developed, which, founded largely on the Sibylline Oracles and on certain New Testament Apocrypha, would include numerous hagiographic texts and crusade narratives, the Old English *Elene*,

---

[60] On the exegetical and iconographic links, see G. O. von Simson, *The Sacred Fortress*, 44–58; E. Dinkler, *Das Apsismosaik*, 77–100; and F. W. Deichmann, *Ravenna: Hauptstadt des spätantiken Abendlandes*, vol. 2/2, 246–254. On the apocalyptic implications of the Transfiguration in patristic exegesis, see once again Peter A. Chamberas, "The Transfiguration of Christ," 49–60.

[61] The full text of the hymn is given in Gretser, vol. 3, 356–357. The Antiphon, cited in the first two verses of the hymn, is sung at first vespers and precedes the singing of the *Magnificat*. In the Saint Yrieix *Gradual* (Ms. Latin 903, Bibliothèque Nationale, Paris) it is listed among the chants in Adoration of the Cross to be sung on Good Friday.

Dream of the Rood, *Christ*, and *Last Judgment*, and even—at least in the heaven of Mars—Dante's *Commedia*.[62]

Some imagined the cross of light as the *etimasía*—the throne of Judgment described in the ninth Psalm—upon which would be placed the Book of Life, and to the left and right of which would

[62] Of these the most interesting is the *Dream of the Rood*, a text which testifies to the continuing existence during the Middle Ages of a literature of cross visions to which Dante's own clearly belongs. From the perspective of cantos 14–18 the most striking feature of the *Dream of the Rood* is its use of a similar red to white (blood to light) symbolism. Dante's essentially "static" superposition of white on red, however, gives way in the Old English poem to actual fluctuations in the appearance of the cross; and this alternation, like the play of foreground and background in the Martial cantos, signifies the two aspects of Christ's sacrifice on the cross: its tragic present and salvific promise. The opening vision, as in canto 14, is of a bejewelled cosmic cross (I quote from the translation of J.A.W. Bennett in *Poetry of the Passion: Studies in Twelve Centuries of English Verse*, 27–31):

> It seemed to me that I saw a most wondrous tree
> Rising in the sky and encircled with light,
> Brightest of beams. The whole of the beacon
> Was decked in gold. Gems gleamed
> Fair at the earth's four corners, and five there were
> High up on the cross beam. Hosts of angels beheld it,
> Timeless in their beauty. It was no felon's gibbet,
> Rather, it held the gaze of holy souls,
> Of men on the earth and the whole glorious creation.   vv. 4–12

As the dream progresses, the cross of light begins to vary in brilliance and hue:

> Attired in gold: gems had covered
> Befittingly the tree of a Ruler.
> Yet beneath that gold I could make out agony
> Once suffered at the hands of wretched men.
> Soon it ran sweat [blood] on its right side. Afflicted with griefs,
> I was terrified by that wondrous sight. I saw this ardent beacon
> Alter in vesture and colour; now it was bedewed with moisture,
> Drenched in flowing sweat, now gleaming with treasure.   vv. 16–23
>   (my insertion)

Finally, as in the vision of Constantine, the cross addresses itself directly to the dreamer, recounting the tale of how a "young warrior"—the "hero" of the cross—mounted upon it to redeem mankind. On the cross in the *Dream of the Rood* see Barbara C. Raw, "The *Dream of the Rood* and its Connections with Early Christian

be distributed respectively the accursed and the blessed.[63] Hence, perhaps, the insistence in 15.19 on Cacciaguida's descent off the right of the cross ("tale dal corno che 'n *destro* si stende" [my italics]). And hence Cacciaguida's reading in that immutable volume (15.50–51) which revealed to him the coming of Dante and his eventual salvation: the hidden "concept" of 15.40–42 that must by necessity ("per necessità") be concealed. To the damned the cross would appear a sign of doom; to the saved it would be seen instead as the martyr's glorious crown, the "sign of victory" cited by Virgil back in *Inferno* 4.54.

Because of a legend in the apocryphal Gospel of Peter which

Art," *Medium Aevum* 39, no. 3 (1970): 239–256; and J.A.W. Bennett, *Poetry of the Passion*, 1–27. For a general survey of interpretations see Annemarie E. Mahler, "*Lignum Domini* and the Opening Vision of *The Dream of the Rood*: A Viable Hypothesis?," *Speculum* 53 (July 1978): 441–443.

[63] On this general subject, see Ernst Wadstein, *Die eschatologische Ideengruppe: Antichrist, Weltsabbat, Weltende und Weltgericht*; and W. Bousset, *The Antichrist Legend*, 232–237. For a comprehensive catalogue of the signs of doom, see Thomas Malavenda's *De Antichristo*. The notion that to the right of the cross would be placed the blessed and to the left the damned is based on a conflation of the story of the two thieves in Luke 23:33–43 with a number of Christ's apocalyptic prophecies, notably that of Matthew 25:34: "Tunc dicet rex his qui a dextris eius erunt: Venite, benedicti Patris mei, possidete paratum vobis regnum a constitutione mundi." According to the conventional view the "good thief" who rebuked the "bad thief" for his mockery and to whom Jesus promises "this day you shall be with me in paradise" (Luke 23:43) as a reward, hung to the right of Christ's cross, and the latter to the left. The Aristotelian belief in an absolute up, down, right, and left in the cosmos allowed for a further adaptation of this notion to the traditional structural dyads of Christ/Antichrist, east/west, salvation/damnation. Hence the terms all tend to fuse, as in Honorius of Autun's *Speculum Ecclesiae*: "Pars quoque utrimque dextrum et sinistrum mundi ostentat, quia per crucis virtutem boni a dextris ad gloriam, et mali a sinistris ad poenam judicabuntur. Illa quippe die signum Filii hominis in coelo apparebit, et lumen solis et lunae non splendebit, quia crux Christi ad judicium praevia tanta luce radiat quod splendorem solis et lunae suae claritate obscurat" ("De Inventione S. Crucis," Migne PL 172, col. 946). On the structural dyads of Christian apocalyptic speculation, see Dölger's *Die Sonne der Gerechtigkeit und der Schwarze: eine religionsgeschichtliche Studie zum Taufgelöbnis*, a study relevant as well to the thematics of the solar Christ.

held that the cross had followed Christ in his ascension, it was also variously conceived as the actual historical rood returning from the heavens. Initially envisioned as returning alone, as in the apse of Sant' Apollinare in Classe, it would in the course of several centuries become associated with the other instruments of the passion: the so-called *arma Christi*. As such, the cross, the nails, the lance, the crown of thorns, and the vinegared sponge—the entire catalogue of signs of Jesus' defeat—were to return at the end of time as the signs of his everlasting victory.[64] Or, in an earlier and more explicitly Apollonian and imperial version of this same apocryphal legend, the cross was seen as the fiery chariot in which Christ was to return as the emperor and sun of the eschatological Jerusalem.

The cross of light commonly was imagined as formed of stars and/or fiery effulgences—the case both at Sant' Apollinare and in Dante's *Paradise*—although no less frequently it was thought to be made up of angels, with Christ enthroned at the center. Its figurative complexity greatly expanded in the first centuries of the Christian era, however, such that it accrued such supplementary attributes as speech, song, and the sort of kinetic writing encountered by Dante in the heaven of Jupiter. Of the many appearances of this expanded iconography, the most illustrious is without a doubt the legendary vision of the Emperor Constantine reported in Eusebius' *Ecclesiastical History* and remembered in the various liturgies of the cross. This vision, which was said to have preceded the decisive battle of Milvia Bridge, was of a coruscating cross of light superimposed over the sun, spelling out (or, alternately, singing out) the message: "In hoc signo vinces" ("in this sign you shall conquer"). The conversion and military victory that ensued leads, in the accounts of Eusebius and Sozomen,

[64] Of the many examples of this standard iconographic program perhaps the best known is Michelangelo's *Last Judgment* fresco in the Sistine Chapel, which shows various groupings of angels bearing the *arma Christi* to one side of the triumphant Christ. For a brief overview of this tradition, see Gertrud Schiller, *Iconography of Christian Art*, vol. 2, 186–187.

to the adoption of the cross as the Empire's military *signum* and to the elaboration of the *labarum*—Constantine's ensign based on the monogram of Christ.⁶⁵

Visions modeled after that of Constantine, the discourse of Matthew 24, the various apocrypha and/or the Sibylline oracles

---

⁶⁵ The vision of Constantine, frequently cited as the origin of his ensign, the *labarum*, is probably a later Christian reworking of a theophany of Apollo (appearing as the Mithraic *Sol Invictus*) and the goddess Victory, reported in Eumenius' *Panegyricus Constantino Augusto* (Migne PL 8, cols. 637–638). In the original vision the two military gods place three laurel crowns—each contains an "X" representing ten years of rule still to come—over the emperor's head after the battle of Milvia Bridge. The fact that in the later version Constantine's vision is said to precede this important battle makes it highly probable that the Christian reworking is modeled after another reported vision: that of the Roman commander Licinius, who, according to Lactantius, saw a "sign of victory in the heavens" only a few days prior to the defeat of Maximian in A.D. 313 (*De Mortibus Persecutorum*, Migne PL 7, cols. 264–265). On this subject, see H. Grégoire, "La Conversion de Constantin," *Revue de l'Université de Bruxelles* 36 (1930-1931): 231–272; cf. Pio Franchi de' Cavallieri, *Constantiniana*, which provides an extensive bibliography. As for Constantine's vision, there are so many Greek and Latin versions that I will refer only to the most important. Eusebius reports the vision as follows: "Horis diei meridianis, sole in occasum vergente, crucis tropaeum in coelo ex luce conflatum, soli superpositum, ipsis oculis se vidisse affirmavit, cum huiusmodi inscriptione: Hac vince" (*De Vita Constantini*, Migne PG 20, col. 943). Other versions include those of Sozomen and Rufinus (Presbyter), the Latin translator of Eusebius, both of whom place the cross to the east and claim that the "In this sign you shall triumph" was sung by angels. Filostorgus also situates the cross to the east but surrounds it with a crown of stars, and imagines the message spelled out in stars. Zonaras, Theophilactus, and a number of hagiographic texts go beyond Eusebius and Filostorgus by insisting that the cross itself was formed of stars and not of light. In the *Historia Ecclesiastica Tripartita* (Migne PL 69, cols. 887–888), Cassiodorus follows the details furnished by Eusebius while shifting the exhortation to: "O Constantine, in hoc vince." There exist in addition such eccentric versions as that of Berengosius the Abbot ("De Laude et Inventione Sanctae Crucis," Migne PL 160, cols. 935–982), in which the vision of the cross arrives just as the Emperor-pilgrim must confront a "Pythagorean bivium." But two that Dante is very likely to have been acquainted with are those present in the liturgies of the Invention and Exaltation of the Cross and in Jacobo de Voragine's *Legenda Aurea* (Graesse, 303–311). For a general survey on this question, see Gretser, *De Sancta*

were reported frequently during the Middle Ages. This was especially true in such periods of political crisis and apocalyptic expectation as the first four centuries after the death of Christ, around the turn of the millennium and in the thirteenth century, (usually in connection with the various radical spiritualist movements).[66] Dante's contribution to this tradition (unmentioned, oddly enough, among the forty or so visions that Gretser documents between A.D. 800 and 1400) occurs in a passage of immense importance to cantos 14–18 of *Paradise*: his discussion in *Convivio* 2.13.20–25 of the planet Mars.

Planet of comets, shooting stars, and all other premonitory "combusted vapors"—the fiery spectacles at the close of canto 14 and at the opening of canto 15 being obvious cases in point— Mars initiates, as I have repeatedly insisted, the endless "passing

---

Cruce, vol. 2, 239–258, and vol. 3, 316–318. An exhaustive bibliography is found in the McGiffert and Richardson translation of Eusebius' *Church History*, 446–455. On Constantine's *labarum*, see Gretser, vol. 2, 239ff.; de' Cavallieri's "Il labaro descritto da Eusebio" in *Scritti agiografici II. 1900–1946*, 201–227; and H. Grégoire, "L'Etymologie de *labarum*," *Byzantion* 4 (1927–1928): 477–482, which suggests that "labarum" may be derived from "lauratum," the crown of the cross from the pagan laurel crown.

[66] On the general subject of apparitions of the cross, see "De Apparitionibus Sanctae Crucis" in Gretser, vol. 1, 316–337, which includes visions from the time of Constantine through the seventeenth century. The most important fourth-century vision, besides those of Constantine and Julian the Apostate, is that reported in the "Epistle to Constance II" (Migne PG 33, cols. 1165–1176), a letter whose author, it is now widely agreed, cannot be Cyril of Jerusalem. Its author reports:

> Crux permagna e luce constructa, in coelo super sanctum Golgotham, et usque ad sanctum Olivarum montem expansa apparuit.... compluribus horis desuper terram oculorum visu conspecta est, solares radios coruscantibus fulgoribus exsuperans. (1170)

The text of the letter is followed by additional testimonies from Jerome, Socrates, Sozomen, and others (cols. 1175–1180). As for the period between the year A.D. 900 and A.D. 1400, Gretser reports no less than thirty-eight apparitions (Gretser, 323–326). On apocalyptic expectation at the turn of the millenium see Henri Focillon, *The Year 1000*, 40–74.

away of kings and transmutation of kingdoms" ("morte di regi e transmutamento di regni" [2.13.22]) that make of the human city a place of wandering and exile. Mars's symbolic presence at the onset of the city's demise should then come as no surprise:

> ... in Fiorenza, nel principio de la sua destruzione, veduta fu ne l'aere, *in figura d'una croce*, grande quantità di questi vapori seguaci de la stella di Marte.
>
> (... in Florence, at the beginning of her downfall, there was seen in the sky *in the figure of the cross* a great mass of these vapors which follow the planet Mars.) [2.13.22; my italics]

This fiery cross, reported by Dino Compagni as vermillion colored ("una croce vermiglia") and probably linked to the apparition of Halley's comet in 1301, belongs to a category of meteorological/cosmological signs that was the stock and trade of Classical and Medieval historiography. Such legendary events as Julius' apotheosis as a comet in *Metamorphoses* 15 (745ff.), the ball of fire seen over Rome at the time of Augustus' death (reported via Seneca in *Convivio* 2.13.22), and the vision of Constantine come to mind in this regard. Yet the specific shape of Dante's cross and its identification as a sign of Judgment clearly suggest that it shares a common ascendancy with the cross of light in the heaven of Mars: both are derived from the eschatological "sign of the Son of man in heaven" of Matthew 24:30.[67]

---

[67] The link between the two crosses has been noted casually at least since the sixteenth century. In his gloss on 14.100–102 Daniello, for instance, writes: "forse allude à quel che dice nel suo *Convivio*, che è che in Firenze nel principio della sua destruttione fù veduta nell'aere in figura d'una croce grandissima quantità di vapori, seguaci della stella di Marte." Besides the obvious eschatological and meteorological connections between the vision of canto 14–15 and the discussion of Mars in *Convivio* 2.13.20–25, there are, as I later show, a number of additional thematic ties between the two texts, as well as between *Convivio* 2.14.1–14 and canto 14. Thomas Bergin has further pointed out (*A Diversity of Dante*, 146) that the phrase "l'affocato riso de la stella" (14.86) recalls the descrip-

The Sibylline Sign of Doom

Of some importance to the interpretation of cantos 14–18 is also the role of the eschatological cross of light in the early Christian Sibyllines. This body of second-century texts, known to the Latin Middle Ages mostly in the form of collected fragments, played a decisive role in the anti-pagan polemics of the early Church Fathers (notably Lactantius), and represents, alongside certain New Testament Apocrypha, the single most important source of lore concerning the apocalyptic cross. Of the ten Sibyls which, according to Varro's lost *Antiquitates Rerum Humanarum et Divinarum*, were reputed to exist in the ancient world, only the Cumaean and Erythrean Sibyls are of interest here, for they alone were universally regarded as the pagan prophetesses of the advent of Christ.[68]

The Cumaean Sibyl was first and foremost associated with a text whose importance to Dante can hardly be overstated: Virgil's Fourth Eclogue. As the testimony of Statius in canto 22 of *Purgatory* confirms, Christians had long interpreted the poem's promise of a new Saturnian age as a description of the "fullness of time" celebrated in Galatians 4:4. Consequently, its "new progeny sent down from heaven on high" ("nova progenies caelo demittitur alto" [*Ecl.* 4.7]), which referred in reality to the birth of a son to Gaius Asinius Pollio, Rome's consul and Virgil's protector, could only signify the first or second advent of Jesus

---

tion of Mars in *Convivio* 2.13.21 as: "affocato di colore, quando più e quando meno, secondo la spessezza e raritate de li vapori che 'l seguono."

[68] Varro's description of the Sibyls (which includes the famous etymology deriving "Sibyl" from *sious boulan* or *theoboule*, "Dei mentem" as rendered by Isidore) was the primary source for Lactantius' *Divinarum Institutionum* 1.5–6, 4.18–19; Augustine's *De Civitate Dei* 18.23; and Isidore's *Etymologiarum* 8.8—the most influential early patristic treatments of the Sibyls. A brief but comprehensive discussion of the Sibylline oracles in the Classical, Judaic and Christian traditions can be found in the Hennecke/Schneemelcher, *New Testament Apocrypha*, vol. 2, 703–709.

Christ.⁶⁹ And this fulfilling the oracles of the same Sibyl ("Ultima Cumaei venit iam carminis aetas" [*Ecl.* 4.4]), whose authority is at stake in Dante's rewriting of Book 6 of the *Aeneid* at the center of *Paradise*.

That Book 6 and the Martial cantos of *Paradise* are involved in an elaborate network of (respectively) anticipations and revisions of one another has, I think, been sufficiently demonstrated by now to permit the consideration of one further and, admittedly, more speculative Sibylline anticipation. Dante must certainly have been familiar with the anonymous Sibylline oracle (the so-called "Eighth Sibylline") contained in the Constantinian *Oratio ad Sanctorum Coetum* and (minus its final six Greek or four Latin verses) in Augustine's *City of God*.⁷⁰ He may well have been ac-

---

⁶⁹ See Pierre Courcelle, "Les Exégèses chrétiennes de la quatrième Eglogue," *Revue des Etudes Anciennes* 59 (1957): 294–319 for a general survey and for bibliography on this subject. On p. 302 Courcelle calls attention to verses 15–16 ("ille deum vitam accipiet divisque videbit / permixtos heroas"), whose allusion to certain divinized heroes was interpreted as a reference to Christ's martyrs. The classic study of Virgil as prophet in the Middle Ages is Doménico Comparetti's *Virgilio nel medioevo*; but see also Henri de Lubac, *L'Exégèse médiévale: Les Quatre Sens de l'Ecriture*, vol. 2, 233–262, dedicated to Virgil as philosopher and prophet; and Theodor Silverstein, "Dante and Vergil the Mystic," *Harvard Studies and Notes in Philology and Literature* 13 (1931): 51–82.

⁷⁰ In the *Oratio ad Sanctorum Coetum* (Migne PL 8, cols. 399–478), the long discourse usually attached to the end of Eusebius' life of Constantine but whose authorship remains uncertain, the Eighth Sibylline is analyzed in the course of a general polemic against Classical philosophy and science. The discussion is situated between an exploration of Plato's debt to Moses (cols. 446–450), and an important interpretation of Virgil's Fourth Eclogue as prophesying the advent of Christ (cols. 458–466). The *Oratio*'s text of Oracle 8 is attributed by the author to the Erythrean Sibyl, and shows numerous divergences from the translation cited by Augustine, the most prominent being the absence in the latter of the closing four verses which complete the full acrostic. The acrostic Augustine gives in both Latin and Greek is thus the truncated: "Jesus Christ Son of God, Redeemer," or "ΙΕSUCS CREISTOS TEVD NIOS SOTER," translated by Augustine as "Iesus Christus Dei filius salvator" (*De Civ. Dei* 18.23.1). On the acrostic *ichthys*, see F. J. Dölger, "ΙΧΘΥS: das Fischsymbol in frühchristlicher Zeit," *Römische Quartalschrift: Supplement* (Rome, 1910): 51–65.

quainted, whether directly or indirectly, with other Sibylline oracles concerned with the cross. Oracle 2, for instance, evokes the arrival of a "great sign" (v.34): both a sign of Judgment (vv. 154ff.) and a radiant crown "for righteous men as guerdon of victory" (vv. 151–152) and "a prize immortal . . . to martyrs who endure the contest even unto death" (vv. 46–47).[71] Oracle 6 strikes a similarly eschatological note:[72]

> O tree most blessed,
>   on which God was stretched out,
> Earth shall not have thee,
>   but thou shalt see a heavenly home,
> When thy fiery eye, O God,
>   shall flash like lightning. (vv. 26–28)

Of Dante's knowledge of the Eighth Sibylline, however, there can be little doubt. This oracle had for a millenium been regarded as the single most compelling proof that the coming (and second coming) of Christ had insinuated itself into even the veiled truths of Apollo's priestesses. Beginning with a prophecy of a certain "sign of Judgment" and concluding with a description of the cross, it formed the famous acrostic "Jesus Christ, Son of God, Redeemer, Cross" ('Ιησοῦς Χρειστὸς Θεοῦ υἱὸς σωτήρ σταυρός). The internal acrostic ΙΧΘΥΣΣ appears by assembling in turn the first letters of the prior acrostic. Signifying ἰχθύς or "fish," it became one of the standard mystical names of Christ: in Augustine's interpretation, "Christ, who in this abyss of mortality as if in the depths of the sea, was able to survive, that is was able to be without sin" ("Christus, eo quod in huius mortalitatis abysso velut in aquarum profunditate vivus, hoc est sine peccato, esse potuerit" [*De Civ. Dei* 18.23.1]). Its ubiquitousness in Christian art is attested to by its presence at Sant' Apollinare in Classe, where it is suspended above an apocalyptic cross of light in a set-

---

[71] *New Testament Apocrypha*, vol. 2, 712–713.
[72] *New Testament Apocrypha*, vol. 2, 720.

ting generally reminiscent of the prophecies of the Eighth Sibylline.

Although usually ascribed to the Erythrean Sibyl, this oracle was often attributed to the Cumaean Sibyl because of its anonymity and the precedent of the Fourth Eclogue. The concluding paragraph of Augustine's important discussion of the Eighth Oracle thus begins: "Furthermore, this Sibyl, whether she be the Erythrean, or as some rather believe, the Cumaean . . ." ("Haec autem Sibylla sive Erythraea sive, ut quidam magis credunt, Cumaea . . ." [*De Civ. Dei* 18.23.2]). But, leaving the question of her identity aside, that a Sibyl here and elsewhere should have prophesied the coming of a "venerable sign" which would accompany the Last Judgment, significantly amplifies a central theme of cantos 14–18: the "completion" of Classical prophecy (and Classical prophecies) through the cross, and the displacement of the veiled circumlocutions of pagan oracles by the prophetic speech of the privileged witnesses of the cross. To the role of Virgil as the prophet of the Fourth Eclogue, and to the prophetic anticipations of the cross that can be read into Book 6 of the *Aeneid* from the revisionist perspective of *Paradise*, then, one must add the Sibyl's anticipation of the cross of light in Dante's heaven of Mars, a cross whose clear and precise oracles would soon disperse her arcane dooms.

Eliòs / Eliso / Eliseo

Whereas the Sibylline oracles tend to emphasize the gloomier aspects of the cross of light, its role as a sign of destruction and doom, what predominates in the Apocrypha and in other early Christian texts is a more "comic" conflation of the cross of light with the solar Christ of the Transfiguration. To cite but a single example, in the Apocalypse of Peter, Jesus' *parousia* is portrayed as a double of his Transfiguration, a notion that will be become a commonplace in patristic exegesis after John Chrysostom: "with my cross going before my face will I come in my glory, shining seven times as bright as the sun will I come in my glory, with all my saints, my angels, when my Father will place a crown upon my head, that I may judge the living and the dead and recompense every man according to his work."[73] With this image of the cross as a cruciform *sol Christi* reminiscent both of cantos 14–18 and of the mosaics of Classe, we rejoin once again the mainstream of scriptures, patristic writings, and liturgies concerned with the cult of the Holy Cross.

For the whole of human history, from Genesis through Golgotha to the apocalyptic "sign of the Son of man in heaven," was to early Christendom but the gradual unveiling of the "comic" meaning of sign of the cross. Not only was every imaginable Old Testament foreshadowing of the cross assiduously documented to justify this view, but also, as I have shown earlier, the cross was itself traced back to the origins of the universe in a effort to show that as the keystone of God's creation it had been in place from the very start. In this same vein, certain messianic prophecies of the Old Testament, such as that of Malachi 4:2 announcing the coming of a "Sun of Justice," Christ's Transfiguration, the opening words of the gospel of John, the various legends concerned with the crucifixion and ascension and the promised "sign

---

[73] Hennecke, vol. 2, 668. Both the phrase "come in my glory with all my saints" and the entire concluding portion cite Matthew 16:27. The sevenfold sun instead recalls Isaiah 30:26: "Et lux solis erit septempliciter sicut lux septem dierum, in die qua alligaverit Dominus vulnus populi sui, et percussuram plagae eius sanaverit." The cross of light and the Transfiguration figure prominently in the Apocrypha, reflecting in the case of the cross the eschatological concerns of a large portion of these texts and, in the case of the Transfiguration, a gnosticizing, Manichean, or simply Hellenizing Christology. On the cross of light, see in Hennecke's edition the *Acts of John* (232–234), and *Acts of Andrew* (418–419); and in *The Apocryphal New Testament*, ed. M. R. James, the *Acts of Phillip* (450). Cf. *Gospel of Peter* (James, 92–93) and *Acts of Peter* (Hennecke, 318–319). On the Transfiguration as an eschatological event, see the *Apocalypse of Peter* (Hennecke, 680–684) and John Chrysostom's *Homiliae in Matthaeum*, Migne PG 58, col. 554, the first patristic source that incorporates the vision of the Apocalypse of Peter into an eschatological interpretation of the Transfiguration.

UNICA SPES HOMINUM 135

of the Son of man," were regarded as directly affiliated with the closing vision of the Johannine Apocalypse: John's vision of an eternal city which was to know neither night nor moon nor sun because "it was lit by the radiant glory of God and the Lamb was a lighted torch for it" (Rev. 21:23; Jerusalem Bible translation).

The ultimate unveiling of the victorious Christ/cross which had first shone at the Transfiguration only to reappear again on the occasion of the crucifixion and/or ascension, was thus to come at the conclusion of history. Then, as described in a sermon long attributed to Saint Augustine, but actually authored by John Chrysostom, it would fill the heavens with its light and, like the magnificent *vexilla regalia* celebrated in Venantius Fortunatus' hymn, precede the coming of Christ into his eschatological kingdom:[74]

> Have you considered how great is the power of the sign of the cross: "the sun shall be darkened, and the moon shall not give her light" (Matt. 24:29). The cross indeed shall shine and with heaven's luminaries darkened and the stars fallen, it shall shine all alone in order that you might see how the cross will be more luminous than the moon and much more radiant than the sun, whose splendor its Divine light, lit up with flashing brightness, will overcome. For just as when a king enters a city, his army precedes him bearing on its shoulders the royal ensigns and banners, and all around the pre-

---

[74] "Considerasti quanta virtus sit signi, hoc est, crucis: *sol obscurabitur, et luna non dabit lumen suum* (Matt. 24:29); crux vero fulgebit, et obscuratis luminaribus coeli, delapsisque sideribus sola radiabit: ut discas quoniam [sic] crux et luna lucidior et sole erit praeclarior, quorum splendorem divini luminis illustrata fulgore superabit. Quemadmodum enim ingredientem regem in civitatem, excercitus antecedit, praeferens humeris signa atque vexilla regalia, et ambitu praeparationis armisonae annuntiat regis introitum: ita Domino descendente de coelis praecedet exercitus Angelorum, qui signum illud, id est, triumphale vexillum sublimibus humeris praeferentes, divinum regis coelestis ingressum terris trementibus nuntiabunt" (Sermon 155 ["De Passione Domini VI, seu de Cruce et Latrone"], Migne PL 39, col. 2051). In the old enumeration of Augustine's sermons this was "De Tempore 130." The sermon is in fact a Latin abridgement of John Chrysostom's "De Cruce et Latrone I," Migne PG 49, cols. 399–408.

paratory sounding of arms proclaims the king's impending entry, so the army of Angels will precede the Lord descending from the heavens, carrying that sign, that is, His triumphal banner, borne aloft on their sublime shoulders, which shall announce the return of the divine celestial king to a trembling earth.

Precursor and military *signum*, this cross is one and the same as the "venerable sign" at the center of Dante's *Paradise* (some seven cantos in fact separate the cross of light from the first triumph of Christ). But, beyond so bellic a role, there is the hint here, as in cantos 14–18, of one both more peaceful and permanent. For the cross of light is imagined by the sermon's author as the supernatural sun which, displacing nature's inconstant stars and planets, would forever illuminate Jerusalem's skies. It is via the presence of such an apocalyptic sign/sun over the heaven of Mars, I should like to suggest in the closing sections of this chapter, that Dante emblematizes post-incarnational man's power to see through to the end of history, piercing the veil of Mars/*mors*. What the cruciform solar Christ in the heaven of Mars opens up is a vision unavailable to Virgil, the Sibyl, Apollo, or Anchises: a vision of peace whose proper name is not Rome but rather Jerusalem. This was the *futura patriae pace* of Isidore's celebrated etymology: "when referring to the peace of the future homeland it [the Church] is called Jerusalem, for Jerusalem is to be understood as signifying 'vision of peace,' since there, all adversity having been swallowed up, peace—which is to say Christ—shall reign in person."[75]

After this excursus we are in a position adequately to confront one of the most puzzling phrases in the entire final canticle and one which has been the source of considerable dissent in the commentary tradition: the "O Eliòs che sì li addobbi" ("O Helios who so adorn them" [14.96]) with which the poet-pilgrim greets the

[75] "Pro futura vero patriae pace Hierusalem vocatur. Nam Hierusalem pacis visio interpretatur. Ibi enim absorpta omni adversitate pacem, quae est Christus, praesenti possidebit obtutu" (*Etym.* 8.1.6).

sudden appearance of the cross of light over the heaven of Mars. Osip Mandelstam's remark that in Dante's poem "the most dadaist of the Romance languages moves forward to take the first place among nations" seems a particularly apt description of this invocation poised on the edge of a sort of mystagogic babble.[76] While not exactly a Hugo Ball *lautgedicht*, Dante's "O Eliòs," with its symmetrical near palindromes (oel-/-lio, ddo-/-obb), alliterative vowel-consonant clusters (el-/-li-/-os ke-/-si-/-li ad-/-ob-/-bi), and with the "I" and "El" that will figure prominently in Adam's discussion of the divine names in *Paradise* 26.133–138, is indeed spoken as if it were glossolalia or a magical incantation.[77] The point is further reinforced by the appearance here of Greek, a language held to be so remote from the pilgrim's native Tuscan in the canto of Ulysses (*Inf.* 26.73–75) that the intercession of a speaker of Lombard, namely Virgil, was required.

The poet-pilgrim's invocation of "Eliòs" cannot, in any case, refer to God the Father—the dominant view since Pietro Alighieri—unless by some stretch of the imagination we attribute to Dante a quite glaring theological imprecision. It is, after all, the sign of Christ that is being addressed: a fact underscored not only by the *Cristo/Cristo/Cristo* rhyme some eight verses later, but also by the presence of the all-important themes of *imitatio Christi* and transfiguration in this portion of canto 14. The verb employed is consequently "addobbare," a highly specialized term like the related verb "decussare," denoting the symbolic act known in the Middle Ages as "cruce signari": an imprinting of the sign of the cross on the crusader's scapulary, signifying his transformation into a knight of the Holy Cross.[78]

---

[76] English trans. by J. G. Harris from "Conversation about Dante," in *Mandelstam: The Complete Critical Prose and Letters*, 400.

[77] "Eliòs" seemingly inverts the historical succession that Adam describes which places the "I" before the postlapsarian "El." Kaske's reading of the DXV prophecy hinges on the theological implications of a comparable inversion; see "Dante's 'DXV' and 'Veltro,' " *Traditio* 17 (1961): 185–252.

[78] On "dubbing" and the taking on of the cross, see Jean Flori, "Les Origines

The traditional view cited by Singleton among many others that "Eliòs" is "the name of God [i.e., God the Father], the spiritual sun," rests in fact on a partial misreading of Uguccione da Pisa's *Magnae Derivationes*.[79] Uguccione is extremely precise on the subject: "Ab *Eli*, quod est deus, dictus est sol *Elios* quod pro deo olim reputabantur" ("from *Eli*, which is to say god, the sun is called *Elios*, since he was once considered a god"). Those who worshipped the sun as their god are the pagans, and their god is unmistakably Apollo: the pagan deity widely regarded among the early Church Fathers as prefiguring the *Apollo vere* (true Apollo), Jesus Christ.[80] Numerous other sources would have in-

---

de l'adoubement chevaleresque: Etude des remises d'armes et du vocabulaire qui les exprime dans les sources historiques latines jusqu'au début du XIIIe siècle," *Traditio* 35 (1979): 209–272; and James Brundage, "Cruce Signari: The Rite for Taking the Cross in England," *Traditio* 22 (1966): 289–310. The literal act of putting on the cross or *decus* is symbolically associated with the proto-apocalyptic marking of the just citizens described in Ezechiel 9:4–6:

> Et dixit Dominus ad eum: Transi per mediam civitatem, in medio Ierusalem, et signa thau super frontes virorum gementium et dolentium super cunctis abominationibus quae fiunt in medio eius. Et illis dixit, audiente me: Transite per civitatem sequentes eum, et percutite; non parcat oculus vester, neque misereamini: senem, adolescentulum et virginem, parvulum et mulieres, interficite usque ad internecionem; omnem autem super quem videritis thau ne occidatis.

On the cross as apocalyptic Thau, see F. J. Dölger, "Beiträge" *JACh* 2 (1959): esp. 15–20.

[79] *Paradiso: 2—Commentary*, 248 (my insertion). Singleton's view is shared by Lana, l'Ottimo, the Anonimo Fiorentino, Landino, Daniello, and most of the other major commentarists. Dissenting views gain the upper hand in some of the nineteenth-century commentaries. On Dante's reliance on Uguccione, see Paget Toynbee, *Dante Studies and Researches*, 97–114. Uguccione's definition of "Elios" is given by Toynbee (113) and Singleton (*ibid.*). Other sources besides Uguccione are extremely consistent in their differentiation of "Elios" from the Hebrew names of God. After discussing the meaning of "Eli" and "Elion" without any reference to "Elios," for instance, Giovanni of Genoa etymologizes the term "Eliades" as follows: "*Eliades*—ab *elios* quod est sol, dicitur hic eliades de filiis vel nepos solis" (*Catholicon*, n.p.).

[80] The phrase *Apollo vere* appears in reference to Apollo's victory over Python

dicated to Dante that Uguccione's "Eli" was in reality either the "Eli" addressed by Christ in Matthew 27:46 or the "El," "Eloi," "Eloe," or "Elion" listed as names of God the Father by Isidore of Seville (the latter three of which would have perfectly satisfied Dante's metric requirements with the mere addition of a diaeresis).[81] Last of all, not a single manuscript of the third canticle proposes a significant variant for "Eliòs."[82] It is fair to assume, then, that Dante intended not "Eli" nor "Elion" but "Elios": one of the titles of Apollo.

Placed within the general setting of cantos 14–18, Dante's cryptic utterance in Greek can be easily shown to celebrate the precedence of the cross of Christ over the oracles of Apollo. The point is reinforced by the philological "status" of the Greek word ἥλιος, greater than that of the Latin *Sol* and the vernacular *Sole* because of its greater antiquity, but lesser than that of the Hebrew *Eli* out of which—at least according to Uguccione—it had descended. Christ's hermeneutic and epistemological ascendancy over Apollo is, as should by now be clear, one of the central themes in Dante's rewriting of the *Aeneid*'s Book 6 at the center of *Paradise*. The rhetorical fulcrum of Dante's revision is

in a poem attributed to Paulinus of Nola: "Salve, o Apollo vere, Paean inclite, / pulsor draconis inferi!" (Carmen 2.51–52, Appendix to Paulinus' *Carmina*, CSEL 30, 349.) A number of elements systematize the Apollo/Christ relation in cantos 14–18: the cross-lyre motif at the opening of canto 15, the frequent references to music (14.118–15.9; 17.42–45; 18.51), the presence of Phaeton as Dante's type, the matter of oracles and prophecy, the discussion of literary posterity at the close of canto 17, and the numerous references, both figurative and literal, to archery (15.43–45, 17.57). As Vettori has shown in "Il centro del Paradiso" (*Letture del Paradiso*, 167–186), the Phaeton/Dante association is of some importance to the theme of "sonship in the sun." But see also Robert Hollander's important reading of the opening invocation to Apollo in *Allegory in Dante's Commedia* (201–232), which suggests how the "Apollo" of the third canticle is from the start suspiciously Christlike; as well as Erich von Richtofen's "Dante 'Appollinian,'" esp. 154–173.

[81] See *Etym*. 7.1.2–11 on the divine names.

[82] Petrocchi lists only two variants: "o elios" in Hamiltonian 203, and "o helyos" (a later addition) in Palatino 313.

the passage which immediately precedes Cacciaguida's prophecy of suffering and exile:

> Né per ambage, in che la gente folle
> già s'inviscava pria che fosse anciso
> l'Agnel di Dio che le peccata tolle,
>   ma per chiare parole e con preciso
> latin rispuose quello amor paterno,
> chiuso e parvente del suo proprio riso. . . .   17.31–36

(In no dark sayings, such as those in which the foolish folk of old once ensnared themselves, before the Lamb of God who takes away sins was slain, but in clear words and with precise discourse that paternal love replied, hidden and revealed by his own smile. . . .)

Here in capsule form are stated the terms of the supplanting of Classical by Christian prophecy. On the one side stands the madness, the sense of paralysis, the semiotic disorder of the Sibylline (and Anchisean) *ambages*; on the other, the unimpaired clarity of Cacciaguida's prophetic disclosures. Separating them is the sacrifice of Christ, joining them a certain "paternal love" and common "latin" that make of Cacciaguida the Christian double of Anchises. I begin with that which apparently unites them so as to set the stage for the more general juxtaposition of prophecies.

That Cacciaguida's *latin* is not precisely the Latin of Virgil we can surmise from canto 16 verse 33, where Dante goes to some trouble to indicate that he is translating his ancestor's speech—an archaic Florentine dialect—into "this modern speech" ("questa moderna favella").[83] But it is clear all the same, that Cacciaguida's

---

[83] On Cacciaguida's "latin" and language at the center of *Paradise*, see André Pézard, "Les Trois Langues de Cacciaguida," *Revue des Etudes Italiennes* no. 13 (1967): 217–238; and "Volgare e latino nella Commedia," *Letture Classensi* no. 2 (1969): 95–111. For a contrary view, see R. Hollander, *Studies in Dante*, 115–131. As should be clear from my discussion, I do not fully accept either interpretation since the reference to Cacciaguida's "latin" must be placed within the larger genealogical network of cantos 14–18. This implies, in my view, an insistence on the irreducible ambiguity of the term "latin," which masterfully continues the

speech stands on the prelapsarian/Virgilian side of the divide which separates Florence's present state of linguistic and political decay from its exalted Roman origins, the origins Dante's own exilic "modern speech" aims at reconstituting. So in a sense Cacciaguida's prophetic "latin" *is* Virgil's Latin: sometimes literally (as in his opening "O sanguis meus" of 15.28), sometimes by translation (as in 15.89), and sometimes only figuratively (as in the prophecies of canto 17). But constantly passed through the intermediary of the Bible's *sermo humilis*, Virgil's Latin has undergone a transformation: humbled in form and content by its yoking to the cross, it has become a speech appropriate for Christian prophecy.[84]

Likewise, the "paternal love" of Anchises and that of Cacciaguida are both similar and yet qualitatively different. Most of all, the great genealogical themes of *Aeneid* 6, the foundation of Anchises' paternal love, are notably missing at the center of *Paradise*. Nowhere is Cacciaguida's heart inflamed, as are Anchises' and, for that matter, Africanus', with visions of a glorious lineage extending off into the horizon of human history. The fate of a single Alighieri is at stake, and, beyond the completion of his book, the future seems to hold only the abandonment of the native place and a promise of ultimate justice. The only explicitly familial debt which the poet-pilgrim is called upon to pay is in fact his grandfather's sin of pride: a sin no doubt of excessive *blood*-pride whose punishment in purgatory "it is right . . . that you should

---

elaborate play of identity and difference between Rome and Florence, Virgil's *Aeneid* and Dante's *Commedia*.

[84] On the *sermo humilis* and its relation to Classical stylistics and genre theory, see the opening chapter of Erich Auerbach's *Literary Language and Its Public in Late Antiquity and in the Middle Ages*, 25–66. Cacciaguida's linguistic register is broader than that of any other character in Dante's poem, deliberately merging the high and the low; the Classical and the Christian; the Latin, latinate, and properly Tuscan. From the lofty rhetorical heights of his Latin greeting, itself a dense conflation of Virgilian and Scriptural Latin, to the extreme creatural realism of such elocutions as "lascia pur grattar dov' è la rogna" (17.129), Cacciaguida programmatically enacts what is in effect Dante's own literary/linguistic program.

shorten through your works" ("si convien che . . . tu li raccorci con l'opere tue" [15.95–96]), Cacciaguida states.

Equally striking is the pointed absence in cantos 14–18 (as in the *Commedia* as a whole) of Dante's own father: a sundering of the symbolic blood-chain right at the decisive link.[85] The omission is of some consequence inasmuch as Cacciaguida is neither the pilgrim's father (i.e., an Anchises), nor his grandfather (i.e., an Africanus), nor even his great-grandfather; but rather is Dante's great-great-grandfather: a thrice-removed "paternal image." This displacement is especially fruitful in that it enables Dante to define his own literary-prophetic mission as both continuous and discontinuous with the past: his role is to reconstitute from exile a distant prelapsarian voice which remains, nonetheless, a familial and a native Florentine voice. Secondly, the displacement permits the conservation of the Aeneas/Anchises (Scipio/Africanus) parallelism and its reelaboration in terms of the theme of brotherhood in Christ—a "figurative" rather than a literal conception of genealogy. Thirdly, by distancing the actual blood-relation, it helps to contain the sort of threat posed by the pilgrim's transgression at the beginning of canto 16, allowing an exaltation of his origins, but always *sous rature*. Finally, it does indeed undercut any literal-minded notion of blood-descent: the theme of 16.1–16, where all illusions of Roman blood nobility are forcefully quashed, with the exemplum of Phaeton, whose obsessive preoccupation with his sonship in the Sun led to the cosmic calamity described in Book Two of Ovid's *Metamorphoses*, serving as a negative prod.[86]

---

[85] Rather than positing a proto-Romantic erasure of the Father as self-creation here, it would seem more probable that for Dante the historical father was too thoroughly enmeshed in the present crisis of the city to be able to provide the empowering exemplary voice required at the center of *Paradise*.

[86] The story of Phaeton takes as its point of departure Epaphus' taunt that he has a "false image of his parentage" (*Met.* 1.754). Phaeton then goes to Clymene to beg: "si modo sum caelesti stirpe creatus / Ede notam tanti generis meque assere caelo" (1.760–761). Clymene, in a speech whose adaptability to a Christian

This is not to say that the epic themes of fulfillment of origins, of living up to one's glorious *cognomen*, of filial imitation of paternal models, all simply evaporate as a result: Cacciaguida remains in a sense Dante's true ancestral father. The logic of this repudiation is such, rather, that it leads to the discovery of an absolute mediating principle: the preeminent reality of Jesus Christ. Cacciaguida's call is thus ultimately modeled less after that of the Sibyl, Anchises, or Africanus than after that which precedes the Transfiguration: "If any man will come after me, let him deny himself, and take up his cross and follow me" (Matt. 16:24). This call is not not so much one to expand the Alighieri lineage as to affiliate oneself with eternity through Christ—through his name, his blood, and his *fraternal* love.

But of even more crucial importance to understanding Dante's rewriting of Book 6 are a number of additional underlying tensions, out of which, once we look back upon the whole of cantos 14–18, emerges a network of oppositions between the prophetic

---

reading is self-evident if we substitute sonship in Apollo (son of Jupiter) for sonship in Christ (son of God), answers:

"Per iubar hoc" inquit "radiis insigne coruscis,
Nate, tibi iuro, quod nos auditque videtque,
Hoc te, quem spectas, hoc te, qui temperat orbem,
Sole satum. . . ."   1.76–77]

The passage is interesting because of the various Apollinian apellations of Cacciaguida ("santa lampa" [17.5], "quella luce" [17.28], "specchio d'oro" [17.123]), which identify him as a double of Dante's tempering cross/Helios, and because of the importance of themes of blood contamination and blood nobility in cantos 14–18. Dante's other mentions of Phaeton reveal a considerable degree of consistency. He is alluded to in *Inferno* 17.107 ("quando Fetonte abbandonò li freni") with reference to Geryon, in *Purgatory* 4.71–72 ("la strada che mal non seppe carreggiar Fetòn"), obliquely in *Purgatory* 29.118 ([il carro] "del Sol che, svïando, fu combusto") and in *Paradise* 31.124–125 ("il temo che mal guidò Fetonte"), always as a negative exemplum. (The latter "temo" recalls the "temo" designation of the cross found in *Purgatory* 32.49; the references to Phaeton's pathway, in turn, the legend of his accidental creation of the Milky Way cited in *Convivio* 2.14.5.) Cf. Marguerite Mills Chiarenza, "Myths of Time and Eternity in *Paradiso* XVII."

methodologies of Cacciaguida and Anchises, the oracles of Christ and of Apollo. For what could be more enigmatic yet controlled and self-assured than Cacciaguida's "paternal love concealed and manifest" ("amor paterno, / chiuso e parvente" [17.35–36]) or than a paternal "smile" ("riso" [17.36]) which accompanies a prophecy of loss and exile? Throughout the central cantos of *Paradise*, the reader is repeatedly struck by the coolness, restraint, and decorum of Cacciaguida, despite the regular allusions to his joy at this extraordinary encounter with his descendant. No tragic embrace marks this encounter of ancestral father and son.[87]

Nothing could be further from the attitude of Anchises, whose wildly fluctuating passions and grandiloquence are everywhere on display. Twice on the verge of tears (in 6.686 at the moment of Aeneas' appearance and at the vision in 6.882 of the tragic Marcellus), greeting his son with outstretched arms as if to invite the impossible embrace of 6.700–702, exalted by the prospect of Rome's ascent, staggered by the tragic price Rome would have to pay: one constantly senses the immediacy of Anchises' affective ties to the imagined spectacle of the city, while Cacciaguida remains consistently aloof. Was it not, after all, a haunting "sad image," a *tristis imago* (6.695), that drew Aeneas to Anchises' side in the first place?

The contrast is symptomatic of the fact that Anchises, unlike Cacciaguida, remains for Dante a figure enclosed within the blindness and flux of earthly perspectives: a limitation which extends to the entire world-view of Classical civilization, its god of poetry and prophecy included. He is a shadowy "ombra" thus as described in 15.25 ("Sì pïa l'ombra d'Anchise si porse").[88] Cac-

---

[87] The last such attempted embrace in Dante's poem was that of Statius in *Purgatory* 21.130. Virgil refuses the gesture, calling attention to its impossibility because they are both shadows: "Frate, / non far, ché tu se' ombra e ombra vedi."

[88] Every soul in Elysium proper, including Anchises, is referred to as a bright "anima" (6.669, 6.713, 6.758), with the sole exception of the tragic Marcellus who is enshrouded in a shadow ("tristi circumvolat umbra" [6.866]). Yet, as might be expected, shadows are abundant in the earlier portions of Book 6: the underworld

ciaguida, on the contrary, is a fulgurant "star" ("stella" [15.16]), a "flame" ("foco" [15.24]) and a "light" ("lume" [15.31]). And he looks at history with the serenity of someone whose feet are firmly planted in the eschatological city. Speaking from this perspective of the end, he is unmoved by the temporary tragedies of history: a reader of God's providential book, he knows precisely how they will end. But in posing the Christian alternative to Classical prophecy, his first task is not to extend the province of human reason over man's future. Quite the opposite: he begins by righting the balance between mystery and revelation, a balance which, in Dante's view, Classical humanism had attempted to upset.

From his opening speech in canto 15 necessarily above the "target of mortals" (15.42) to his words in canto 17 concerning the non-causal relation of divine omniscience to temporal events (17.37–42), Cacciaguida will consequently insist on the limitations of human knowledge and the evanescence of the concerns of human history. In dramatic counterposition to the confident tone of Anchises' historical predictions and metaphysical/cosmological exposition, he will invoke the final impenetrability and radical otherness to man of the divine μυστήριον τοῦ Θεοῦ, the eternal plan which, implemented through the cross, governs human history from its grandest events to its most intimate details.

The same can be said of the beginnings of the two encounters of father and son. Cacciaguida's encounter with Dante opens, not with the glorification of the son's heroism or of the filial piety which overcame the epic *iter durum* (6.688), but with a recogni-

---

itself is a place of shadows ("umbrarum . . . locus" [6.390]), Aeneas' descent is a descent into the shadows ("descendit ad umbras" [6.404]), and Dido, Palinurus, and Deiphobus are all described as shadows. That Dante should thus refer to Anchises as an "ombra" chooses to emphasize his role as *tristis imago* (6.695), as the empty paternal image that escapes Aeneas' triple embrace like the wings of sleep (6.700). This is an Anchises who shares in the fate of the damned, or who at the very best remains tragically enshrouded, like Marcellus, in the "hemisphere of shadows" of *Inferno* 4.69.

tion of the power which made possible the son's ascent: the "superinfusa gratïa" (supernatural grace) of man's creator (15.28). Again in his next intelligible words, Cacciaguida turns away from the poet-pilgrim's epic endeavor: first to the trinitarian godhead "who to my seed show so much favor" ("che nel mio seme se' tanto cortese" [15.48]), and then to its mediatrix: "she who for the high flight clothed you with wings" ("colei / ch'a l'alto volo ti vestì le piume" [15.53–54]).[89]

But most pointed of all is the juxtaposition of Anchises' individualized *calculation* of his son's arrival in Elysium—for whose accuracy he ironically congratulates himself, although the event occurs in a context of great pathos and uncertainty—with Cacciaguida's *act of reading* faithfully performed in the text of divine foresight, the *Liber de Praescientia Dei*: that immutable volume of the past, present, and future "in which white and dark are never altered" ("du' non si muta mai bianco né bruno" [15.51]). Not only is this book above all Martial mutability, but it is so radically all-encompassing that in it are inscribed the very words of Cacciaguida's responses to Dante's apparently—the delusion is ours—spontaneous questions: "la mia risposta è già decreta" ("my answer is already decreed" [15.69]).[90]

---

[89] At first glance the term "cortesia" may appear out of context here, but, as Aldo Vallone has pointed out in *La "cortesia" dai provenzali a Dante*, it is associated in Dante's later works with grace: "la cortesia è dote umana e sovrumana, ed è degli uomini e di Dio" (39), "nel mondo in contrasto all'Inferno, nel Paradiso, cortesia è qualcosa di veramente alto, è grazia, è felicità" (49). See esp. 45–73 concerning the *Commedia*.

[90] The precise identity of Cacciaguida's immutable "volume" is deliberately obscured, but is clear nonetheless that in terms of both content and form it is to be associated with: (a) the "Book of Life" referred to in Psalm 68:29, Philippians 4:3, and, most importantly, Revelations 3:5, 20:12–15, 21:27, and 22:19; (b) the "scroll written on the back and on the front" of Ezechiel 2:9 and Revelations 5:1; and (c) the heavenly inscription of the blessed described in Luke 10:20 ("Gaudete autem, quod nomina vestra scripta sunt in coelis"). The three are in fact closely linked in the exegetical tradition, being placed under the general rubric of the "Book of Divine Foreknowledge": a book necessarily inaccessible to mortals in which are contained the names of the saved, the details of God's providential plan governing history, and the secrets of individual and collective predestination. On

Here we touch upon an illusion which is essential to the strategy of the third canticle as a whole, but nowhere more so than in cantos 14–18, where it serves to differentiate the oracles of Christ from those of Apollo. While, from the perspective of pilgrim and reader, the action of the text seems one of looking forward into a murky and undecided future from the solidity of the present, the reverse is actually the case: it is a fully dictated providential future that rapidly advances upon *us* as we travel toward the anticipatory apocalypse of canto 33, and it is *we* who remain the undecided factor.[91] If the Virgilian parallel is still operative, then, its logic has been transformed. The future scenario comes upon us not, as was the case of Aeneas, in the form of an inexorable fate: the drama of *individual choice* is fully foregrounded, our need to respond to Christ's call, putting on or putting off our personal cross. And inasmuch as the scenario is both universal (like that of Anchises) as well as personal (unlike Anchises') its scope has been vastly expanded to encompass even the most trivial and private of historical actions.

---

this subject, see Leo Koep, *Das himmlische Buch in Antike und Christentum: eine religionsgeschichtliche Untersuchung zur altchristlichen Bildersprache*.

[91] The gap between human and divine perspectives is evoked right before Cacciaguida's history of the city and his prophecies regarding Dante's future; that is, at the opening of cantos 15 (37–47, 73–84) and 17 (13–18, 37–42). The function of these reminders is to edge the *perpetüa vista* of the divine perspective on history up against the perpetual blindness of the living, in order to set the stage for Cacciaguida's prophetic disclosures. But the outcome of the future's rushing toward historical eyes and ears cannot be a sense of passive resignation, or a belief that divine prevision imparts necessity and inevitability to human events, Cacciaguida states:

> La contingenza, che fuor del quaderno
> de la vostra matera non si stende,
> tutta è dipinta nel cospetto etterno;
> necessità però quindi non prende
> se non come dal viso in che si specchia
> nave che per torrente giù discende.   17.37–42

Rather, the contrary is true: the spotlight is on the present, on the success or failure of man's conversion to Christ's cross.

The usual laws of succession and causality are thus continuously suspended in cantos 14–18 while the dialectic of mystery and revelation works itself out. Writing in the "great volume" precedes the speech acts which would normally be presumed to be their source ("la mia risposta è già decreta" [15.69]). Or in canto 15.8–9 the spirits that form the cross of light collectively anticipate Dante's desire to question them even before such a desire comes into being: "per darmi voglia / ch'io le pregassi, a tacer fur concorde" ("to make me want to beg of them, they became silent with one accord"). The same is true of the rapturous harmonies that envelop the heaven of Mars. Always testing the limits of intelligibility, this music, like a record playing backward from eternity into time to the straining ears of pilgrim and reader, is continually heard yet never fully comprehended. Occasional passages do overcome the din of history and are overheard: the sweet resurrectional hymn of 14.125 heard as one who hears and understands not ("come a colui che non intende e ode" [14.126]), the secret smile concealed in Cacciaguida's prophecies which comes "like the sweet harmony of an organ to the ear" ("sì come viene ad orecchia / dolce armonia da organo" [17.43–44]). Other passages are necessarily obscured, as when "the spirit added to his first words things I understood not, so deep did he speak; nor did he conceal himself from me by choice, but by necessity" ("giunse lo spirto al suo principio cose, / ch'io non lo 'ntesi, sì parlò profondo; / né per elezïon mi si nascose, / ma per necessità" [15.38–41]). But the music that does penetrate this barrier of intelligibility is relentlessly upbeat; and its sweet harmonies, like the enigmatic smiles of cantos 14–18—Mars's "fiery smile" (14.86) and Cacciaguida's "smile" both "concealed and manifest" ("chiuso e parvente" [17.36])—belie its origin in the universal harmony of the eschatological city.

The implications of this network of contrasts and oppositions are self-evident: Cacciaguida, as the Christian Anchises, does not speak for himself. Rather, he speaks as an intermediary directly transmitting the message of the divine text. He is for the poet-pilgrim the personalized projection of that text: the divine appendage that condescending to human faculties raises them up to a vision of transcendent mysteries. As such, despite all appearances to the contrary, he is at least as much an exemplary *figura Christi* as the originary progenitor of the Alighieri clan. Descending out of the cross and reascending at the beginning of canto 17, he speaks as the authoritative voice of the cruciform solar Christ—a voice uncontaminated by Mars/*mors* or the flux of history, a voice in which are foreshadowed the distant strains of a universal symphony.

The cross for which he speaks is the same cross prophesied by Virgil, Anchises, and the Sibyls. With its "perpetual insight" (15.65) it promises the translation of Classical tragedy into Christian comedy, Virgil's epic of history into Dante's epic of redemption, the paralyzing riddles of Apollo into the "clear words and precise Latin" of Christian revelation. And in so doing it delimits the powers of human reason and restores the claims of mystery over the province of history. Through this cross Virgil and his prophetic text are completed, but in the process they are superseded and their humanist illusions undercut. This transcendence of Virgil and Apollo is itself encompassed within a broader symbolic act: the inscription of Dante's own poem (whatever its necessary limitations) in God's providential "great volume" through its symbol, the cross of light; and the binding of Dante's own poetic voice through Cacciaguida to the divinely empowered speech of Christ's martyr-prophets. As such, transcribing his ancestor's prophetic utterances, Dante symbolically affiliates his text with eternity itself, over and above all merely human and historical (literary) genealogies. This is the sense in which he touches the limit of his glory and of his paradise ("lo fondo / de la mia gloria e del mio paradiso" [15.35–36]).

Harmonia est Discordia Concors

Beyond the complex matter of Dante's rewriting of Book 6 of the *Aeneid*, however, there is a second and complementary purpose to the *Eliòs* address: to call attention to the centrality and the harmonizing role of the cruciform "Sun of Christ" in the Christian universe. That the sign of Christ should be designated as *Eliòs* just as the poet-pilgrim abandons the heaven of the sun, where Christ's place at the center of the circular dance of the Church Fathers was occupied by Dante and Beatrice, would seem to insist on the symbolic implications of the transition from the planetary sun to the figurative (or cosmic) Helios.

Here Dante may have been thinking of an etymology cited in the *praeconium Solis* of the pseudo-Dionysius' treatise on the divine names but at least as ancient as Plato's *Cratylus*:[92]

[92] "Secundum eamdem manifestae imaginis rationem, et lumen congregat et convertit ad se ipsum omnia, videntia, quae moventur, quae illuminantur, quae calefiunt, quae totaliter a fulgoribus ejus continentur. Propter quod et *helios* appellatur, quoniam omnia indestructibilia facit et congregat dispersa. Et omnia sensibilia ipsum desiderant, aut sicut videre aut sicut moveri aut sicut illuminari et calefieri et totaliter contineri a lumine concupiscentia" (*De Divinis Nominibus* 4.3, par. 123). The Latin translation is the twelfth-century version of John the Saracen, which I quote from the *Dionysiaca*, ed. Ph. Chevalier, vol. 1, 169–171. Hilduin translates ἥλιος as "helios," John Scotus Eriugena and Robert Grosseteste simply as "sol." Thomas Aquinas merely touches upon the "helios" etymology in his commentary (*In Librum Beati Dionysii De Divinis Nominibus Expositio*, ed. Pera, 104f.), but a full discussion can be found in Albertus Magnus' *Super Dionysium De Divinis Nominibus*, ed. Simon, 166–168 (pars. 59–61). The etymology originates with Plato's *Cratylus* (409a): "The origin of the sun will probably be clearer in the Doric form, for the Dorians call him ἅλιος, and this name is given to him because when he rises he gathers (ἁλίζοι) men together or because he is always rolling in his course (ἀεὶ εἰλεῖν ἰών) about the earth, or from αἰολεῖν, of which the meaning is the same as ποικίλλειν (to variegate), because he variegates the productions of the earth" (B. Jowett trans.). For the intellectual background of the pseudo-Dionysius' "praeconium" see Plato's *Republic* 6.507a–509b, and Julian the Apostate's "Discourse on Helios the King" in *Oeuvres complètes*, ed. C. Lacombrade, vol. 2/2, 100–138. For bibliography and a general introduction to the solar religions of late antiquity and their role in early Christian thought, see the articles of Kerenyi, Willi, Schmidt, Pulver, and H. Rahner in *Eranos-Jahrbuch* 10 (1943), an issue entirely devoted to the ancient sun cults and light symbolism in Gnosticism and early Christianity. For late antiquity, see Gaston H. Halsberghe, *The Cult of Sol Invictus*, which includes a short selection of texts and relevant bibliography. See also Marie-Madelaine Davy et al., *Le Thème de la lumière dans le Judaisme, le Christianisme et l'Islam*.

> According to the *logos* of its visible image [the sun], the light both gathers and turns to itself all things, seeing things, things which move, which are illuminated, which are heated by it, all are entirely encompassed within its flashing forth. Thus it is called *helios* since it makes all things indestructible and gathers together all that which is dispersed. And all sensible beings feverishly desire it, for they desire to see, to move, to be illuminated, to be warmed, and to be totally embraced within its light.

This second sun, the pseudo-Dionysius contends, is not the sensible sun or the Roman god *Sol*, but the suprasensible Helios (the neo-Platonic supreme Good) whose rays illuminate all of creation. While the metaphysical themes of this passage may not seem immediately relevant to cantos 14–18, the etymology remains suggestive inasmuch as it touches upon a number of important attributes of the cross, and provides an important link to certain musicological and arithmetic themes I am about to explore. The idea that this sun makes all things indestructible recalls the early Christian faith in the apotropaic value of the cross: its role, especially, in shielding the adubbed crusader or martyr.[93] The theme of binding together what is dispersed throughout the universe in turn recalls the early Christian understanding of the cosmic implications of Christ's cross: its role of reconciling the dispersed (cf. Col. 1:19), establishing the unstable, binding the circumference of the universe, and bringing earth into contact with heaven. Last of all, the emphasis here on the cleaving of all phenomena to the universal "Helios" recalls a related belief in the mysterious omnipresence of the sign of the cross in creation, from the very shape of the cosmos to the form of the human body to even the climatology and geography of the terrestrial sphere. "From the beginning God divided this world into four separate *climata*, because assuredly he predestined them to be restored from their collapse via the cross," writes Honorius of Autun,

---

[93] See the first section of part 6 of Dölger's "Beiträge" *JACh* 6 (1963): 7–18, on this subject.

"and man too he patterned after the form of cross, because he predestined that the fallen one be renewed through the cross."[94]

The "Eliòs" of the heaven of Mars must in any event be viewed as a further unveiling of what was prefigured in the cantos of the sun: namely, the future triumph of Christ (here worked out in its most personal implications, while at the same time looking forward to Christ's eventual triumph in the heaven of the fixed stars and in the Empyrean). I would submit, moreover, that in the opening invocation of canto 14 we are invited to consider the cross of light, towering over the actual solar sphere, as the *true* sun of *Paradise*: the rightful occupant of the central planetary circle because of its symbolic centrality to the Christian cosmos.[95] The terms of this succession are not primarily those of the neo-Platonic distinction between *sol sensibilis* (sensate sun) and *sol intellectualis* (intellectual sun), despite their importance in cantos 10–13, but rather the traditional Christian distinction of the planetary sun from the messianic "Sun of Justice" which would shine eternally at the end of time.[96] An emblem of the new epis-

---

[94] "Deus ab initio hunc mundum in quatuor clymata partitum creavit, quia profecto eum collapsum per crucem restaurare praedestinavit. Hominem quoque in modum crucis formavit, quia perditum per crucem reparare praedestinavit" ("De Inventione Sanctae Crucis," *Speculum Ecclesiae*, Migne PL 172, col. 945). On the sign of the cross in nature, see Dölger, "Beiträge" *JACh* 10 (1967): 7–11.

[95] Cf. Victor Castellani, "Heliocentricity in the Structure of Dante's *Paradiso*," in *Studies in Philology* 78 (Summer 1981): 211–223, which argues for the centrality of the sphere of the sun. There are actually two central heavens: one which stands at the center of the seven planetary spheres (that of the sun), and one which is at the center of all the heavenly spheres, both planetary and supra-planetary (that of Mars).

[96] Commenting on Matthew 17:2, John of Damascus writes "ejus, inquam, qui ingenti sua potentia solem hunc lumine perfundit: ejus qui lucem sole antiquiorem creavit, ac solis luminare, ut lucis conceptaculum esset, postea fabricatus est. Ipse enim est lux vera, qui ex vera et materiae experte luce perpetua gignitur; Patris utique substantiale Verbum, ille gloriae splendor, ille naturalis Dei ac Patris substantaie character." John continues later: "ac corpore in seipso manente lumen in omnis terrae partes extremas diffunditur: eodem modo Christus quoque, cum sempiternum et inaccessum lumen de lumine sit, dum in tempora-

temological and hermeneutic conditions of the era of Christ, this sun is in fact the Christian *sol intellectualis*: the sun that rules the cosmos, balances the heavens, tunes the universal symphony. But, as befits its Christianization, it takes on a specifically historical dimension which is distinctly non-Platonic. It is that sun of Gregory of Nyssa's gloss on Revelations 21:23 and 22:5: "The great day (of everlasting life) will no longer be illuminated by the visible sun but by a true light, the Sun of Justice, which is called Orient (the rising sun) by the prophets because it is no longer hidden by any setting."[97]

Dante's motivations in this matter were, in any case, both structural and thematic, for he needed to preserve the heliocentric epistemology of neo-Platonism (which thoroughly permeated Christian speculations on the solar Christ as well as Christian theories of contemplation), while remaining faithful to the Ptolemaic planetary scheme which places Mars at the center of *Paradise*. The problem was one that Dante had already confronted with considerable ingenuity in the *Convivio*, where, in a dramatic departure from the Macrobian-Boethian analysis of the harmonic ratios of the heavenly spheres, he had transferred the musical attributes of the sun, the heaven universally regarded as the bearer of harmony and reason, to Mars, the heaven of discord by antonomasia. The gesture is all the more radical in that it assigns to Mars the middle note (or "mean") in the full octave which was thought by some to extend from earth to Empyrean: the decisive swing-vote, or better swing-*note*, through whose tempering and harmonizing action the cosmic symphony was kept in order.[98]

---

rio et creato corpore existit, unus est justitiae sol" ("Homilia de Transfiguratione Domini," Migne PG 96, cols. 563d–566b).

[97] Migne PG 44, col. 505a. The passage is cited in Jean Daniélou's *The Bible and the Liturgy* (p. 32), which is useful on eschatology and the solar Christ in the early Christian liturgies (27–34).

[98] On harmonies and the music of the spheres see *Commentarii* 2.1–5, which represents Macrobius' exposition on *De Re Publica* 6.18. Cf. Boethius, *De Institutione*

Mars was thus imagined as the heaven of music because of its:[99]

> più bella relazione, ché, annumerando li cieli mobili, da qualunque si comincia o da l'infimo o dal sommo, esso cielo di Marte è lo quinto, esso è lo mezzo di tutti, cioè de li primi, de li secondi, de li terzi e de li quarti.
>
> (most beautiful relation [to the other planets], for in counting the revolving heavens, whether one begins at the base or the summit [of the cosmos] this same heaven of Mars is the fifth, which is to say, the mean of each [planetary] pair, that is of the two first, the two second, the two third and the two fourth.)

Dante's allegory could hardly be more heterodox from the point of view of the Classical hierarchy of the planets or more suggestive in terms of Medieval arithmetic and harmonics. For what is described is the suspension of Mars, the central heaven of Dante's universe, between two symmetrical quaternary *tetractys*:

Musica 1.10–28. For the Greek background, see Bouché-Leclercq, *L'Astrologie grecque*, 7ff., and on the speculative use of music in the Middle Ages, Manfred F. Bukofzer, "Speculative Thinking in Mediaeval Music," *Speculum* 17 (April 1942): 165–180. On the metaphysics and aesthetics of music in the Middle Ages, see Edgar de Bruyne, *Etudes d'esthétique médiévale*, vol. 1, 3–35, 306–338, and vol. 2, 108–123; and von Simson, *The Gothic Cathedral: Origins of Gothic Architecture and the Medieval Concept of Order*, 21–58. In the opening canto of *Paradise* (1.76–78) Dante accepts the idea of the harmony of the spheres which had been rejected by figures as authoritative as Aristotle and Thomas Aquinas, but perhaps only as a *bella menzogna*: a symbol of the divine origin and rational construction of the universe.

[99] *Convivio* 2.13.20. In his insistence on the symmetrical relation of the heaven of Mars to the two extremes of the planetary system, Dante might have had in mind Macrobius' discussion of the "numerical" centrality of the sun: "nam sol quartum locum obtinens mediam regionem tenebit numero, spatio non tenebit. si inter ternos enim summos et imos locatur, sine dubio medius est numero" (*Commentarii* 1.19.15). Dante's idea that Mars stands at the center of the cosmos is somewhat unusual but can be found in *De Mundi Coelestis Terrestrisque Constitutione*, Migne PL 90, col. 898, a treatise attributed to Bede: "Mars positus [est] in centro mundi."

UNICA SPES HOMINUM 155

the founding numerical progression of Pythagorean/neo-Platonic speculations about the construction of the universe. The quaternary *tetractys*, the first and foremost of the ten noted in Theon Smyrnaeus' *Mathematikon* (the second being the famous "Lambda" diagram employed by Plato's demiurge in structuring the World Soul), consists of the simple addition of 1 + 2 + 3 + 4 whose sum is the perfect number 10 or the *decad*: a number viewed in this mystical arithmetic as the universal number embracing all other numbers, the nature of number itself, the very embodiment of universal harmony and reason.[100]

Hence Chalcidius describes the first *tetractys* as the fountain out of which spring all other harmonies:[101]

---

[100] The *tetractys* was usually thought of as an equilateral triangle of dots (the same pattern as that of bowling pins):

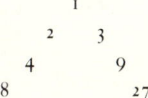

In the "first" or "quaternary" *tetractys* its components are simply added up to produce the decad. In the "second" *tetractys* they are multiplied producing the Lambda diagram:

$$\begin{array}{ccc} & 1 & \\ 2 & & 3 \\ 4 & & 9 \\ 8 & & 27 \end{array}$$

The individual digits on opposing axes are then combined in various ratios to produce the musical octaves. Each of these images serves to describe the derivation of the multiple out of the one, an image present in canto 15: "Tu credi che a me tuo pensier mei / da quel ch'è primo, così come raia / da l'un, se si conosce, il cinque e 'l sei" (55–57). (The "se si conosce" here sharply underscores the hermetic character of this sort of numerology.) The key texts as far as Dante is concerned are Macrobius' *Commentarii*, which only briefly treats the actual *tetractys* (1.6.40–41) but is filled with speculations about magic numbers and musical proportions; and Chalcidius' commentary on the *Timaeus*, which contains extensive discussions of the *tetractys*, Pythagorean harmonics, and arithmetic (see *Platonis Timaeus Interprete Chalcidio* 35–55). On Plato's use of Pythagorean harmonics and arithmetic in the *Timaeus*, the best introduction is Cornford's *Plato's Cosmology*, 66–72.

[101] "Decimanum numerum Pythagorici adpellant primam quadraturam, propterea quod ex primis quattuor numeris confit: uno, duobus, tribus, quattuor. Symphoniae quoque ratio ex eorundem numerorum, qui decimanum numerum

The Pythagoreans refer to the tenth number as the first tetrad [set of four], therefore, because it is the product of the first four numbers: one, two, three and four. Out of these numbers which form the tenth, the ratio of harmony flows as from a fountainhead: since from them 4:3 and 3:2 and double and triple and quadruple numbers and sounds come into being.

Confirmation of Dante's extensive familiarity with speculations of this sort can be found in a portion of the *Convivio* which immediately follows the above-cited discussion of Mars: his allegorization in 2.14.3 of the Milky Way and the heaven of the fixed stars. Considering the "one thousand and twenty-two sidereal bodies" which the "ancient Egyptians" believed to occupy the starry heavens, he offers the following numerological interpretations:

> per lo due s'intende lo movimento locale, lo quale è da uno punto ad un altro di necessitate. E per lo venti significa lo movimento de l'alterazione; ché, con ciò sia cosa che *dal diece in su non si vada se non esso diece alterando con gli altri nove e con se stesso*, e la più bella alterazione che esso riceva sia la sua di se medesimo, e la prima che riceve sia venti, ragionevolemente per questo numero lo detto movimento significa.

> (By the number two, local movement [locomotion] is to be understood, for it is by necessity from one point to another. And by the number twenty the movement of alteration [motion with change of quality] is signified; since it is the case that *to proceed upwards of ten one can but modify ten by the other nine numbers and by itself*, and the most beautiful alteration to which it is subject is alteration by itself [10 + 10 + . . .], the first product of which is twenty, it is logical that said movement should be designated by this number.) [italics and insertions mine]

The reference to the all-encompassing character of the decad here might in itself seem insignificant were it not for the impor-

---

conplent, quasi quodam fontem demanat: siquidem ex his epitriti et sescuplares et duplices et triplices et quadruplices numeri sonique nascuntur" (*Platonis Timaeus Interprete Chalcidio* 35).

tant verbal and thematic strains that connect *Convivio* 2.14 to the heaven of Mars.

That this chapter from the *Convivio* was fresh in Dante's mind when he composed the Martial cantos we can surmise from 2.14.7, where he writes:

> Ne la Vecchia dice [Aristotile] che la Galassia non è altro che moltitudine di stelle fisse in quella parte, tanto picciole che *distinguere* di qua giù non le potemo, ma di loro apparisce *quello albore*, lo quale noi chiamiamo Galassia.

> (In the old translation he [Aristotle] says that the Galaxy is nothing more than a multitude of fixed stars in that part, so small that we cannot *distinguish* them from here below, but from them comes *that whiteness* which we call the Milky Way.) [my italics]

Of the many echoes of this passage in canto 14, two are particularly salient: the description in 14.97–98 of the galactic cross as "pricked out" or *distinta* with greater and lesser lights ("Come distinta da minori e maggi / lumi"), recalling the first of the extracts I have italicized; and the reference in 14.108 to "that whiteness" (*quell' albor*) in which Christ shines forth ("vedendo in quell' albor balenar Cristo"), which recalls the second.[102] Both passages also insist on whiteness ("bianco cerchio" [*Conv.* 2.14.1], "biancheggia tra' poli" [14.98]), on dense multitudinous constellations ("molte stelle" [*Conv.* 2.14.1], "minori e maggi / lumi" [14.97–98], "sì costellati" [14.100], "molte corde" [14.119]), and on the minuteness of the individual lights ("moltitudine . . . tanto picciole" [*Conv.* 2.14.1], "le minuzie d'i corpi" [14.114]). In addition, both are associated with the fable of Phaeton: noted in *Convivio* 2.14.5 as the mythological account for the origin of the Milky Way, and

---

[102] Although some manuscripts read "arbor," Dante almost certainly intended the play on "albor" as both "dawn" and "whiteness." As in the later white-on-white images of cantos 15 and 18, the emphasis is on the superimposition of light on light: the metamorphosed Christ flashing forth on the fulgurant cross just like the star-souls shuttling up and down and from horn to horn in 14.109–111 along the crossbeams of light.

cited at the beginning of canto 16 (as it is in *Inferno* 17.107 and *Purgatory* 4.72 and 29.118) as a negative exemplum.

Perhaps most interesting of all, however, is the eschatological focus of both passages: in *Convivio* 2.14.13 Dante concludes on the basis of the galaxy's rotation that "we are now in the last age of the world and truly await the consummation of the celestial movement" ("noi siamo già ne l'ultima etade del secolo, e attendemo veracemente la consummazione del celestiale movimento"). I take it for granted that the apocalyptic character of the "venerable sign" of cantos 14–18 hardly needs to be argued at this point. There is, last but not least, the matter of Dante's allegory of the two celestial poles in *Convivio* 2.14.9–13, whose relevance to the cross of light cannot be discounted. The Northern pole, because it is visible to man, represents, Dante suggests, the natural and corruptible things which are the concern of the science of Physics. The Southern pole, because of its invisibility, represents the suprasensate and incorruptible things which are the concern of Metaphysics. Inasmuch as the Martial cross of light at the center of Dante's *Paradise* overspans the cosmic poles, bridging the gap between the visible and invisible, the natural and supernatural, the historical and eternal, its links to this allegorical "Galaxy" are less than casual.

Now, to return from this brief digression to the numerological question, it just so happens that there is a prominent and all-embracing musical 10 in the central heaven of the final canticle which is itself composed of a pair of "elegant" modifications of 10: the two 270 ($[3 \times 3 \times 3] \times 10$) verse sections which divide canto 16 into 77 verse halves. According to the account from *Convivio* 2.13, it is indeed the source out of which four ordinal numbers proceed in symmetrical fashion: "the two first, the two second, the two third, and the two fourth." This "ten" is Christ's cross: the X-shaped "joining of quadrants in a circle" (14.102) which rises over Mars, signifying the Roman numeral ten—the sum of $4 + 3 + 2 + 1$ and $1 + 2 + 3 + 4$, whether one counts from Mars toward the Empyrean or the earth or vice versa.[103] While this interpretation is a hermetic and admittedly quite speculative one, it suggests just how, by shifting the special tempering and harmonizing role of the sun onto an eschatological cruciform *Eliòs* located in the central heaven of Mars but nevertheless a galactic "X" spanning the poles of the universe,

[103] Peter Dronke has noted the importance in *Paradise* 14 of images of flux, reflux, and of numerical reflectivity in "*Orizzonte che rischiari*: Notes toward the Interpretation of *Paradiso* XIV," in *Romance Philology* 29 (August 1975): 1–19. The canto opens with the simile of a vase ("Dal centro al cerchio, e sì dal cerchio al centro" [14.1]), which would seem to in turn recall a simile from Boethius' *De Institutione Musica* 1.14 ("quod crescentes undas possit offendere, statim motus ille revertitur et quasi ad centrum"). Some thirty verses later we find the following description of the mystery of the Trinity:

> Quell' uno e due e tre che sempre vive
> e regna sempre in tre e 'n due e 'n uno,
> non circunscritto, e tutto circunscrive   14.28–30

These arithmetic-musical references clearly prepare the way for the later allusion to the procession of the five and six out of the one ("raia / dal un, se si conosce, il cinque e 'l sei" [15.57]), the reversible 1–2–3–4's that surround the heaven of Mars, and the musical imagery of cantos 14–18. Links between the *decad*, Plato's Timaean "Chi," and the cross are not infrequent in texts from the Chartrian milieu. The opening *prosa* of Alan of Lisle's *De Planctu Naturae*, for instance, makes use of the verb *decussare* in a description of the double part which makes Natura's head an image of the cosmos:

> A twofold hair-band, parting the hair, did not ignore the regions above nor disdain to grant earth a caressing smile. What one might call a length of lily-white path, forming a crosswise demarcation [decussata], separated struggling locks.

The Plaint of Nature, trans. James J. Sheridan, 73–74. *Decussare* is a relatively common verb in this text as well as in the *Anticlaudianus*, and, like *addobbare*, means primarily to ornament or decorate, being derived from "decus" and the Greek *doxa*: "ornament, grace, embellishment, splendor, glory, honor, dignity" (Lewis and Short, *A Latin Dictionary*, 524). Its secondary, and in the case of the cross, complementary, meaning is to shape "in the form of a Roman ten (X), crosswise" (*ibid.*). In his notes, Sheridan points out various usages of the verb from Cicero's lost *Timaeus* to Christian texts such as the *Vita Sancti Gerardi* and *Vita Sancti Diecoli* (in which its usage is precisely analogous to that of "addobbare").

Dante adapts a heliocentric neo-Platonic cosmology, epistemology, and harmonics to Christian ends, giving Classical solar imagery, I repeat, a new historical and apocalyptic focus. The result is a series of deliberate inversions: a Martial heaven which is oddly enough the heaven of harmony and music, a blinding Mars who opens up clear and precise visions of an eternally peaceful future. But they are paradoxes uniquely suited to the Christian theology of the cross.

For once Dante seems to have followed the planetary symbolism of the *Convivio* in the third canticle, since from the opening invocation of Christ/*Eliòs*/(Apollo), so rich in hymnic echoes and allusions, to the closing reference to Cacciaguida's lyrical artistry ("qual era tra i cantor del cielo artista" [18.51]), the heaven of Mars is indeed enclosed in the rapturous music of the cross. Only half intelligible to human ears, it is produced by the body of Christ, his "holy strings" ("sante corde" [15.5]), invisibly strummed by the "right hand of heaven" ("la destra del cielo" [15.6]), whether Christ himself or the hand of God:

> Benigna volontade in che si liqua
> sempre l'amor che drittamente spira,
> come cupidità fa ne la iniqua,
>   silenzio puose a quella dolce lira,
> e fece quïetar le sante corde
> che la destra del cielo allenta e tira.
>   Come saranno a' giusti preghi sorde
> quelle sustanze che, per darmi voglia
> ch'io le pregassi, a tacer fur concorde?   15.1–9

(Gracious will, wherein right-breathing love always resolves itself, as cupidity does into grudging will, imposed silence on that sweet lyre and quieted the holy strings which the right hand of Heaven slackens and draws tight. How shall those beings be deaf to righteous prayers, who, in order to prompt me to beg of them, became silent with one consent?)

Once again we must return to the language of paradox, for the actual instrument of Christ's torture (a *fidicula*) is imagined as transformed into an instrument of joy and faith: a celestial lyre (or *fides*) which, in the heaven of discord, wrath and war, provides a sublime example of utopian *concordia*.[104]

From an iconographic standpoint, the cross as lyre is not an unusual motif.[105] It is as much a product of the association of Christ with the figures of Apollo, god of poetry and music, and Orpheus, musical tamer of nature and beasts, as of the patristic identification of the cross with the lyre of David.[106] A number of

[104] The play on *fides* (or "lyra") and *fidicula* (or "fidis") would be too oblique here to be of any significance, but in Manilius' *Astronomica* it allows for some fancy footwork in explaining away the existence according to Classical tradition of two musical constellations in the heavens: Lyra and Fides (in reality a single constellation with two names). Manilius imagines the former, and this was the conventional view, as the transfigured lyre of Orpheus: once it led the forests and rocks in its train, "nunc ducit et rapit immensum mundi revolutionibus orbem" (*Astronomica* 1.329–330). The latter he imagines as the sign of the torturer ("poenaeque minister"), who brings to light all that lies hidden under the silence of deceit. On the celestial Lyra, see Isidore, *Etym*. 3.22.8–9 and 3.62.36; and Hyginus, *Poeticon Astronomicon* 2.7 and 3.7 in *Authores Mythographi Latini*, ed. A. von Staverin, 439–441, 504–505.

[105] For examples of this iconography, see in Greenhill (361–362 and plate 1) the twelfth-century South German Psalter which represents David with his harp as a *typus Christi*; and in Füglister (147–148 and plate 7) the fifteenth-century German Old Testament illuminated by Berthold Furtmayr, which shows David playing a cross that is a harp (Bayerische Staatsbibliothek, Munich, cgm 8010 a, fol. 388ʳ). The famous miniature in the eleventh-century Book of Pericopes of Uta, Abbess of Niedermünster in Regensburg, offers an interesting variation, depicting the crucifixion as a cosmic event linked to the music of the spheres (Bayerische Staatsbibliothek, Munich, clm 13601, fol. 3ᵛ).

[106] For a contemporary identification of Apollo with Christ, see Pierre Bersuire, *Ovidius Metamorphoseos Moralizatus*, ed. F. Ghisalberti, *Studij Romanzi* 13 (1933): 107–108. On Orpheus and Christ, see John Block Friedman, *Orpheus in the Middle Ages*, 38–39; and H. Rahner, "The Christian Mystery," 379. The association of Christ's cross with the lyre of David is a commonplace found among other places in the *Allegoriae in Vetus Testamentum* of Richard of Saint Victor: "David adhuc puer in cithara suaviter, imo fortiter canens, malignum spiritum qui exagitabat Saulem compescebat: non quod ejus cithara tantam virtutem haberet, sed figura crucis Christi, per lignum et chordarum extensionem mystice gerebat, quae jam tunc daemones effugabat" (Migne PL 175, col. 692). The heptachord lyre was of course the conventional Pythagorean image of the cosmos as

additional exegetical traditions, growing up around Psalms 32 (33) and 143 (144), further reinforced the figurative ties between the cross and lyre in the minds of the Church Fathers. In one particular version, Christ's bodily self-extension over the X (or number 10) of the cross was even allegorized as the stringing of the ten-stringed psaltery, a psaltery on which the ten imperative interdictions of the Mosaic father were replaced by the "new song" (Ps. 143.9) of Jesus' incarnate love. Another version, found in Bonaventure's *Vitis Mistica*, conceives Jesus' final seven phrases on the cross as alternatively the stringing or the resonating of his cross/heptachord lute: "Your Spouse, formed to the shape of the cross, is become a harp; His body, stretching over the cross's surface, its chords."[107] Such traditions might well have had an impact on Dante's vision, especially given the arithmetic/musicological themes already considered.

But the sweet lyre of cantos 14–18 overflows the boundaries of these various exegetical traditions, and its music bears certain "urban" implications that, as I have hinted in my earlier treatment of this passage, give an added eschatological dimension to whatever harmonic and numerical mysteries it might contain.

---

a whole, a notion echoed by the *Aeneid's* Medieval commentators. The brief allusion to Orpheus and his lyre in *Aeneid* 6.645–647 was thus glossed by Servius and Isidore as a description of Orpheus as a cosmic *poeta theologus*: "Orpheus . . . qui primus etiam deprehendit harmoniam, id est circulorum mundanorum sonum, quos novem esse novimus, e quibus summus, quem anastron dicunt, sono caret, item ultimus, qui terrenus est" (*Commentarius in Vergilii Aeneidos* 6.645, Thilo/Hagen, vol. 1, 89–90). Isidore cites the passage from Virgil in *Etym.* 3.22.4–5, commenting: "Discrimina autem ideo, quod nulla chorda vicinae chordae similem sonum reddat. Sed ideo septem chordae, vel quia totam vocem implent, vel quia septem motibus sonat caelum."

[107] "Cithara tibi factus est sponsus, cruce habente formam ligni; corpore autem suo vicem supplente chordarum per ligni planitiem extensarum" (*Vitis Mistica* 7.1, Migne PL 184, col. 655). The X as Moses' *decalogus* is also a common gloss, as in Honorius of Autun: "Quae littera X in numeris decem exprimit et decalogum legis innuit. Quam Dominus non solvere, sed adimplere venit, dum crucem sustinuit" (Migne PL 172, col. 945).

Simply put, the musical cross of light foreshadows the Holy Jerusalem, an action very much in keeping with its iconographic origins, its relationship to the Transfiguration, and its role in cantos 14–18 as the oracle of Christ. Composed of *sante corde*—the play on *chorda* (or string) and *cor* (or heart) is almost certainly deliberate—the cross/lyre provides a scandalous countersign to anarchic discord of the human city.[108] Its holy chords, as will be seen in the next chapter, are also, like Dante's ancestral "living topaz" (15.85), the fulgurant gemstones out of which the apocalyptic city was to be constructed according to Revelations 21. But whether of gemstones or strings, it is masterfully ordered and tuned by the hand of its king: "the right hand of the heavens" which "slackens and draws tight" ("la destra del cielo [che] allenta e tira" [15.6]).

The vision is a utopian one, staging a symbolic integration of the anarchic and heterogeneous strings of the city of man into the transcendent unity of the sign of Christ in anticipation of history's end. "Minori e maggi / lumi" (14.97–98), "diritte e torte, / veloci e tarde" (14.112–113), "lunghe e corte" (14.114), "minori e' grandi" (15.61), equal and unequal, great and small: all are one in the cross of light. This mysterious procession of the one out of the multiple and the multiple out of the one is seconded by the plurality of instruments indentified with the musical cross: first a "viol and harp, in tempered harmony strung with many chords" ("giga e arpa, in tempra tesa / di molte corde" [14.118–119]), then a chorus of human voices (the hymn of high praise of 14.123–124), and finally a "sweet lyre" composed of "holy chords" (15.5). The terms of this integration are musical because music has always offered the discourse of the city a most powerful set of metaphors for describing the process whereby a single political subject, whether the "body politic" of Classical political theory or the Christian "body of Christ," emerges out of the chaos of the

---

[108] Isidore writes: "Chordas autem dictas a corde, quia sicut pulsus est cordis in pectore, ita pulsus chordae in cithara" (*Etym.* 3.22.6).

urban mob (the "joyous throng" or "turba gaia" of 15.60). It cannot then be coincidental that in so "urban" a portion of the poem and in a heaven identified with music, Dante should call into play one of the most venerable of urban/political themes: the theme of *concordia discors* (discordant concord) or, as Augustine would have it, *discordia concors* (concordant discord).[109]

Following Plato, Cicero had envisioned the government of the city as an illustration of this musical principle:[110]

> For, as in the music of lyre and flute and as even in singing and spoken discourse there is a certain melody [*concentus*] which must be preserved in the different sounds—and if this is altered or discordant it becomes intolerable to the ears of a connoisseur—and as this melody is made concordant and harmonious in spite of the dissimilar sounds of which it is composed, so the state achieves harmony by the agreement [*consensu*] of unlike individuals, when there is a wise blending of the highest, the lowest and the intervening middle

---

[109] The itinerary of this analogy through history has been traced, although by no means exhaustively, by Leo Spitzer in his *Classical and Christian Ideas of World Harmony*. The most influential single statement is almost certainly that of Plato, who in the *Republic* constantly imagines the well-ordered life, the well-ordered household, well-ordered city and well-ordered universe (in ascending order) as a telescoping of harmonious and law-bound forms of organization. It is sometimes forgotten that the *Timaeus* also mirrors this progression and particularly so in Chalcidius' incomplete text: beginning with the history of the city and ascending into the musical laws which are the structuring principle of the World Soul (the heavenly model for the government of the city). Law is inseparable in this tradition from music: just as Orpheus "civilized" nature, Amphion moved stones by music to build Thebes, Solon sang the laws, Parmenides and Tyrtaeus were oral poets, city founders, and lawmakers. See Horace, *Ars Poetica*, 391–407, for a brief summation.

[110] "Ut enim in fidibus aut tibiis atque ut in cantu ipso ac vocibus concentus est quidam tenendus ex distinctis sonis, quem inmutatum aut discrepantem aures eruditae ferre non possunt, isque concentus ex dissimillimarum vocum moderatione concors tamen efficitur et congruens, sic ex summis et infimis et mediis interiectis ordinibus ut sonis moderata ratione civitas consensu dissimillimorum concinit; et quae harmonia a musicis dicitur in cantu, ea est in civitate concordia" (*De Re Publica* 2.42). Eng. trans. by G. H. Sabine and S. B. Smith from *On the Commonwealth*, 193.

classes in the manner of tones. And what musicians call harmony in song is concord in a state.

Saint Augustine, having already cited the Ciceronian passage in Book Two of *De Civitate Dei* (2.21.1), adapts the same notion to a Christian end, imagining the *pax urbana* in the image of musical concord:[111]

> The peace of the political community is an ordered harmony [*concordia*] of authority and obedience between citizens. The peace of the heavenly City lies in the perfectly ordered and harmonious communion of those who find their joy in God and in one another in God. Peace, in its final sense, is the calm that comes of order. Order is the arrangement of like and unlike [*parium disparium*] things whereby each of them is disposed in its proper place.

But as Leo Spitzer has pointed out in *Classical and Christian Ideas of World Harmony*, what is striking in Augustine's use of musical imagery is the sudden disappearance of any emphasis on *dissonance*.[112] Dissonance, discord, war and alterity: the Martial forces which in the Stoic and Heraclitean cosmos must be violently constrained in order to produce the mysterious fusion out of which emerges a higher harmony, are all transformed into mere perceptual and hermeneutic obstacles—a reduction which is an essential part of the scenario of Dante's "interpretive conversion" in cantos 14–18.

In Augustine's eschatological city all illusions of difference fall

---

[111] "Pax civitatis ordinata imperandi atque oboediendi concordia civium, pax caelestis civitatis ordinatissima et concordissima societas fruendi Deo et invicem in Deo, pax omnium rerum tranquillitas ordinis. Ordo est parium disparium rerum sua cuique loca tribuens dispositio" (*De Civ. Dei* 19.13.1). Trans. by Walsh et al., *The City of God*, 456.

[112] "Whereas the Stoics (like Heraclitus) had thought of harmony as forcing together the inimical, Augustine has in mind rather the ability of harmony to smooth out apparent discord—as the 'inner ear' of the believer hears the unity underlying diversity. Thus the *concordia discors* foreshadows the differentiated harmony of the saints—and the organ is symbol of the *discordia concors* of world music" (*Classical and Christian Ideas of World Harmony*, 40).

away once we open up our inner ear to history's secret harmony:[113]

> So even at that time there shall be differences between God's saints, yet they shall be consonant and not dissonant differences, assenting and not dissenting differences: just as the sweetest harmony emerges from sounds indeed diverse [*diversis*] from one another, but not opposed to one another [*inter se adversis*].

This same eschatological concordant discord informs Richard of Saint Victor's vision of the celestial *ecclesia* with Christ as its lutist/king and brings us even closer to the vision of cantos 14–18:[114]

---

[113] "Habebunt enim etiam tunc sancti Dei differentias suas consonantes, non dissonantes, id est consentientes, non dissentientes; sicut fit suavissimus concentus ex diversis quidem, sed non inter se adversis sonis" (*Ennarationes in Psalmos*, Migne PL 37, col. 1964). Boethius comes closer to the Stoic/Pythagorean insistence on discord: "est enim harmonia plurimorum adunatio et dissententium consensio" (*De Institutione Arithmetica* 2.32). The shift in emphasis that Spitzer has noted results from the availability to Christians of a divine (and I would suggest "utopian") model of temporal succession which claims to abolish all difference and negativity: that of "promise" and "fulfillment." Christ comes not to "replace" or "abolish" the Mosaic father and his law, but rather to "fulfill" both. The "New" Testament is not the conqueror of the "Old" Testament but its "fulfillment." The Trinity is the other Christian model, and through its insistence on consubstantiality within the diversity of the divine persons, it again claims to extricate father and son, eternity and history, past and present, from any Oedipal or competitive network.

[114] "Superius iam assignavimus quam sint multiplices, vel multiformes, humani cordis affectus. Hos utique ille Domini Spiritus quotidie in electis suis paulatim contemperat, et in unam harmoniam conformat, et gratiae suae plectro quasi citharoedo doctissumus hos extendendo, illos relaxando ad concordem quamdam consonantiam coaptat, donec reboet ex his in auribus Domini Sabaoth melodia quaedam melliflua et supra modum dulcis, tanquam citharoedorum multorum citharizantium in citharis suis. Sed si tam mira harmonia et tam multiplex consonantia surgit de corde uno in tanta pluralitate tam multiplicium affectionum, quae, quaeso, vel quanta erit illa supercoelestium animorum consona concordia, concorsque consonantia in tanta multitudine tot milium angelorum, tot animarum sanctarum exsultantium et laudantium viventem in saecula saeculorum" (*Benjamin Maior* 3.24, Migne PL 196, col. 134) Eng. trans. from Zinn, *The Twelve Patriarchs*, 257–258. A similar notion is found, according to Spitzer (p.

We have already indicated above how manifold and diverse the affections of the human heart are. Yet the Spirit of the Lord daily combines [*contemperat*] them little by little in His elect and skillfully forms [*conformat*] them into one harmony and by the plucking instrument of His graces fits them together in a certain harmonious consonance like a learned harp player who stretches [*extendendo*] these and loosens [*relaxando*] those, until a certain melody, mellifluous and sweet beyond measure, resounds from them into the ears of the Lord Sabaoth as if from the playing of many harpers upon their harps [cf. Rev. 14:2]. But if so marvelous a harmony and so mainfold a consonance arises from one heart [*corde*] in so great a plurality of so many affections, what, I ask, or how much will be that consonant concord [*consona concordia*] and concordant consonance [*concorsque consonantia*] of supercelestial souls in so great a multitude of so many thousands of angels and so many holy souls exulting and praising Him who lives without end?

With its focus on the paradox of singleness in multiplicity and of harmony in apparent dissonance, its image of the Lord as the expert instrumentalist now relaxing (*allentando/relaxando*) now tightening (*tirando/extendendo*) the heavenly city's heartstrings, Richard's "melody, mellifluous and sweet beyond measure" could hardly be closer to the *melode* of 14.122 with its rapturously sweet shackles ("dolci vinci" [14.129]), or, for that matter, to the vision of the celestial rose in the Empyrean. But with characteristic brilliance Dante injects such utopian imagery into a more properly epic-dialectical setting, often bringing us right to the edge of a sort of Stoic-Heraclitean dualism, while never fully abandoning Augustine's concordant discord.

So the cross of light does not appear in cantos 14–18, as an unmotivated or autonomous sign. Rather, it is indissociable from the turbulent text of history against which it is profiled. The dynamic interchange that results between eternal cross and historical cross, eternal city and historical city, eternal Father and his-

---

35), in Honorius of Autun: "Summus opifex universum quasi magnam citharam condidit in qua veluti varias chordas ad multiplices sonos reddendos posuit."

torical son, powerfully dramatizes the very real difficulties of achieving any grand harmonization of opposing terms. And yet what prophecy reveals at the center of *Paradise* is ultimately more akin to Augustine's *discordia concors* than to the more conflictual *concordia discors*: not conflict but the essential identity of apparent contraries, and this whether their actual reconciliation is an immediate or distant prospect.

An important clue to understanding this mystery may be found by returning to Dante's description of the heaven of Mars as the heaven of music in *Convivio* 2.13. There he founds the association of Mars with music on two common properties: the "most beautiful relation" of Mars to the other heavens (2.13.20) and the dryness of its heat, able to ignite surrounding vapors creating comets and shooting stars like the spinning souls of cantos 14–18 (2.13.21–22). Dante continues:

> E queste due proprietadi sono ne la Musica, *la quale è tutta relativa*, sì come si vede ne le parole armonizzate e ne li canti, de' quali tanto più dolce armonia resulta, quanto più la relazione è bella; la quale in essa scienza massimamente è bella, perché massimamente in essa s'intende. Ancora: la Musica trae a sé li spiriti umani, che quasi sono principalmente vapori del cuore, sì che *quasi cessano da ogni operazione*; sì è l'anima intera, quando l'ode, e la virtù di tutti quasi corre a lo spirito sensibile, che riceve lo suono.
>
> (And these two properties are present in Music, *which is entirely a matter of relative proportion*, as one can observe in verse and in song, from which as sweet a harmony results as the [chosen] proportion itself is beautiful; and it is always most beautiful in that science, for this is its special domain. Furthermore: with such power does Music draw unto itself the spirits of men, which are as if principally vapors of the heart, that *they nearly cease all operation*; such is the state of the entire being when listening to it, and the vital spirits of all almost rush to the sensate faculty that receives the sound.)
> [2.13.23–24; my italics]

While in the first italicized passage Dante is referring to such beautiful "relations" as the symmetrical one's, two's, three's, and four's to either side of Mars, his description seems particularly cogent when applied to Cacciaguida's representation of *historical relativity*. History under Mars is a place of constant flux subject to endless cycles of generation and degeneration. It is a "fallacious world" (15.146) where "cities have their end" (16.78) and where "your affairs all have their death, as do you" ("vostre cose tutte hanno lor morte, / sì come voi" [16.79–80]). The source of this founding negativity is death itself, a state mimed by the sensual transport that Dante describes as the effect of music: the human faculties that "nearly cease all operation."

And yet this negativity we call history is none other than the divinely authored text of revelation: God's *allegoria in factis*, his providential "great volume in which white and dark are never altered" (15.51), whose seeming contingencies are "all depicted in the Eternal Vision" ("tutta è dipinta nel cospetto etterno" [17.39]. The apparent cacophony of history, with all of its blindness, madness, confusion, and flux is then no less than the music of eternity. Its relativity is God's mysterious *disciplina*, serving to elevate man to a higher perspective, to an understanding of the beautiful and harmonious logic which pervades the text of history. It opens up our inner ear to the universal symphony of hymning harps, viols, organs, and sweet lyres. And the privileged instrument of this transcendence is the venerable sign of the cross: the hermeneutic moment of the divine text, its crux and turning point. Through it the eschatological harmony of God's *organum* (17.44) finally reaches mortal eyes and ears.

V

SANT' APOLLINARE IN CLASSE AND DANTE'S POETICS OF MARTYRDOM

> . . . dentro al templo
> che si murò di segni e di martìri.
>
> *Paradise*, 18.122–123

Introduction

Virgil, it seems, was not entirely mistaken in his identification of Christ as a "Mighty One" and of his sign as a "sign of victory." Yet beyond the reach of Virgil's gaze was what Dante believed to be the ultimate reality of Christ's power and victory on the cross: a promise that all Martial categories and perspectives would be abolished once and for all. Beyond, then, the transcendence of history implicit in the Classical formula *harmonia est concordia discors*, Christ's sign of victory opens up the prospect of an apocalyptic transfiguration of history modeled after the differentiated harmony of the saints: Augustine's "concordant discord."

Yet, despite this promise of peace, it should not be forgotten that cantos 14–18 remain an apology for the necessity of war, or, to be more exact, *just* war. The epic equations between sacrifice and deification, historical loss and eternal gain, present war and ultimate peace, so central to Virgil's Book 6, Cicero's *Somnium*, and Dante's Martial cantos, remain fully in force. Cyclical violence continues to haunt the earthly city (be it Florence or Rome), requiring the supplement of prophecy as a temporary remedy, the supplement of the otherworld as a definitive one. But superadding an eschatological—which is to say, historical—dimension onto this otherworld, Dante also appends an intimate and subjective one, calling attention to the mysterious sign which joins the former to the latter, the universal drama of apocalypse to that of the individual's success or failure to participate in Christ's victory on the cross.

In the preceding chapter I have emphasized the hermeneutic and epistemological background of the poet-pilgrim's interpretive conversion at the center of *Paradise*, the cross's iconographic origins and exegetical background, its role as oracle, archetype, and eschatological sign. In this final chapter I should like instead to turn by way of the mosaics of Sant' Apollinare in Classe toward the more immediate implications of both interpretive conversion and cross. In particular I should like to bring into clearer focus the role of Cacciaguida as martyr, model, and mediator, and to elucidate further the literary program that emerges at the end of canto 17 as the central message of the Martial cross of light. This program, I suggest, is one which bridges the gap between epic hero and author, opening the way for Dante's own autobiographical reenactment of Book 6 of Virgil's *Aeneid* in the *Commedia*, and in turn for a revisionary reading of Virgil's poem which identifies the fate of Aeneas with Virgil's own. Such a move is part and parcel of the "internalization" of epic instanced in Dante's own *Comedy*. It is founded on the belief that all individual biographies are potentially rooted in the model biography of Jesus Christ; all sacrificial acts, whether military or literary, potentially rooted in his cross.

Per la pineta in su 'l lito di Chiassi

Meshing the narrative of the Transfiguration with the iconography of the Exaltation of the Cross, Dante had a number of important precedents in patristic exegesis, but only one in the visual arts: the apsidal mosaics of Sant' Apollinare in Classe, Ravenna—the site, it is widely agreed, of the composition of much of the final canticle of the *Commedia*. Thematic and iconographic correspondences between the various mosaic ensembles of Ravenna and certain portions of *Paradise* have been noted casually at least since Corrado Ricci's *L'ultimo rifugio di Dante Alighieri*. In documenting Dante's final years, Ricci conclusively demonstrated not only the extent of Dante's familiarity with Ravenna and its region, but also its importance in the *Commedia* as a whole: "The Romagna region, consequently, was second only to Tuscany in its contribution of names and facts to the divine poet: undisputable proof that his life principally took place in those two regions."[1]

Others, Giovanni Pascoli among them, have seen particular affinities between the mosaics of San Vitale and the canto of Justinian, or the mosaics of Sant' Apollinare and cantos 14–18, or even between the procession depicted on the walls of Sant' Apollinare Nuovo and that of *Purgatory* 29.[2] In the impassioned dedication of *La mirabile visione* to "Ravenna, homeland of the *Divine Comedy*," Pascoli thus writes of a *Dante bizantino* whose poem is but a literary basilica in the image of San Vitale and Sant' Apollinare in Classe:[3]

---

[1] "La Romagna per tal modo offerse, dopo la Toscana, il maggior contributo di nomi e di fatti al divino poeta e nessuno vorrà certo negare non esser anche questa una prova che la sua vita si svolse massimamente in quelle due provincie." Corrado Ricci, *L'ultimo rifugio di Dante Alighieri*, 119. On Ravenna in Dante's poem, see 111ff. Ricci makes occasional references to Ravenna's mosaics but denies any real interest on Dante's part. Since the time of Ricci a voluminous bibliography has accumulated on the subject of Dante's stay in Ravenna, but for a recent *mise au point*, and one with interesting things to say about the possible role of Ravenna's mosaics in the *Commedia*, see Eugenio Chiarini, "Riflessioni su un vecchio problema: Dante e Ravenna" in *Atti del Convegno Internazionale di Studi Danteschi* (Ravenna, Sept. 10–12, 1971): 217–237.

[2] For a fairly complete bibliography on the Ravenna mosaics and Dante's *Commedia*, see Chiarini, "Riflessioni su un vecchio problema," 231–232. Most of the studies Chiarini cites, including those of Bosco, Cosmo, Momigliano, Apollonio, Santi Muratori, and Zovatto, are no more rigorous in their approach than is Pascoli, and hence are of limited interest.

[3] "Il bello di queste basiliche è l'insieme, è il tutto, è il complesso di oro vecchio e di legno putre, è il sentor d'umido e di sepolcro, è l'aria di mistero e di sogno: e di queste basiliche quale è più alta, quale è più profonda, quale è più misteriosa, quale è più ricca d'oro mezzo scomparso, di musaici mezzo rotti, di strani geroglifici, di marmi, di alabastri, di madreperle d'ogni parte venute, che il Poema Sacro?" (*La mirabile visione*, xxi). On Ravenna in the *Commedia*, see esp. 258–289. Pascoli's writings on Ravenna have been assembled into a single volume entitled *Giovanni Pascoli: Ravenna e la Romagna negli "Studi Danteschi."*

The beauty of these basilicas is their total effect, the whole, the comingling of antique gold and of moldering wood, the musty and sepulchral aroma, the air of mystery and of dreams: and of these basilicas which is more sublime, which more profound, which more mysterious, which more ornamented with half-vanished gold, with mosaics half-crumbled, with dark hieroglyphs, with marbles, with alabasters and with mother of pearl come from the world over, than the Sacred Poem?

Pascoli's remarks have in a sense been followed up by William Stephany and Christie Fengler, who have more recently suggested certain analogies in technique between the final canticle and the mosaic method.[4] But the casual and impressionistic character of Pascoli's observations remains typical, and regrettably so, of the majority of contemporary references to the entire question of thematic and iconographic links between the Ravenna churches and Dante's *Paradise*.[5] The lack of a single systematic

---

[4] "The Visual Arts: A Basis for Dante's Imagery in *Purgatory* and *Paradise*," in *The Michigan Academician* 10 (Fall 1977): 127–141. "Dante's artistic problem in *Paradise* is to create visual images for such a heaven, where light retains its conceptual unity even while its reflections are scattered abroad. One of his principal solutions, especially after the Circle of the Sun, is to describe his several visions of the saved as mosaic images akin to the ones he would have encountered in the city of Ravenna, where he completed *Paradise*. The dominant artistic character of Ravenna, then as now, was found in its many splendid sixth-century Byzantine mosaics. These works embody visual principles which, in direct contrast with the practices of Dante's contemporaries, are intentionally non-naturalistic, abstract, and other-worldly" (137–138). The affinity between Ravenna's mosaics and *Paradise* is then not only an iconographic and conceptual one, but also one of pictorial/poetic technique, of a common attitude toward pictorial/poetic "materials," and desire for similar pictorial/poetic "effects." Fengler and Stephany go on to make the most radical proposal for a "visual" rereading of the *Commedia* of which I am aware. On the heaven of Mars, see especially 138, 140–141.

[5] Notable exceptions are the Fengler/Stephany article cited above and Rachel Jacoff's forthcoming "Sacrifice and Empire: Thematic Analogies in San Vitale and the *Paradiso*" (in vol. 1, *Renaissance Studies in Honor of Craig Hugh Smyth*, eds. A. Morrogh et al.), a suggestive exploration of the political/sacrificial language of canto 6 of *Paradise* in relation to the iconographic program of the mosaics of San Vitale.

study of this matter is all the more striking given the fairly voluminous bibliography devoted to the illuminated manuscripts of the *Commedia* and the poem's presence in the visual arts from Botticelli through Doré and Blake.[6]

As for the question of a possible dependence on Dante's part upon the apsidal mosaics of Sant' Apollinare, the state of affairs is essentially the same: scattered remarks here and there but not a single in-depth study. Much has been made by Ricci and Pascoli, and in the case of the latter not without a certain *campanilismo*, of Dante's comparison in *Purgatory* 28.20 of Eden with the pine forest on Classe's shore ("la pineta in su 'l lito di Chiassi"), the location of the church of Sant' Apollinare. Unless we assume that Dante chose to restrict his wanderings to the grounds, the simile would indeed seem to suggest the particular esteem which Dante reserved for both site and structure.

But despite this reference in *Purgatory*, few Dantists—the *pauci, quos aequus amavit Iuppiter?*—appear to have ventured inside for a closer look at the apsidal mosaics, or, having done so, they appear to have recoiled at the prospect of "lowering" the "sacred poem" to the level of a work of art which they believed to belong to a simpler less sophisticated era. One exception is Hermann Gmelin, who in the third volume of his great *Commentary* raises the possibility of an interdependence only to reject it on the grounds that the cross at Sant' Apollinare is not perfectly symmetrical:[7]

---

[6] The fundamental text is the two-volume Peter Brieger, Millard Meiss, and Charles S. Singleton, *Illuminated Manuscripts of the Divine Comedy*. For further bibliography on Dante and the Visual Arts, see the entry under "Arti Figurative" by Fortunato Bellonzi in the *Enciclopedia Dantesca* 1.401.

[7] "Die Vision des im Kreuze aufleuchtenden Christus ist vermutlich eine Bild-Imitatio: er könnte in dem Apsismosaik von Sant' Apollinare in Classe bei Ravenna ein Kreuz auf Sternengrund sehen, in dessen Mitte das Antlitz Christi steht; es ist allerdings kein griechisches Kreuz wie das des Mars-himmels." *Kommentar: III Tiel—Das Paradies*, 280. Another exception is Eugenio Chiarini, who in the already cited article and in his entry on Ravenna in the *Enciclopedia Dantesca* 4.862 anticipates a few of my own arguments.

The vision of Christ flashed forth on the cross is possibly derived from a visual prototype: in the apse mosaic at Sant' Apollinare in Classe, in Ravenna, Dante could have seen a cross against a background of stars, at whose center stands the visage of Christ; it is not, however, a Greek cross, as is that of the heaven of Mars.

Without any pretense here of fully answering this objection, it should be said from the outset that even if it were valid, there is a great deal more than the simple cross of light that links cantos 14–18 to the mosaics of Sant' Apollinare: structural resemblances of such importance as to render the detail of the Latin versus Greek cross practically irrelevant.

Gmelin in fact arrived at the same conclusion, openly retracting the noted objection in the final essay of his scholarly career: the posthumous "L'ispirazione iconografica nella *Divina Commedia*."[8] In a brief survey of several passages from Dante's poem that are particularly rich in their iconographic implications—*Inferno* 28, *Purgatory* 29, *Paradise* 30, for example—Gmelin not only affirms the importance of the Ravenna mosaics to the interpretation of Dante's cross of light ("this image corresponds precisely to the cross of Sant' Apollinare in Classe and also to that of the Archbishop's Chapel"), but also announces his intention to assemble a new and important exegetical work:[9]

> I insist . . . on the almost neglected number of iconographic sources as direct and as instrumental as many well-known and frequently discussed literary ones. It is my intention to collect materials for a seventh volume to be added to my other works on Dante:

---

[8] Gmelin died in November of 1958, and this essay appeared in *Veltro* 3 (1959): 13–16.

[9] "Insisto . . . sulla quasi negletta quantità di fonti iconografiche dirette ed altrettanto effettive come molte fonti letterarie assai conosciute e discusse. Ho intenzione di raccogliere il materiale per un settimo volume della mia opera dantesca, il quale sarebbe un *Bildkommentar der Göttlichen Komödie*, cioè un commento iconografico della Divina Commedia" ("L'ispirazione iconografica nella *Divina Commedia*," 13–14).

a *Bildkommentar der Göttlichen Komödie*, that is, an iconographic commentary on the *Divine Comedy*.

Gmelin's project was of course never realized, and its legacy has been modest. Aside from recent work by a number of American Dante scholars, the promised iconographic commentary on the *Commedia* is no closer to completion than it was in 1958, the year of Gmelin's death.[10]

Another apparent exception to the flight from iconography is Giovanni Fallani, who in a recent book devoted to Dante's relation to the visual culture of the Middle Ages dedicates a page or two to San Vitale and Sant' Apollinare. In the absence, however, of any real analysis of either the relevant passages in *Paradise* or of the mosaics, Fallani arrives at the terminally meek conclusion that:[11]

> the cross which presides over Sant' Apollinare in Classe, at the center of whose bejeweled arms is Christ, calls to mind the cross which the poet conceived for the heaven of Mars, so placing the fulgurant spirits of the martyrs within the kingdom of the saved. There is a

---

[10] See, for instance, Robert Durling, "Farinata and the Body of Christ," *SIR* 2 (Spring 1981): 5–35; Anthony K. Cassell, "Dante's Farinata and the Image of the *Arca*," *Yale Italian Studies* 1 (1977): 335–370; Nancy J. Vickers, "Seeing Is Believing: Gregory, Trajan, and Dante's Art," *DS* (forthcoming), and the aforementioned articles by R. Jacoff, W. Stephany, and C. Fengler. Their distinguished predecessor was Ernest Hatch Wilkins' "Dante and the Mosaics of His *Bel San Giovanni*," *Speculum* 2 (1927): 1–10; reprinted in *Dante in America: The First Two Centuries*, ed. A. Bartlett Giamatti, 144–159.

[11] "La croce dominante in S. Apollinare in Classe, che reca al centro del motivo gemmato il Cristo, ci fa pensare alla croce che il poeta ideò per il cielo di Marte, immettendo nel regno della salvezza gli spiriti luminosissimi dei martiri. Tra le basiliche ravvenate di S. Vitale e S. Apollinare e il poema dantesco vi è un rapporto; nella *Commedia* vi è 'un nucleo poetico operante, un gusto simbolico coloristico che potrebbe definirsi approssimativamente come bizantino' " (*Dante e la cultura figurativa medievale*, 119). Ravenna is discussed on pp. 118–120, which conclude: "sembra che Ravenna (più che negli accenni espliciti), sia presente a Dante per quegli elementi che ne constituiscono l'interna forza e magico significato" (120).

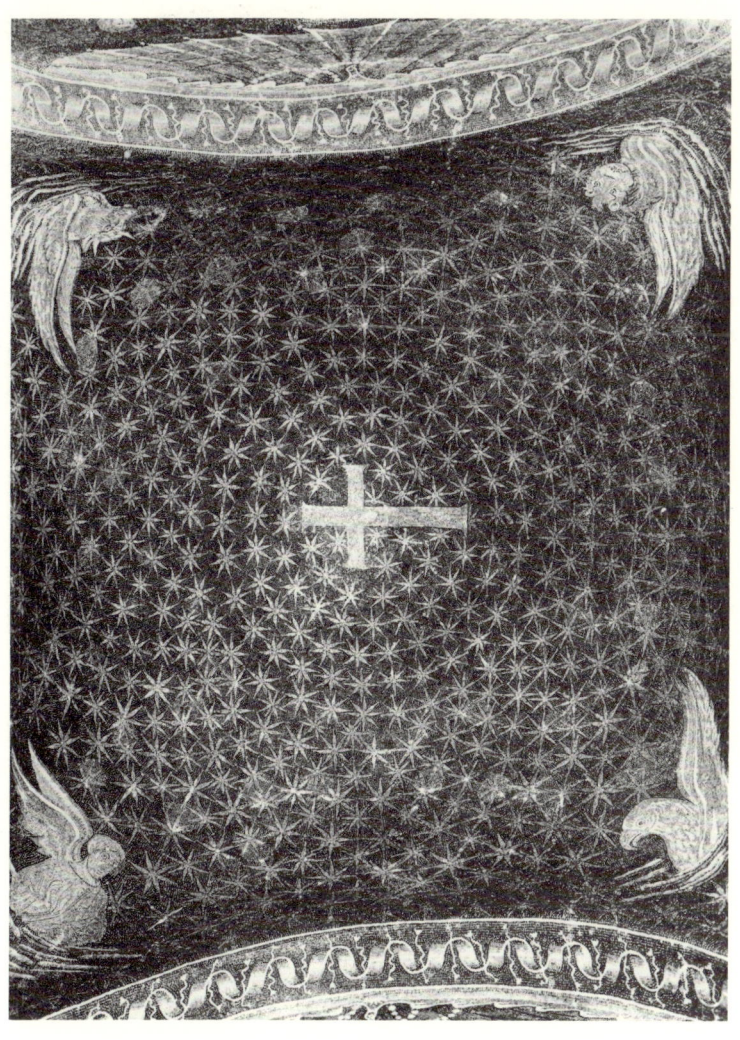

1. *The Cross against a background of stars with the four Evangelists. Mosaic, central vault of the mausoleum of the Galla Placidia, Ravenna.*

2. *The Cross against a background of stars over altar. Mosaic, chapel of the Archbishop's Palace, Ravenna.*

3. Four Angels supporting central Christogram surrounded by the four Evangelists. Mosaic, central vault of the Archbishop's Palace, Ravenna.

4. *The Lamb of God against a background of stars supported by four angels. Mosaic, central vault of the Presbyterium, San Vitale, Ravenna.*

5. *Saint Apollinaris as orant. Detail from apse mosaic, Sant' Apollinare in Classe, Ravenna.*

6. *The Vision of the Cross against background of the heavens. Central area of apse mosaic, Sant' Apollinare in Classe, Ravenna.*

7. *Clipeus with portrait of Christ. Detail from cross, apse mosaic, Sant' Apollinare in Classe, Ravenna.*

8. *Christ as universal sovereign with attendant angels, presenting martyr's crown to Saint Vitalis. Apse mosaic, San Vitale, Ravenna.*

10. *The Evangelists John and Matthew (above); procession of sheep out of Jerusalem (below). Mosaic, left side of triumphal archway, Sant' Apollinare in Classe, Ravenna.*

9. *The Transfiguration with figure of orant Saint Apollinaris below, accompanied by sheep. Full horizontal view of apse mosaic, Sant' Apollinare in Classe, Ravenna.*

11. *The Evangelists Mark and Luke (above); procession of sheep out of Bethlehem (below). Mosaic, right side of triumphal archway, Sant' Apollinare in Classe, Ravenna.*

12. The Transfiguration. Full vertical view of apse mosaic, including triumphal arch, portraits of Ravenna's Bishops and altar, Sant' Apollinare in Classe, Ravenna.

13. *The Granting of Ravenna's* Privilegia. *Left panel, apse mosaic, Sant' Apollinare in Classe, Ravenna.*

14. *The Symbolic Sacrifices. Right panel, apse mosaic, Sant' Apollinare in Classe, Ravenna.*

15. *The Vision of the Cross with orant Saint Apollinaris. Central axis of apse mosaic, Sant' Apollinare in Classe, Ravenna.*

16. *The Good Shepherd and the story of Jonah, with accompanying orant figures. Ceiling painting, chamber of the Good Shepherd, catacomb of Saints Peter and Marcellinus, Rome.*

17. *Pagan orants. Roman sarcophagus, Vatican Museum, Rome.*

18. Pagan orant. Roman Statue, Vatican Museum, Rome.

19. Christian orant (the "Donna Velata"). Wall painting, chamber of the Velatio, *catacomb of Priscilla, Rome.*

20. Noah as orant. Ceiling painting, catacomb of Pamphillus, Rome.

21. Veiled Christian orant. Ceiling painting, catacomb of Saint Callixtus, Rome.

22. *Saint Agnes as orant. Altar façade, Sant' Agnese fuori le Mura, Rome.*

connection between the Ravennate basilicas of San Vitale and Sant' Apollinare and Dante's poem; there is in the *Commedia* "an operative poetic nexus, a symbolic and coloristic taste that could, roughly speaking, be defined as Byzantine."

With the closing quotation from Pascoli we come full circle: a general "Byzantine tone" joins *Paradise* to the mosaics. (Even the unspecified "connection" is about to be partially retracted.) Again we are locked outside the basilica, left to explore the Edenic pine forest with Matelda.

In the argument that follows, but upon which the entire edifice of my interpretation of cantos 14–18 does not rest, I examine Dante's relation to the apsidal mosaics of Sant' Apollinare in Classe from an iconographic, thematic, and structural standpoint. I am not, needless to say, asserting that Dante simply translated these mosaics from visual into literary form, nor that there exists any literal-minded one-to-one correspondence between mosaics and text. Rather, I am first and foremost suggesting that these sixth-century mosaics played a decisive mediating role in Dante's Christian reworking of his Virgilian-Ciceronian models in the central cantos of *Paradise*. I am proposing, secondly, that the iconographic, thematic, and structural affinities are much greater than has been suspected. The evidence is such that the entire matter must be reopened but with a greater sensitivity to both visual and literary text. If the present study cannot pretend to fully answer Gmelin's call for an iconographic commentary on Dante's *Commedia*, it aims at least to pose in a new and provocative manner the question of the importance of the visual arts to Dante's poetics, and in particular to the poetics of the final canticle.

The Apsidal Mosaics of Sant' Apollinare in Classe

The apsidal mosaics of Sant' Apollinare represent a unique synthesis of two usually disparate types of early Christian images. Both are especially ubiquitous in the churches of Ravenna. The

CHAPTER FIVE

first type is represented by the abstract jewel-studded cross of light which occupies the upper portion of the apse at Classe. In its most elementary form, encountered for instance at the mausoleum of the fifth-century Galla Placidia and in the semi-dome of the sixth-century Archbishop's Chapel, it appears against the simple background of a night sky filled with stars (Figs. 1 and 2). Linked both directly and indirectly to the decorative images of martyr's crowns, imperial *labara*, cruciform halos, christograms, enthroned crosses, medallion-crosses and wreath-crosses characteristic of the art of Ravenna, this cross of light usually appears centered on the keystone of an archway or spherical vault, a vault which clearly stands for the dome of the heavens. This is the case not only at the Galla Placidia but also in the vault of the Archbishop's Chapel, where we encounter a central nimbus-encircled christogram supported by four angels and surrounded by the evangelists, and in a more oblique sense, in the vault at San Vitale, where the *Agnus Dei* appears against a starry background in a central orb supported by four angels perched on globes (Figs. 3 and 4).[12] The structural allegory is self-evident: Christ the *cosmoscrator* is the keystone of the universe, an idea which the central placement of the cross in the apses of Classe and the Archbishop's Chapel attempts to translate to the semi-dome.

The second type of image that contributes to the unusual synthesis of Sant' Apollinare is that which is encountered in the lower portion of the apse. Here Saint Apollinaris, like the many other saints, martyrs, bishops, and emperors ornamenting the walls of Ravenna's churches, is represented frontally in the *orant* pose, imitating Christ as he attests to his own Christlike piety (Fig. 5). The figure of Apollinaris, with its personalized facial features and identifying liturgical robe, represents a relatively advanced stage in the development of the orant from the entirely

---

[12] For an interesting comparison, see the vault mosaics of the baptistry of the cathedral of San Giovanni in Fonte, Naples, where a double-crowned Constantinian *labarum* appears against the backdrop of the starry heavens.

schematic representations of Classical *Pietas* in late Antiquity to the full-fledged orant portraiture of the later Byzantine period.

The combination of these two elements in a single unified ensemble gives to the mosaics of Sant' Apollinare the distinctive two-tier structure which certain art historians, demonstrating not only insensitivity to the pictorial logic of the mosaics but also a general ignorance of their theological program, once supposed to have resulted from the simple superimposition of two unrelated compositions. A similar move has characterized much of the scholarship concerned with the Martial cantos of *Paradise*, and as a result here too the vision of the cross in cantos 14–18 has been divorced from Cacciaguida's discourse and prophecies, or their relation reduced to a largely circumstantial one.[13] The dynamic interplay of universal and personal crosses, so central to the meaning of the Martial cantos, has thus been lost.

This coincidence of misprisions is no accident, for the structural parallels between cantos 14–18 and the sixth-century mosaics could hardly be more striking. Both are indeed characterized by a two-tier composition; they are, as André Grabar has put it with reference to Sant' Apollinare, *mi-abstrait* and *mi-historique*.[14] But the doubling of hieratic abstraction and of historical detail, of cosmic cross and imitator of Christ, is not symptomatic of a schism in the artist's vision. Rather, it provides at Sant' Apollinare and in the *Commedia* the foundation for an extraordinarily concise thematic program, dramatizing the participation of the human city—the Christian *ecclesia* and its individual citi-

---

[13] In de Sanctis' Zurich lectures on the *Paradiso*, thus, the cross is barely noted in passing. It becomes but a decorative backdrop for the "vere pitture fiamminghe, scene di vita domestica" of canto 15 (*Lezioni*, 301).

[14] André Grabar, *Martyrium: Recherches sur le culte des reliques et l'art Chrétien antique*, vol. 2, 193. Though Grabar is specifically referring to the contrast between the "historical" Moses and Elijah and the abstract Christ, his remarks are equally if not especially applicable to the even more marked juxtaposition of Apollinaris and Christ. From the perspective of the congregation, after all, Apollinaris is the more vividly "historical" figure.

zens—in the eschatological cross of light through the person of Christ and through His privileged historical witness: *the Christian martyr*.

The cross of light at Sant' Apollinare is thus suspended, as in cantos 14–18, above the figure of a martyr who belongs to the viewers' historical collectivity: in the case of Ravenna, Saint Apollinaris, the first of the city's bishops and its only martyr. Profiled against the night sky and enclosed within a bejewelled red *tondo*, the apsidal cross appears surrounded by ninety-nine stars representing synecdochically the *magno volume* of the cosmos and also, as will later be seen, the eschatological city (Fig. 6). The one hundredth star in this symbolic cosmos of ninety-nine stars, and the one whose cruciform rays literally extend from Alpha to Omega and earth to Empyrean, is the transfigured Christ, whose visage ("sicut sol") appears on a medallion at the center of a Latin cross studded with pearls and gemstones (Fig. 7).

The cross at Classe is not, as Gmelin correctly points out, a geometrically exact "giuntura di quadranti in tondo" ("joining of quadrants in a circle" [14.102]): its bottom two quadrants are greater in size than the two upper ones because the fourth or bottom arm of the cross is exactly twice as long as the other three (which are of equal length). In a less technical sense, however, and most certainly from a symbolic standpoint, it *is* a "giuntura di quadranti in tondo": a cosmic cross of light embracing the universe, congregating the dispersed through the binding and transfiguring action of a central *sol Christi*.[15] Like Dante's galactic cross, it provides not a literal figuration of the cosmic archetype, but rather a synthetic emblem: a sign which points to the univer-

---

[15] As if to underline the cross's specifically book-like role, a Christ inscribed within a circle and crowned with a perfectly symmetrical "sign of victory" ornaments the later triumphal arch. Holding the Book of Life in his left hand, he appears immediately above the cross of light with the symbols of the four evangelists to his left and right, each bearing in turn a book. The enthroned Christ, who occupies the apse of San Vitale, also holds the Book of Life in his left hand.

sal role of the cross without pretending to mime it in any literal-minded fashion.

Confirmation of the cosmic character of the Ravenna cross can be found by turning to the nimbus which surrounds the *crux gemmata* (Fig. 6). Although this bejewelled red circle of light has not received any particular attention from art historians (due almost certainly to its conventional character), it is of some significance I believe to cantos 14–18.[16] First and foremost, it renders plausible the connection between the mosaics of Sant' Apollinare and the Martial cantos, inasmuch as in both color and function this *tondo* is amenable to one of the most distinctive and symbolically charged eccentricities of Dante's own cross of light: Dante's is a cosmic cross in the image of the Milky Way ("biancheggia tra' poli del mondo" [14.98]) which appears not among the fixed stars of cantos 22–27, where one might expect it, but rather in the central heaven of Mars. It is this astronomical doubleness that permits the powerful dramatization of the themes of the Exaltation of the Cross that I have called attention to in an earlier chapter. Only against a Martian backdrop "ruddier than its wont" (14.87) can the cross of light so vividly illustrate the triumph of resurrected life over death, light over blood, Christ/Helios over Mars/*mors*. This astronomical doubleness, furthermore, permits Dante to have it both ways in terms of the positioning and scale of his cross: enabling it to be located at the planetary hub of *Paradise*—a move which in turn leads to the shifting of numerous attributes onto it from the sun—without sacrificing the idea that it is all-embracing, like the Milky Way, the outermost sphere of the Ptolemaic universe.

While the coloristic link with the red sphere of Mars is entirely self-evident, there is admittedly no clear indication that the be-

---

[16] One largely speculative interpretation advanced by Nordström among others is that the red circle illustrates the apocalyptic "rolling up of the heavens like a scroll" described in Isaiah 34:4 and Revelations 6:14. See Carl-Otto Nordström, *Ravennastudien: ideengeschichtliche und ikonographische Untersuchungen über die Mosaiken von Ravenna*, 132. Cf. Deichmann, *Ravenna*, vol. 2/2, 254.

jewelled red nimbus of Sant' Apollinare bears any specific cosmological meaning. There are, nevertheless, reasons besides those already adumbrated for associating it with that galactic "reddish royal crown and diadem, glittering with circling gems" flashing like lightning around the goddess Natura's head in the opening prose section of Alan of Lille's *Plaint of Nature*.[17] For the Milky Way had long been envisioned as a golden celestial crown or girdle ornamented with constellated jewels. The fable of the Milky Way's origin in Phaeton's mad voyage (*Convivio* 2.14.5) and, similarly, its reputation, akin to that of Mars, for being the site of celestial vapors and fires, make the linkage tenable in the case of Sant' Apollinare, especially so given the unmistakably cosmic character of the cross with its ninety-nine stars. The jewel-studded *tondo* must in some sense mark the vertical and horizontal limit of the cross of light, just like that celestial circle which Dante describes in canto 14 as stretching between the poles of the universe.[18]

[17] "Regalis autem diadematis corona rutilans, gemmarum scintillata choreis, in capite superne fulgurabat." English version from the J. J. Sheridan translation (p. 76). The attribution of a reddish hue to the Milky Way is far from illogical in that, like the zodiac, it was considered one of the fiery pathways of the sun. It might also be noted that the zodiac itself, or at the very least, the portion of the zodiac in the immediate vicinity of the sun, was often described as "ruddy" (as in the "Zodïaco rubecchio" of *Purgatory* 4.64).

[18] A number of traditions going back as far as Philo had connected the lapidary lists of the Old and New Testament to the heaven of the fixed stars. The zodiacal interpretation Philo proposed of the Ephod (Exodus 28:14–19) is a case in point and was often transposed to the description of the Holy Jerusalem in Revelations 21–21. On the celestial lapidary, see Jean Daniélou, "Les Douze Apôtres et le zodiaque," *Vigiliae Christianae* 13 (1959): 14–25. One further symbolism is at work in Alan's image of the "reddish crown" that is much easier to verify but no less suggestive with regard to cantos 14–18: the association of the apsidal cross inscribed within a circle with the martyr's crown and the cruciform nimbus. This is due not only to the extraordinary frequency in Ravenna of abstract representations of this kind, but also to the mosaics' visual construction: the apse's central red *tondo* is reflected in the reddish halo of Saint Apollinaris which is aligned below it. The cosmic "tropaeum," the crown of God's creation, is thus translated

Further evidence concerning the astronomical identity of the bejewelled circle as well as the cosmic character of the cross of light comes from the earlier mosaics at San Vitale, the most immediate of Sant' Apollinare's sources. In the apse of San Vitale, a youthful Christ appears as the universal sovereign enthroned on the celestial globe (Fig. 8). This globe served as an important visual prototype for the red *tondo* for a number of interlocking pictorial, exegetical, and iconographic reasons. Both ensembles are fundamentally eschatological in focus, and share a concern with martyrdom and with the dialectics of historical sacrifice and eternal reward. The intersection of horizon line and circle is identical in both compositions: a thin band of light causing each Edenic landscape apparently to fold in at the precise junction of sphere and line (Figs. 6 and 8).

Beyond this compositional device it would appear, moreover, that the apse of Sant' Apollinare essentially appropriates the entire central complex of celestial globe, throne of Judgment, Messiah, and cruciform nimbus, and translates it (leaving its compositional placement unaltered) into the unitary cross of light spanning the poles of the cosmos, an image long associated with Christ's eschatological throne (Fig. 9). The overall format of San Vitale is thus largely preserved, although in the process the paradisiac landscape which occupies its foreground more than doubles in scale. While this expanded foreground ultimately transforms the meaning of the central complex at Sant' Apollinare, staging the more "personal" and less "juridical" drama of the martyr's exemplary intercession between celestial sign of victory and individual cross, the identification of San Vitale's celestial globe with the universal *tondo* nevertheless holds.

If the cosmic *crux gemmata* of Sant' Apollinare is open to a number of the most important astronomical peculiarities of Dante's cross, the connection becomes all the more apparent

---

through Apollinaris into the more personal sign of victory available to those who answer Christ's call in a line of descent reminiscent of cantos 14–18.

when one considers the iconographic origins of the Ravenna cross. Like the "venerable sign" of cantos 14–18, there can be no question that it too is that sign celebrated in the Antiphon sung at the vespertine masses of the Invention and the Exaltation: "Hoc signum crucis erit in caelo, cum Dominus ad iudicandum venerit" ("This sign of the cross shall be in the heavens when the Lord comes in judgment"). Appearing over the horizon in a sea of clouds, it provides an anticipatory fulfillment of Christ's prophecy in Matthew 24:29–31:[19]

> And immediately after the tribulation of those days, the sun shall be darkened, and the moon shall not give her light, and the stars shall fall from heaven, and the powers of the heavens shall be moved: And then shall appear the sign of the Son of man in heaven . . . and they shall see the Son of man coming in the clouds of heaven with great power and majesty.

Its apocalyptic character is further underscored by the Johannine "Alpha" and "Omega" (Rev. 21:6, 22:13) present at the extremes of its lateral crossbar, identifying it as the sign of the Aeon, history's *arche* and *telos*, its *protos* and *eschatos* (Fig. 6). The ninety-nine stars, as has been suggested by Erich Dinkler, may stand in turn for the ninety-nine angels which, according to Cyril of Jerusalem, would accompany Jesus' *parousia* at the end of time.[20] If

---

[19] "Statim autem post tribulationem dierum illorum sol obscurabitur, et luna non dabit lumen suum, et stellae cadent de caelo et virtutes caelorum commovebuntur: et tunc parebit signum Filii hominis in caelo . . . et videbunt Filium hominis venentiem in nubibus caeli cum virtute multa et maiestate."

[20] Erich Dinkler, *Das Apsismosaik*, 64ff. The relevant text of Cyril of Jerusalem in his *Cathechism* ("De Secundo Advento"), Migne PG 33, col. 901. Although Cyril refers to the ninety-nine as lambs (with Matthew 18:12 no doubt in mind), Dinkler offers sufficient evidence to make the connection at least tenable. On the ninety-nine stars and their numerological implications, see also Deichmann, *Ravenna*, vol. 2/2, 256–258. The notion that the cross itself might be the one-hundredth star, completing thus an eschatological *saeculum* of ninety-nine plus one, is strangely absent from the art historians' discussions. This logic of 1 + 99 = 100 of course structures the *Commedia*: a poem of 1 + 99 cantos whose outermost projections—the final words of each canticle—are "stelle" in a mode analogous to

we add the cosmic cross of light with its Christ-Helios to these ninety-nine, a perfect eschatological *saeculum* of course takes form.

Perhaps even more interesting from the perspective of cantos 14–18, this sign arrives not only like the transfigured Christ to fulfill Old Testament prophecy and law—Elijah and Moses stand respectively to the left and right—but also as a sign of Judgment fulfilling the Sibyl's eighth oracle, whose acrostic ΙΧΘΥΣΣ, or "Jesus Christ, Son of God, Redeemer, Cross," appears at the apex of the vertical crossbar (Fig. 6). The presence here of the most famous of Sibylline *ambages* might well have seemed to place upon the apocalyptic sign of Sant' Apollinare the sort of specialized hermeneutic burden that it bears at the center of *Paradise*.

Although the cross of light provides a powerful clarification of the cryptic Sibylline message, its ultimate "reality"—to paraphrase von Simson—must be sought in the Transfiguration, which it invests with a singularly eschatological meaning. That the Transfiguration is the other iconographic point of reference at Sant' Apollinare, besides the Exaltation of the Cross, is attested to by the figures of Moses and Elijah, the three sheep occupying the background of the paradisiacal landscape (representing the three apostles), the hand descending out of the layer of clouds (signifying the divine "This is my beloved Son in whom I am well pleased: hear ye him"), and by the solar symbolism implicit in the placement of the medallion at the center of the cross's crossbars (Fig. 9). The dense bands of clouds which bend over the circular nimbus form a point of transition between San Vitale, the "bright cloud" of Matthew 17:5 ("nubes lucida obumbravit eos"), and the apocalyptic "clouds of heaven" of Matthew 24:30.

Yet from almost every point of view the most audacious visual association made by the creators of the apsidal mosaics was their iden-

---

the construction of the cosmos. Might not Dante have seen in the central portion of the apse at Classe a figuration of his own completed book and of its ultimate model, God's completed *magno volume*? (See, once again, Nordström, 132, on this subject.)

tification of the transfigured Christ with the "sign of the Son of man in heaven," which, as I have shown in the prior chapter, had frequently been envisioned as the eschatological "Sun of Justice" (*sol iustitiae*) which would shine eternally over the Holy Jerusalem. The scene represented in the mosaics of Sant' Apollinare, then, is quite literally the anticipatory dawning of the *sol Christi* over the eschatological city: Christ's Transfigurational sun, placed appropriately to the east, displaces the sensible sun as it rises over an earthly landscape that has been restored to its originary Edenic state. This sun which comes as the apocalyptic Tau, as a sign of cosmic recapitulation joining the four quadrants of the cosmos, the four corners of the earth, the four winds and the terrestrial climates, also arrives, consequently, as sign of Judgment: a crown rewarding the martyrs and the just, an instrument of torture to the unjust. The former are represented by Saint Apollinaris as well as by the sheep surrounding Ravenna's martyr, each symbolizing one of the twelve tribes of Israel (each of which, according to Revelations 7:5–8, was in turn to provide twelve thousand chosen souls).

Once the iconographic network produced by the conflation of Christ's Transfiguration with the Exaltation of the Cross has been brought into focus, many additional elements in the possible equation between Dante's Martial vision and the mosaics at Sant' Apollinare fall into place. The "venerable sign" of cantos 14–18, like the apsidal cross, also emerges out of the collapsing of a past event, the Transfiguration, into a future event, the Apocalypse celebrated in the mass of the Exaltation. The result is a unique fusion: a vision of the cross as the true sun of the Christian universe, a vision of the transfigured Christ as the eschatological "sign of the Son of man." This unique association of cross with sun, and substitution of cross/sun for Christ, I believe, provides a key to understanding Dante's Martial cantos.

That in cantos 14–18 the "venerable sign" joining the cosmic quadrants takes the place of an eschatological transfigured Christ seems particularly clear from the various addresses to the cross in canto 14. The cross is first invoked in canto 14 as "*O Eliòs*," although this "Eliòs" is subsequently described not as radiating *light* but rather as "radiating" or "flashing forth" *Christ*: "quella croce lampeggiava Cristo" (14.104), and in the next tercet "vedendo in quell' albor balenar Cristo" (14.108). While there is a sense in which this can be understood as the description of a semiotic spectacle, the phosphorescent X flashing Jesus' initial like a Times Square billboard, the apsidal cross offers a more precise answer: the bars of the cross which "radiate Christ" combine the fulgurant appearance of Christ at the time of his *parousia* with that his visage ("resplenduit . . . sicut sol") and vestments ("facta alba sicut nix") at the time of the Transfiguration, into a single solar sign.

This hybrid sign, like that of Sant' Apollinare, is so much the ultimate exemplar and cosmic archetype that only the most all-encompassing of similes can do it justice: similes like the galactic one of 14.99, whose pictorial double is the enclosure of the Ravenna cross within the orb of the heavens. Even so lavish an astronomical simile will be found wanting in the end: "lampeggiava Cristo, / sì ch'io non so trovare essempro degno" ("Christ so flashed forth that I can find no fit comparison" [14.104–105]). But the solution upon which Dante settles, a "profound Mars" (14.100) which circumscribes the cross with its constellated lights, could hardly be closer to the visual configuration of the mosaics at Classe, with their cross suspended against a cosmic backdrop and encircled by a red band of light.

A particular concern with the cosmic centrality of the cruciform sun further unites the cantos of Mars to the Byzantine mosaics: the former rendering the notion of "center" in terms of planetary order, the latter pictorially through the placement of Christ's visage at the symbolic hub of a celestial *tondo* (Fig. 6). Related and no less important is the shared insistence on the contrast between natural and supernatural suns: implicit at Sant' Apollinare but quite explicit in the case of cantos 14–18. Each cruciform sun arrives with the precise attributes of the natural sun: centrality, eastern rising, all-embracing rays. But it introduces the imminent prospect of an end to all flux and cyclicality. Under the cross of light the cyclical succession of seasons gives way to the perpetual spring of paradise, the violent revolutions afflicting the human city mysteriously produce the eschatological Jerusalem.

The Shepherd and the Pastoral City

This figurative link between the restoration of the eternal spring of Eden through the cross and the eternal peace of the Holy Jerusalem is of special importance to the Christian discourse of the city. If there is a single reason that garden and city are for Christians typologically one, it would have to be found in the very structure of biblical history: garden and city mark the Book's absolute historical and narrative limits. The Scriptures open with the vision of a garden and they close with advent of a (garden)/city. In an earlier chapter, I have alluded to the presence of such hybrid urban-pastoral language in cantos 14–18, and its symbiotic relationship with the Classical discourse of the city. Now I should like to turn at least briefly to its role in the mosaics of Sant' Apollinare, where, as in Dante's Martial cantos, the abstraction of the cross is surrounded by a text of history in which pastoral symbolism figures prominently.

When I say "surrounded" I mean this quite literally. Above the cross of light, on the triumphal archway that extends over the concave apse, is represented the symbolic procession of two Christian cities toward Christ.[21] On the left, or above the figure of Moses, six sheep ascend out of Jerusalem toward a Christ placed above the arch's keystone who appears sandwiched between a small cruciform nimbus rising behind him and a larger nimbus that encircles him (Fig. 10). Immediately above the figure of Elijah appears the mirror-image of this scene, except for the fact that the city out of which the flock emerges is now Bethlehem (Fig. 11). Art historians have differed in their interpretations of the triumphal archway: some, like von Simson, interpreting the symmetrical processions as symbols of the *ecclesia ex*

[21] It should be pointed out that the archway's composition contains a number of internal discontinuities in style and is of a somewhat later date than the mosaics of the apse.

circumcisione (Jerusalem) and *ecclesia ex gentibus* (Bethlehem) joined through Christ; others identifying the sheep with the twelve apostles as representatives of the church.

In any event, the symbolic implications of the scene seem indisputable: in an atmosphere replete with apocalyptic clouds, the two historical cities are abandoned by their respective citizens in order to embark on a pilgrimage up a mountain at whose apex stands Jesus Christ. Because of the hybrid iconography of the scene below, their pilgrimage must be viewed simultaneously as an individual and urban allegory. From the former perspective what appears is the individual's mystical ascent toward a vision of the transfigured (and transfiguring) Christ. As an urban allegory, we see instead a procession of the historical city out into the eschatological Jerusalem. Through Christ the divided cities and citizens are symbolically united. The immediate model for this reconciliation is found in the uppermost panel of the triumphal arch, where the four evangelists, each with their respective volume in hand, appear in symmetrical pairings to each side of Christ (Figs. 10 and 11). It is the exemplary "harmony" of their gospels, a frequent patristic topos, that is symbolized: despite the apparent disharmony of their texts, all were the bearers of a single identical message—Christ's message of salvation. Of this portion of the mosaics von Simson writes:[22]

> In this magnificent passage as in the mosaic, the dual imagery of the lambs and the two churches symbolizes the vision of mankind's ultimate reconciliation under the Divine Shepherd; in both works this vision is, moreover, related to the architecture of the basilica, the opposite walls of which, united in the *lapis angularis* (keystone), are an image of the Heavenly Jerusalem.

Indeed, nothing could be truer of the entire mosaic ensemble, whose central pictorial statement would seem to be the reconciliation of contraries (opposing scenes, walls, cities) through Christ and his cross. It is not that the visual "opposites" of Sant' Apollinare, whether groupings of sheep or opposing walls, represent

[22] von Simson, *Sacred Fortress*, 62.

true contraries: the asymmetries are of a more subtle kind, like the diverging visages of Moses and Elijah, the extra sheep to the right side of the cross, the seeming disjunction between the two lower panels. Rather, the oppositions are only apparent ones: signs of a *discordia concors*, of a multiplicity harmonized along the central compositional axis.

This is the central pictorial drama of the apse at Classe in my view. The function of this central axis is to establish a perfectly symmetrical descending chain of Christ-symbols, from the bust of Christ in the uppermost panel down through the mountaintop (at the archway's keystone), through the divine hand naming Christ as prophet and beloved Son of God, to the cross of light, to the orant figure of Saint Apollinaris, to the marble altar on which the mystery of the eucharist is celebrated (Fig. 12). This symbolic progression suggests not only the interchangeability of these signs, but also the unifying presence of Christ, his cross and sacrifice, in the hermeneutic drama of revelation. (To insist on the slight stylistic-chronological discontinuities of the upper panels would be to miss this important point.)

The horizontal tiers, to the contrary, from the four evangelists to the twelve sheep of the archway to Moses and Elijah to the three apostles to the lower twelve sheep to the four portraits of bishops with the opposing scenes of the *Autokephalia* and Symbolic Sacrifices, stage the text of history in all of its diversity, constantly structuring a play of symmetrical opposites along the central Christological axis. Out of this structural warp and woof (or intersection of syntagms and paradigms) emerges a synthetic statement of the Christian theology of history. The centering and unifying point in this statement, both vertically and horizontally, literally and figuratively, is rendered by the mosaics of Sant' Apollinare in the form of the great eschatological *signum* enclosed within a radiant circle, the point of anchorage of the entire pictorial edifice.[23]

---

[23] An examination of the geometry of the apse and triumphal arch bears this out. To note only a few of the most obvious geometrical relationships:

From the images of abandoning the city for the mountaintop of Christ's Transfiguration (or proto-*parousia*) to the downward procession of Christ-signs to the promise of an eschatological reconciliation of discordant perspectives, the analogies with Dante's vision are powerfully suggestive. If the pastoral language of Sant' Apollinare ultimately leads, as in cantos 14–18, to a fusion of the utopian and apocalyptic, there remains in these mosaics an equally important and specifically *political* dimension which could hardly have escaped Dante's keen eye. The exceptional contribution of von Simson must be recognized in this area, for of the many studies of the Ravenna mosaics only his has fully succeeded in bringing to the fore the political aspirations and program that underlie these monumental artistic gestures. The mosaics of San Vitale, as von Simson has shown, can only be fully understood once we recognize the stamp of Justinian's political vision in their conception, a vision whose importance, at least to canto 6 of Dante's *Paradise*, is considerable. They speak eloquently of the eschatological implications of the respective rules of Christ and Emperor, of the necessary symbiosis of *sacerdotium* and *imperium* (priesthood and empire), of the common or-

(a) The diameter of Apollinaris' aureole appears to be based on the two parallel lines that extend from the upper to the lower "horns" of the vertical bar of the cross of light. The figure of Apollinaris, as I later point out, is precisely crafted to the scale of the cross of light.

(b) Numerous angles in the landscape below the cross clearly are based on lines extending symmetrically either out of the medallion, or out of the arms. For instance, the half-figures of Moses and Elijah are encompassed within the two parallel arcs passing through the lower horns of the horizontal crossbar and the horns of the uppermost extremity of the cross. The neck angles of the three sheep representing the three apostles present at the Transfiguration are derived from the central medallion.

(c) Although I have not been able to confirm this through actual measurement, it would appear on the basis of photographs that the Christ medallion at the center of the cross is also at the center of the rectangle formed by the triumphal arch from its uppermost ornamental frame to the window-line. The sides of the rectangle seem to be based on a 2 to 3 ratio.

igin of their authority, of the mutuality of their law and of their participation in and imitation of Christ's universal sacrifice.[24]

Although the mosaics of Sant' Apollinare are less immediately bound to the political aspirations of Justinian, the gulf is far from absolute. There is perhaps a shift in emphasis at Sant' Apollinare away from the Justinian vision of *imperium* toward a more "local" thematics concerned in particular with Ravenna's ecclesiastical autonomy from Rome. Even so, the latter theme still bears strong imperial connotations. As von Simson has shown, a symbolism of this kind was at work in the cult of Saint Apollinaris from the very start. The martyr and first bishop of Ravenna "at the period of rivalry with the papacy, confirmed the apostolic origin of the see of Ravenna and became, in fact, the instrument of the latter's struggle for complete equality with, and eventually for independence from Rome."[25]

The scenes which appear in the lower panels of the apse at Classe, with their themes of independence from Rome and dependence upon the Emperor, are informed by such ambitions. On the panel to the left of the central altar, the ceremony of the *autokephalia*, or the granting of "self-authority" to the city, is represented (Fig. 13). The event, which actually occurred in A.D. 666, is placed under the aegis of the Roman Emperor, Constantine IV, who is shown handing the document granting Ravenna's *privilegia* to a figure who is doubtless the city's archbishop Maurus. In a manner recalling the organization of the mosaics at San Vitale, this scene is contrasted with that of the "Symbolic Sacrifices" of Melchizedek, Abraham and Abel which ornaments the opposing wall (Fig. 14): a juxtaposition powerfully identifying lawmaker with priest, and suggesting the Christological dimension of the Emperor's rule.

[24] See von Simson, 23–39. See also R. Jacoff's forthcoming "Thematic Analogies in the *Paradiso* and San Vitale," which develops many of von Simson's insights in terms of canto 6 of *Paradise*.
[25] von Simson, 51.

If not exactly part of the mosaic's foreground, then, the imperial imagery of San Vitale provides at least a significant backdrop at Sant' Apollinare. It paints the martyrdom of Apollinaris in distinctively pro-imperial shades, raising his city to the dignity of Rome through the harmonious interaction of *imperium* and *sacerdotium*. These themes are of some importance to cantos 14–18, where the martyr Cacciaguida represents himself as a Good Shepherd and Good Roman, an ideal follower both of Christ and of the Emperor Conrad III. But the symbolic reconciliation of priesthood and empire is most of all effected through the Martial cross of light: a sign of the victory and power of Christ but also, like the sign of Constantine, a military *signum* of the Emperor's crusade "against the iniquity of that law whose people usurps, through fault of the shepherds, what is your right" (15.142–144).

If in cantos 14–18 such thematic affinities with the Ravenna mosaics seem more of the oblique than of the direct kind, they at least shed some light on one of the unique features of the pastoral imagery which predominates in both works. Eden, both at Classe and at the center of Dante's *Paradise*, is a hybrid Roman and Christian construction. This is particularly true of cantos 14–18, where, from the opening remembrance of Virgil's Elysium in 15.27, to the references to "paradise" in 15.36 and 18.21, to the unornamented and chaste Florentine "ancient circle" (15.97ff.), to Cacciaguida's description of the later imbalance of "shepherds" (the Popes) and "justice" (15.144), to the description of Florence as the "sheepfold of Saint John" (16.25) forever "at rest" (16.149) and "in peace" (15.99), to finally the mention of Christ as the "Lamb of God" in 17.33, the language of the sheepfold is utilized in order to make of originary Florence an Eden in the image of the Rome of Augustus and Christ. The case of Sant' Apollinare is of course a more subtle one. Yet both the mosaics of Classe and Dante's Martial cantos look back upon this origin only to look forward in anticipation of a future apocalypse. The paradisiac landscape they reveal is a lost origin but also, more importantly, an imminent future: the return to Eden and/or Elysium is in reality the anticipation of an entirely new Eden.

In the hiatus between these images of man's beginning and his possible end, emerges what must be regarded as the central message of both works: an appeal specifically couched in the language of the sheepfold, yet calling not for immutability but rather for radical change. A pastoral language is thus heard which is addressed quite specifically to the historical present: the sacrificial language of Christ "the Lamb of God who takes away sin" ("l'Agnel di Dio che le peccata tolle" [17.33]), present through the crusader Cacciaguida and the martyr Apollinaris, figured in the sign of the cross and celebrated on the apsidal altar. It calls upon the celebrant, viewer, reader, or poet-pilgrim to participate in the mysterious metamorphosis of the sacrificial lamb, to imitate the exemplary imitators of Christ, making a symbolic "holocaust" (14.89), a literal or figurative "sacrifice" (14.92) of oneself.

The Martyr as Living Gemstone

In rehearsing the various points of contact between the celestial cross of cantos 14–18 and that of the apsidal mosaics at Sant' Apollinare, I have left one area for last because it introduces a subject of the utmost importance to both works: the role of the martyr as privileged mediator for the cross of light. While in cantos 14 and 15 Dante's cross emerges initially as a kinetically coruscating constellation of lightning bolts, meteors, and shooting stars, it is subsequently described in a manner befitting its possible artistic source of inspiration: appearing as a precious gem bejewelled—the verb is *ingemmare*—with precious living stones like the "living topaz" (15.85) who is Dante's glorious ancestor: "Ben supplico io a te, vivo topazio / che questa gioia prezïosa ingemmi" ("Yet I beg of you, living topaz who bejewel this precious gem").

The topic of the cross as a *preciosa gemma* is of course a conventional one, found in the liturgy of the Invention of the Cross (see "Ad Primas Vesperas" for the prior phrase), and in numerous Holy Cross homilies and hymns. The copious ornamentation typical of early sacramental crosses renders the theme all the more obvious. It appears transferred to the iconography of the cross of light early on, as, for example, in the Old English *Elene* in which the Emperor Constantine is described beholding a cross of light "clothed with treasure / O'er the roof of the clouds" splendidly adorned with gold and precious stones.[26] A separate tradition, present in many portions of the third canticle, notably in the vision in canto 30 of the river of Grace and celestial rose with its rubies (66) and topazes (76), had long imagined Christ's apostles, saints, and martyrs as the celestial gemstones which formed the larger gemstone of the City of God.

The metaphorical slippage between gemstones and luminary effulgences throughout Dante's *Paradise* is a natural one within the canons of Byzantine art. Originally employed to increase surface reflectivity and to achieve kinetic optical effects, gemstones soon became fully conventionalized pictographic signs for representing the presence of supernatural light. (The lapidary tradition, with its celebration of the magical, medicinal, and moral properties of stones, also played an important part.) This practice was given a special theological resonance by the words in the first Epistle of Peter concerning the construction of God's spiritual house out of *living* stones:[27]

> approaching the living stone, rejected indeed by men, but chosen and precious to God: Be you also as living stones built up [*lapides vivi superaedificamini*], a spiritual house, a holy priesthood, to offer up spiritual sacrifices, acceptable to God by Jesus Christ. (1 Peter 2:4–5)

[26] *Early English Poetry*, trans. C. W. Kennedy, vv. 88–95 (p. 181).
[27] "Accedentes lapidem vivum, ad hominibus quidem reprobatum, a Deo autem electum, et honorificatum: et ipsi tanquam lapides vivi superaedificamini, domus spiritualis, sacerdotium sanctum, offerre spirituales hostias, acceptabiles Deo per Iesum Christum."

These precious living stones, which are themselves sacrificial offerings or *spirituales hostiae*, were long interpreted in the Middle Ages as specifically referring to Christ's martyrs and to their relics. To the common themes of Christ as cornerstone, of the precious "treasure hidden in a field" which is the eternity of the heavenly realm (Matt. 13:44), of Peter as founding rock or *petra*, was thus appended a symbolism which emphasized the resurrectional implications of the martyr's self-sacrifice in lapidary terms.[28] This is the theme of God's *exaedificatio animam* found in Ambrose's *Commentary on Luke*: "[God] wishes to fully build up every soul; His wish is to conform each to salvation; His desire is to transport living stones from earth to heaven"—a construction of the city of God here on earth as well as in the heavens.[29]

---

[28] For a general introduction to the background of this tradition, see J. C. Plumpe, "*Vivum saxum, vivi lapides*: The Concept of 'Living Stone' in Classical and Christian Antiquity," *Traditio* 1 (1943): 1–14.

[29] "[Deus] vult omnem exaedificari animam; vult eam ad salutem informare; vult lapides vivos a terra ad coelum transferre" (*Expositiones in Lucam* 2.94, Migne PL 15, col. 1670). Cf. 1 Cor. 3:10–16 and Jude 1:20. The theme of the martyr or saint as a living gemstone is especially frequent in Medieval hymns, as for instance in the following portion of a hymn of Peter Damian's:

—Nunc serenum victor coelum,
O beate coronate,
Post triumphum
Martyr invictissime.

—In aeterni luce regni
Radians lapis vivus,
Clarum sidus cum ignitis
Angelorum agminibus.

(Strophes C–D of Hymn 95 ["Rythmus de S. Vincentio Martyre"] from *Carmina*, Migne PL 145, col. 948.) Similar imagery recurs in Peter Damian's hymn to Saint Apollinaris. It is also frequent in Augustine, as, for instance, in *De Civitate Dei* 8.24.2: "Aedificatur enim domus Domino civitas Dei, quae est sancta ecclesia, in omni terra post eam captivitatem, qua illos homines, de quibus credentibus in Deum tamquam lapidibus vivis domus aedificatur, captos daemonia possidebant." Cf. 18.45.1: "Talibus enim electis gentium domus aedificatur Dei per tes-

That the description of Cacciaguida as the living topaz which bejewels the precious cruciform gem of the heaven of Mars (15.85–86) participates in this tradition there can be no doubt. Cacciaguida is a brilliant living "topaz" first and foremost through his sacrificial imitation of Christ. For the central attribute of the gemstone known to the Middle Ages as topaz—the actual identity of the gem is disputed—was in fact its mysterious property of containing the colors, which is to say the virtues, of all other gemstones: "They say that it includes the colors of all gems," affirms the *glossator* of the *Glossa Ordinaria*, "and hence it takes its name from *pan*, that is to say 'all.' "[30] This etymological derivation of to-paz from the Greek formula *to pan*, meaning "totality," "world soul," or "cosmic body," was employed to demonstrate that it was the most resplendent of all stones when contacted by the sun's rays: "It shines most brightly when struck by the sun, surpassing in splendor all gemstones."[31] Hence its role

---

tamentum novum lapidibus vivis, longe gloriosior, quam templum illud fuit, quod a rege Salomone constructum est et post captivitatem instauratum."

[30] On the lapidary tradition in Dante, see Angelo Lipinsky, "La simbologia delle gemme nella *Divina Commedia* e le sue fonti letterarie," in *Atti del I Congresso Nazionale di Studi Danteschi: "Dante nel secolo dell'unità d'Italia"*, 127–58, which includes a relatively comprehensive bibliography. On the general subject, see Léon Baisier, *The Lapidaire Chrétien: Its Composition, Its Influence, Its Sources*, and Joan Evans, *Magical Jewels of the Middle Ages and the Renaissance*.

[31] *Biblia Sacra cum Glossa Ordinaria*, vol. 6, 1681, gloss on Revelations 21:20. The full exposition follows:

Nonus ponitur hic lapis, quia rarior et preciosior. Et habet duos colores ex auro et aetherea claritate. Maxime lucens cum splendore solis tangitur superans omnium gemmarum claritates. In aspectum suum singulariter provocans ascipientes, quem si plus polis, obscuras: si naturae relinquis, clarior est. Et nihil est carius regibus inter divitias. Contemplativam vitam significat, quam sancti reges omnibus operum divitiis et gemmis virtutum praeserunt et in eam maxime aspectus suos dirigunt et tancto amplius, quanto frequentius divina illustrantur gratia. Ex interna charitate color aureus, ex dulcedine contemplationis aethereus, quae ex attritu saeculi semper obscurascit, vix enim potest quis simul doloribus attingi et tranquilla mente coeli gaudia intueri. Vel si polis, quod si dignitatibus saeculi honoras eos, et or-

as, in a sense, the central stone in the Medieval lapidary: the stone of Christ and of his earthly imitators, first and foremost among them emperors and kings.[32] And hence its association with Cacciaguida, an *imitator Christi* and the central ornament of the final canticle's celestial lapidary.

---

nas, obscuras: quia contemplationi minus vocant, vel minoris meriti fiunt. Et sicut in octavo est activa vita, sic in nono contemplativa quae est angelorum, quorum sunt novem ordines [the *pan* etymology follows].

The emphasis here on the strictly contemplative properties of the stone is somewhat at variance with the lapidary tradition, the usual view being that, as the name *to-paz* or *to pan* implies, the stone signifies (and its two colors are cited as evidence) the duality of contemplation and action required of kings. In any case, one additional reason for Cacciaguida's being a "living topaz" is that the purity of the rustic Roman and Christian values he embodies would be falsified and obscured—the case of postlapsarian Florence—by being polished. For a general survey of the attributes of topaz, see Manfred Bambeck, "Topaz (15, 85–87; 30, 76–78)," in *Studien zu Dantes Paradiso*, 115–123; and John Conley, "The Peculiar Name *Thopas*," in *Studies in Philology* 73 (Jan. 1976): 42–61, which is concerned with Chaucer's "Sir Thopas" but suggests that Chaucer may have intended a parody of Cacciaguida. The etymology of topaz as *to pan*, the foundation of the stone's entire lapidary tradition, recalls the important Plotinian formula *en to pan*, which (as earlier indicated) Macrobius connects with the cosmological discourses of Africanus and Anchises and with the Platonic *anima mundi*. The formula is also associated with the person of Christ in his cosmic and eschatological role as Alpha and Omega, especially in Pauline discussions of the universality of his body (Gal. 3:28, for example). On Christ as the *en to pan*, see Eduard Norden, *Agnostos Theos: Untersuchungen zur Formengeschichte religiöser Rede*, 240ff.

[32] *Glossa Ordinaria* (*ibid.*). For an extended allegorization of the topaz as Christstone, see Giovanni of San Gimignano's *Summa de Exemplis* 2.30. Giovanni insists that Christ is a topaz because it is the most beautiful, luminous, and useful of all gemstones. It is associated with Christ's cross because Pliny's four-cubit topaz statue recalls the four varieties of wood that made up the cross, and the four directions of Christ's outstretched body on the cross. It is linked to Christ's virgin birth and to his appearance at the Resurrection because of its clarity. It signifies the "kingdom of heaven like a treasure hidden in a field" described in Matthew 13:44, because it too is found underground and is a precious treasure like Christ himself. And, like the Messiah, it is one in a thousand: a perfect entity and a rarity. Finally, and here Giovanni is once again Christianizing a commonplace from the lapidary tradition, the topaz restrains the flow of blood and keeps water from

Besides a topaz, of course, Cacciaguida is also described as a treasure: "il mio tesoro ch'io trovai lì" ("my treasure that I found there" [17.121–122]), a living historical treasury unearthed from the soil of Dante's personal history. Or, as André Pézard suggested in *Dante sous la pluie du feu*, he is Dante's "treasure" in pointed contrast with Brunetto Latini's *Tresor*: the speaker of a prelapsarian Florentine dialect and authentic Christian father and teacher, who contrasts the linguistically and philosophically corrupt humanist paternal *image* (*Inf.* 15.83) of Brunetto.[33] But whether topaz or treasure, Cacciaguida, like Apollinaris, presents himself as a living mirror of the kingdom of the heavens, the living embodiment of the entire *pan*oply of Christian virtues.

This association between the martyr's exemplarity and the translucency/reflectivity of gemstones represents only one aspect of the Christian lapidary tradition, and must be placed within the larger context of the most important lapidary passage in the New Testament: the enumeration in Revelations 21:19–22 of the precious gemstones that would make up the Holy Jerusalem's foundations. As a result, a specifically eschatological meaning was given to the spiritual architectonics of 1 Peter 2:5, its precious *spirituales hostiae* interpreted as the actual building blocks of the apocalyptic city.

In his 48th Sermon (the "Second Homily on the Exaltation of the Cross"), Peter Damian, the eleventh-century cardinal-bishop of Ostia who appears in canto 21 of *Paradise*, offers us an example of this hybrid tradition in a form strongly reminiscent of both cantos 14–18 and of the apsidal mosaics at Classe (the latter I suspect quite deliberately):[34]

---

boiling, just as Christ protects his followers against the wrath of persecutors and calms all stormy seas (Matt. 8:24–27). Cf. Giordano da Rivalto, whose seventh sermon ("Domenica, dì 2 di Febbraio, in Santa Maria Novella") compares the incarnate Mary with the topaz on the basis of its qualities as a convex mirror (*Prediche inedite*, 35–36).

[33] *Dante sous la pluie du feu*, 401–405.

[34] "O crux purior vitro, rutilantior auro, quae tanquam vernantibus gemmis et

O cross more translucent than glass, more glowing than gold, you who flower as much with gems and pearls as with the Saviour's limbs! O cross more sparkling than the moon, more brilliant than the sun, who by the greatness of the Divine light precede the radiance of the stars and all the bodies in the heavens! You alone among all the trees in the forest were chosen for the task of man's redemption. You alone were worthy of bearing that weight, whose power turns the heavenly spheres, supports the earth, and balances the whole cosmic mechanism such that it never falls. Tartarus fears you, the angels venerate you, and all created things look upon you with awe. O most noble tree, you who indeed rise up from the earth's soil, but who extend your joyous branches over the starry heavens! Once your fruit was punished with damnation, now it brings forth cedars in paradise; and *from you procede the living stones from which the buildings of the Heavenly Jerusalem are constructed.*

The Ravenna mosaics and the central cantos of *Paradise* fall within this tradition for what by now should be entirely obvious iconographic reasons: the presence of such themes as those of the cross as cosmic tree, as celestial X, as universal sun, and as precious gemstone itself composed of gems.

But as is at least implicit in the passage cited above, they are joined by an additional structural feature: Cacciaguida and Apollinaris alike present themselves as martyrs who have descended out of Christ's celestial cross in an act which *anticipates and imi-*

---

margaritis, membris ornata es Salvatoris! O crux luna micantior, sole splendidior, quae prae divini magnitudine luminis, stellarum jubar, et omnia coeli astra praecedis! Tu sola inter omnia ligna silvarum electa es ad humanae redemptoris officium. Tu pondus illud sustinere meruisti, cujus virtute coelum volvitur, terra suspenditur, et universa mundi machina nunquam casura libratur. Te tartara metuunt, angeli venerantur, et omnis rerum creatura miratur. O vere nobilis arbor, quae de terreno quidem cespite orta procedis, sed super astra coeli felices ramos expandis! Olim quidem fructus tuus gehennae erat obnoxius, tunc cedros germinas paradiso; et *vivi ex te lapides prodeunt, quibus supernae Hierusalem aedificia construuntur*" (*Sermones*, Migne PL 144, col. 776; my italics). The entire sermon (cols. 766–777) is an encyclopedia of just about every major attribute of the cross that I have run across. The affinity with the *crux gemmata* of Classe is probably not casual, since Ravenna was Peter's place of birth and of study.

tates Christ's coming at the end of time. In the case of Cacciaguida the narrative is quite clear as regards this action: in canto 15 he comes sliding like a gemstone on a ribbon or like a shooting star across the heavens, down to the base of the cross of light, only to reascend at the conclusion of the encounter in canto 18. Dante's ancestral "sudden fire" ("sùbito foco" [15.14]) in fact proceeds in a *rightward* arc from the right horn of the cross ("tale dal corno che 'n destro si stende" [15.19]) through its center to its base: a motion which, if translated into the absolute coordinates of Aristotelian cosmology, imitates the daily "eastward" or "rightward" rotation of the sun.[35] Leaving aside the imperial connotations of such a *translatio*—the subject of Justinian's discourse on the imperial sign in *Paradise* 6—the action is unmistakeably apocalyptic in character, for it mimes the "rightward" lightning flash of Matthew 24:27: "like a lightning-flash coming out of the east and shining into the west: so also shall be the coming of the Son of man ("Sicut enim fulgur exit ab oriente, et paret usque in occidentem: ita erit et adventus Filii hominis").[36]

---

[35] The solar symbolism is reinforced by the conventional association of the right arm of the cross with the sun (not to mention the New Testament) in early representations of Christ's crucifixion. On the applicability of Medieval cosmology to the pilgrim's own motions, see John Freccero, "Dante's Pilgrim in a Gyre," *PMLA* 76 (March 1961): 168–181.

[36] In Medieval science, shooting-stars and lightning bolts were both imagined as *accendimenti di vapori* or "ignited exhalations" and hence appertained to the field of meteorology. The former were thought characteristic of clear skies (15.13–14), and the latter of clouded skies in the process of cooling and condensing. The characterization of Cacciaguida's descent as fiery (15.14–17), clearly visible (13), extremely rapid (18), unexpected (14), and supernatural (17–18) would seem to satisfy Cornelius a Lapide's gloss on Matthew 24:27. To compare Christ's coming with a bolt of lightning is appropriate, Cornelius suggests, because it shall be: "*primo*, subitus; *secundo*, inexpectatus; *tertio*, omnibus manifestus; *quarto*, gloriosus; *quinto*, efficax, ut nemo ei resistere valeat; *sexto*, non in terra, sed in aere" (*Commentaria in Quatuor Evangelia*, vol. 2, 227). All these attributes, it might be noted, confirm that Christ (and hence Cacciaguida) is not one of the pseudo-Christs and pseudo-prophets described in Matthew 24:24; rather, he comes as a true *imago Christi* and prophet.

Because of the synchronic character of the mosaic medium, to find an exact equivalent one must look to the visual relationship of martyr-saint and cross. I have already suggested that the figure of Apollinaris serves as a key link in the vertical chain of Christ-signs described earlier. When one considers, however, the perspectival structure of the apse, this vertical axis can be shown to constitute a diagonal "line of descent," running from the cross of light to Apollinaris to the altar to the base of its steps, entirely analogous to that of canto 15 (Fig. 12). Like Cacciaguida, Apollinaris occupies the spatial and temporal middleground between an indefinite eschatological future and an imminent sacrificial present. Behind and above him appear the coming cross of light and its radiant circle, which rise over the eastern horizon but at a considerable distance as if pictorially locked to the rearmost edge of the Edenic landscape. Before and below him (within the actual space of the basilica), to the west of the cross and to the east of a spectator kneeling at the steps, extends the altar: site of the liturgical reenactment of Christ's sacrifice by his living imitators. Suspended between the two, Apollinaris is thrust forward from east to west into a zone at the very border of the pictorial foreground: an unstable space linked to the apocalyptic future figured behind his back, yet promising to intrude into the spectatorial present.

A close examination of the relative scale of Apollinaris and the cross of light bears out even more persuasively the notion that as an imitator of Christ, the Ravenna martyr "descends" out of the cross: the two are in fact doubles, they are literally made for one another (Fig. 15). The mosaic is precisely designed so that if one were to cut out the figure of Apollinaris and to superimpose it over the cross the fit would be exact: his arms would extend some three-quarters of the distance between the center and extremity of the horizontal crossbar, his head and aureole occupy the center of the top section of the vertical bar, and his feet the two horns of the cross' lower extremity.

Just as Cacciaguida is the "Christ" of cantos 14–18, then,

Apollinaris is the "Christ" of the Ravenna cross. As exemplary "living stones," each offers himself as proof of the well-foundedness of Christian hopes and an example of the spiritual metamorphosis that lies beyond the opaque reality of the cross. If the structural hub of both works is in an ultimate sense the eschatological cross of light, in a more immediate sense, it is the martyr's role as *didactic intermediary*: translating the language of faith into the language of exemplarity, eternal theological mysteries into historically immediate terms, the universal cross of Christ into an individualized one in the community's own image. The martyr thus serves as a natural earthward projection of the cross. He provides one further bridge between history and the transcendent mysteries of eternity, one further genealogical link between Christ and the individual.

Sì pïa l'ombra d'Anchise si porse

This conception of martyrdom, I believe, is the crux of Dante's narrative fiction and poetics in the *Commedia*. It provides, moreover, a key to the "internalization" of Classical epic that will be the subject of my concluding sections. But before turning to the general subject of the poetics of martyrdom, I should like to focus specifically on the immediate "sign" of the martyr's mediation: his adoption of the so-called "orant" pose—the sign of Classical and, later, Christian *pietas*. In so doing, I propose an additional link between cantos 14–18 and the mosaics at Classe: the mediating figure of the orant Saint Apollinaris, who serves as bridge between Virgil's Anchises and Dante's Cacciaguida. Saint Apollinaris, I suggest, is not only a mediator between cross of light and reader/viewer, but also between Classical and Christian images of paternal piety and epic heroism.

Orant figures are one of the most ancient types of Christian representations, appearing with great frequency in Christian mural paintings and on sarcophagi as early as the first century A.D. (Fig. 16). Yet the frontal depiction of the individual with his or her hands symmetrically upraised in the attitude of prayer is in reality not of Christian but of Classical origin (Figs. 17 and 18). Such figures are allegorical signs standing for Classical *pietas* or εὐσέβεια, a virtue whose preeminent role in Book 6 of Virgil's *Aeneid* hardly requires any comment. The idea was rapidly assimilated by Christian artists and "in the series of abstract ideas [characteristic of paleo-Christian art] there is," writes André Grabar, "the notion of piety, which has as an image-sign the orant."[37] The equivalence was incontrovertible in early Christian art.

But in the process of adaptation the meaning of the gesture would gradually shift. "Piety" in the Classical context had been defined in a mostly "vertical" or hierarchical sense. It was the network of legal debts and constraints governing the behaviour of social inferior to superior and (to a much lesser extent) vice versa: a mechanism guaranteeing the individual's subordination to all genealogical, political, and religious fathers. In Christian art, the "piety" signified by the orant gesture would be derived less from the individual's debt to the historical father and/or secular authority, whether legal, familial, or religious, than from humanity's collective debt (all hierarchical distinctions aside) to a *transcendent* Father who sacrificed his only Son for the redemption of humankind as whole. The model for all human acts of piety thus becomes Christ's sacrifice on the cross: a radical act of both filial and paternal self-abasement, addressed not to any hierarchical "superior" but rather to those "below," promising no less than a complete reconciliation of divine father and human children.

What this implies in terms of the history of the orant figure is that the Classical orant, a stylized type without particularized features, becomes increasingly particularized and this-worldly. Initially, the divergence is by no means absolute: Classical and Christian types follow a parallel course for some time, with ab-

[37] *Christian Iconography: A Study of its Origins*, 10.

stract *pietas* "image-signs" giving way to orant representations of a concrete deceased individual in both a Classical and Christian context (Fig. 19). But as the interest in portraiture expands, the emphasis shifts away from simple depictions of the orant subject's own piety. Instead, the increasingly concrete historical individual described appears typologically identified with the Son of God and with his exemplary sacrifice on the cross; or in turn identified with a number of standard Christ-figures: Noah and Jonah in particular (Figs. 20, 21, and 22). The gesture of prayer comes to be envisaged as the gesture of taking on one's own personal cross. This serves to underscore not only the subject's pious imitation of Christ and symbolic sonship in God, but also his adoption of an additional Christological role: that of *mediator* between man and his creator, of prophet and messenger from the beyond.

The orant in Christian art is consequently a martyr and/or a saint, and he prays, not for his own salvation, which is already a given, but rather for the salvation of the viewer and the historical collectivity. It is for the viewer that the orant descends from the beyond, and this intercession is directly modelled after Christ's own condescension into human history, his self-lowering on the cross. So becoming this-worldly in the process of its Christianization, the Classical orant figure was, paradoxically, transformed into an "otherworldly" sign at the same time.[38]

I have already drawn attention to the various themes and compositional devices present in the apsidal mosaics at Classe which figuratively enrich the implications of Saint Apollinaris' own adoption of the orant pose. Yet from the perspective of the *Commedia* the martyr's pose takes on an even more suggestive feature which, interestingly enough, recalls the orant figure's Classical origins. For the attitude of Apollinaris might well have struck

---

[38] On the paradox of "otherworldliness" and "realism" in Dante's aesthetics, see Erich Auerbach's classic essay "Figura," in *Scenes from the Drama of European Literature*, 11–76.

Dante as a splendid literalization and Christianization of Anchises' greeting of Aeneas in Elysium. Apollinaris, just as Anchises, extends outward both of his palms. "Palmas utrasque tetendit" (6.685) writes Virgil: an ambiguous phrase which can be read either as a precise description of the orant pose (of the Ravenna martyr, for instance), or, as is almost certainly intended, as referring to Anchises' hands *stretching forward* to greet his son. Indeed the emotional volatility of Anchises, the rapidity of the gesture ("alacris palmas" [6.685]), the effusiveness of his tears ("effusaeque genis lacrimae" [6.686]), all lend credence to the latter interpretation. Nothing could be more unlike the silence and immobility of the gesture of Apollinaris, situated too in an eternal landscape that is quite explicitly Elysian.

The analogy might seem of secondary interest if the encounter of Anchises and Aeneas did not occupy so prominent a place in cantos 14-18. Like Anchises sighting his son, Cacciaguida too, at the center of Dante's celestial Elysium, *palmas utrasque tetendit*:

> Sì pïa l'ombra d'Anchise si porse,
> se fede merta nostra maggior musa,
> quando in Eliso del figlio s'accorse.   15.25-27

(With like piety did the shade of Anchises show himself, if our greatest muse merits faith, when in Elysium he first beheld his son.) [my translation]

That the bodily pose referred to is the orant gesture seems entirely beyond question here, for the term of comparison is *pïa*, and the orant, the Classical and Christian sign of *pietas*, as earlier shown. The point is strongly seconded by the dramatic setting: the crusader Cacciaguida has just descended off the cross; he is one of those who have taken on the cross and followed Christ; he is a "living cross," as Georg Rabuse has put it.[39]

But the most telling confirmation of all comes from Cacciagui-

---

[39] *Gesammelte Aufsätze*, 196. Rabuse was the first, I believe, to draw any particular attention to the character of the gesture itself and to clarify its relation to the cross.

da's opening speech. Like Anchises, Cacciaguida calls out to his descendant, but only to turn immediately in thankfulness to the divine source of Dante's extraordinary privilege: "God's grace infused from above." This he does in Latin, the language of Virgil, but, more importantly, of Christian liturgy and *prayer*:

> "O sanguis meus, o superinfusa
> gratïa Deï, sicut tibi cui
> bis unquam celi ianüa reclusa?"   15.28–30
>
> ("O blood of mine, O lavish grace of God! To whom was Heaven's gate ever twice opened, as to thee?")

So while it is the overflow of emotion that is dramatized in Anchises' Elysian greeting of Aeneas, the pathos of a family reunion after death, the blood-love that binds father to son, in cantos 14–18 an entirely new element comes into play. The Virgilian themes are recast in the image of the Christian orant, whose piety is exhibited not only through his personal devotion to a spiritual son, but also through the acts of prayer and intercession that occupy the entire opening portion of canto 15, from the speech quoted above through the "deep speech" or *parlar profondo* (15.39) beyond the grasp of mortals to the vernacular prayer of intercession: "Benedetto sia tu . . . trino e uno" ("Blessed be Thou . . . three-fold and one" [15.47]).

What is staged in this crucial passage of Dante's text is another of the many instances studied by Robert Ball in a recent article, of a superposition of Christian piety, with its insistence upon sonship in God over and above all socially conditioned relations, onto Classical *pietas*, which places the emphasis instead on the son's blood-debt to the historical father.[40] This is not to say that Dante entirely abandons the "family romance" of Book 6: the *pietas* of Cacciaguida too, as is evident in his greeting "O sanguis meus," involves a special love for those of his own blood (as does the pilgrim's assertion in canto 16.16 that "You are my father"

---

[40] Robert Ball, "Theological Semantics," 59–79.

["Voi siete il padre mio"]). Yet such themes appear in cantos 14–18 always mediated by an insistence on the primacy of a Christian inheritance and genealogy which exceeds the bonds of human blood-relations. Hence the pilgrim's switch to the honorific "voi" first spoken in Rome ("che prima a Roma s'offerie" [16.10]) is presented, not as an example of filial piety, but, on the contrary, of the "*poca* nostra nobiltà di sangue" (16.1; my italics), the petty and trifling nobility of blood. Hence also in Cacciaguida's self-naming, the family cognomem is inextricable from man's affiliation with Christ: "insieme fui cristiano e Cacciaguida" ("I became at once a Christian and Cacciaguida" [15.135]). Last of all, it should be remembered that Cacciaguida is neither Dante's father (cf. Anchises) nor his grandfather (cf. Africanus), but rather his great-great-grandfather—a paternal image thrice removed.

At first glance it would appear that the same parallelism is observed in Cacciaguida's opening anaphora: "O sanguis meus," addressing Dante on the basis of their historical kinship, the subsequent "O superinfusa gratïa," on the basis of their Christian fellowship. The invocation is, however, even more complex and brings us once again to the very heart of Dante's Christian rewriting of Book 6. Cacciaguida's anaphora, and for that matter the entirety of his discourse from canto 15 to canto 18, systematically fuses the Classical and Christian literary horizons of the *Commedia* as a whole. This is true, as should by now be clear, not only of his narrative role as the Christian Anchises, but also of his language, his *pietas*, his manner, his prophetic *latin* and distinctively Christian exemplification of epic heroism. But of no portion of the Martial cantos is this more true than of the opening half of canto 15, where the Virgilian background is everywhere emphasized in order that it be transformed.

The invocation of 15.28–30 thus represents only one of a number of dense symbolic crossroads placed at the beginning of the father-son encounter. In the third vocative of canto 15, again spoken by Cacciaguida to Dante, the fusion of Virgilian/Christian horizons is all the more dramatically on display:

> O fronda mia in che io compiacemmi
> pur aspettando, io fui la tua radice.   15.88–89

(Oh branch of mine, in whom I was well pleased, even in expectation, I was your root.) [my translation]

Here, some fifty verses before the *cristiano/Cacciaguida* self-identification of 15.135, we see once again the ultimate priority granted to their bond as Christians, figuratively joined through their sacrificial imitation of Christ, over all literal blood ties. Cacciaguida is unmistakably echoing Anchises' greeting in Book 6 (a passage already implicitly present in the orant simile of 15.25 ["Sì pïa l'ombra d'Anchise si porse"] and the paternal expectation of 15.49–52 ["Grato e lontano digiuno . . ."]):

> Venisti tandem, tuaque *exspectata parenti*
> vicit iter durum pietas?   6.687–688

(Have you come at last? Did piety, *as your father long anticipated*, conquer the arduous path?) [italics mine]

But the apparent similarity masks the actual gap that separates Classical *pietas* from Christian *pietà*. Not only is Cacciaguida adopting a genealogical language of trees, roots, and branches strongly reminiscent of the Old Testament genealogies associated with the birth of Christ (such as Isaiah 11:1, cited in Gmelin's commentary: "And there shall come forth a rod out of the root of Jesse, and a flower shall rise up out of his root"); but also he is addressing himself to his descendant in the precise manner in which the celestial Father spoke to Christ at his Baptism and Transfiguration: "Hic est Filius meus dilectus, *in quo mihi bene complacui*" ("This is my beloved Son in whom I am well pleased" [my italics]). The transfigured imitator of Christ thus speaks to the poet-pilgrim as a fellow imitator of Christ, implicitly answering the rhetorical question posed at the beginning of the encounter: "sicut tibi cui bis unquam celi ianüa reclusa?" or "for whom was the door to heaven twice opened as to you?" The answer to the question is self-evident: only to God's own Son and to the most well-beloved of his imitators, the adoptive Sons of God.

We are now in a better position to reexamine Cacciaguida's opening invocation, a passage that makes use of the same layering technique. The parallelism between a human and Christological kinship that I have earlier suggested reveals an additional Virgilian and Christian dimension. While the Latin of Cacciaguida's rhetorical question and the appeal to God's infused grace is clearly the Latin of the Scriptures and of Christian liturgy and prayer, it is thoroughly permeated with the Latin of Virgil. The entire speech would in fact seem to occupy a role precisely analogous to that of the famous speech of the Sibyl at the opening of Book 6, to which it provides in my view the Pauline equivalent:

> Sate sanguine divum,
> Tros Anchisiade, facilis descensus Averno;
> noctes atque dies patet atri ianua Ditis;
> sed revocare gradum superasque evadere ad auras,
> hoc opus, hic labor est. Pauci, quos aequus amavit
> Iuppiter aut ardens evexit ad aethera virtus,
> dis geniti potuere.   6.125–131

> (Offspring
> Of gods by blood, Trojan Anchises' son,
> The way downward is easy from Avernus.
> Black Dis's door stands open night and day.
> But to retrace your steps to heaven's air,
> There is the trouble, there is the toil. A few
> Whom a benign Jupiter has loved or whom
> Fiery heroism has borne to heaven.
> Sons of gods, could do it.)   vv. 185–193, Fitzgerald

This speech, concerned as it is with the genealogical preconditions of the hero's epic *labor*, has as its referent the double crossing of the Stygian water and of the night of Tartarus ("bis Stygios innare lacus, bis nigra videre Tartara" [6.134–135]), which constitutes the infernal double of Cacciaguida's rhetorical question.

The "ianua Ditis" of one are the "celi ianüa" of the other, Virgil's ascensional "revocare" is Dante's double "ianüa reclusa," and the Sibyl's infernal *bis*, the poet-pilgrim's "*bis* unquam celi ianüa" (a possibility only Gmelin seems to have considered).[41] More importantly, the epic *labor* of the one is the *labor* in imitation of Christ of the other. The full prophetic foreshadowing of the son's endeavor of course provides the culminating moment in each of these otherworldly encounters. That the conflation of Anchises with the Sibyl is essential to Dante's later juxtaposition of Classical and Christian oracles I take for granted from my earlier argument.

What, then, of Cacciaguida's opening address to the poet-pilgrim as "O sanguis meus"? There can be no question that this too is involved in a complex Christian/Classical superposition. As in the later prayer of thanksgiving to the Trinitarian godhead "who show such favor to my seed" ("che nel mio seme se' tanto cortese" [15.48]), Cacciaguida is drawing attention to the hybrid seed that binds father and son together: the seed of a Rome of both Augustus and Christ. The standard view has long been that Dante's "sanguis meus" quotes from Anchises' demand at the conclusion of Book 6 that his distant descendant, Julius Caesar, put down the sword and end Rome's civil wars: "tuque prior, tu parce, genus qui ducis Olympo; / proiice tela manu, sanguis meus" ("Be first, spare us, you who trace your line from Olympus; throw down your sword, child of my blood" [6.834–835]). If this interpretation is an accurate one, which it may well be, the meaning of the phrase, a common one preserved even in modern colloquial Italian, has undergone an important shift in meaning. For the literal context of Anchises' call runs entirely counter to the militant thrust of cantos 14–18: their imprecation to rise up and

---

[41] Gmelin writes: "Das pathetische *bis* für die zweimalige, d.h. für die vorzeitige und die endgültige Himmelsreise Dantes ist ebenso wie das *sanguis meus* eine virgil-Imitatio; vgl. Aen. VI, 134 . . . Da hier die Frageform steht, schliesst die Stelle den Gedanken an die Himmelsvision des Paulus nicht aus" (*Kommentar—III Tiel*, 289).

conquer (14.125), to take up the cross and follow Christ (14.106), to complete the epic task and combat evil without fear or hesitation (17.128).

Might not the blood referred to in Cacciaguida's Latin greeting be equally thought of as the Christian equivalent to the Virgilian blood of the gods? After all, Anchises' "sanguis" in 6.835 is none other than that of Olympus. While at face value this may seem an outrageous suggestion, the phrase "sanguis meus" is particularly rich in liturgical associations and inevitably calls to mind Christ's institution of the eucharist in Matthew 26:28: "Hic est enim *sanguis meus* novi testamenti, qui pro multis effundetur in remissionem peccatorum" ("For this is *my blood* of the new testament which shall be shed for many, for the remission of sins" [italics mine]).[42] It is this sacrificial symbolism that is re-enacted literally by Christ's martyrs, who, in taking on their personal crosses, make sacrificial offerings, ardent sacrifices (14.92), spiritual holocausts (14.89) of themselves.[43] Through this baptism of

---

[42] The phrase is alluded to twice in Dante's treatise on monarchy. It first appears in a quotation from Ephesians 1:5–8, which serves to buttress Dante's assertion of the providentiality of Imperial Rome: "Qui praedestinavit nos in adoptionem filiorum per Iesum Christum in ipsum secundum propositum voluntatis suae, in laudem gloriae gratiae suae, in qua gratificavit nos in dilecto Filio suo. In quo habemus redemptionem per *sanguinem eius*, remissionem peccatorum secundum divitas gratiae eius, quae superabundavit in nobis" (quoted in *Monarchia* 2.11.22). The second reference comes at the beginning of Book 3 and is preceded by an allusion to the need to sacrifice even that which is most dear in the name of the truth (cf. 17.54ff.) and by an assertion of prophetic *fiducia* (Daniel, the Seraphim and Isaiah being cited as models). Next follows Dante's self-identification as a prophet devoted to speaking the uncensored truth: "et in brachio Illius qui nos de potestate tenebrarum liberavit in *sanguine suo* impium atque mendacem de palestra, spectante mundo, eiciam. Quid timeam, cum Spiritus Patri et Filio coecternus aiat per os David: 'In memoria ecterna erit justus, ab auditione mala non timebit?' " (*Monarchia* 3.1.27; my italics). The unspeakable "truth" in question is, naturally, his own theory of Empire and vision of Rome's redemptive role in history.

[43] On early Christian conceptions of martyrdom and eucharistic symbolism in the cult of martyrs, see the entry by Rordorf and Solignac in the *Dictionnaire de spiritualité mystique et ascétique*, fasc. 66/67, 726–736.

blood they are symbolically integrated into the body of Christ, transformed into adoptive sons of God. The call that issues forth from the eternal father of cantos 14–18 cannot as a result be identical to that of Anchises to Julius Caesar. It is an activist call: a call to sacrifice, to put on the cross, and not to "put down the sword." Yet the ultimate reward for this militant combat unto death against sin is, as Cacciaguida describes it, not really at odds with the result of Julius' abandonment of the sword. Both inaugurate an era of peace: one, the *pax Augusta* which accompanied the birth of Christ, the other, the eternal peace of salvation that is the end result of history's martyrdom (15.148).

In her famed speech on the difficulty of returning from Hell to a vision of the heavens, the Sibyl had insisted on the need for a divine affiliation as a precondition for otherworldly quests: the literal maternity of Venus in the case of Aeneas, the superinfused grace of God in the case of the poet-pilgrim. The onerous responsibilities, as well as the immense privileges, that result from Aeneas' divine ancestry are recurring subjects in the course of Book 6.[44] As Dante saw it, Classicism had erred (like those contemporaries of his who considered nobility in a strictly genealogical sense) when it imagined such a relation as a literal blood-tie. The metamorphosis of the self into a well-beloved Son of God could only be the result of a thoroughgoing askesis modeled after Christ's sacrifice on the cross.

In *De Vulgari Eloquentia* 2.4.9–11 Dante had thus interpreted the Sibyl's words as referring to those poets who, through assid-

[44] References to Aeneas' divine origins and blood are extremely frequent toward the beginning of Book 6. Already in 6.90 Achilles is described as "born also a goddess' son" ("natus et ipse dea"). Next follows in 6.123 Aeneas' affirmation that he too is of Jove's line ("et mi genus ab Iove summo"), the Sibyl's response ("Sate sanguine divum" [6.125]), and then her reference to Jove's chosen: the "sons of god" ("dis geniti" [6.131]). Next comes Aeneas' call to his mother Venus in 6.197 ("diva parens"), followed by the Sibyl's address to him as a true descendant of the gods ("deum certissima proles" [6.322]). Finally comes the boatman's disgust at the sight of Aeneas, whom he identifies as another of those "sons of gods and unconquered heros" ("dis quamquam geniti atque invicti viri" [6.394]), who occasionally render his job somewhat unpleasant.

uous study and the strenuous development of their *ingenium*, had achieved a *figurative* sonship in God:[45]

> Caveat ergo quilibet et discernat ea que dicimus, et quando pure hec tria [Salus, Amor et Virtus] cantare intendit, vel que ad ea directe ac pure secuntur, prius Elicone potatus, tensis fidibus ad supremum, secure plectrum tum movere incipiat. Sed cautionem atque discretionem hanc accipere, sicut decet, hic opus et labor est, quoniam nunquam sine strenuitate ingenii et artis assiduitate scientiarumque habitu fieri potest. Et hii sunt quos Poeta Eneidorum sexto Dei dilectos et ab ardente virtute sublimatos ad ethera deorumque filios vocat, quanquam figurate loquatur.

> (Let everyone therefore beware and discern what we say; so when intending to sing of these three subjects [Welfare, Love, and Virtue] in their essence, or of matters immediately deriving from them, drink first from the Helicon, tune your strings to the highest: only then move the plectrum with confidence. But to exercise the needed caution and judgement—this is the toil and task—for never without the mind's strenuous exertion, diligent practice in the arts and frequenting the sciences is this attainable. And such are those to whom the Poet in Book 6 of the *Aeneid* refers as the "beloved of God and raised by fiery virtue into the heavens" and as "sons of Gods," though he speaks figuratively.)

---

[45] The text continues: "Et ideo confutetur illorum stultitia qui, arte scientiaque immunes, de solo ingenio confidentes, ad summa summe canenda prorumpunt; et a tanta presumptuositate desistant; et si anseres natura vel desidia sunt, nolint astripetam aquilam imitari" (*De Vulgari Eloquentia* 2.4.11). This passage is powerfully suggestive with regard to cantos 14–18, especially in its contention that Virgil's passage is concerned with poetic ascent and (an at least figurative) divine descent. That the figurative children of God are here referred to as "dilecti"—the word is not found in *Aeneid* 6.125–131—recalls the baptismal and transfigurational: "Hic est Filius meus dilectus, in quo mihi bene complacui." The theme of heavenly ascent attempted only via the individual wit or *ingenio*, furthermore, seems particularly reminiscent both of the story of Daedalus (present at the opening of Virgil's Book 6) and of the Medieval allegorists' understanding of the fable of Phaeton: the standard example of the secular philosopher's attempting a fruitless ascent into transcendent mysteries.

At the center of *Paradise* he would seem to append to this secular allegory an all-important qualification: such a transformation, whether figurative and anticipatory, or literal and definitive, is possible only through the imitation of Christ. Whether the cross that is borne is like that of the adubbed crusader, or instead a prophetic lyre battering the highest summits with its paracletic wind, the supreme exemplar is the universal cross of Christ: the only true *celi ianua*.

Martyrdom and the Internalization of Epic

In the concluding portion of this study I hope to sketch out in general terms how the entire network of concerns that has emerged from this and earlier chapters, embracing themes as apparently diverse as the authority of oracles and prophecy, the relation of individual to universal cross, the discourse of the city, and the dialectics of historical sacrifice and eternal reward, gravitates toward a central theme which unifies all others: that of the identification of the poet-pilgrim himself as a martyr and of his poetic task with the public witness borne by Christ's martyrs. The itinerary from abstraction to history, from the cross of light to the palpable immediacy of history, that joins the Martial cantos to the mosaics of Sant' Apollinare can only be completed by turning to the early Christian conception of martyrdom, for it alone provides the key to the Christianization of Virgilian epic which is at the heart of Dante's endeavor in the Martial cantos and in the *Commedia* as whole.

If the abstract cross is the "anagogical hub" of cantos 14–18 of *Paradise* and of the apsidal mosaics of Sant' Apollinare, the orant martyr provides the literal hub around which the reader/viewer's experience more immediately revolves. It is through the figure of the martyr that the text of history is filled out in all its concreteness, that the language of faith is translated into the language of exemplarity, that the universal cross of Christ is transformed into an individualized cross in the reader/viewer's own image. This role of the martyr as didactic intermediary, as both prophet and facilitator of the individual's conversion to the sacrificial task, is founded on the deeply paradoxical relationship of the martyr to the historical collectivity.

It is not by accident that the theme of martyrdom should arise in the heaven of Mars, for the martyr is the precise Christian equivalent to the Classical epic hero. Indeed, as is well known, the Christian cult of martyrs bears considerable resemblances to the Classical cult of heroes. The martyr is the "athlete of God" who enters the ring of history, the Pauline agon, Dante's literary *aringo* (*Par.* 1.18), to struggle for the attainment of the ultimate Christian laurel: the glory of Christian paradise. His virtues are persistence, courage, detachment from worldly concerns. He struggles "not against the flesh and blood, but against principalities and powers, against the rulers of the world of this darkness, against the spirits of the wicked in high places" (Eph. 6:12): the destructive forces that constantly encircle the human city. Hence Cacciaguida's own martyrdom: his joining of the *militia Christi* of Ephesians 6, his battle against iniquity (15.142) under the ensign of the cross.

If such attributes would seem to make of the martyr an exemplary citizen of the human city, the relationship is in reality a more ambiguous one. For like Aeneas, Ulysses, and Jason, the martyr is also a being always at the margins of the earthly city: a wanderer, a pilgrim, the eternal foreigner. But in the case of the Christian martyr this is not because he is in pursuit of some personal *aristeia*, or driven, like Dante's Ulysses, by an insatiable appetite for "virtue and knowledge" ("virtute e canoscenza" *Inf.* 26.120). Rather, it is due to the fact that even while he is here among us he is already the citizen of another city. Like Dante's Ulysses, the Christian martyr does indeed abandon a cherished son, an aged father and a beloved Penelope (26.94–96). But in doing so his goal is not to make a name for *himself*; his sacrifice of familial ties is instead a sign of absolute adhesion to the name of Jesus Christ. He is one of those referred to by Jesus in Matthew 19:29

"who have left behind house, or brothers, or sisters, or father, or mother, or wife, or children, or lands, *in my name*" (my italics) and who as a reward "shall possess life everlasting."

It is this identification of the martyr with the name of Christ that defines his paradoxical relation to the historical collectivity: he is both one of "us" and radically unlike "us." In the early Christian conception, once the martyr had undergone his epic ordeal, the so-called "baptism of blood," he emerged immediately as someone radically "other"—and this irrespective of whether he survived. Having survived, he became the living sign of the persistence of Christ in the human city: a *figura Christi* living in exile among us, a priest and prophet. Deceased, he was identified as one of those referred to by Jesus before the Transfiguration: "there are some standing here among us, who shall not taste death, till they see the Son of man coming in his kingdom" (Matt. 26:28). The martyr was believed to be instantaneously transfigured at the precise moment of death.[46]

While many martyriological themes are entirely analogous to Classical epic themes, there is one area where the divergence is absolute, and this difference is of the greatest relevance to Dante's Christianization of Book 6. The martyr's acts of valour, his *aristeiai*, are conceived not only as exterior feats, but also as interior ones, acts of heroic self-discipline and ascetic self-abnegation. And with this "internalization" of epic action comes a new emphasis on the heroism of the spoken word. In countless martyriological narratives it is the martyr's refusal to take any

---

[46] For a contemporary statement of this doctrine, see Giordano da Rivalto's sermon 21 ("26 di Dicembre, Domenica, a vespro, in Santa Liperata"): "Per santo Istefano s'intende la quarta generazione di quegli a cui è aperto il cielo immantanente, cioè sono i santi martiri; a quegli è aperto il cielo sanza nullo indugio, perchè il martirio purga tutti i peccati quanti ne avessi nè meno nè più che al battesimo; martirio fu tanto quanto battesimo, chè si purga l'anima da colpa e da pena immantanente, o di piccola pena o lieve che sia martire, non ci ha nulla forza se è egli martire per Cristo" (*Prediche inedite*, 116). See also sermons 16 (16 giugno, 1303) and 27 (26 luglio, 1304) among Giordano's *Prediche*, vol. 1, 104 and 211–212.

oath of loyalty to earthly rulers, accompanied by his or her open profession of faith to Christ, that sets the stage for his or her actual martyrdom. If Virgil's Aeneas, with all his interior struggles to satisfy the contradictory demands of filial *pietas*, already represents a significant departure from the action-oriented Homeric epic hero, this Christian "internalization" of epic action combined with a verbal conception of heroism implies an even more significant departure.

In the Christian construct, *act* and *word* are radically fused. The martyr's task is to wield not only a material sword against the opponent but also the "sword of the spirit" that is God's all-powerful Word (Eph. 6:17). The notion of enemy too finds itself radically figuralized. He is at once within and without, visible and invisible, verbal and physical. So the Christian "hero" is to go into combat on the battlefield of revelation as much as on any concrete material battlefield, struggling with words as well as works. Hence Dante's ability to characterize Saint Dominic as a "holy athlete" (56), Dominic and Francis as "champions" (44) and soldiers in the "army of Christ" (37), and Joachim of Fiore as a valiant "paladin" (142), to cite only examples from the twelfth canto of *Paradise*.[47]

Consequently, martyrdom is defined first and foremost as a discursive act, as a production of sacrificial signs:[48]

> "Martyrs" in Greek are called "witnesses" [*testes*] in Latin, and this is why acts of testimony in Greek are referred to as "martyrdoms."

[47] The blessed in the Empyrean are of course described as the "milizia di paradiso" (30.43–44). An especially telling example is found in Fra Giordano: "Santo Augustino fu campione grandissimo; questi fu Scipione Affricano, che liberò Roma dall'ultima sua distruzione; liberò e fece franca la Chiesa; che come quelli combatte con Annibale, e cacciolo; così questi contro a le resie del Demonio, e contro a ogne eretico, e peccatore combatte, cacciogli, e dispersegli, ed abbattegli" (sermon 39 [28 agosto, 1304], in *Prediche*, vol. 2, 15).

[48] "Martyres Graeca lingua, Latine testes dicuntur, unde et testimonia Graece martyria nuncupantur. Testes autem ideo vocati sunt, quia propter testimonium Christi passiones sustinuerunt, et usque ad mortem pro veritate certaverunt" (*Etym.* 7.11.1).

They are called "witnesses" because they endured great sufferings in bearing witness to Christ, and struggled unto death to defend the truth.

It is not that the literal act of self-sacrifice recedes into the background, but rather that this holocaust is itself understood in a verbal context: as a making manifest, a confession, a bearing witness, even an act of prophecy.[49] For the martyr's heroic self-abnegation and/or courageous speech was viewed as an active reinforcement of Christ's resurrectional message. Like a powerful sermon, a mystical vision, or a miracle, it provides a direct and fully intelligible restatement of Christ's message for the Christian collectivity. Through the martyr Christ speaks—an idea central to cantos 14–18 and the apse at Sant' Apollinare.

If in martyrdom speech and action are already one, then the special honor which martyrs' dreams and visions were accorded should come as no surprise. The result of risking and/or suffering death in defense of the faith was in the view of the Church Fathers a special grace: that Pauline *fiducia* or *parrhesía* (παρρησία) which makes possible an almost lawlessly bold frankness of speech. This is the apocalyptic/prophetic speech founded in hope which Paul refers to in II Corinthians 3:12–13: "Habentes igitur talem spem, multa *fiducia* utimur, et non sicut Moyses ponebat velamen super faciem suam" ("Having, therefore, such hope, we use much confidence: *and not like Moses who put a veil over his face*" [italics mine]).

In order to grasp the rich connotations of the term *parrhesía* as employed in the Christian Scriptures, it is worth briefly examining its Classical roots.[50] In ancient Greece the concept of *parrhesía*

---

[49] This is the case of Boethius, who in canto 10 is strategically represented as both a *poeta-teologo* and a martyr in order to set the stage for Cacciaguida's proclamation of Dante's own prophetic mission as a "making manifest."

[50] For a general introduction to the historical development of the term *parrhesía*, see the entry in Gerhard Kittel's *Theologisches Wörterbuch zum Neuen Testament* and G.J.M. Bartelink, "Quelques Observations sur παρρησία dans la littérature paléo-chrétienne," *Graecitas et Latinitas Christianorum Primaeva: Supplementa* 3 (1970): 7–57. For a more specialized treatment, see W. C. van Unnik, "The

first appears in a strictly juridical and political setting, signifying the individual citizen's right to untrammeled free speech in the city's public forums. As this privilege was gradually extended to broader and broader sectors of the Greek population and even to foreigners, the term accrued an increasingly marginal semantic coloring, implying either uncontrolled, subversive, and lawless speech (Plato), or speech that endangers its speaker: for instance, the courageous exercise of free speech in the name of justice under a tyrant's rule (the orators), and public discourses pronounced before a hostile assembly (an idea present in John 7:13). A number of less "public" meanings come into play as the word evolves a less political and more properly "moral" connotation in the Hellenistic period. A case in point is its use to refer to the free and uncensored exchanges of views and opinions, even ones negative in character, that define human friendship.

Given this semantic register, it is not surprising that *parrhesía* should have been classed among the "figures" of Classical rhetoric. Known as *licentia* or *oratio libera*, it was first authoritatively defined for the Latin west in the pseudo-Ciceronian *Rhetorica ad Herennium*: "Frankness of Speech [is practiced] when, before those to whom we owe reverence or fear, we yet exercise our right to speak out, because we seem justified in reprehending them, or persons dear to them, for some fault."[51] As a matter of

---

Christian's Freedom of Speech in the New Testament," *Bulletin of the John Rylands Library* no. 44 (1961/1962): 466–488; Jean Daniélou, *Platonisme et théologie mystique: Doctrine spirituelle de Saint Grégoire de Nysse*, esp. 103–115; L. Engels, "*Fiducia* dans la Vulgate: Le Problème de traduction παρρησία—*fiducia*," *Graecitas et Latinitas Christianorum Primaeva: Supplementa* 1 (1964): 99–141, and by the same author, "*Fiducia*: Influence de l'emploi juridique sur l'usage commun et paléo-chrétien," *Graecitas et Latinitas Christianorum Primaeva: Supplementa* 3 (1970): 61–118. Barthelink and Engels both supply extensive bibliographies on the subject.

[51] "Licentia est cum apud eos quos aut vereri aut metuere debemus tamen aliquid pro iure nostro dicimus, quod eos aut quos ii diligunt aliquo in errato vere reprehendere videamur" (*Rhetorica ad Herennium* 4.36; Eng. trans. Harry Caplan). Although Quintillian rejects *parrhesía* as a rhetorical figure (*Institutio Oratoria*

fact, this is the rhetorical figure at the heart of Juvenalian satire, a key literary model, as earlier indicated, for Cacciaguida's own anti-urban discourse of cantos 15–16. In the first of his *Satires*, Juvenal defiantly affirms that he will exercise the poetic *licentia* that was that of the ancients: "From whence shall you obtain that beautiful frankness with which your forefathers wrote of all that inflamed their souls?" asks a mocking interlocutor, to which the satirist responds "What? You think me afraid to mention names? What does it matter to me if Mucius approves or disapproves of what I say?"[52]

The Christian Scriptures will absorb this entire panoply of juridical, political, and oratorical meanings of the term *parrhesía* into their theology of prophecy, balancing the themes of danger and courage, lawlessness and truthfulness, intimate friendship with God and the hostility of human listeners, and (with Juvenal) linking them to the restoration of an ancestral freedom of speech. In the Acts of the Apostles, for instance, *parrhesía* is the force that transforms the individual into a fearless instrument of the Lord. Hence the sudden courage of the recent convert Saul, who at Damascus "acted boldly" in the name of Jesus ("fiducialiter egerit in nomine Iesu" [Acts 9:27]), and who on the road to Jerusalem "fearlessly preached" in the name of the Lord ("fiducialiter agens in nomine Domini" [Acts 9:28]). Renamed Paul, we find him in the final episode of the apostles' Acts in captivity and awaiting trial, yet still proclaiming the kingdom of God and teaching of Christ with complete *parrhesía* and without prohibition: "cum omni fiducia, sine prohibitione" (Acts 28:31).

In the Pauline Epistles, the emphasis is equally on the absolute *parrhesía* with God that Adam had enjoyed and its restoration through the sacrifice of Christ. Man's originary birthright was a

---

9.2.27–29), the figure is preserved in Isidore (*Etym.* 2.21.31) and in such modern treatises as Heinrich Lausberg's *Elemente der literarischen Rhetorik* (par. 438).

[52] " 'Unde illa priorum / scribendi quodcumque animo flagrante liberet / simplicitas?'—'Cuius non audeo dicere nomen? / Quid refert, dictis ignoscat Mucius an non?' " (*Saturae* 1.151–154.)

free and open exchange with his creator. Lost through sin, this birthright had been regained through Christ and his cross, and would be fully restituted in the eschatological republic. Such a freedom of access to God was understood by the Church Fathers from the time of Origen onward, in both the "gnostic" and "activist" sense: that is, as both a mystical accession to certain *arcana Dei* (divine secrets) as well as an actual practice of prophecy in the human city.

For the Church Fathers, such powers of mystical and prophetic insight were the special province of the martyr. Having endured his or her sacrificial ordeal, the martyr was thought to achieve a quite literal "familiarity" with God: he or she now belonged, just like the prelapsarian Adam and Eve, to God's immediate family. In his *Exhortation to Martyrdom* Origen thus addresses an imaginary assembly of martyrs as intimates of God, referring to the precedent of Paul's rapture:[53]

> You yourselves will as a matter of course know secrets both more and greater than the ineffable words then revealed to Paul. . . . If you remain united with His [Jesus'] followers, you, too, will pass into the heavens, passing beyond not only the earth and its mysteries, but also the heavens and all that concerns them.

The relevance of such visionary powers to Dante's depiction of Cacciaguida, a crusader and martyr, are quite obvious. From the very beginning of canto 15 to his disappearance in canto 18 among the lights of the cross, Cacciaguida is represented as a prophet and spokesman of Christ's venerable sign. He is a divinely empowered reader of the book of divine foreknowledge, the apocalyptic *liber de praescientia Dei*, that "great volume in which white and dark are never altered" (15.51). He sees with "perpetual vision" ("perpetüa vista" [15.65]), exemplifies an ideal equilibrium of love and intelligence ("l'affetto e 'l senno" [15.73]), heat and light ("caldo e . . . luce" [15.77]), looks at the text of history from that "point to which all times are present" ("il punto a

[53] *Prayer-Exhortation to Martyrdom*, trans. John J. O'Meara, 154.

cui tutti li tempi son presenti" [17.17–18]), and arrives from his "martyrdom to this peace" (15.148), the paradoxical peace of Mars.

In so doing Cacciaguida mimes the spiritual itinerary of no less a visionary than Boethius, represented in the heaven of the Sun as:

> l'anima santa che 'l mondo fallace
> fa manifesto a chi di lei ben ode.
>   Lo corpo ond' ella fu cacciata giace
> giuso in Cieldauro; ed essa da martiro
> e da essilio venne a questa pace.   10.125–129
>
> (the sainted soul . . . who makes the fallacious world manifest to any who listen well to him. The body from which it was driven lies down below in Cieldauro, and he came from martyrdom and exile to this peace.)

Together the twin sainted souls ("anime sante") of 10.125 and 17.101 reveal the full extent to which Dante viewed martyrdom and theological/philosophical *gnosis* as indissociable. (Cacciaguida's unmasking of the fallaciousness of our world is in fact but a collage of extracts from Boethius' *Consolatio*.) In the martyr's words and in his works, be they literary or military, a prospect is opened up on the landscape of history which makes visible the providential peace that lies beyond the tragic immediacy of exile and misery. But only for those who, unlike the pilgrim at the opening of canto 16, listen attentively to wisdom's voice ("a chi di lei ben ode").

If in the cases of Boethius and Cacciaguida the applicability of the martyr's attributes is entirely beyond question, the case of the poet-pilgrim requires a more careful examination. First of all, it should be said that the poet-pilgrim is not *yet* a martyr in the literal sense: thus far he has not been made a victim on history's sacrificial altar. But, as I will shortly demonstrate, Cacciaguida's prophecy suggests unequivocally that Dante shall certainly be a martyr, if not literally, then at least figuratively.

The distinction between literal and figurative martyrdom is an oft-repeated one in patristic exegesis, and represents a natural corollary to the "figuralization" of the enemy and "internalization" of epic heroism that I have alluded to earlier. Isidore writes:[54]

> There exist then two forms of martyrdom, one made up of actual physical torments [*in aperta passione*] and the other of the hidden virtues of an individual soul [*in occulta animi virtute*]. Since many, by virtue of having endured the treacheries of the enemy and resisted all carnal temptation, make in their hearts a sacrificial offering of themselves to all-powerful God, they become martyrs in times of peace, since they would certainly have been [literal] martyrs if they had lived in a time of persecution.

If we return to the precise Latin of Cacciaguida's prophecies, I think it becomes perfectly clear that Dante's fate is modeled not only after that of Aeneas but also after that of Christ. This is to say that he belongs among Isidore's martyrs, who either *in aperta passione* or *in occulta animi virtute* re-enact the passion of Christ: a fact whose foundation is of course to be found in the paschal chronology of the poem.

Beyond the epic themes of sacrifice, exile, and battle, a distinctly martyriological pattern can be discerned in Dante's fu-

---

[54] "Duo sunt autem martyrii genera, unum in aperta passione, alterum in occulta animi virtute. Nam multi hostis insidias tolerantes, et cunctis carnalibus desideriis resistentes per hoc, quod se omnipotenti Deo in corde mactaverunt, etiam pacis tempore martyres facti sunt, qui etiam si persecutionis tempus existeret, martyres esse potuerunt" (*Etym.* 7.11.4). Giordano da Rivalto refers to this point in sermon 27 (26 luglio, 1304): "Ed oggidì ne sono di martiri; gli uomini tribolati, che sostengono la povertà, le tribolazioni, che ti fanno mali uomini, che ti spogliano, e tolgono il tuo, se sostieni in pace se' quasi martire. Avvengnachè non si pigli di volontà, ma molti fuggiano, se poteano, e cessavano il martirio; ma pur essendo presi, e non potendo fuggire, allora sosteneano il martirio, ed abbracciavanlo con grande fervore, e con grande amore, ed erano martiri preziosi: incorporata in loro la passione di Cristo passavano a Dio fatti imperadori" (*Prediche*, vol. 1, 212). For a more elaborate discussion of this distinction, see Richard of Saint Victor, *Explicatio in Cantica Canticorum*, Migne PL 196, cols. 465–467.

ture, and this pattern is the sign of a special grace: a *superinfusa gratia*. Like the martyrs who "have left behind house, or brothers, or sisters, or father, or mother, or wife, or children, or lands" (Matt. 19:29), the poet-pilgrim shall be called upon to make a total sacrifice: "Tu lascerai ogne cosa diletta / più caramente" ("You shall leave everything most dearly cherished" [17.55–56]). He shall be forced to abandon all hopes of an earthly peace and home in order to set out upon exile's arduous path (17.59), constantly ascending and descending by another's stairs (17.60), tasting the salt of another's bread (17.59), and all the while with a wicked and senseless company (17.62) weighing heavily on his shoulders (17.61).[55] He shall not only undergo these various trials and humiliations, but also be tempted, as Isidore's definition prescribes, by the advances of an impudic Phaedra-like *Fiorenza*, haunted by the insidious plots of foes (17.95), and thrust into a personal vale of tears ("tu cadrai in questa valle ... tutta ingrata, tutta matta ed empia" [17.63–64]).

But, like those martyrs who have endured such sufferings in the name of Christ (Matt. 19:29), he shall be rewarded for his perseverance with that salvific honor (17.135) and eternal peace that comes from boldly speaking the uncensored truth. The poet-pilgrim will indeed be one of Christ's martyrs, a literary bearer of the cross, and justice will be done. Vengeance will testify to the truth that dispenses it: "la vendetta / fia testimonio al ver che la dispensa" (17.53–54). The punishment of the perfidious acts of Boniface and Corso Donati will come well before even Dante's own death (17.98–99). Victory is assured once Dante completes the term of (literary) warfare Providence has prescribed ("anzi

---

[55] Cf. 6.688 for Aeneas' own *iter durum*. Although the *calle/spalle/valle* rhyme of 17.59–61–63 is not infrequent in Dante's *Commedia*, it is probably not accidental, given the obvious thematic affinities with the crisis delineated in canto 17, that it appears (in inverted order) in the poem's opening description (*Inf.* 1.14–16–18). It returns once again in *Inferno* 15.50–52–54, as the pilgrim describes his predicament in canto 1 to Brunetto, and canto 15 of course looks forward explicitly to Cacciaguida's *chiose*.

che 'l militar li sia prescritto" [25.57]). Like the Emperor Constantine, he too shall rise up and conquer under the sign of the cross. And like the blessed souls of the third canticle, he shall live forever in the memory of "those who shall call this time ancient" ("coloro che questo tempo chiameranno antico" [17.119–120]).

How, then, is it that the story of Aeneas' foundation of Rome can be retold as the story of the writing of a poem? The approximation may seem untenable at first glance, but it is made possible by certain peculiarities of the Christian theology of the cross. First of all, this cross, as I have earlier insisted, has a single exemplar—the universal cross of Christ—but it can be figuratively dispersed into an infinity of individualized crosses. These personalized "crosses" encompass the most external and military of enemies and obstacles as well as those enemies and obstacles hidden away in the depths of the individual's heart. The Christian's war is, thus, like that of the pilgrim of *Inferno* 2.4–5, a double war of the journey and the pity ("la guerra / sì del cammino e sì de la pietate"): a combat involving body as well as soul, a crusade that is both exterior and interior.

So in each and every individual Christian's conversion or aversion to Christ, taking on or putting off of the cross, is an inchoate epic narrative replete with violent battles, miraculous reversals, stunning victories and defeats. And each of these private epics, whose heroes are no longer exclusively the noble Scipios and divine Aeneas' but rather "Jew and Greek, slave and free, male and female" (Gal. 3:28), is cast in the image of the biography of Jesus Christ. This is possible inasmuch as all are bound together by the mysterious logic which rules human history from its grandest events—Aeneas' foundation of Rome—to the most intimate details—the exile of a poet.[56]

---

[56] No two texts play a more crucial role in this "internalization" of epic than Virgil's *Aeneid* and Augustine's *Confessions* (the two of which are in fact closely related if only "negatively," that is, by the asperity of Augustine's repression of the Virgilian precedent. The same is true of the *City of God*, which from beginning to end presents itself as a Christian response to the vision of Roman history articu-

Secondly, this seemingly improbable assimilation of the act of writing to the foundation of a city is accomplished through that peculiar synthesis of *word* and *act* that is characteristic of the Christian concept of martyrdom. The *parrhesiastes*, he who speaks out dangerously, at the risk of losing his life, is a figure who joins the epic action of the Classical hero to the verbal action of the Christian prophet. In so doing he becomes a sort of Christian Amphion who through divinely empowered words helps to construct that Rome in which Christ is a Roman: "quella Roma onde Cristo è romano" (*Purg.* 32.102). Was not the temple built, after all, both of miraculous *signs* and of *martyrdoms* ("di segni e di martìri" [*Par.* 18.123])?

Such is the program which Dante is called upon to fulfill. His epic task, as mapped out in canto 17, is a simple one: to tell all and spare none, irrespective of the risk. At his descendant's expression of fear, his statement that he feels he is confronted with a choice between the literary posterity of his *carmi* or songs ("temo di *perder viver* tra coloro / che questo tempo chiameranno antico" [119–120; my italics]), and a compromise with history, Cacciaguida's response is unequivocal:

---

lated in Book 6 by Anchises). As Brooks Otis has shown in *Vergil: A Study in Civilized Poetry* (esp. 5–96), Aeneas embodies a wholly new type of epic heroism with respect to the Greek epic tradition. He is the hero of a complex metropolitan civilization, constantly torn between competing demands, always enmeshed in his collectivity's past and future. He is less the protagonist of great epic *aristeiai*, of athletic feats or adventurous wanderings, than the embodiment of those moral virtues which Virgil conceived as the foundation of *Romanitas* itself: such virtues as *pietas*, *iustitia*, and *fortitudo*. The result is a "psychological" dimension absent in the Homeric prototypes: an epic of moral, ethical, and psychic struggles and of personal sacrifices whose overarching theme is history as exodus. In the *Confessions* we are brought one step further and this preoccupation with the unfolding of the individual subject comes to dominate the entire foreground of the text. The language of war and conquest, of epic sacrifice and reward, are all preserved, as are such characteristic epic themes as those of the circular journey, the founding of the city, the temptations of eros and of illusory homelands. But they are "figuralized" and "internalized," and thus redefined in individualized Christian terms.

> Ma nondimen, rimossa ogne menzogna,
> tutta tua visïon fa manifesta;
> e lascia pur grattar dov' è la rogna.
>
> Ché se la voce tua sarà molesta
> nel primo gusto, vital nodrimento
> lascerà poi, quando sarà digesta.
>
> Questo tuo grido farà come vento,
> che le più alte cime più percuote;
> e ciò non fa d'onor poco argomento.   17.127–135

(But none the less, all falsehood set aside, make manifest all that you have seen; and then let them scratch where the itch is. For if at first taste your voice be grievous, yet shall it leave thereafter vital nourishment when digested. This cry of yours shall do as does the wind, which smites most upon the loftiest summits; and this shall be no little cause of honor.)

The call is one to bring into play the full etymological force of the word *martyr*: bearing full and uncompromising witness to the realities of the otherworld, no matter how great the price.[57] "Qui enim voluerit animam suam salvam facere, perdet eam: qui autem perdiderit animam suam propter me, inveniet eam" ("For whosoever will save his life, shall lose it, and he that shall lose his life for my sake, shall find it" [Matt. 16:25]): such is the paradoxical economy of sacrifice, and Dante's literary survival (or *viver*), over both the short term and the long, depends upon it. Answering to this call—the poem is of course Dante's answer—the poet-pilgrim is to add one last link to that "condescensional" and "di-

---

[57] Boethius' own martyrdom as described in *Paradise* 10.124–129 serves as an indirect model here. For Boethius was he who, like Cacciaguida in his own exemplary discourses: " 'l mondo fallace / fa manifesto a chi di lei ben ode" (125–126). The phrase "rimossa ogne menzogna" seems to recall the frequent references in the *Consolation of Philosophy* to removing the various obstacles ("nubila," "tenebrae," "nube caligantia") which impair human vision and judgment. Making like Boethius "all manifest," Dante would achieve, not the illusory honor of literary fame, but rather the eternal honor of the Christian martyr, philosopher, and prophet. On this general subject, see once again the discussion in *Monarchia* 3.1.1–27 of the prophet's loyal service to "Truth's unwavering throne."

dactic" chain that we have discovered at Sant' Apollinare and in cantos 14–18.

Just as through his crucifixion Christ demonstrated the glorious light that lies beyond the humiliations and sacrifices of history, just as Cacciaguida and Apollinaris re-enacted Christ's metamorphosis and in so doing bear witness for the benefit of the reader/viewer (poet-pilgrim included) to the comic perspectives opened up to humankind by Jesus' sacrifice, the poet-pilgrim is now to adopt this very same role. His task is a literary intercession in the image of that of the martyr. On the one hand, by making the full vision manifest, he takes on his personal cross and is assured of the ensuing rewards. On the other hand, issuing forth linguistic signs that shall be a bitter cross to some, he advances the cause of Christ's redemption of mankind. For, like the secret comedy that underlies his own tragic fate, *these cruciform words shall be converted into signs of eternal life*: a "vital nourishment" ("vital nodrimento" [17.131]) for those who endure their initial bitter taste. God's transfiguring *paideia*, with its sometimes sweet, sometimes bitter lessons and cures, shall now be Dante's own.[58]

This literary task, cast in the image of the martyr's imitation of Christ, has a further complementary aspect, discussed only briefly in an earlier chapter. If the full disclosure of Dante's prophetic text is to initiate the same hermeneutic conversion in the reader that was accomplished in the poet-pilgrim in cantos 14–18, in Aeneas in Book 6 and in Scipio in his dream, one further

---

[58] As Scartazzini and others have indicated, the specific image in 17.130–132 quotes from Lady Philosophy's speech in 3, prosa 1.13–14 of Boethius' *Consolation of Philosophy*: "talia sunt quippe quae restant, ut degustata quidem mordeant, interius autem recepta dulcescant." This line is preceded by one that, as I have earlier suggested, may illuminate the pilgrim's opening speech in canto 17.13–27: "O . . . summum lassorum solamen animorum quam tu me vel sententiarum pondere vel canendi etiam iucunditate refovisti! Adeo ut iam me post haec inparem fortunae ictibus esse non arbitrer. Itaque remedia quae paulo acriora esse dicebas non modo non perhorresco, sed audiendi avidus vehementer efflagito" (3, prosa 1.3–9). On Fortune's sweet/sour medicine, see also 4, prosa 6.109–119; on Fortune's negative pedagogy, see 2, prosa 8.7–18.

literary support is required: exemplary figurations of historical individuals such as Christ, his imitators Cacciaguida and Apollinaris, or for that matter, the souls of the damned, to serve as negative or positive models that will buttress the reader's faith. Like the Juvenalian satirist, the Christian poet is called upon to name names, famous names, renowned examples of sin and virtue, whether Mucius likes it or not. Cacciaguida's concluding words in canto 17 thus describe a poetics of exemplarity which completes Dante's literary imitation of Christ in his future *Commedia*:

> Però ti son mostrate in queste rote,
> nel monte e ne la valle dolorosa
> pur l'anime che son di fama note,
>   che l'animo di quel ch'ode, non posa
> né ferma fede per essempro ch'aia
> la sua radice incognita e ascosa,
> né per altro argomento che non paia.   17.136–142

(Therefore only the souls known of fame have been shown to you within these wheels, upon the mountain, and in the woeful valley; for the mind of him who hears rests not nor confirms its faith by an example that has its roots unknown or hidden, nor for other proof that is not manifest.)

I have already suggested the relevance of this passage to the figure of the poet-pilgrim, of whom Cacciaguida himself is the symbolic root. It represents, as earlier indicated, a quite deliberate inversion of the Pauline definition of faith:

> Est autem fides sperandarum substantia rerum, argumentum non apparentium. In hac enim testimonium consecuti sunt senes. Fide intelligimus aptata esse saecula verbo Dei: ut ex invisibilibus visibilia fierent.
>
> (Now faith is the substance of things hoped for, the conviction of things that appear not. For by this the ancients obtained a testimony. By faith we understand that the world was framed by the

word of God; that from invisible things, visible things might be made.) [Hebr. 11:1–3]

Seen through the eye of faith, creation discloses its invisible mysteries. Yet faith requires a foundation in appearance: these invisible mysteries must condescend into visible figures in order that they remain intelligible to human faculties (limited as they are). The literary program of Dante's *Commedia* is thus to provide a diversity of visible/readable exemplary figurations that "shore up faith" inasmuch as they provide the negative double of the hermeneutic of faith described in Hebrews 11. In Dante's poem the narrative movement from visible to invisible, outer to inner vision, earthly to divine perspectives which is the movement of faith, must be doubled by an inverse move from unintelligible mystery to fully intelligible revelation. Such is the foundation of Dante's poetics, a poetics modeled on the Incarnation and sacrifice of Christ. Its ultimate consequence is the production not only of a gallery of exemplary "souls of noted fame" ("anime che son di fama note" [17.138]), not only of a central exemplum—the poet-pilgrim—who is the reader's double, but also an act of writing which is in itself an exemplary cross, an exemplary imitation of Christ.

The Empowered Voice

In my opening chapters I have insisted on the importance to cantos 14–18 and to Dante's Classical models of the theme of the "transmission of the mantle": the father's empowerment of the son as the privileged spokesman for and bearer of the paternal seed, his responsibility for the symbolic *cognomen*. In my later chapters, I have underscored the sense in which Christianity absorbs this same complex of themes, but transforms them by insisting on the primacy of an alternative genealogy: the transcendental affiliation of man with God through the cross of Christ. In this last chapter, the key to the translation of the language of epic into that of Christian conversion and sacrifice has emerged as the concept of *martyrdom*: martyrdom as a poetics and as a new epic construct joining Classical and Christian models, martyrdom as a biographical key to Dante's conception of his own personal history and as a link between "personal" and "universal" history, and, finally, martyrdom as a precondition for mystical visions and epic endeavors. Last of all, I should like to recapitulate one final question that is essential to Dante's use of martyrdom and martyr in cantos 14–18: the matter of speech and epic action, or, better, speech *as* epic action.

We have seen how at the climactic moment in cantos 14–18, Book 6 of the *Aeneid*, and Cicero's *De Re Publica*, the father proclaims the son's historical mission. In an important departure from his Classical prototypes, however, Dante exploits the duality of speech and action inherent in the Christian concept of martyrdom, preserving the underlying logic of the epic encounter of father and son, yet transforming the character of the epic mission itself. For the son's task in cantos 14–18 is first and foremost a literary one: "tutta tua visïon fa manifesta" commands Cacciaguida; reveal all, no matter how great the cost.

If there is a symbolic "mantle" transmitted at the center of *Paradise*, then it must in some sense be a "verbal" one. But although it is an act of writing—or, in the fiction of the poem, of prophetic "speech" or "song"—that replaces the mission of founding or defending the integrity of Rome, the epic dimension is preserved by identifying the writing of the poem with that courageous public speech or *parrhesía* which was considered the special province of Christian martyrs like the crusader Cacciaguida. The symbolic "mantle" that Cacciaguida transmits to his descendant Dante, I would suggest, is none other than the bold and vigorous voice that Cacciaguida himself will exemplify in the course of cantos 14–18: an ancestral voice in which the strains of Scripture, liturgy, Virgilian Latin, Juvenalian satire, and Boethian *Philosophia* are clearly audible, but, all the same, a distinctively *native* Florentine voice.[59]

---

[59] The theme of prophetic investiture brings to mind the scene in II Kings 2:1–

From the opening reference to that interior "speech that is one for all" ("quella favella / ch'è una in tutti" [14.88–89]) to the closing mention of Cacciaguida as a lyrical "artist" (18.51), the Martial cantos are filled with references to the sounding of the human voice in prophetic speech and song. Some of the implications of this recurrent theme I have already explored. The theme of the transmission of the father's voice, for example, involves an affiliation of Dante's book with God's immutable volume. Transcribing Cacciaguida's prophetic discourse, the poet-pilgrim's own transcript is symbolically bound to the immutable divine Book.

As the Christian double of Anchises, Cacciaguida also serves as a vehicle for the prophetic voice/text of Virgil. Indeed, as I have shown, it is through Cacciaguida's own voice that the two literary horizons of Dante's *Commedia*, Virgil's *Aeneid* and the Christian Scriptures and liturgy, are systematically fused. Likewise, between Cacciaguida's prophetic *latin*, his Latin greeting, and the various other references to languages ancient and modern, sensate and suprasensible, a pattern emerges whose principal objective is the identification of Dante as the privileged inheritor of these languages: he is their translator into "this modern tongue" ("questa moderna favella" [16.33]). The voice that Dante inherits is thus one empowering him as the successor to both Virgil and Paul, as both epic singer of Rome and as Christian prophet. That the dualism of Aeneas and Paul cited at the outset of the journey (*Inf.* 2.32) is here displaced by that of *Virgil* and Paul, I think suggests the extent to which Dante imagines Virgil's poem (as for that matter, the *Thebaid* of Statius) as a mirror image of his own; that is, as an ultimately autobiographical, even confessional, high Tragedy (*Inf.* 20.113). But, to return to the earlier argument, it is this dual literary genealogy that is the point of the systematic overlayering of scriptural and Virgilian language in Dante's Martial cantos.

---

18 in which Elisha receives Elijah's prophetic mantle as the latter ascends into the heavens in a fiery chariot. The parallel may be of some significance inasmuch as Cacciaguida describes himself as a brother of Elijah: "Moronto fu mio frate ed Eliseo" (15.136).

The term "voce" (or voice) in cantos 14–18, however, often extends far beyond these genealogical boundaries, becoming, for instance, the Christian signifier whose Classical equivalent is *fama*. The Christian Hall of Fame we encounter in the heaven of Mars is thus composed of spirits who, before coming to heaven, were literally of "great voice" (meaning "renowned"): "spiriti son beati, che giù, prima / che venissero al ciel, fuor *di gran voce*, / sì ch'ogne musa ne sarebbe opima" (18.31–33; italics mine). Such a usage of the term "voce" is admittedly conventional, yet once again it implies the all-important conflation of verbal action (*gran voce*) with bodily action that is essential to Dante's "internalization" and/or "figuralization" of Classical conceptions of heroism. To define the greatest epic heroes of Christendom as "of great voice" is to place the literary-prophetic endeavor of the poet-pilgrim within the semantic field of "heroism." Likewise, to attach the adjective "opima" (or *opimus*), a privileged term in the description of relics and battle spoils, to the literary "wealth" of the above-cited epic "muses" is implicitly to compare the literary endeavor with that of a victorious warrior seizing the *opima spolia* that will bring honor to him.[60]

Such details might perhaps seem incidental if it were not for the opening vision of the warriors of the cross as the singers or holy chords of Christ's cruciform lyre. The theme is especially important because the closing image in the heaven of Mars brings us back to the theme of song:

> Indi, tra l'altre luci mota e mista,
> mostrommi l'alma che m'avea parlato
> qual era tra i cantor del cielo artista.   18.49–51

---

[60] Although literally "opimus" means fat, rich, plump, or corpulent, this specialized military usage is fairly common, found, for instance, in Anchises' description of Marcellus at the close of Book 6: "Aspice ut insignis *spoliis* Marcellus *opimis* / ingreditur, victorque viros supereminent omnis" (6.855–856; my italics). See also 10.449: "Aut spoliis ego iam raptis laudabor opimis." The point to remember here is that, like a martyr's relics, such spoils are a badge of honor to their bearer, just as singing the exploits of a glorious hero in turn brings honor to the singer.

(Then, moving and mingling among the other lights, the soul which had spoken with me showed me how great an artist it was among the singers of that heaven.)

Not only are the heroes once again seen as singers of Christ, but Cacciaguida is envisioned as one of the most accomplished of these singers: a veritable "artist." This artistic attribute firmly establishes the completeness of Cacciaguida's exemplarity at the close of Dante's Martial vision: he is truly the resplendent topaz of the final canticle, the bearer of the full range of heavenly virtues, and an ideal double of his equally artistic descendant. One is the literal crusader and singer of the cross enrolled in the company of heroes "of great voice," the other the literary crusader who in cantos 14–18 symbolically comes into his own voice.

If, then, Dante's use of the term "voce" further explores certain Classical/Christian parallels and contrasts, while expanding on the theme of martyrdom as both testimony and action, its central role is to dramatize the empowerment of Dante's own literary endeavor. This endeavor, as Cacciaguida defines it, is an unabashedly prophetic one. But the adverse historical setting in which it is circumscribed, as well as the mortal risk involved, identify it more precisely with the *parrhesía* of Christ's martyrs. Time and again in cantos 14–18, Cacciaguida actively solicits Dante's speech, and often with unusually strong words of encouragement. On two occasions in particular his requests are of the utmost significance.

The first comes in canto 15 and immediately follows that mysterious colloquium necessarily above the "target" of the human intellect (15.37–42) and Cacciaguida's prayer of thanksgiving for an act of grace bestowed upon his "son" (15.47–48). After describing the perpetual vision of the emparadised souls, he emphatically calls upon Dante to sound his voice: "la voce tua sicura, balda e lieta / suoni la volontà, suoni 'l disio" ("let your voice, self-assured, bold and joyous, sound forth the will, sound forth the desire" [15.67–68]). Such verbal self-assurance, boldness, and joy can only be understood as the sign of an extraordinary privilege: a "grace" ("cortesia" [15.48]) at least as great as that bestowed upon Paul when he was allowed to penetrate the *arcana Dei* and to speak of them, albeit darkly. Hence the subject of Cacciaguida's unintelligible "conception" ("concetto") in 15.37–42 must be taken as a confirmation of the truly unprecedented glorious destiny that awaits his descendant: for him as for Paul (and in a sense Aeneas), the doors of the heavens shall indeed open twice.[61]

The second and final instance of Cacciaguida's prophetic empowerment of Dante's voice comes in the midst of the climactic speech which marks the conclusion of canto 17. The call to sound freely the instrument of his prophetic voice is turned on this occasion not only into a full literary manifesto ("tutta tua visïon fa manifesta"), but also into a conventional image of the prophet filled with the *pneuma* of the Holy Spirit:

> Questo tuo grido farà come vento,
> che le più alte cime più percuote;
> e ciò non fa d'onor poco argomento.   17.133–135

---

[61] The mysterious "deep speech" at the opening of canto 15 may well concern the fulfillment of Brunetto's promise back in *Inferno* 15.55–56 that: "Se tu segui tua stella, / non puoi fallire a glorïoso porto." As has been recognized since Dante's earliest commentators, there are unmistakable and important links between *Inferno* 15 and the Cacciaguida cantos. Brunetto's statement that such shall be the pilgrim's fame that both Florentine parties shall hunger for him ("La tua fortuna tanto onor ti serba, / che l'una parte e l'altra avranno fame / di te" [*Inf.* 15.70–72]), for instance, recalls Cacciaguida's own description of the importance of Dante's neutralism: "a te fia bello / averti fatta parte per te stesso" (17.68–69). The mention of *onor* in turn recalls both the ineffable honor described in the opening of canto 15 (28–30), as well as the prophetic honor Cacciaguida will evoke in 17.135. As for Brunetto's vision of Florentine history, I take it for granted that it is essential to the capsule history of Florence presented by Cacciaguida in cantos 15–17. (Both make ample use, in any case, of the chronicle tradition.) Numerous other affinities can of course be found between *Inferno* 15 and *Paradise* 15–18, in particular Dante's mention of his readiness for the blows of fortune: a statement which once again mirrors the attitude of Aeneas in Book 6, Scipio in Cicero's *Somnium*, and Boethius in Book 3 of the *Consolation of Philosophy*.

(This cry of yours shall do as does the wind, which smites most upon the loftiest summits; and this shall be no little cause of honor.)

Here the prophetic cry from his exile in the desert of history is quite literally imagined as a fusion of word and action. The pilgrim's word emerges as a natural force, an apocalyptic wind extending from history's valleys to its symbolic mountain tops. This is both the wind of Revelations 6:13 that reaches even the stars ("et stellae de caelo ceciderunt super terram, sicut ficus emittit grossos suos cum a vento magno movetur") and, as Sarolli and Mineo among others have pointed out, the apocalyptic shout of Isaiah 40:9: "Super montem excelsum ascende, tu qui evangelizas Sion; exalta in fortitudine vocem tuam, qui evangelizas Ierusalem; exalta, noli timere" ("Ascend upon a high mountain, you who bring good tidings to Sion; lift up your voice with strength, you who bring good tidings to Jerusalem; lift it up, fear not").[62]

From the powerlessness of his exile in Ravenna, Dante must have maintained with an anguished intensity this secret faith in the power of the poetic voice and word: its capacity to transform the landscape of history, even to strike down the most imposing of political mountaintops. The dream of a triumphal return to the fallen city sadly persists even as late as canto 25 of *Paradise*, the dream of a historical reward, of a public honor not unlike that achieved by Virgil under the reign of Augustus: "con altra voce omai, con altro vello / ritornerò poeta, e in sul fonte / del mio battesmo prenderò 'l capello" ("with another voice now, with another fleece, a poet I shall return, and at the font of my baptism take the crown" [25.7–9]). And yet, while completing the final canticle he must have been well aware of the futility of such

---

[62] On Dante as martyr and prophet, the most exhaustive study is Niccolò Mineo's *Profetica e apocalittica in Dante*, esp. 210–222, 254–296. Mineo has particularly interesting things to say about the Cacciaguida cantos in their relation to the rest of the *Commedia*. See also Gian Roberto Sarolli, "Dante's Katabasis and Mission," in *Prolegomena alla Divina Commedia*, 381–419, a study which insists in particular on Dante's self-representation as prophet.

hopes. Between the dirgelike theme of Mars, *mors*, and martyrdom, and the rapturous eschatological music of the cross, the Martial cantos ultimately promise no such historical apotheosis. The rise of Cangrande remains the sole locus in cantos 14–18 of all immediate "historical" hopes. And while such hopes are far from negligible at the center of *Paradise*, they are nonetheless placed in a context of growing skepticism about any imminent resurrection of the Roman holy seed. History may indeed be transfigured and history's tragedies revealed as eternity's comedy; but this transfiguration of history can only be completed from the perspective of history's end. So to the madness of a fallacious world, to a city of man plunged in eternal turmoil, the Martial cantos finally propose only the consolation of self-sacrifice in imitation of Christ's cross, the consolation of a literary cry.

BIBLIOGRAPHY

Primary Sources

Alan of Lille. *Anticlaudianus*. Ed. R. Bossuat. Paris: J. Vrin, 1955.
— *Anticlaudianus or the Good and Perfect Man*. Trans. and comm. James J. Sheridan. Toronto: Pontifical Inst. of Mediaeval Studies, 1973.
— *Opera Omnia*. Migne PL 210.
— *The Plaint of Nature*. Trans. and comm. James J. Sheridan. Toronto: Pontifical Inst. of Mediaeval Studies, 1980.
Albert the Great (Albertus Magnus). *Super Dionysium De Divinis Nominibus*. Ed. Paul Simon. Vol. 37/1 of *Opera Omnia*. Ed. B. Geyer. Aschendorff: Monasterii Westfalorum, 1972.
— *Opera Omnia*. Ed. Auguste Borgnet. Paris: Vivès, 1890–1899. Vol. 4, *De Caelo et Mundo, De Generatione et Corruptione, De Meteoris*. Vol. 8, *Politicorum*. Vol. 14, *Commentarii in Operae B. Dionysii Areopagita*.
Albumasar (Abu Ma'shar). *De Magnis Coniunctionibus*. Venice: Erhard Ratdolt, 1489.
Alighieri, Dante. *La Commedia secondo l'antica vulgata*. Ed. Giorgio Petrocchi. Vols. 7/1, 7/2, 7/3, and 7/4 of *Le opere di Dante Alighieri*. Edizione Nazionale a cura della Società Dantesca Italiana. Verona: A. Mondadori, 1966–1967.
— *The Divine Comedy*. Ed., trans. and comm. C. S. Singleton. 6 vols. Bollingen Series 80. Princeton: Princeton University Press, 1975.
— *Il Convivio*. Edizione critica a cura di Maria Simonelli. Testi e Saggi di Letterature Moderne, Testi 2. Bologna: Casa Editrice Prof. Riccardo Pàtron, 1966.
— *Il Convivio ridotto a miglior lezione e commentato*. Eds. G. Busnelli and G. Vandelli, 2nd ed. rev. A. E. Quaglio. Vols. 4–5 of *Opere di Dante*. Fondazione Giorgio Cini. Florence: Le Monnier, 1964.
— *Epistolae*. 2nd ed., ed. and trans. Paget Toynbee. Oxford: Clarendon Press, 1966.
— *Monarchia*. Ed. Pier Giorgio Ricci. Vol. 5 of *Le opere di Dante Alighieri*. Edizione Nazionale a cura della Società Dantesca Italiana. Verona: A. Mondadori, 1965.
— *Rime*. 2nd ed., ed. Gianfranco Contini. Turin: Einaudi 1946.

Alighieri, Dante. *Vita Nuova*. Ed. Domenico di Robertis. Milan and Naples: Riccardo Ricciardi, 1980.
— *De Vulgari Eloquentia*. Ed. Pier Vincenzo Mengaldo. Vol. 2 of *Opere minori*. La Letteratura Italiana: Storia e Testi, no. 5. Milan and Naples: Riccardo Ricciardi, 1979.
Alighieri, Pietro. *Super Dantis Ipsius Genitoris Comoediam Commentarium*. Ed. Vincenzo Nannucci. Florence: A. Garinei, 1846.
Ambrose, Saint. *Expositio Evangelii Secundum Lucam*. Migne PL 15.
Analecta Sacra Spicilegio Solesmensi. Ed. Jean Baptiste Pitra. 5 vols. Paris: Jouby and Roger, 1876–1884.
The Apocryphal New Testament being the Apocryphal Gospels, Acts, Epistles and Apocalypses. Trans. M. R. James. Oxford: Clarendon Press, 1924.
New Testament Apocrypha. Eds. Edgar Hennecke and W. Schneemelcher; trans. R. M. Wilson. 2 vols. Philadelphia: Westminster Press, 1965.
Aquinas, Saint Thomas. *In Librum Beati Dionysii De Divinis Nominibus Expositio*. Ed. Ceslai Pera. Turin: Marietti, 1950.
— *Sententia Libri Ethicorum Aristoteles*. Vol. 47, part 1 of *Opera Omnia*. Ed. fratrum predicatorum Scta. Sabinae. Rome: Sancta Sabina, 1969.
— *Summa Theologiae*. Ed. by the Ottawa Institute of Medieval Studies. 4 vols. Ottawa: Impensis Studii Generalis Ordinis Predicatorum, 1941–1944.
Aristotle. *The Complete Works of Aristotle: The Revised Oxford Translation*. Ed. Jonathan Barnes. 2 vols. Bollingen Series 71–2. Princeton: Princeton University Press, 1984.
Augustine of Hippo, Saint. *La Cité de Dieu*. Ed. G. Bardy. Trans. G. Combès. Vols. 33–38 of *Oeuvres de Saint Augustin*. Bruges: Desclée de Brouwer, 1959.
— *The City of God*. Ed. Vernon J. Bourke. Trans. Gerald G. Walsh et al. Garden City, New York: Image Books, 1958.
— *Confessions*. Ed. W.H.D. Rouse. Trans. William Watts. 2 vols. Loeb Classical Library. London: Heinemann, 1912.
— *Ennarationes in Psalmos*. Migne PL 36–37.
— *In Joannis Evangelium*. Migne PL 35.
— *Sermones*. Migne PL 38–39.
— *On the Soul and Its Origins in Saint Augustine: Anti-Pelagian Writings*. Ed. and trans. Phillip Schaff. Library of the Nicene and Post-Nicene Fathers, vol. 5. Grand Rapids: Eerdmans, 1971.

Bacon, Roger. *The Opus Majus of Roger Bacon*. Ed. John Henry Bridges. 2 vols. Oxford: Clarendon Press, 1897.
Bede ("The Venerable"). *De Mundi Coelestis Terrestrisque Constitutione*. Migne PL 90.
— *Opera Rythmica*. Part 4 of *Opera*. CCSL 122.
pseudo-Bede. *In Evangelium Matthaei Expositio*. Migne PL 92. (A version of Hrabanus Maurus' commentary on Matthew.)
Benvenuto de Rambaldis de Imola. *Comentum super Dantis Aldigherij Comoediam*. Ed. Jacobus Philippo Lacaita. 5 vols. Florence: G. Barbera, 1887.
Berengosius, the Abbot. *De Laude et Inventione Sanctae Crucis*. Migne PL 160.
Bernard Silvestris. *Commentary on the First Six Books of Virgil's Aeneid*. Eds. and trans. E. G. Schreiber and T. E. Maresca. Lincoln: University of Nebraska Press, 1979.
Bersuire, Pierre. *Ovidius Metamorphoseos Moralizatus*. Ed. Fausto Ghisalberti. *Studij Romanzi* 13 (1933): 5–132.
The Holy Bible, translated from the Latin Vulgate: The Old Testament, first published by the English College at Douay (1609) and The New Testament, first published by the English College at Rheims. Notes by George L. Haydock, ed. F. C. Husenbeth. 2 vols. London and New York: Virtue, Emmins and Roberts, 1850.
The Jerusalem Bible. General ed. Alexander Jones. Garden City: Doubleday and Co., 1966.
Biblia Sacra cum Glossa Ordinaria. With postillae, commentary of Nicholas of Lyra. 6 vols. Duaci: B. Belleri typ., 1617.
Biblia Sacra Iuxta Vulgatam Clementinam. Eds. Alberto Colunga and Lorenzo Turrado. 5th ed. Madrid, Biblioteca de Autores Cristianos, 1977.
Boccaccio, Giovanni. *Genealogie Deorum Gentilium Libri*. Ed. Vincenzo Romano. Vols. 10–11 of *Opere*. Scrittori d'Italia nos. 200–201. Bari: Laterza, 1951.
— *Teseida delle nozze d'Emilia*. Ed. Aurelio Roncaglia. Vol. 3 of *Opere*. Scrittori d'Italia no. 185. Bari: Laterza, 1941.
Boethius. *De Institutione Arithmetica. De Institutione Musica*. Ed. G. Friedlein. Leipzig: Teubner, 1867.
— *The Theological Tractates, The Consolation of Philosophy*. Eds. and trans. H. F. Stewart and E. K. Rand. Loeb Classical Library. London: Heinemann, 1946.

Bonaventure, Saint. *Opera Omnia*. Ed. PP. Collegii a S. Bonaventura. Quaracchi, 1882-1902. Vol. 5, *Collationes in Hexaemeron*. Vol. 9, *Sermones de Tempore*.
— *Vitis Mystica*. Migne PL 184. (Erroneously attributed to Bernard of Clairvaux by Migne.)
Cassiodorus. *Chronica sive Historia Ecclesiastica Tripartita*. Migne PL 69.
Chalcidius. *Platonis Timaeus Interprete Chalcidio cum eiusdem Commentario*. Ed. J. Wrobel. Leipzig: Teubner, 1876.
Chronica de Origine Civitatis. (See Hartwig)
Chrysostom, Saint John. *Homiliae in Matthaeum*. Migne PG 57–58.
Cicero. *De Finibus Bonorum et Malorum*. Ed. T. Schiche. Leipzig: Teubner, 1919.
— *De Officiis*. Ed. Paolo Fedeli. Milan: Mondadori, 1965.
— *De Re Publica*. Ed. K. Ziegler. Leipzig: Teubner, 1915.
— *On the Commonwealth*. Trans. G. H. Sabine and S. B. Smith. Indianapolis: Bobbs-Merrill, 1976.
— *Tusculanarum Disputationum*. Ed. O. Plasberg. Leipzig: Teubner, 1917.
Constantine the Great, Emperor. *Opera*. Migne PL 8.
Cornelii a Lapide. *Commentaria in Quatuor Evangelia*. Ed. A. Padovani. 4 vols. Turin: Marietti, 1922.
Cyril of Jerusalem. *Epistola ad Constantinum*. Migne PG 33.
Damian, Peter. *Opera Omnia*. Migne PL 144–145.
Daniello, Bernardino. *Dante con l'espositione di M. Bernardo Daniello da Lucca sopra la sua Comedia dell'Inferno, del Purgatorio, & del Paradiso*. Venice: Pietro da Fino, 1568.
del Virgilio, Giovanni. *Allegoriae Librorum Ovidii Metamorphoseos*. Ed. Fausto Ghisalberti. *Il Giornale Dantesco* 34 (1931): 43–109.
pseudo-Dionysius ("the Areopagite"). *De Caeleste Hierarchia*. Trans. John Scotus (Eriugena). Migne PL 122.
— *De Divinis Nominibus*. Migne PG 3.
— *Dionysiaca*. Ed. Ph. Chevalier. 2 vols. Bruges: Desclée de Brouwer, 1936.
Donne, John. *The Complete English Poems*. Ed. A. J. Smith. Middlesex: Penguin Books, 1971.
Eumenius. *Panegyricus Constantino Augusto*. Migne PL 8.
Eusebius of Caesaria. *Eusebius: Church History, Life of Constantine the Great and Oration in Praise of Constantine*. Trans. Arthur C. McGiffert and

Ernest C. Richardson. Vol. 1 of *A Select Library of Nicene and Post-Nicene Fathers of the Christian Church*, second series. Eds. P. Schaff and H. Wace. Grand Rapids: Eerdmans, 1952.

— *Historiae Ecclesiasticae, Vita Constantini.* Migne PG 20.

Firmicii Materni, Iulius. *Matheseos Libri VIII.* Ed. W. Kroll and F. Skutsch. 2 vols. Leipzig: Teubner, 1968.

Fulgentius. *Opera.* Ed. R. Helm. Leipzig: Teubner, 1898. (See also van Staverin)

— *Fulgentius the Mythographer.* Ed. and trans. Leslie G. Whitbread. Columbus: Ohio State University Press, 1971.

Giordano da Rivalto. *Prediche del beato fra Giordano da Rivalto.* 2 vols. Florence: Il Magheri, 1831.

— *Prediche inedite del beato Giordano da Rivalto dell'ordine dei Predicatori.* Ed. Enrico Narducci. Bologna: G. Romagnoli, 1867.

Giovanni of Genoa (Johannes Balbus). *Catholicon.* Strassburg: Adolph Rusch, 1470.

Giovanni of San Gimignano (Johannes de Sancto Geminiano). *Summa de Exemplis.* Venice: Joannes and Gregorius de Gregoriis, 1497.

Godefridus of Viterbo. *Pantheon.* Migne PL 198.

Gregory I, Saint (Gregorius Magnus). *Moralia in Job.* Migne PL 75-76.

Gretser, Jacob. *De Sancta Cruce.* Vols. 1-3 of his *Opera Omnia.* Ratisbon: Peez/Baader, 1734.

Hartwig, Otto (ed.). *Quellen und Forschungen zur ältesten Geschichte der Stadt Florenz.* 2 vols. Marburg: N. G. Elwert, 1875.

Honorius of Autun. *Speculum Ecclesiae.* Migne PL 172.

Horace. *Opera.* Eds. O. Keller and A. Holder. 2 vols. Leipzig: Teubner, 1864.

Hrabanus Maurus. *De Laudibus Sanctae Crucis.* Migne PL 107.

— *De Universo.* Migne PL 111.

Hyginus, Gaius Iulius. (See van Staverin)

Isidore of Seville. *Etymologiarum sive Originum.* Ed. W. M. Lindsay. 2 vols. Oxford: Clarendon Press, 1911.

Jacobi a Voragine. *Legenda Aurea Vulgo Historia Lombardica Dicta.* 3rd. ed., ed. Johann Theodore Graesse. Ratisbon: G. Koelner, 1890.

Jerome, Saint. *Commentarius in Evangelium Matthaei.* Migne PL 26.

Joachim of Fiore. *Il libro delle figure.* Ed. Leone Tondelli. 2 vols. Turin: Società Editrice Internazionale, 1940.

John of Damascus. *Homiliae, Carmina.* Migne PG 96.

John of Salisbury. *Policratici sive de Nugis Curalium et Vestigiis Philosophorum Libri VIII*. Ed. C. J. Webb. 2 vols. Oxford: Oxford University Press, 1909.

John the Scot (Eriugena). *Annotationes in Marcianum*. Ed. Cora E. Lutz. Cambridge, Mass.: Mediaeval Academy of America, 1939.

— *De Divisione Naturae*. Migne PL 122.

Julian (the "Apostate"). "Discours sur Hélios-Roi." In Vol. 2/2 of *Oeuvres complètes*. Ed. and trans. Christian Lacombrade. Paris: Les Belles Lettres, 1964.

Juvenal (Decimus Junius Juvenalis) *Saturae*. Eds. and trans. P. de Labriolle and F. Villeneuve. Paris: Les Belles Lettres, 1931.

Lactantius. *Divinarum Institutionum*. Migne PL 6.

— *De Mortibus Persecutorum*. Migne PL 7.

Latini, Brunetto. *Li Livres dou Tresor*. Ed. Francis J. Carmody. Berkeley and Los Angeles: University of California Press, 1948.

Leo the Great, Pope. *Homiliae*. CCSL 138–A.

Il libro fiesolano. (See Hartwig)

Lucan. *The Civil War (Pharsalia)*. Ed. and trans. J. D. Duff. Loeb Classical Library. London: Heinemann, 1977.

Lucretius. *De Rerum Natura*. Ed. Martin Ferguson Smith. Trans. W.H.D. Rouse. Loeb Classical Library. London: Heinemann, 1975.

Macrobius. *Commentarii in Somnium Scipionis*. Ed. Jacob Willis. Leipzig: Teubner, 1970.

— *Commentary on the Dream of Scipio*. Ed. and trans. William Harris Stahl. Records of Civilization, Sources and Studies 48. New York: Columbia University Press, 1952.

Malavenda, Thomas. *De Antichristo*. Lugundi, 1647.

Malispini, Ricordano. *Storia Fiorentina*. Rome: Multigrafica Editrice, 1976.

Manilius. *Astronomica*. Ed. and trans. G. P. Goold. Loeb Classical Library. Cambridge, Mass.: Harvard University Press, 1976.

Masha 'Allah. *The Astrological History of Masha 'Allah*. Eds. and trans. E. S. Kennedy and D. Pingree. Cambridge, Mass.: Harvard University Press, 1971.

Origen. *Commentarius in Evangelium Secundum Mattheum*. Migne PG 13.

— *Prayer, Exhortation to Martyrdom*. Trans. John J. O'Meara. London: Newman Press, 1954.

Orosius, Paulus. *Historiarum Adversum Paganos Libri VII*. Ed. Karl Zangemeister. Leipzig: Teubner, 1889.

Ottimo. *L'Ottimo commento della Divina Commedia*. 3 vols. Ed. Accademia della Crusca. Pisa: N. Capurro, 1827–1829.

Ovid. *Fasti*. Ed. and trans. J. G. Frazer. Loeb Classical Library. London: Heinemann, 1931.

— *Les Métamorphoses*. Ed. and trans. Georges Lafaye. 3 vols. Paris: Les Belles Lettres, 1961.

Ovide Moralisé. Ed. Christian de Boer. *Verhandelingen der koninklijke Nederlandsche Akademie van Wetenschappen te Amsterdam*, Afdelling Letterkunde, no. 15 (1915), no. 21 (1920), no. 30 (1931), no. 37 (1936), no. 43 (1938). Reprint. Amsterdam: North-Holland Pub. Co., 1954.

Paulinus of Nola. *Carmina*. CSEL 30.

Plato. *The Collected Dialogues*. Eds. E. Hamilton and H. Cairns. Bollingen Series 71. Princeton: Princeton University Press, 1973.

— (See also Chalcidius and Cornford)

Ptolemy (Claudius Ptolomeus). *Tetrabiblios*. Ed. and trans. F. E. Robbins. Loeb Classical Library. Cambridge, Mass.: Harvard University Press, 1940.

Quintillian. *Institutio Oratoria*. Ed. and trans. H. E. Butler. 4 vols. Loeb Classical Series. Cambridge, Mass.: Harvard University Press, 1976.

Restoro d'Arezzo. *La composizione del mondo colle sue cascioni*. Ed. Alberto Morino. Scrittori Italiani e Testi Antichi. Florence: Accademia della Crusca, 1976.

Rhetorica ad Herennium. Ed. and trans. Harry Caplan. Loeb Classical Library. Cambridge, Mass.: Harvard University Press, 1981.

Richard of Saint Victor. *Allegoriae in Vetus Testamentum*. Migne PL 175. (Attributed to Hugh of Saint Victor by Migne.)

— *Opera Omnia*. Migne PL 196.

— *The Twelve Patriarchs, The Mystical Ark, Book Three of the Trinity*. Trans. Grover A. Zinn. The Classics of Western Spirituality. New York: Paulist Press, 1979.

Servius ("the Grammarian"). *Commentarii in Vergilii Carmina*. Eds. G. Thilo and H. Hagen. 2 vols. Hildesheim: Georg Olms, 1961.

The Sibylline Oracles. (See *New Testament Apocrypha*)

Statius. *Thebaid*. Ed. and trans. J. H. Mozley. 2 vols. Loeb Classical Series. London: Heinemann, 1967.

Sylvestris, Bernard. *Commentary on the First Six Books of Vergil's Aeneid.* Eds. and trans. E. G. Schreiber and T. E. Maresca. Lincoln: University of Nebraska Press, 1974.

Uguccione of Pisa. *Magnae Derivationes.* Ms. Misc. 626 Laud (a), Bodleian, Oxford.

van Staverin, August. *Authores Mythographi Latini.* Amsterdam, 1742. Contains: Hyginus' *Fabulae* and *Poeticon Astronomicon,* Lactantius Planciades' *Narrationes Fabularum,* and Fulgentius' *Mythologia* and *De Virgiliana Continentia.*

Virgil. *Opera.* Eds. T. L. Papillon and A. E. Haigh. 2 vols. Oxford: Clarendon Press, 1892.

— *Aeneidos: Liber Sextus.* Commentary by R. G. Austin. Oxford: Clarendon Press, 1977.

— *The Aeneid.* Trans. Robert Fitzgerald. New York: Random House, 1983.

Villani, Giovanni. *Cronica.* Ed. Francesco Gherardi Dragomanni. 4 vols. Florence: S. Coen, 1844-1845. Reprint. Frankfurt: Minerva GMBH, 1969.

Secondary Sources

Ahern, John. "Binding the Book: Hermeneutics and Manuscript Production in *Paradiso* 33." *PMLA* 97 (October 1982): 800-809.

Aquilecchia, Giovanni. "Dante and the Florentine Chroniclers." *Bulletin of the John Rylands Library* 48 (1965): 30-55. Reprinted in *Schede di Italianistica,* 45-72. Turin: Einaudi, 1976.

Arseniev, Nicholas A. "Resurrection and Transfiguration." *Saint Vladimir's Seminary Quarterly* 1 (October 1957): 28-39.

Auerbach, Erich. *Scenes from the Drama of European Literature.* Trans. Ralph Manheim. New York: Meridian Books, 1959. Reprint. Theory and History of Literature series, no. 9. Minneapolis: University of Minnesota Press, 1984.

— *Literary Language and Its Public in Late Antiquity and in the Middle Ages.* Trans. Ralph Manheim. Bollingen Series 74. New York: Pantheon, 1965.

Avalle D'Arco, Silvio. *Modelli semiologici nella Commedia di Dante.* Studi Bompiani 13. Milan: Bompiani, 1975.

Baisier, Léon. *The Lapidaire Chrétien: its Composition, its Influence, its Sources.* New York: AMS Press, 1969.

Bakhtin, Mikhael. *Rabelais and his World*. Trans. Helen Iswolsky. Cambridge, Mass.: M.I.T. Press, 1968.
Ball, Robert. "Theological Semantics: Virgil's *Pietas* and Dante's *Pietà*." *SIR* 2 (Spring 1981): 59–80.
Bambeck, Manfred. *Studien zu Dantes "Paradiso"*. Wiesbaden: Franz Steiner Verlag, 1979.
Bartelink, G.J.M. "Quelques Observations sur παρρησία dans la littérature paléo-chrétienne." *Graecitas et Latinitas Christianorum Primaeva: Supplementa* 3 (1970): 7–57.
Bennett, J.A.W. *Poetry of the Passion: Studies in Twelve Centuries of English Verse*. Oxford: Clarendon Press, 1982.
Bergin, Thomas. *A Diversity of Dante*. New Brunswick, N. J.: Rutgers University Press, 1969.
Bernardo, Aldo S., and Anthony L. Pellegrini, eds. *Dante, Petrarch, Boccaccio: Studies in the Italian Trecento in Honor of Charles S. Singleton*. Medieval and Renaissance Texts and Studies 22. Binghamton: Medieval and Renaissance Texts and Studies, 1983.
Bouché-Leclercq, Auguste. *L'Astrologie grecque*. Paris, 1899. Reprint. Brussels: Culture et Civilisation, 1963.
Bousset, Wilhelm. *The Antichrist Legend: A Chapter in Christian-Jewish Folklore*. Trans. A. H. Keane. London: Hutchinson and Co., 1896.
— *Kyrios Christos: A History of Belief from the Beginnings of Christianity to Irenaeus*. Trans. John E. Steely. Nashville: Abingdon Press, 1970.
— "Platons Weltseele und das Kreuz Christi." *Zeitschrift für die Neuetestamentliche Wissenschaft* 14 (1913): 273–285.
Brieger, Peter, Millard Meiss, and Charles S. Singleton, eds. *Illuminated Manuscripts of the Divine Comedy*. 2 vols. Bollingen Series 81. Princeton: Princeton University Press, 1969.
Brundage, James A. "Cruce Signari: The Rite for Taking the Cross in England." *Traditio* 22 (1966): 289–310.
Bukofzer, Manfred F. "Speculative Thinking in Mediaeval Music." *Speculum* 17 (April 1942): 165–180.
Busnelli, Giovanni. *Il concetto e l'ordine del 'Paradiso' dantesco. Parte I: Il concetto*. Città del Castello: S. Lapi, 1911.
Cassell, Anthony K. "Dante's Farinata and the Image of the *Arca*." *Yale Italian Studies* 1 (1977): 335–370.
Castellani, Victor. "Heliocentricity in the Structure of Dante's *Paradiso*." *Studies in Philology* 78 (Summer 1981): 211–223.

Chamberas, Peter A. "The Transfiguration of Christ: A Study in Patristic Exegesis of Scripture." *Saint Vladimir's Theological Quarterly* 14, nos. 1–2 (1970): 48–65.
Chiarenza, Marguerite Mills. "Boethian Themes in Dante's Reading of Virgil." *SIR* 3 (Spring 1983): 25–35.
— "Hippolytus' Exile: *Paradiso* xvii, vv. 46–48." *DS* 84 (1966): 65–68.
— "Time and Eternity in the Myths of *Paradiso* xvii." In *Dante, Petrarch, Boccaccio*, eds. Aldo S. Bernardo and Anthony L. Pellegrini, 133–150.
Chiarini, Eugenio. "Riflessioni su un vecchio problema: Dante e Ravenna." In *Atti del Convegno Internazionale di Studi Danteschi*, a cura del commune di Ravenna e della Società Dantesca Italiana (Ravenna, Sept. 10–12, 1971): 217–237. Longo: Ravenna, 1979.
Cioffari, Vincenzo. *The Conception of Fortune and Fate in the Works of Dante.* Cambridge, Mass.: Dante Society of America, 1940.
Cochrane, Charles Norris. *Christianity and Classical Culture: A Study of Thought and Action from Augustus to Augustine.* Oxford: Clarendon Press, 1940. Reprint. New York: Oxford University Press, 1977.
Comparetti, Domenico. *Virgilio nel medio evo.* New ed., ed. Giorgio Pasquali. 2 vols. Florence: La Nuova Italia, 1937.
Conley, John. "The Peculiar Name Thopas." *Studies in Philology* 73, no. 1 (1976): 42–61.
Cornford, Francis MacDonald, trans. and comm. *Plato's Cosmology: The Timaeus of Plato.* Library of Liberal Arts no. 101. Indianapolis and New York: Bobbs-Merrill, n.d.
Courcelle, Pierre. "Les Exégèses chrétiennes de la quatrième Eglogue." *Revue des Etudes Anciennes* 59 (1957): 294–319.
— "Interprétations néo-platonizantes du livre VI de l'*Enéide*." Fondation Hardt, *Entretiens sur l'Antiquité Classique 3*: "Recherches sur la Tradition Platonicienne" (1955): 95–136.
— "Les Pères de l'église devant les enfers virgiliens." *Archives d'Histoire Doctrinale et Littéraire du Moyen Âge* 22 (1953): 5–69.
Cullmann, Oscar. *Christ and Time: The Primitive Christian Conception of Time and History.* Trans. Floyd Filson. Philadelphia: Westminster Press, 1950.
— *The Christology of the New Testament.* Trans. S. C. Guthrie and Charles A. M. Hall. The New Testament Library. London: SCM Press, 1963.

BIBLIOGRAPHY 249

Curtius, Ernst Robert. *European Literature and the Latin Middle Ages*. Trans. Willard R. Trask. Bollingen Series 37. Princeton: Princeton University Press, 1973.

Daniélou, Jean. *The Bible and the Liturgy*. University of Notre Dame Liturgical Studies 3. Notre Dame: University of Notre Dame Press, 1956.

— "Les Douze Apôtres et le zodiaque." *Vigiliae Christianae* 13 (1959): 14–25.

— *Platonisme et théologie mystique: Doctrine spirituelle de Saint Grégoire de Nysse*. Paris: Aubier, 1944.

Davidsohn, Robert. *Geschichte von Florenz*. 4 vols. Berlin: E. S. Mittler, 1896–1908.

Davis, Charles Till. *Dante and the Idea of Rome*. Oxford: Clarendon Press, 1957.

— *Dante's Italy and Other Essays*. Philadelphia: University of Pennsylvania Press, 1984.

Davy, Marie-Madelaine, Armand Abécassis, Mohammad Mokri, and Jean-Pierre Renneteau. *Le Thème de la lumière dans le Judaisme, le Christianisme, et l'Islam*. Clamecy: Berg International, 1976.

de Bruyne, Edgar. *Etudes d'esthétique médiévale*. 3 vols. Rijksuniversiteit te Gent, Werken uitgegeven door de Faculteit van de Wijsbegeerte en Letteren no. 97–99. Bruges: De Tempel, 1946.

de' Cavallieri, Pio Franchi. *Constantiniana*. Studi e Testi no. 171. Vatican City, 1953.

— *Scritti agiografici II: 1900–1946*. Vatican City, 1962.

de Gaiffier, Baudoin. *Etudes critiques d'hagiographie et d'iconologie*. Brussels: Société des Bollandistes, 1967.

Deichmann, Friedrich Wilhelm. *Ravenna: Hauptstadt des spätantiken Abendlandes*. 3 vols. plus portfolio. Wiesbaden: Franz Steiner, 1969.

Delehaye, Hippolyte. *Les Légendes hagiographiques*. 4th ed. Brussels: Société del Bollandistes, 1955.

— *Les Passions des martyrs et les genres littéraires*. Brussels: Société des Bollandistes, 1921.

de Lubac, Henri. *L'Exégèse médiévale: Les Quatre Sens de l'Ecriture*. 4 vols. Paris: Aubier, 1959–1964.

de Sanctis, Francesco. *Lezioni sulla Divina Commedia*. Ed. Michele Manfredi. Scrittori d'Italia no. 214. Bari: Laterza, 1955.

de Santillana, Giorgio, and Hertha von Dechend. *Hamlet's Mill: An Essay on Myth and the Frame of Time*. Boston: Gambit, 1969.

Dictionnaire de spiritualité ascétique et mystique. Eds. M. Viller et al. Paris: Beauchesne, 1932–.

Dinkler, Erich. *Das Apsismosaik von S. Apollinare in Classe*. Wissenschaftliche Abhandlung der Arbeitsgemeinschaft für Forschung des Landes Nordrhein-Westfalen, Band 29. Cologne and Opladen: Westdeutscher Verlag, 1964.

Dölger, Franz Joseph. 1958–1967. "Beiträge zur Geschichte des Kreuzzeichens." *JACh* 1: 5–20; 2: 15–30; 3: 5–17; 4: 5–18; 5: 5–23; 6: 7–35; 7: 5–39; 8/9: 7–53; 10: 7–30.

——— "ΙΧΘΥΣ: das Fischsymbol in frühchristlicher Zeit." *Römische Quartalschrift: Supplement* (Rome, 1910): 51–65.

——— *Sol Salutis: Gebet und Gesang im Christlichen Altertum*. Liturgiegeschichtliche Forschungen. Münster: Aschendorff, 1925.

——— *Die Sonne der Gerechtigkeit und der Schwarze: eine religionsgeschichtliche Studie zum Taufgelöbnis*. Liturgiegeschichtliche Forschungen 2. Münster: Aschendorff, 1918.

Dronke, Peter. "*Orizzonte che rischiari*: Notes towards the Interpretation of *Paradiso* XIV." *Romance Philology* 29 (August 1975): 1–19.

Dunbar, H. Flanders. *Symbolism in Medieval Thought and its Consummation in the Divine Comedy*. New Haven: Yale University Press, 1929.

Durling, Robert M. "Farinata and the Body of Christ." *SIR* 2 (Spring 1981): 5–35.

——— "*Io son venuto*: Seneca, Plato and the Microcosm." *DS* 93 (1975): 95–129.

Enciclopedia Dantesca. Dir. Umberto Bosco; ed. Giorgio Petrocchi. 5 vols. plus Appendix. Rome: Istituto dell'Enciclopedia Italiana, 1970–1978.

Engels, L. "*Fiducia* dans la Vulgate: Le Problème de traduction παρρησία—*fiducia*." *Graecitas et Latinitas Christianorum Primaeva: Supplementa* 1 (1964): 99–141.

——— "*Fiducia*: Influence de l'emploi juridique sur l'usage commun et paléo-chrétien." *Graecitas et Latinitas Christianorum Primaeva: Supplementa* 3 (1970): 61–118.

Evans, Joan. *Magical Jewels of the Middle Ages and the Renaissance*. Oxford: Oxford University Press, 1922.

Fallani, Giovanni. *Dante e la cultura figurativa medievale.* Bergamo: Minerva Italica, 1971.
Fengler, Christie K., and William A. Stephany. "The Visual Arts: A Basis for Dante's Imagery in Purgatory and Paradise." *The Michigan Academician* 10 (Fall 1977): 127–141.
Ferrante, Joan M. *The Political Vision of the Divine Comedy.* Princeton: Princeton University Press, 1984.
Fleming, John V. "The Dream of the Rood and Anglo-Saxon Monasticism." *Traditio* 22 (1966): 43–72.
Flori, Jean. "Les Origines de l'adoubement chevalresque: Etude des remises d'armes et du vocabulaire qui les exprime dans les sources historiques latines jusqu'au début du XIIIe siècle." *Traditio* 35 (1979): 209–272.
Focillon, Henri. *The Year 1000.* Trans. F. D. Wieck. Harper Torchbook reprint; New York: Harper and Row, 1971.
Freccero, John, ed. *Dante: A Collection of Critical Essays.* Englewood Cliffs: Prentice Hall, 1965.
—— "Dante's Pilgrim in a Gyre." *PMLA* 76 (March 1961): 168–181.
—— "Dante's Prologue Scene." *DS* 84 (1966): 1–25.
—— "*Paradiso X*: The Dance of the Stars." *Dante Studies* 86 (1968): 85–111. Reprinted in *Dante in America: The First Two Centuries*, ed. A. Bartlett Giamatti, 345–371.
—— "The Significance of Terza Rima." In *Dante, Petrarch, Boccaccio*, eds. Aldo S. Bernardo and Anthony L. Pellegrini, 3–17.
Friedman, John Block. *Orpheus in the Middle Ages.* Cambridge, Mass.: Harvard University Press, 1970.
Füglister, Robert L. *Das Lebende Kreuz: Ikonographisch-ikonologische Untersuchung der Herkunft und Entwicklung einer spätmittelalterlichen Bildidee und ihrer Verwurzelung im Wort.* Diss. Fribourg, Switzerland, 1961. Einsiedeln: Benziger Verlag, 1964.
Gardner, Edmund G. *Dante and the Mystics: A Study of the Mystical Aspect of the Divina Commedia and its Relations with some of its Mediaeval Sources.* London and New York: Dent/Dutton, 1913.
Garin, Eugenio. *Studi sul platonismo medievale.* Florence: Le Monnier, 1958.
Giamatti, A. Bartlett, ed. *Dante in America: The First Two Centuries.* Medieval and Renaissance Texts and Studies 23. Binghamton: Center for Medieval and Early Renaissance Studies, 1983.

Gilson, Etienne. *La Philosophie au Moyen Âge des origines patristiques à la fin du XIVe siècle.* Paris: Payot, 1962.

Gmelin, Hermann. *Die Göttliche Komödie: Kommentar.* 3 vols. Stuttgart: E. Klett, 1955.

— "L'ispirazione iconografica nella Divina Commedia." *Il Veltro: Rivista della Civiltà Italiana* 3 (1959): 13–16.

Grabar, André. *Christian Iconography: A Study of its Origins.* Bollingen Series 35–10. Princeton: Princeton University Press, 1980.

— *Martyrium: Recherches sur le culte des reliques et l'art chrétien antique.* 2 vols. Limoges: Collège de France/Fondation Schlumberger, 1946.

Greenhill, Eleanor S. "The Child in the Tree: A Study of the Cosmological Tree in Christian Tradition." *Traditio* 10 (1954): 323–371.

Grégoire, Henri. "La Conversion de Constantin." *Revue de l'Université de Bruxelles* 36 (1930–1931): 231–272.

— "L'Etymologie de *labarum*." *Byzantion* 4 (1927–1928): 477–482.

Halsberghe, Gaston H. *The Cult of Sol Invictus.* Leiden: Brill, 1972.

Hardie, Colin. "Cacciaguida's Prophecy in *Paradiso* 17." *Traditio* 19 (1963): 267–294.

Hirsch-Reich, Beatrice. (See Reeves)

Hollander, Robert. *Allegory in Dante's Commedia.* Princeton: Princeton University Press, 1969.

— *Studies in Dante.* Ravenna: Longo Editore, 1980.

Jacoff, Rachel. "Sacrifice and Empire: Thematic Analogies in San Vitale and the *Paradiso*." In vol. 1, *Renaissance Studies in Honor of Craig Hugh Smyth*, eds. A. Morrogh, F. Superbi Gioffredi, P. Morselli and E. Borsook. Florence: Giunti Barbera, 1985.

Jaeger, Werner. *Early Christianity and Greek Paideia.* Cambridge, Mass.: Belknap Press of Harvard University Press, 1961.

— *Paideia: The Ideals of Greek Culture.* Trans. Gilbert Highet. 3 vols. New York: Oxford University Press, 1943.

Johnson, W. R. *Darkness Visible: A Study of Virgil's Aeneid.* Berkeley: University of California Press, 1976.

Kaske, Robert E. "Dante's 'DXV' and 'Veltro.'" *Traditio* 17 (1961): 185–252.

— "A Poem of the Cross in the Exeter Book: 'Riddle 60' and 'The Husband's Message.'" *Traditio* 23 (1967): 41–73.

— "The Seven *Status Ecclesiae* in *Purgatorio* XXXII–XXXIII." In *Dante, Pe-*

trarch, Boccaccio, eds. Aldo S. Bernardo and Anthony L. Pellegrini, 89–113.

Kennedy, Charles W., ed. and trans. *Early English Christian Poetry*. New York: Oxford University Press, 1963.

Kermode, Frank. *The Genesis of Secrecy: On the Interpretation of Narrative*. Cambridge, Mass.: Harvard University Press, 1979.

Kittel, Gerhard, ed. *Theologisches Wörterbuch zum Neuen Testament*. 10 vols. Stuttgart: W. Kohlhammer Verlag, 1938–1979.

Koep, Leo. *Das himmlische Buch in Antike und Christentum: eine religionsgeschichtliche Untersuchung zur altchristlichen Bildersprache*. Theophaneia 8. Bonn: Peter Hanstein, 1952.

Kristeva, Julia. *Sèméiôtiké: Recherches pour une sémanalyse*. Paris: Eds. du Seuil, 1969.

Lausberg, Heinrich. *Elemente der literarischen Rhetorik*. Munich: Max Hueber Verlag, 1967.

Le Goff, Jacques. *Time, Work, and Culture in the Middle Ages*. Trans. Arthur Goldhammer. Chicago: University of Chicago Press, 1980.

Lehmann, Paul. *The Transfiguration of Politics*. New York: Harper and Row, 1975.

Lewis, Charlton T., and Charles Short. *A Latin Dictionary*. Oxford: Clarendon Press, 1879.

Lewis, C. S. *The Allegory of Love: A Study in Medieval Tradition*. New York: Oxford University Press, 1958.

Lipinsky, Angelo. "La 'Crux Gemmata' e il culto della Santa Croce nei monumenti superstiti e nelle raffigurazioni monumentali." *Felix Ravenna* 81 (July 1960): 5–62.

—— "La simbologia della gemme nella *Divina Commedia* e le sue fonti letterarie." In *Atti del I Congresso Nazionale di Studi Danteschi: "Dante nel secolo dell'unità d'Italia,"* 127–158. Florence: Olschki, 1962.

Logan, J. L. "The Poet's Central Numbers." *MLN* 86 (1971): 95–98.

MacPherson Oliver, Mary Anne. "Mystical Experience and the Literary Technique of Silence." *Studia Mystica* 1 (Spring 1978): 5–20.

Mahler, Annemarie E. "*Lignum Domini* and the Opening Vision of the *Dream of the Rood*: A Viable Hypothesis?" *Speculum* 53 (July 1978): 441–453.

Mandelstam, Osip E. *Mandelstam: The Complete Critical Prose and Letters*. Ed. and trans. Jane Gary Harris. Ann Arbor: Ardis, 1979.

Marcovaldi, Gaetano. *Tre studi danteschi*. Rome: Vivarelli and Giulia, 1969.
Martinez, Ronald L. "Dante, Statius, and the Earthly City." Diss. University of California, Santa Cruz, 1977.
Marx, Karl, and Friedrich Engels. *The Marx-Engels Reader*. 2nd ed., ed. Robert J. Tucker. New York: Norton and Co., 1978.
Mazzeo, Joseph Anthony. "Dante's Sun Symbolism." *Italica* 33 (December 1956): 243–251.
— "Light Metaphysics, Dante's 'Convivio' and the Letter to Can Grande della Scala." *Traditio* 14 (1958): 191–229.
Mazzotta, Giuseppe. *Dante, Poet of the Desert: History and Allegory in the Divine Comedy*. Princeton: Princeton University Press, 1979.
Mazzotti, Mario. *La basilica di Sant' Apollinare in Classe*. Studi di Antichità Cristiana, vol. 21. Rome: Pontifical Institute of Christian Archeology, 1954.
Meiss, Millard. (See Brieger, Peter)
Mineo, Niccolò. *Profetica e apocalittica in Dante*. Catania: Università di Catania, Facoltà di Lettere, 1968.
Moore, Clifford Herschel. "Prophecy in Ancient Epic." *Harvard Studies in Classical Philology* 32 (1921): 99–175.
Moore, Edward. *Studies in Dante: First Series—Scripture and Classical Authors in Dante*. Oxford: Clarendon Press, 1896.
— *Studies in Dante: Second Series—Miscellaneous Essays*. Oxford: Clarendon Press, 1899.
— *Studies in Dante: Third Series—Miscellaneous Essays*. Oxford: Clarendon Press, 1903.
The Mysteries: Papers from the Eranos Yearbooks. Eds. Joseph Campbell and Olga Froebe-Kapteyn. Trans. Olga Froebe-Kapteyn. Bollingen Series 30–2. Princeton: Princeton University Press, 1955.
Nardi, Bruno. *Saggi di filosofia dantesca*. 2nd ed. Florence: La Nuova Italia, 1967.
Norden, Eduard. *Agnostos Theos: Untersuchungen zur Formengeschichte religiöser Rede*. Leipzig: Teubner, 1913.
Nordström, Carl-Otto. *Ravennastudien: ideengeschichtliche und ikonographische Untersuchungen über die Mosaiken von Ravenna*. Stockholm: Almquist and Wiksell, 1953.
Otis, Brooks. *Vergil: A Study in Civilized Poetry*. Oxford: Clarendon Press, 1964.

Palgen, Rudolf. *Dantes Sternglaube: Beiträge zur Erklärung des Paradiso.* Heidelberg: C. Winter, 1940.
Pannier, Leopold, ed. *Les Lapidaires français du Moyen Âge.* Bibliothèque de l'Ecole des Hautes Etudes, no. 52. Paris: Vieweg, 1882.
Pascoli, Giovanni. *La mirabile visione: Abozzo d'una storia della Divina Commedia.* 3rd. ed. Bologna: N. Zanichelli, 1923.
— *Ravenna e la Romagna negli 'Studi Danteschi.'* Ed. Francesco Giugni. Ravenna: Longo, 1966.
Patch, Howard E. *The Goddess Fortuna in Medieval Literature.* Cambridge, Mass.: Harvard University Press, 1927.
— *The Tradition of Boethius.* New York: Oxford University Press, 1935.
Pegis, Richard. J. "Numerology and Probability in Dante." *Medieval Studies* 29 (1967): 370–373.
Pézard, André. *Dante sous la pluie de feu.* Etudes de Philosophie Médiévale 40. Paris: J. Vrin, 1950.
— "Les Trois Langues de Cacciaguida." *Revue des Etudes Italiennes* no. 13 (1967): 217–238.
— "Volgare e latino nella *Commedia.*" *Letture Classensi* no. 2 (1969): 95–111.
Plumpe, J. C. "*Vivum saxum, vivi lapides*: The Concept of 'Living Stone' in Classical Antiquity." *Traditio* 1 (1943): 1–14.
Rabuse, Georg. *Der kosmische Aufbau der Jenseitsreiche Dantes: ein Schlüssel zur Göttlichen Komödie.* Graz: Hermann Böhlaus, 1958.
— *Gesammelte Aufsätze zu Dante.* Eds. E. Kanduth, F. P. Kirsch and S. Loewe. Wiener Romanistische Arbeiten. Vienna: Wilhelm Braumüller, 1976.
Rahner, Hugo. "The Christian Mystery and the Pagan Mysteries." In *The Mysteries: Papers from the Eranos Yearbooks,* ed. Joseph Campbell and ed.-trans. Olga Froebe-Kapteyn, 337–401.
Ramat, Rafaello. *Il canto XV del Paradiso.* Lectura Dantis Scaligera. Florence: Le Monnier, 1965.
— *Il mito di Firenze e altri saggi danteschi.* Florence: Casa Editrice d'Anna, 1976.
Raw, Barbara C. "The *Dream of the Rood* and its Connections with Early Christian Art." *Medium Aevum* 39, no. 3 (1970): 239–256.
Reeves, Marjorie, and Beatrice Hirsch-Reich. *The Figurae of Joachim of Fiore.* Oxford-Warburg Series. Oxford: Clarendon Press, 1972.

Ricci Corrado. *L'ultimo rifugio di Dante Alighieri*. Milan: U. Hoepli, 1891.
Roscher, Wilhelm Heinrich, ed. *Ausführliches Lexikon der griechischen und römischen Mythologie*. 6 vols. Leipzig-Berlin: Teubner, 1884–1937.
Sarolli, Gian Roberto. *Analitica della Divina Commedia: Struttura numerologica e poesia*. Bari: Adriatica, 1974.
— *Prolegomena alla Divina Commedia*. Biblioteca dell'Archivium Romanicum 1/112. Florence: Olschki, 1971.
Scartazzini, G. A., ed. and comm. *La Divina Commedia di Dante Alighieri*. 3 vols. Leipzig: Brockhaus, 1874–1882.
Schiller, Gertrud. *Iconography of Christian Art*. Trans. Janet Seligman. 2 vols. Greenwich, Conn.: New York Graphic Society, 1972.
Seymour William Wood. *The Cross in Tradition, History and Art*. New York: G. P. Putnam/Knickerbocker, 1898.
Silverstein, Theodor. "Dante and Virgil the Mystic." *Harvard Studies and Notes in Philology and Literature* 13 (1931): 51–82.
Singleton, Charles S. *Dante's Commedia: Elements of Structure* (Dante Studies I). Cambridge, Mass.: Harvard University Press, 1954. Reprint. Baltimore: Johns Hopkins, 1977.
— *Journey to Beatrice* (Dante Studies II). Cambridge, Mass.: Harvard University Press, 1958. Reprint. Baltimore: Johns Hopkins, 1977.
— "The Poet's Number at the Center." *MLN* 80 (1965): 1–10.
— (See also Brieger)
Spitzer, Leo. *Classical and Christian Ideas of World Harmony: Prolegomena to an Interpretation of the Word "Stimmung."* Ed. Anna Granville Hatcher. Baltimore: Johns Hopkins, 1963.
Stephany, William A. (See Fengler)
Stockbauer, Jacob. *Kunstgeschichte des Kreuzes: die bildliche Darstellung des Erlösungstodes Christi im Monogramm, Kreuz und Crucifix*. Schaffhausen: Fr. Hurter'schen Buchhandlung, 1870.
Stockmeier, Peter. *Theologie und Kult des Kreuzes bei Johannes Chrysostomus: ein Beitrag zum Verständnis des Kreuzes im 4. Jahrhundert*. Trierer Theologische Studien, Band 18. Trier: Paulinus Verlag, 1966.
Szövérffy, Joseph. "*Crux Fidelis*: Prolegomena to a History of the Holy Cross Hymns." *Traditio* 22 (1966): 1–41.
— *Hymns of the Holy Cross: An Annotated Edition with Introduction*. Medieval Classics: Texts and Studies 7. Brookline and Leyden: Classical Folia Editions, 1976.

Tarrant, R. J. "Aeneas and the Gates of Sleep." *Classical Philology* 67 (January 1982): 51–55.
Tate, George S. "Chiasmus and Metaphor: The *Figura Crucis* Tradition and *The Dream of the Rood.*" *Neuphilologische Mitteilungen* 79, no. 2 (1978): 114–125.
Thoby, Paul. *Le Crucifix des origines au Concile de Trente: Etude iconographique*. Nantes: Bellanger, 1959.
Thorndike, Lynn, ed. *Latin Treatises on Comets between 1238 and 1368 A.D.* Chicago: University of Chicago Press, 1950.
Tondelli, Leone, ed. *Il libro delle figure*. 2 vols. Turin: Società Editrice Internazionale, 1940.
Toynbee, Paget. *Dante Studies and Researches*. London: Methuen and Co., 1902.
Valesio, Paolo. "The Language of Madness in the Renaissance." *Yearbook of Italian Studies* (1971): 199–234.
Valli, Luigi. *Il segreto della croce e dell'aquila nella Divina Commedia*. Bologna: N. Zanichelli, 1922.
Vallone, Aldo. *La 'cortesia' dai provenzali a Dante*. Palermo: Palumbo, 1950.
van Unnik, W. C. "The Christian's Freedom of Speech in the New Testament." *Bulletin of the John Rylands Library* no. 44 (1961/1962): 466–488.
Vessey, David. *Statius and the Thebaid*. Cambridge: Cambridge University Press, 1973.
Vettori, Vittorio. "Il centro del Paradiso." In *Letture del Paradiso*. Ed. Vittorio Vettori. Lectura Dantis Internazionale. Milan: Marzorati, 1970.
Vickers, Nancy J. "Seeing Is Believing: Gregory, Trajan and Dante's Art." *DS*. Forthcoming.
von Richtofen, Erich. "Dante 'Apollinian.' " *Annali dell'Istituto Universitario Orientale; Sezione Romanza* 12 (Naples, 1970): 147–244.
von Simson, Otto Georg. *The Gothic Cathedral: Origins of Gothic Architecture and the Medieval Concept of Order*. Bollingen Series 48. Princeton: Princeton University Press, 1974.
—— *Sacred Fortress: Byzantine Art and Statecraft in Ravenna*. Chicago: University of Chicago Press, 1948.
Wadstein, Ernst. *Die eschatologische Ideengruppe: Antichrist, Weltsabbat, Weltende und Weltgericht*. Leipzig: O. R. Reisland, 1896.

Wilkins, Ernest Hatch. "Dante and the Mosaics of *Bel San Giovanni*." *Speculum* 2 (1927): 1–10. Reprinted in *Dante in America: The First Two Centuries*, ed. A. Bartlett Giamatti, 144–159.

Wind, Edgar. *Pagan Mysteries of the Renaissance*. New York: Norton and Co., 1958.

Zöckler, Otto. *Das Kreuz Christi*. Religionshistorische und kirchlicharchäologische Untersuchungen. Gütersloh: C. Bertelsmann, 1875.

INDEX TO PASSAGES CITED FROM DANTE'S WORKS

The Divine Comedy
—Inferno
1.14–16–18, 225n
2.4–5, 87, 226
2.32, 44n, 233
4.52–54, 3, 4, 5, 125
4.68–69, 34
4.69, 145n
6.63, 37
6.74, 37
7.91–93, 57n
8.78, 16n
9.54, 37
10.81, 37
10.130–132, 64n
12.37–43, 22–23
13.58–63, 112n
13.145, 37
15.50–52–54, 225n
15.55–56, 236n
15.70–72, 236n
15.83, 199
15.88–90, 64n
15.106–108, 113n
17.107, 143n, 158
19.17, 46
19.93, 112
20.113, 233
23.124–126, 28n
24.143–151, 37
26.73–75, 137
26.94–96, 216
26.120, 216
31.51, 51n
34.1, 62n
—Purgatory
4.64, 182n

4.71–72, 143n, 158
5.88, 44n
6.76–151, 53n
11.98–99, 33n
11.100–102, 33n
14.125, 115
22.73, 44
28.20, 174
28.23, 45
29.118, 143n
32.38–39, 115
32.46–47, 75
32.49, 75, 143n
32.61, 116
32.66, 118
32.73–75, 116, 118
32.90, 116
32.102, 116, 227
—Paradise
1.18, 216
1.70, 9, 107
1.71–72, 107n
1.76–78, 154n
1.130–135, 110n
4.40–42, 40
5.19–45, 54n
6.10, 44n
8.75, 113n
9.127–142, 53n
10.7–9, 67
10.7–21, 78
10.52–60, 105n
10.59–60, 104
10.124–129, 48, 49n, 223, 228n
10.125–126, 38, 228n
10.126, 49n

12.37, 218
12.44, 218
12.56, 218
12.71–73–75, 74n
12.142, 218
14.1, 67
14.10–60, 106
14.28–29, 67
14.37–60, 67
14.69, 67
14.72, 67
14.85–87, 67, 148
14.86, 129n–130n
14.87, 181, 194
14.89, 68, 194, 212
14.92–93, 68
14.94–95, 73
14.95–108, 108
14.96, 59n, 106, 136
14.97–98, 157, 163, 181
14.97–108, 76, 89
14.100–101, 80, 157, 187
14.103, 88
14.104–106–108, 74, 101, 187
14.105, 81, 90, 187
14.105–108, 107n
14.108, 67, 71, 157
14.109–111, 157n
14.114, 157, 163
14.115–116, 89
14.118–119, 163
14.119, 157
14.122, 167
14.123, 88

—Paradise (cont.)
 14.123–124, 163
 14.125, 90, 104, 148, 212
 14.126, 88
 14.127–129, 104, 167
 14.130–139, 104
 15.1–9, 102, 160
 15.5, 160, 163
 15.6, 160, 163
 15.8–9, 148
 15.10–12, 102
 15.13, 89, 90
 15.13–18, 201n
 15.13–21, 89, 90, 125
 15.14, 201, 201n
 15.16, 145
 15.24, 89, 90, 145
 15.25, 144
 15.25–27, 206, 209
 15.26, 103
 15.27, 193
 15.28–29, 89, 141
 15.28–30, 206, 208
 15.31, 145
 15.35–36, 89, 149, 193
 15.36–42, 68, 145
 15.37–47, 147n, 235, 236
 15.38–41, 148
 15.39, 207
 15.42, 90, 125
 15.47, 207
 15.48, 146, 211, 235, 236
 15.49–52, 209
 15.50–51, 125, 169
 15.51, 146, 222
 15.53–54, 146
 15.60, 164
 15.61, 163
 15.65, 149, 222

15.67–68, 235
15.67–72, 102n
15.69, 146, 148
15.73, 222
15.73–84, 147n
15.77, 222
15.85, 163, 197
15.86, 85n, 197
15.88, 106
15.89, 47n, 141n, 209
15.92, 41
15.95–96, 142
15.97, 39, 45, 45n, 90, 103, 193
15.99, 193
15.100–102, 43
15.100–111, 50
15.107, 51
15.109–117, 103
15.126, 43
15.129, 43
15.130–132, 45
15.135, 209
15.136, 233n
15.138, 41
15.142–144, 54
15.142–146, 16, 193, 216
15.142–148, 49n
15.146, 12, 48n, 169
15.148, 48, 48n, 87, 213, 222
16.1, 208
16.1–16, 142
16.10, 48, 49n, 208
16.16, 41, 47n
16.22, 41, 47n
16.33–34, 45, 140, 233
16.34–39, 65n
16.46–47, 43
16.49, 193
16.59–60, 55

16.67, 55
16.73–81, 57
16.76, 55
16.77, 73
16.78–80, 169
16.88–90, 55
16.90, 47n
16.91–93, 55
16.100–108, 55
16.145–147, 53
16.154, 90
17.13, 41, 47n
17.13–18, 147n
17.13–27, 229n
17.17–18, 223
17.23–24, 61
17.31–36, 31–32, 32n, 140
17.32, 30
17.33, 193–194
17.34–35, 89, 119
17.35–36, 144, 148
17.37–42, 145, 147
17.39, 169
17.43–44, 148, 169
17.46–48, 55
17.48, 64n
17.53–54, 225
17.55, 64, 225
17.59, 64, 225, 225n
17.60–61, 225, 225n
17.62–64, 55, 225
17.76, 65
17.77, 66
17.80, 67, 74
17.83, 72, 74
17.92–93, 66–68
17.95–96, 38, 225
17.98–99, 225
17.101, 49n, 223
17.118, 62
17.119–120, 226, 227
17.121, 40, 47n

INDEX

17.122–123, 199
17.127–129, 64n
17.127–135, 228
17.128, 10, 49n, 212
17.130–132, 229n
17.131, 229
17.133–135, 236
17.135, 225
17.136–142, 39–40
17.138, 231
17.141, 41
18.1, 49n
18.21, 193
18.28, 120
18.28–30, 119
18.29–30, 75n, 80, 120
18.31–33, 234
18.32–33, 103
18.49–51, 234
18.51, 49n, 233
18.52, 73
18.123, 227
19.104–106–108, 74
20.46–47, 105
23.28–33, 108
23.37–38, 109
23.40–51, 109
23.61–63, 107
24.29–30, 122

24.64–66, 40
25.7–9, 237
25.33, 110
25.57, 226
25.95, 110
25.119–120, 105n
25.123, 105n
26.133–138, 137
27.22–36, 87n
27.28–36, 86n, 87n
27.35, 105n
27.40–66, 53n
29.102, 105n
30.66, 195
30.76, 195
30.95–97–99, 74n
31.124–125, 143n
32.49, 119
32.71–82, 116–117
32.83–85–87, 74n
33.85–87, 80
33.116–117, 81n
33.131–138, 81n
Convivio
1.2.13, 12, 12n
1.6.3, 45
2.1.2–4, 111
2.1.5, 111, 112n
2.1.6–8, 112
2.13, 9, 15, 78n

2.13.20, 154n, 168
2.13.20–25, 128, 129n
2.13.21–24, 168
2.13.22, 66, 129
2.14.1, 157
2.14.1–4, 129n
2.14.1–13, 78
2.14.3, 156–157
2.14.5, 143n, 157, 182
2.14.6, 83n
2.14.7, 157
2.14.9–13, 158
2.14.13, 158
4.5.3–4, 120n
4.5.6–8, 82n–83n
Epistolae
  Epistle to Can Grande, 88n, 107, 107n, 117
Monarchia
  3.1.1–27, 228n
  3.1.27, 212
  3.9.11, 112
Vita Nuova
  14.7–15.2, 112–113
  14.8, 118
  15.4–8, 113n
De Vulgari Eloquentia
  2.4.9–11, 213
  2.4.11, 214

SUBJECT INDEX

Adam, 47n, 137, 221–222
Aegidius Romanus, 51n
Aeneas, 6, 9, 11, 14, 19, 20, 26, 29n, 34, 38, 59, 64, 69, 72, 87, 118, 142, 147, 216–218, 224, 226
Africanus, 13, 15, 24, 49n, 60, 61n, 62, 84n, 141n, 142, 226
Ahern, J., 82n
Alan of Lille, 14, 70, 159n, 182
Albertus Magnus, 15, 51n, 78n, 91, 150n
Albumasar (Abu Ma'shar), 15, 65n
Alighieri, Pietro, 51n, 59n, 137
Ambrose, 96
Anaxagoras, 83n
Anchises, 6, 7, 9, 13, 19, 20, 24, 31–32, 39, 49n, 59, 61n, 62, 64n, 65, 72, 82, 136, 140, 141, 142, 144, 145n, 209, 211, 212, 213
Andrew of Crete, 71n
Apollinaris, Saint, 10, 178, 179n, 186, 193–194, 199–203, 205, 229–230
Apollo, 10, 25–26, 29, 32–33, 121, 127n, 132, 136, 138–139, 143n, 144, 147, 149, 161
Aquilecchia, G., 42n
Aquinas, Saint Thomas, 67, 91n, 112n, 150n, 154n
Aristotle, 44, 51n–52n, 78n, 154n
arma Christi, 126
astrology, 14–16, 19, 65, 66n
Auerbach, E., 5, 141n
Augustine, Saint, 7, 11, 20, 23n, 26–27, 34n, 41n, 51n, 71n, 91n, 96, 97, 116n, 130, 131–133, 165, 167n, 168, 170, 226n, 227n
Augustus Caesar, 19, 22, 39
Avalle, D. S., 45n
Averroes, 78n

Bacon, Roger, 65n
Bakhtin, M., 53n
Ball, R., 29n, 44n, 207
Barthelink, G., 219n
Beatrice, 28–29, 32n, 104, 105n, 109, 114, 117
Bede, 96, 154n
Bennett, J.A.W., 124n–125n
Benvenuto of Imola, 59n, 79
Berengosius the Abbot, 127n
Bergin, T. G., 129n
Bernard Silvestris, 41n
Bersuire, Pierre, 161n
Bible. *See* Old Testament; New Testament
Boccaccio, Giovanni, 17n, 59n, 84
Boethius, 11, 12, 23, 38, 48n–49n, 58n, 60n, 64n, 75n, 153n–154n, 159n, 166n, 219n, 228n–229n, 236n
Bonaventure, Saint, 3, 67, 91n, 162
book, 78, 80–81, 81n–82n, 125, 146–149, 180, 185; Book of Divine Foreknowledge, 146, 222; Book of Life, 124, 146n
Bouché-Leclercq, A., 14, 15n, 16n, 19n, 154n
Bousset, W., 77, 92n, 121n, 125n
Brundage, J., 138n
Brunetto Latini, 36, 43, 199, 236n
Bukofzer, M., 154n
Busnelli, G., 109n, 112n

Cacciaguida, 12, 24, 39, 41n, 58–60, 84n, 103, 223–230; as crusader, 39, 48, 90, 232; his descent from the cross, 90, 125; as double of Anchises, 146–149, 233; his "Latin," 44, 140–141, 208–210, 233; as martyr, 10, 48, 49n, 58n, 64, 101, 171,

INDEX

193–194, 200–203; as paternal image, 40–41, 44, 141–149; as prophet, 5, 10, 13, 32n, 47n, 56, 64, 66, 74, 140, 146–149
Can Grande della Scala, 39, 65, 107, 108n, 117
carnival, 50n, 53, 56, 105
Cassell, A., 176n
Cassiodorus, 127n
Castellani, V., 152n
Catiline, 18, 19, 42, 51
Cavalcanti, Guido, 33n, 59n, 113n
Chalcidius, 155, 155n–156n, 164n
Chamberas, P., 91n, 123n
Chiarenza, M. M., 32n, 55n–56n, 64n, 65n, 143n
Chiarini, E., 172n
Christ: as *Sol Christi*, 28, 101, 125n, 133–134, 136, 149–153, 180; as "Sun of Justice," 4, 92–93, 98, 109, 134, 152–153, 186. *See also* Cross; New Testament; Transfiguration
Chrysostom, Saint John, 70, 91n, 134n, 135, 135n–136n
Church, 44, 75, 114–115, 179
Cicero, 19n, 42, 43–44, 50n–52n, 55n, 164–165, 232; *De Re Publica*, 6, 7, 13, 59, 62, 86n, 99, 170, 236n; *6.11*, 41n; *6.13*, 84; *6.14*, 60; *6.15*, 30–31; *6.17*, 15n, 61n, 86n; *6.18*, 74, 155n; *6.23*, 61–62
Cioffari, V., 23n
city, 12, 18, 22, 44, 50, 54n, 57, 87, 105, 129, 144, 145, 162–163, 179–180, 188–194, 217–222
Cochrane, C. N., 22n, 44n
comedy, 10, 26, 28, 35, 36, 56n, 134, 149
Compagni, Dino, 129
Comparetti, D., 131n
Constantine, 85n, 124n, 126–129, 195
conversion, 25–26, 47n, 99–100
Cornelius a Lapide, 121n, 201n
Cornford, F. M., 75n, 155n

Cornutus, 58n
Cosmo, U., 5, 172n
Courcelle, P., 34n, 131n
Croce, B., 5
Cross, 36, 57, 61, 231–238; cross of light, 9, 10, 40, 68, 73, 76, 77, 81n, 86–87, 90, 102n, 108, 119, 121, 123, 128–129, 133, 136, 149–153, 171, 175, 178, 180–181, 187, 193, 203; as crucifix, 57, 87, 120; Exaltation of the Cross, 6, 9, 10, 62n, 75, 77, 84, 84n–85n, 86, 123, 127n–128n, 184; hymns to the Holy Cross, 62–63, 114, 123; Invention of the Cross, 84n–85n, 123, 127n–128n, 152n, 184, 195; and numerology, 72–74, 158–159; sign of the Son of man, 76, 121, 129, 134–135, 184, 186
Cullmann, O., 24n
Curtius, E. R., 45n
Cyril of Jerusalem, 184

Daniello, Bernardino, 129n, 138n
Daniélou, J., 153n, 220n
Davidsohn, R., 47n
Davis, C. T., 11n, 24n, 27n, 42n, 45n, 55
de Bruyne, E., 154n
de' Cavallieri, P. F., 127n–128n
de Gaiffier, B., 56n
Deichmann, F. W., 123n, 181n, 184n
del Lungo, I., 5
de Lubac, H., 131n
de Sanctis, F., 5, 179n
de Santillana, G., 120n
Dinkler, E., 122n, 123n, 184
pseudo-Dionysius (the Areopagite), 91n, 96, 150, 151
Dis, 16, 18, 36
Dölger, F. J., 77, 103n, 125, 131n, 138n, 151n, 152n
Dominic, Saint, 67, 218
Donne, John, 85n

264 INDEX

Dream of the Rood, 86n, 124
Dronke, P., 159n
dubbing, 137, 137n–138n, 157, 159n, 215
Durling, R. M., 66n, 176n

Eden, 75–76, 114, 116n, 117, 118–119, 174
Elene, 195
Elijah, 93–94, 117–118
Eliös, 104n, 109, 133–140, 150–151
Elysium, 5, 6, 8, 25, 31, 33, 34, 41n, 68, 71, 76, 206
Empedocles, 22–23
eschatology, 47n, 57, 68, 100, 105, 114, 121, 123, 126, 129n, 145, 153n, 162, 164–166, 170, 180, 183, 188, 220
Eumenius, 127n
Eusebius of Caesaria, 126, 127n–128n, 131n
exile, 55, 58, 64, 129, 140, 144, 237

Fallani, G., 176
fame, 33, 101
Fengler, C., 173
Ferrante, J. M., 11n
Fiesole, 19, 42, 51, 54
Filostorgus, 127n
Firmicius Maternus, 15
Florence, 7, 8, 11, 12, 18, 19, 25, 28, 36–69, 102n, 105, 141, 170, 193
Florentine civic chronicles, 42, 42n–43n, 46n–47n, 51n
Foçillon, H., 128n
Fortuna, 7, 23, 59, 60n–61n
Francis of Assisi, Saint, 67, 218
Freccero, J., 29n, 40n, 74n, 99n, 201n
Friedman, J. B., 161n
Füglister, R., 71n, 161n
Fulgentius, 41n

Gardner, E., 88n

Gilson, E., 44n
Giordano di Rivalto, 99n, 111n, 199n, 217n, 218n, 224n
Giovanni of San Gimignano, 78n–79n, 138n, 198n
Gmelin, H., 174–177, 211
Godefridus of Viterbo, 86n
Grabar, A., 179, 204
Greenhill, E., 75n, 161n
Grégoire, H., 127n–128n
Gregory of Nyssa, 153
Gregory the Great, Saint, 91n
Gretser, J., 70n, 75n, 77n, 85n–86n, 121n, 123, 127n–128n, 128
Grosseteste, R., 150n
Guinizelli, Guido, 33n

Hardie, C., 65n
harmony, 10, 23, 74n–75n, 120, 149–169, 170, 190
Hippolytus, 55, 55n–56n, 106
Hollander, R., 139n, 140n
Homer, 34n
Honorius of Autun, 125n, 151n, 162n, 167n–169n
Horace, 37n, 164n
Hrabanus Maurus, 58n–59n
Hyginus, 78n, 161n

imitatio Christi, 10, 11, 39, 44, 56n, 68, 90, 100–106, 121, 137, 179, 198, 202, 205, 209–211, 215, 229–231
insomnium, 33, 38, 118
Isidore of Seville, 30n, 54n, 58, 130n, 136, 139, 161n, 162n, 218, 221n, 224

Jacobi a Voragine, 115n, 127n
Jacoff, R., 173n, 192n
Jaeger, W., 99n
James, Saint, 91–94, 109, 112n, 117, 122

Jason, 11, 216
Jerome, Saint, 91n, 93, 96, 128n
Jerusalem, 13, 69, 71, 87, 99, 126, 136, 163, 186, 188–194
Joachim of Fiore, 81n, 218
John, Saint (the Evangelist), 55, 91–94, 109, 112n, 117, 122
John Chrysostom, Saint, 70, 91n, 134n, 135, 135n–136n
John of Damascus, 91n, 92n, 96, 104n, 152n
John of Salisbury, 33n
Johnson, W. R., 22
John the Baptist, 46, 94
John the Scot (Eriugena), 58n, 91n, 150n
Julian "the Apostate," 128n, 150n
Julius Caesar, 42, 51, 54, 213
Jupiter, 16, 21, 65, 81n, 126
Justinian, 191–192, 201
Juvenal, 51n, 54, 221, 230, 232

Kaske, R. E., 71n, 115n, 137n
Kermode, J. F., 94n
Kittel, G., 219n
Koep, L., 147n
Kristeva, J., 53n

Lactantius, 130n
Lady Philosophy, 23, 24, 38n, 57n, 60n
Lausberg, H., 221n
Le Goff, J., 46n
Lehmann, P., 94, 97n
Leo the Great, Pope, 91n, 96, 97–98
Lewis, C. S., 16
locus amoenus, 44–53
Logan, J. L., 72n
Lucan, 51
Lucretius, 17, 18, 20, 23

Macrobius, 15n, 33, 34, 38, 38n–39n, 61n, 75n, 153n–155n

Mahler, A. E., 125n
Malavenda, Thomas, 125n
Malisipini, Ricordano, 42n
Mandelstam, O., 137
Manilius, 78n, 161n
Marcellus, 20, 28–29, 145n
Mars: in the *Aeneid*, 18, 19, 21, 31–35, 37n; as city founder, 8, 18, 19, 46–47, 51n; as god, 9, 14, 14n, 23, 36–38, 54, 57; as heaven of music, 9, 157–169; and *mors*, 7, 15n, 28, 34–35, 58–62, 68, 86, 113, 117, 181; as planet, 5, 6, 7, 9, 13, 14, 15, 16, 17, 22, 25, 27, 36, 37, 65n, 88, 107, 128–129
Martinez, R. L., 19n
martyrdom, 6, 10, 11, 49n, 56n, 63–64, 69, 87, 90, 149, 171, 180, 183, 202–238
Maximus of Turin, 71n
Mazzotta, G., 11n, 23n, 24n, 45n
Milky Way, 70, 78, 82–85, 89, 108–109, 156–157, 181–182
Mineo, N., 237
Momigliano, A., 5, 172n
Moore, E., 75n, 115n
mosaics: Ravenna, 171–178; Sant' Apollinare in Classe, 6, 10, 77, 121, 123, 126, 132, 134, 170–203, 219; San Vitale, 172, 176, 178, 191–192, 193
Moses, 69, 93–94, 117–118, 162
music. *See* harmony

Nebuchadnezzar, 80, 120
New Testament:
—Matthew: *3:17*, 93; *13:44*, 196, 197n; *16:1–4*, 86n; *16:16*, 99; *16:16–17*, 93; *16:18–19*, 112n; *16:21*, 86n; *16:22–23*, 98; *16:24–27*, 101, 104, 105, 122, 143; *16:27–17:6*, 86n, 100; *17:1*, 96n–97n; *17:2*, 92, 142n; *17:3*, 93n; *17:5*, 93,

266 INDEX

—Matthew (*cont.*)
106, 185; *17:6*, 108n, 110; *17:7*, 93; *17:9*, 93; *18:12*, 184n; *19:29*, 216–217, 225; *24:19*, 184; *24:27*, 201, 201n; *24:29–31*, 100, 122n, 129, 135; *25:34*, 125n; *26:28*, 212, 217; *26:36–47*, 92n, 110; *27:46*, 139
—Mark: *5:37*, 91, 112n; *8:32–33*, 98; *9:1–2*, 92n, 96; *9:3*, 93n; *9:6*, 93n; *14:33*, 91, 112n; *14:32–43*, 92n
—Luke: *1:32*, 65; *8:50–56*, 110; *9:27*, 114; *9:29–31*, 92n, 93; *9:32*, 93; *9:35*, 93n; *10:20*, 146n; *22:39–47*, 92n; *23:33*, 125n; *23:43*, 125n
—John: *7:13*, 220; *12:36*, 105; *19:6*, 113n
—Acts: *9:27–28*, 24; *28:31*, 221
—I Corinthians: *1:18*, 70; *1:23–24*, 70; *3:10–16*, 196n
—II Corinthians: *3:12–13*, 219; *3:18*, 104; *12:2*, 107
—Galatians: *3:28*, 226; *4:4*, 116, 130
—Ephesians: *1:5–8*, 212n; *6:17*, 218
—Colossians: *1:17–20*, 80; *1:19*, 157
—I Thessalonians: *4:13*, 34n
—Hebrews: *11:1*, 40, 68–69; *11:1–3*, 230–231; *11:13*, 58; *11:27*, 69
—I Peter: *2:4–5*, 195
—II Peter: *1:16–21*, 95–96
—I John: *2:18*, 76
—Jude: *1:20*, 196
—Revelations: *3:5*, 146n; *5:1*, 146n; *6:13*, 237; *6:14*, 181n; *7:5–8*, 186; *20:12–15*, 146n; *21:6*, 184; *21:20*, 197n; *21:23*, 135, 153; *21:27*, 146n; *22:2*, 80, 120; *22:5*, 153; *22:13*, 184; *22:19*, 146n
New Testament Apocrypha, 79, 123, 125–126, 130, 132n, 133, 134n
Norden, E., 198n
Nördstrom, C. O., 181n, 185n

Old Testament:
—Genesis: *2:9*, 75; *2:17*, 115
—Exodus: *28:14*, 182n
—Psalms: *32*, 162; *143*, 162; *143:9*, 162
—Isaiah: *11:1*, 209; *34:4*, 181n; *40:9*, 237
—Ezechiel: *2:9*, 146n; *9:4–6*, 138n
—Daniel: *4:7–10*, 80, 120
—Malachi: *4:2*, 92–93, 134
orant gesture, 10, 178–179, 190, 203–206
Origen, 86n, 91n, 97n, 108n, 222
Orosius, 27, 51n
Orpheus, 161
Otis, B., 227n
Ovid, 55n, 56n, 116–117, 129, 142, 142n–143n

paideia, 39, 43, 229
Palgen, R., 66n
parrhesia, 219–222, 227, 232
Pascoli, G., 5, 74n, 172, 174, 177
pastoral, 44–53, 188
Patch, H., 23n
Paul, Saint, 11, 49n, 222, 233
Paulinus of Nola, 139n
Pegis, R. J., 72n
Peter, Saint, 91–93, 98–99, 109, 112n, 122
Peter Damian, 71n, 85, 85n–86n, 199–200
Petrocchi, G., 139n
Pézard, A., 140n, 199
Phaeton, 55n, 106, 139n, 142, 142n–143n, 214n
Piero della Francesca, 115n
Plato, 25, 50n, 51n, 60n, 75n, 77–78, 150, 159n, 164
prophecy, 62–63, 64n–65n, 106, 117, 121–122, 130–149, 170, 219, 221–222, 232–233, 236–237
Ptolemy, 15n

Quintillian, 220n–221n

INDEX

Rabuse, G., 36n, 66n, 79n, 86n, 120, 150n
Rahner, H., 77, 119, 121n, 161n
Rajna, P., 5
Ramat, R., 45n
Ravenna, 171, 192, 199n–200n
Raw, B., 124n–125n
Restoro d'Arezzo, 15n, 19n, 83n–84n
Rheinfelder, H., 5
Rhetorica ad Herennium, 220
Ricci, C., 171, 172n, 174
Richard of Saint Victor, 88, 96, 108n, 161n, 166n, 224n
Rome, 7, 11, 12, 14n, 15, 18, 19, 20, 24, 26–27, 37n, 39, 42, 44, 51, 65, 71, 82, 87, 114–115, 141, 144, 170, 192, 212n, 226
Rufinus (Presbyter), 127n

Sardanapalus, 50–51, 51n–52n
Sarolli, G. R., 72n, 237
Saturn, 14, 15n, 16n, 20, 65, 81n, 130
Scartazzini, G. A., 229n
Scipio, 15, 41, 60, 84n, 118, 226
sermo humilis, 140
Servius, 37n, 61n, 162n
Seymour, W. W., 71n
Sibyl, 14, 30n, 31–34, 64n–65n, 80, 149, 185, 210–214
Sibylline oracles, 123, 127, 130–149, 185
Silverstein, T., 131n
Singleton, C. S., 58n, 72, 99n, 115n, 116n, 138, 174n
Solomon, 67
Sozomen, 126, 127n–128n
Spitzer, L., 17, 164n, 165, 167n
Statius, 4, 130; the *Thebaid*, 16, 17, 18, 19n, 36, 233
Stephany, W. A., 173
Stockbauer, J., 77n, 103n
Stockmeier, P., 71n, 77n, 122n
Szövérffy, J., 86n

Tarrant, R. J., 34n
tetractys, 154–155
Thebes, 14, 18, 21, 28
Theophilactus, 127n
Theseus, 37
Tondelli, L., 81n
topaz, 194–199
Toynbee, P., 51n, 78n
tragedy, 10, 26, 35, 36, 86, 106, 149
Transfiguration, 6, 9, 10, 13, 69, 91–123, 133, 180, 185–186, 217
Tree of Knowledge, 75, 114
Tree of Law, 115, 117, 120
Tree of Life, 75, 79–80, 119, 120
Troy, 18, 20, 25, 28, 32n

Uguccione of Pisa, 14n, 58n, 138
Ulysses, 11, 216

Valesio, P., 29n
Valli, L., 44n
Vallone, A., 5, 146n
Vandelli, G., 112n
van Unnik, W. C., 219n–220n
Varro, 19n, 130, 131n
Venantius Fortunatus, 62n–63n, 135
Venus, 17, 18, 20, 21, 23
Vessey, D., 16n
Vettori, V., 139n
Vianello, N., 5
Villani, Giovanni, 19n, 42n–43n, 46n, 47n, 51n
Virgil:
—in the *Commedia*, 3, 4, 22, 23, 28n, 29, 57n, 64n, 81, 87, 99, 140
—*Aeneid*: *3.456–460*, 64n; *3.458–460*, 32n; *5.730–731*, 32n; *6.38–41*, 29; *6.83–86*, 14; *6.83–90*, 32n; *6.90*, 213n; *6.95*, 69; *6.96*, 32n; *6.99–100*, 29; *6.123*, 213n; *6.125–131*, 210, 213n, 214n; *6.134–135*, 210; *6.149–155*, 29; *6.197*, 213n; *6.249–267*, 29; *6.270–280*, 16n, 21n; *6.278*, 34; *6.322*, 213n; *6.332*, 30;

—*Aeneid (cont.)*
6.390, 145n; 6.394, 213n; 6.404,
145n; 6.556–576, 16n; 6.629–630,
69; 6.641, 34; 6.645–647, 162n;
6.653, 31; 6.662, 26; 6.682, 144;
6.683, 83; 6.685, 206; 6.686, 144,
206; 6.687–688, 209; 6.688, 64,
145, 225n; 6.695, 144; 6.700–702,
144, 145n; 6.719–721, 30; 6.724,
61n; 6.730–734, 59; 6.791–797, 82;
6.834–835, 211; 6.851–853, 26–28;
6.853, 65; 6.855–856, 234; 6.878,
28; 6.883, 28; 6.890–892, 32n, 64n;
6.896, 33n, 34; 7.550, 21; 8.700–
703, 21n; 9.565–566, 37n; 12.332,
21; 12.335–336, 21
—*Fourth Eclogue*: 82–83, 130–131
von Dechend, H., 120n
von Richtofen, E., 36n, 139n
von Simson, G., 91, 123n, 154n, 188,
189, 191, 192
Vossler, K., 5

Wadstein, E., 125n
Wind, E., 17

Zöckler, O., 71n
Zonaras, 127n

Library of Congress Cataloging-in-Publication Data

SCHNAPP, JEFFREY T. (JEFFREY THOMPSON), 1954–
THE TRANSFIGURATION OF HISTORY AT THE CENTER OF
DANTE'S PARADISE.

BIBLIOGRAPHY: P.
INCLUDES INDEX.
1. DANTE ALIGHIERI, 1265–1321. PARADISO.
2. DANTE ALIGHIERE, 1265–1321—SYMBOLISM.
3. HEAVEN IN LITERATURE. 4. HISTORY—PHILOSOPHY.
I. TITLE.
PQ4406.S3 1986 851'.1 85-43309
ISBN 0-691-06679-5 (ALK. PAPER)